Singlewomen in the
European Past, 1250–1800

Singlewomen in the European Past, 1250–1800

EDITED BY

Judith M. Bennett

AND

Amy M. Froide

PENN

University of Pennsylvania Press

Philadelphia

10 9 8 7 6 5 4 3 2 1

Published by
University of Pennsylvania Press
Philadelphia, Pennsylvania 19104-4011

Library of Congress Cataloging-in-Publication Data
Singlewomen in the European past, 1250–1800 / edited by Judith M.
Bennett and Amy M. Froide.
    p.   cm.
Includes bibliographical references and index.
ISBN 0-8122-3464-2 (cloth : alk. paper). —
ISBN 0-8122-1668-7 (pbk. : alk. paper)
    1. Single women — Europe — History.   2. Single women — Europe — Social
conditions.   3. Single women — Europe — Economic conditions.   4. Sex
role — Europe — History.   I. Bennett, Judith M.   II. Froide, Amy M.
HQ800.2.S59   1998
305.48'9652'094 — dc21   98-35172
                                                                    CIP

Contents

Acknowledgments

We would like to thank the nine contributors to this volume for their patience, promptness, and generosity. With their agreement, all royalties on the sale of *Singlewomen in the European Past, 1250–1800* will be donated to the graduate fellowship endowment of the Coordinating Council for Women in History. The idea for this volume began in October 1995 at a conference organized by the North Carolina Research Group on Medieval and Early Modern Women. We are grateful to the members of the Research Group as well as to Ronald Witt (who took on the bulk of fundraising responsibilities for the conference). Thanks also to Jerry Singerman, whose editorial enthusiasm helped to bring this project to a successful conclusion. Finally, and as always, thanks to Cynthia Herrup and Terry Bouton.

I

A Singular Past

Judith M. Bennett and Amy M. Froide

WHEN WE IMAGINE THE VILLAGES, towns, and cities of Europe before 1800, we see these places bustling with nuclear families — husbands, wives, and their children. We know, of course, that some people were neither spouses nor children, but they appear to us as random individuals caught temporarily at awkward points in the game of making marriages and sustaining conjugal families. Orphans needed surrogate parents; adult daughters and sons awaited marriage; widows and widowers missed old partners and perhaps sought new ones. Indeed, marriage was so much the destiny of most adults in traditional Europe that in some languages — English among them — the words for "wife" and "husband" could be synonyms for "adult female" and "adult male."[1] To be grown up was to be married.

What we imagine is largely true. Most women and men in Europe before 1800 did marry and raise children together. Their songs, stories, and art consistently represented marriage as the usual life for both sexes, and in the lessons of their rabbis, priests, and ministers, they drank even more deeply from the cup of marriage. Unlike Protestants and Jews, Catholics were taught to revere holy celibacy above marriage, but even they learned that ordinary lay folk could expect to take good comfort from married life. In traditional Europe, boys and girls grew up expecting that they should and would find partners of the opposite sex, get married, and breed children. In both theory and practice, marriage was normative.

Yet what we imagine is only part of the story. Marriage might have been normative, but many people never married, and many others lived single for many years — through their teens, twenties, and sometimes even thirties — and then later lived alone as widows and widowers. Unmarried persons — singlewomen, bachelors, widows, and widowers — were more common in some times and places than others, but they always constituted a significant minority of adults and sometimes a majority. From among the many unmarried people found in western Europe before 1800, this collection focuses on one particular group: singlewomen — that is, women who had never married. Today, we usually call such women "spinsters," for during the seventeenth century "spinster" came to mean not only a female spinner of wool (its older meaning) but also a never-married woman. (The two definitions neatly coincided, since many singlewomen then earned their livings by working as spinsters.)[2] Today, "spinster" carries a negative connotation shaped by pseudoscientific research and popular culture during the past three hundred years.[3] For the study of Europe before 1800, "singlewoman" — a word found (in the compound form used here) in English documents from the fourteenth century — more neutrally describes a woman who lived without having married.

The term "singlewomen" encompasses both women who would eventually marry and those who never would. Some adult women lived and worked as singlewomen for five, ten, fifteen years or more, and then married. It is useful to think of these women as *life-cycle singlewomen*, for they lived single only for the years between childhood and marriage. Other women might have expected to marry while they were young but, for a variety of reasons, never did. For these *lifelong singlewomen*, the single state was a permanent one. Whether they eventually married, or not, singlewomen lived in ways very different from another group of never-married women who are not included in this collection: virginal nuns. Christian ideas about virginal celibacy were probably well known to most Europeans, but not all singlewomen were celibate virgins, and, in any case, their day-to-day lives included possibilities, challenges, and responsibilities very different from those of cloistered nuns. As Sharon Farmer's essay in this collection shows, some women bridged the gap between secular single life and monastic virginity, but for most people nuns (who were, after all, "brides of Christ") seemed very different from the singlewomen they knew as neighbors, servants, and friends.

In Europe between 1250 and 1800, lifelong singlewomen were quite common, usually accounting for 10 to 20 percent of all adult women. Their numbers were always swelled by life-cycle singlewomen, who would eventually marry but had not yet done so. In England in 1377, almost one-third of all adult women were single; in Florence fifty years later, singlewomen accounted for about one-fifth of women; and in Zurich fifty years after that, nearly half of all women had never taken a husband. In most places, proportions of singlewomen grew even larger in the sixteenth century and peaked thereafter.[4] At any given moment, a quite startling number of single-women — including middle-aged and older ones — lived in the cottages, town houses, lanes, and streets of Europe.

Despite their numerical prominence, singlewomen — both those who would eventually marry and those who would not — have been mostly ignored in European history. In part, singlewomen have been neglected because they are so difficult to find in the archives and sources of past times. Often poorer than their married sisters, often living in marginal circumstances, and often without descendants who might have preserved their memory, singlewomen have left precious few diaries, letters, or other personal memorabilia for historians to study today. These problems of documentation are very real and significant, but, as the essays in this volume demonstrate so clearly, they are not insurmountable. Indeed, because marital status was such an important marker of female identity, singlewomen — much more so than bachelors — were often explicitly distinguished from their married or widowed counterparts in censuses, tax records, and other nominal listings. Captivated with the vision of a preindustrial Europe shaped by conjugal households, we have too often overlooked single people in the historical record.[5]

The essays in this volume illustrate some of the insights to be gained not only by recognizing that singlewomen lived in the towns and villages of preindustrial Europe but also by studying their lives. Offering wide-ranging examples of how to observe, approach, and study the lives of singlewomen, these essays offer new perspectives on a hitherto neglected subject. Maryanne Kowaleski traces what demography reveals about how and why the presence of singlewomen varied within Europe between 1250 and 1800; Sharon Farmer explores how the social elites of thirteenth-century Paris were so unable to conceive of the single state that they responded inadequately to the real needs of the actual singlewomen around them; Susan Mosher Stuard argues that singlewomen were essential to systems of slavery in the Middle Ages; Ruth Mazo Karras examines how the close association of heterosexual sex and venality in medieval Europe linked singlewomen with prostitutes; Roberta Krueger finds that singlewomen in the courtly literatures of medieval France enjoyed considerable autonomy and forged strong relationships with other women; Merry Wiesner shows how singlewomen in early modern German towns supported themselves in often difficult circumstances; Monica Chojnacka examines institutional responses to the proliferation of singlewomen in sixteenth-century Venice; Amy Froide traces the very different ways in which the city fathers of early modern English towns treated widows and singlewomen; Margaret Hunt argues that the same social structures that accommodated singlewomen in eighteenth-century England also facilitated lesbian love and sexuality; and Susan Lanser suggests that English nationalism in the eighteenth century fostered a particular harshness and cruelty towards singlewomen.

This collection does not attempt to offer genuine coverage, an impossibility in a field as nascent as the study of premodern singlewomen.[6] Instead, these essays lay out new possibilities, provoke new questions, and facilitate future research. In so doing, they establish the importance of singlewomen in the European past, for the histories of European women, European families, and European societies look very different when singlewomen are a part of the story. In this introduction, we seek, by assessing what is now known and what still needs to be known about singlewomen, to sketch out the general importance of these women in European history. The questions that frame this discussion have developed from the collaborative production of this volume, and, as they have been ever-changing, they reflect both the concerns that shaped these essays initially and the final fruits of their research findings. These questions address the numbers of singlewomen; distinctions among them; their experiences of work, family, friendship, and sex; their representations in narratives, songs, and commentary; and the ways in which we can best understand their choices, actions, and relationships. In posing these questions and offering observations on them, we hope our discussion will be provocative and productive. We look forward to both further debates about singlewomen and further research into their histories.

How, Why, and with What Significance Did Numbers of Singlewomen Vary Across Time and Region?

In her essay for this collection, Maryanne Kowaleski tackles the challenging task of collating demographers' many estimates of the presence of singlewomen — life-cycle as well as lifelong — in Europe before 1800. For demographers, singlewomen are one piece in a larger puzzle. Because population was likely to fall whenever female marriage was delayed or restricted, two measures of female nuptiality — the age at first marriage for women, and the proportion of women who never married — profoundly affected trends of population growth and decline.[7] Numbers of singlewomen varied enormously across region, time, and locale; generally speaking, there were more singlewomen in the north than in the south, more in the seventeenth and eighteenth centuries than earlier, and more in cities than in villages.

Ever since John Hajnal showed in 1965 that marriage in northwestern regions of early modern Europe was distinctive in two respects — late age of first marriage for both sexes, and large numbers of never-married adults — demographers have traced the origins, extent, and varieties of what is now known as the "Northwestern European Marriage Pattern."[8] They have also suggested that there might have been two distinct marriage regimes — northwestern and Mediterranean — in Europe. In the Mediterranean, it is argued, marriage was almost universal and usually contracted between young women and older men; in the northwest, singleness was more common, marriage occurred relatively late (in the mid-twenties for both sexes), and husbands and wives tended to be of roughly similar ages.[9] Nevertheless, it does not follow that singlewomen always proliferated in the north and were rarely to be found in the south. Within both general regions, diverse factors could affect rates of singleness quite dramatically: migration, residence in urban areas, economic fluctuations, sex ratios, inheritance strategies, social status, and cultural ideas about female honor and virginity.[10] Moreover, as Kowaleski observes, by the eighteenth century rising numbers of singlewomen in both northern and southern European countries muted these two marriages systems.

Inadequate data make it difficult to compare medieval rates of singleness to early modern patterns, but Kowaleski shows that singlewomen were common in some regions as early as 1350, and that their numbers increased in the centuries after 1500. For example, there were significantly more singlewomen than before in seventeenth-century England and Scandinavia, as well as in eighteenth-century Scotland and Switzerland; numbers of singlewomen in Italy and Spain also rose well above their medieval levels in the eighteenth century. The overall trend was one of increasing numbers of singlewomen during the centuries covered by this volume, but there were some significant variations. In England, for example, numbers of singlewomen were exceptionally high in the seventeenth century, but fell thereafter. Moreover, these long-term trends were always marked by volatility; numbers of singlewomen could shift quite quickly, with one generation producing many more — or many fewer — singlewomen than the next.

Each woman's life was, of course, shaped by her own circumstances, but in general, she was more likely to remain single if she lived in a town rather than the countryside.[11] Pamela Sharpe has argued that where women outnumbered men (as was usually the case in urban areas), lifelong singlewomen tended to be especially numerous, and Vivien Brodsky has shown that female migrants to towns also tended to marry late. In the countryside, where apprenticeship, service, and migration were less likely to delay marriage, people usually married earlier than their urban cousins. Sex ratios were often (but not invariably) more balanced in rural areas, so peasant women also found husbands with greater ease.[12]

Singlewomen were also more common in poor households than in rich ones. In the opulent castles and town houses of Europe, singlewomen were rarely found, perhaps because rich families valued women's reproductive capacities over their productive abilities. Monarchs, aristocrats, and rich merchants tended to marry off their daughters at quite young ages. Throughout Europe during the Middle Ages and in Catholic countries thereafter, elite parents were also able—unlike more humble parents in town and country—to place unmarried daughters in monasteries. Elite status, however, did not always guarantee that a woman would marry. Whenever marriage settlements grew prohibitively expensive (for example, in fifteenth-century Florence, sixteenth-century Venice, and eighteenth-century Britain), singlewomen proliferated among the urban and landed elites.[13]

Hard times could delay marriage or even preclude it. When working people found it difficult to obtain land or employment, they often postponed marriage or avoided it altogether. When an elite family fell into financial difficulties or found marriage to be especially costly, a few children married and the rest lived without spouses. Better times led to earlier marriages and more of them. Yet the specific economic circumstances of women—that is, whether women did or did not control resources—must be distinguished from generalities about good or bad times. Women almost never found occupations that paid as well as the work of men, but when women's work was more abundant than usual, women married less frequently, at least in England.[14] Among elites, it similarly seems that wealthy heiresses who controlled their own destinies were better able than other women to forego marriage. Elizabeth I of England was a powerful woman as well as a wealthy heiress, but she is an obvious example of the link between female control of property and singleness. Historians argue about her motivations for remaining single, but there can be little doubt that the absence of a father, brother, or husband facilitated Elizabeth I's ability to determine her own fate.[15] In other words, it seems possible that *female* prosperity inhibited marriage whereas *general* prosperity promoted it. If so, women might have sought husbands not only for sexual and emotional needs but also as a result of simple calculations about how best to survive; in other words, women's economic disadvantages in preindustrial Europe might have been a critical part of what Adrienne Rich has called "compulsory heterosexuality."[16]

How Did the Experiences of Singlewomen Differ by Class, Age, Sexuality, Race, Ethnicity, and Religion?

Differences among singlewomen could be quite striking, and they ran along many different lines: rich and poor; young and old; celibate and sexually active; native and foreign; Catholic, Protestant, and Jew. As several essays in this collection show, these differences were often relational, creating advantages for some singlewomen out of the disadvantages of others.[17] For example, Chojnacka explores how the plight of poor singlewomen in sixteenth-century Venice created opportunities for elite singlewomen. In 1568, Venetian donors established the Casa delle Zitelle [Home of Unmarried Girls] in order to direct poor women away from prostitution and toward either marriage or monastic life. Yet other women were also assisted by the Casa; single noblewomen occupied the top administrative positions, and other staff positions were taken by former inmates who had decided neither to marry nor to enter a monastery. In the Casa delle Zitelle, charity dispensed to poor singlewomen provided vocations for better-off singlewomen. This charitable exchange also tended to distinguish life-cycle singlewomen (who were helped by the Casa toward marriage or monasticism) from lifelong singlewomen (who made careers out of managing the Casa).[18]

A woman's class shaped not only whether she might remain single but also, if single, the kind of life she might expect to lead. As Olwen Hufton and Christine Adams have shown for France, and Virginia Cox for Venice, elite singlewomen did not have to worry much about income; they busied themselves helping their parents and siblings and performing works of piety and charity.[19] Mary Astell, Jane Barker, Moderata Fonte, and other singlewomen from the middle and upper classes were even able to envision lives of intellectual and pious retreat, with days filled by educational and charitable pursuits.[20] Poorer singlewomen had quite different experiences. Hufton has surmised that some singlewomen without supportive friends or relatives survived only by resorting to petty crime and prostitution, and Hans Johansen has traced the prominence of elderly singlewomen among beggars and recipients of charity in Danish towns.[21] Poor singlewomen sometimes found help from friends, kin, and neighbors, or, more rarely, from charitable institutions, but they often numbered among the poorest and most pathetic members of their communities. For well-off women, singleness offered certain challenges and opportunities, but it did not necessarily raise the specter of poverty; for poor women, the economic hardships of the single state often loomed very large indeed.

Age was also as a critical factor distinguishing some singlewomen from others. Young singlewomen were often readily accommodated within contemporary structures of adolescence, service, and apprenticeship; older singlewomen were more anomalous, and their experiences more varied. Most research on adolescence has focused on males, who tended to drink a great deal, sing a great deal, and cause a great deal of trouble in many cities and towns.[22] Young women were less rowdy, but they found adolescence to be a time of exceptional autonomy. As children, girls were subject to their parents, and once married, women were subject to their husbands; as adolescents, young women were able to do some things — such as hold land in their own right and live apart from relatives — that neither girls nor wives could usually do.[23] As Krueger explores for courtly literature in her essay for this volume, the theme of female autonomy in adolescence was a familiar one in European literature. Adolescents were not fully independent adults, not especially flush with funds, and not free of authoritative regulation, but for both singlewomen and bachelors, the years between about fifteen and twenty-five could be filled with some change and some opportunity — perhaps new employment, perhaps residence away from the parental home, perhaps travel to a nearby town or city, and perhaps, of course, sexual experimentation.[24]

Many young singlewomen worked for at least a few years as servants, living and laboring in the households of other people.[25] Service was ubiquitous in many regions of preindustrial Europe, with even modest households taking in a young woman or man to help with domestic chores, farmwork, the workshop, or, indeed, all three sorts of tasks at once. Providing a place to live and work, service also enabled adolescents to acquire new skills, meet new people, earn relatively high wages (due to the room and board included in their salaries), and because of this, even save some money.[26] Yet servants were also subjected to the authority of masters and mistresses who could be unreasonable and cruel, often with impunity. For women, in particular, the intimate living arrangements of domestic service could lead to sexual harassment, rape, pregnancy, and, in most of these cases, dismissal.[27]

Service was closely linked to singleness in at least some parts of Europe, encouraging young women and young men to delay marriage into their mid-twenties or beyond.[28] The link between singleness and domestic employment was not invariable, but, as Stuard's essay in this volume suggests, it was very strong. She calls our attention to the presence of domestic slaves as well as servants in the households of medieval Italy, demonstrating that the inability of slaves to marry was a critical part of their day-by-day exploitation and continued enslavement. To be a slave in the cities of the medieval Mediterranean was to be both female and single. As epitomized by the sad plight of slaves, the social deference and flexible work expected from domestic laborers made young, never-married women especially suitable for the task.

Apprenticeship was one alternative to service. It worked at two levels, one privileged and the other very poor. Well-off parents apprenticed their sons and sometimes daughters in skilled trades. They hoped that, in return for the apprentice's labor for a set period of years, he or she would be taught the trade, and might eventually proceed, if male, to membership in a guild and citizenship in a town. Throughout Europe, young men constituted the vast majority of those apprenticed in skilled trades, and the small numbers of female apprentices seem, in some places, to have dwindled even more by the seventeenth and eighteenth centuries.[29] Nevertheless, apprenticeship continued to be seen by some middle-class parents as useful for daughters who might some day need to support themselves, especially if they never married.[30] At the other end of the social scale, orphaned or poor children were sometimes apprenticed by the local authorities into whose care they fell. Eager to support poor children and to teach them useful skills, officers apprenticed them into very humble occupations: "housewifery" (that is, domestic service) was the most common apprenticeship for pauper or orphaned girls. Among pauper apprentices, women were much more common than among those apprenticed in skilled trades.[31] Some poor singlewomen spent their teens and early twenties as pauper apprentices before beginning paid work as domestic servants.

Adolescence, service, and apprenticeship were especially important in the lives of young singlewomen, for all three customarily ended before or at marriage.[32] The circumstances of older singlewomen were quite different. Many continued to work as servants, and others supported themselves by piecework, wage-labor, petty trading, civic employment, inheritances, and even shop-owning.[33] For some singlewomen, aging brought improved circumstances and more independent living.[34] As Froide and Wiesner point out in their essays, older singlewomen sometimes managed to work for themselves and live on their own, opportunities that were often denied to younger singlewomen who usually lived with their parents, kin, or employers. Older singlewomen were more likely to live as lodgers, to share housing with other singlewomen (forming what Hufton has termed "spinster clusters"), or to establish independent households for themselves alone.[35] Moreover, as Farmer and Froide observe, older singlewomen were sometimes viewed as quasi-widows by their neighbors, enabling them to receive approbation and charity denied their younger counterparts. Yet the experiences of older singlewomen could also be quite difficult. A singlewoman aged fifty was unlikely to marry, regardless of her intentions or circumstances, and she was likely to be more subject to suspicion and ridicule than her younger counterparts; the "old" in the eighteenth-century formulation of "old maid" was a critical modifier. And, as many studies in this volume stress, poverty was the final fate of many aged singlewomen.[36]

In addition to class and age, sexuality also shaped the experiences and meanings of singleness for women. Some singlewomen were celibate, but many others were not, engaging in relationships that we would today label as either heterosexual or lesbian. Evidence of premarital sex is common enough for Europe before 1800 to make it abundantly clear that many singlewomen enjoyed sexual relations with male partners, lovers, or acquaintances.[37] Indeed, just as some wives lived without husbands (because of desertion, male service at sea, informal divorce, or other similar reasons), so some singlewomen lived with men who were husbands in all but name. For the very poor in particular, marriage was an expensive and unnecessary luxury; it was often cheaper and easier simply to live together.[38] Other singlewomen worked as prostitutes, profiting from the heterosexual trade in sex. Karras's essay in this collection explores how deeply prostitution was associated with women who were not married. A poor woman who "belonged" to no man was often assumed to "belong" to all men.

Other singlewomen found emotional comfort and sexual pleasure with women. The history of same-sex relations between women in medieval and early modern Europe is exceedingly difficult to study, but there can be no doubt of its existence. Church leaders worried about lesbian sex; women expressed, practiced, and were sometimes imprisoned or even executed for same-sex love; and some women cross-dressed in order to live with other women as married couples. The use of the word "lesbian" to denote woman-to-woman sexual practices, once thought to be a very modern usage and identity, has now been traced back to 1732, and there is good reason to conclude that at least some lesbians then saw themselves as part of a distinctive social group.[39] Nevertheless, we certainly should not equate the single state with lesbian practices. Hunt's essay explores how same-sex relations between women easily moved across boundaries of married and unmarried; as she shows, it would be foolish to equate heterosexuality with married folk and homosexuality with the unmarried. Without rendering female singleness equivalent to lesbianism, however, it seems clear that some women in some places may have opted for a single life because it offered their best opportunity for same-sex love and sexual practice.

Differences of ethnicity and race have, as yet, been little studied for premodern Europe. Because migration tended to delay marriage, immigrant women — such as the Welsh, Scots, Irish, Flemish, Dutch, German, and French women found in London — were probably single longer than native women. They were also more likely to fall into prostitution.[40] To date, race has been little studied. The few African women who appear in the historical records of early modern England were usually single and supported themselves either through service or poor relief. Perhaps their race put barriers in the way of marriage. Although African males often married Englishwomen, it seems to have been less common for African women to marry native men.[41]

Religion also differentiated the experiences of singlewomen, especially distinguishing pious women from those who pursued more secular vocations. Monastic life provided a respectable alternative to marriage, but nuns, as "brides of Christ," were not strictly single. Taking final vows in ceremonies that mimicked secular weddings, many nuns probably thought themselves as irrevocably bound to a husband as were wives in secular marriages.[42] In the gap between brides of Christ and singlewomen were many other women who combined religious piety with the unmarried life. Most of these women lived informally, but some took vows of celibacy, others attached themselves as tertiaries to the mendicant orders, and still others lived semireligious lives in informal communities of like-minded women. One of the most important of these groups, the beguines, flourished in northern European cities in the thirteenth century. Gathering into communities known as beguinages, widows and singlewomen agreed to live chastely during their time together; they took in work or sometimes labored outside the beguinage during the day; and they studied, prayed, and worshiped together. Unlike the vows of nuns, the obligations of beguines endured only for the duration of their stay in the community. Pious beguines, some of whom came from rich families and others of whom were quite poor, commanded a great deal of respect from local people. But they began to suffer ecclesiastical persecution in the fourteenth century and, although never completely eliminated, their numbers dwindled thereafter. Other secular orders continued to provide an option for early modern women, such as the *Stifte* in Germany discussed by Merry Wiesner in this volume, as well as the Ursulines in Italy and the beatas in Spain.[43] Beguines and other tertiaries have been studied mostly for their religious piety and mysticism, but, as Farmer's essay in this collection suggests, they are also an important part of the history of singlewomen in preindustrial Europe. In beguinages and similar institutions, singlewomen found supportive homes that addressed not just their religious piety but also their needs for shelter, support, and employment.

Among ordinary laywomen, religion could also be an important point of difference. On the one hand, singlewomen in Protestant countries did not have the option of entering into a convent, nor did many Protestant singlewomen have institutions such as Venice's Casa delle Zitelle to assist them. On the other hand, singlewomen in Catholic countries may have found it more difficult to leave their homes and strike out on their own as servants, lodgers, or other sorts of independent workers. Perhaps these differences were due to religion, but they might also reflect cultural preferences that made the enclosure of women (in either male-headed households or institutions) more of a priority in Mediterranean regions than in the north. (The issue is complicated by the geographical bifurcation of Europe into Protestant and Catholic zones, the former mostly lying in the north and the latter mostly located around the Mediterranean.) In any case, differences were not limited to Catholics and Protestants, for non-Christian singlewomen may have had distinct experiences from their Christian counterparts. Among Jewish populations, lifelong singlewomen may have been less common, regardless of whether they lived in northern or southern Europe, or in city or country. Stefanie Siegmund has found that Jewish communities encouraged universal marriage, did not produce any institutional outlets for never-married women, and even lacked a term to describe such women. Yet, because the age at which Jewish women first married was quite variable, Siegmund surmises many Jewish women would have spent a good portion of their lives as life-cycle singlewomen.[44] Did Jews accept life-cycle singlewomen more readily than Christian societies, but virtually eliminate the possibility of living permanently as a singlewoman? Questions such as this illustrate our need for more research into how race, ethnicity, and religion differentiated the lives of European women, singlewomen among them, in the premodern era.

In What Ways Were Singlewomen Different from Wives and Widows? Were Singlewomen a Different Gender?

All women in premodern Europe faced some common circumstances. Women were considered to be inferior to men in body and mind; they were generally excluded from public office at all levels; and they had less access than men to wealth, collected through gifts, inheritance, or sheer earning power. Some women, of course, were very rich and powerful, enjoying privileges denied to many men. But as a rule, women were — compared to men of their class or status — disadvantaged. Marital status divided wives, widows, and singlewomen, but it was a fluid and vague marker. Still, although wives, widows, and singlewomen shared a great deal, they also differed from each other in some fundamental respects.

Relationships with men seem to have divided women along two distinct boundaries. First, *marital status* shaped women's lives, for wives, widows, and singlewomen generally faced quite different opportunities and limitations. Wives were assumed to be better governed than other women (thanks to the supervision of their husbands); wives could exercise some informal political power through their husbands; and wives enjoyed, of course, the material benefits of their husbands' greater wealth. Without husbands to support them, widows faced more difficult circumstances. Nevertheless, they sometimes wielded political influence through their sons; they often enjoyed considerable claims over the goods and properties of their dead husbands; and as the "deputies" of their deceased husbands, they were allowed some economic and residential independence. Singlewomen usually enjoyed no such advantages. Some singlewomen were aided by fathers, brothers, sons, or lovers, but many — especially older singlewomen — had no men at all on whom to rely or through whom to claim any economic or social privileges. A few managed very well indeed, but many others faced very hard lives. As the essays of Wiesner, Froide, and Farmer especially stress, in the towns and villages of Europe, the most maligned, least powerful, and poorest women were often those who had never married. Second, *living arrangements* also shaped women's lives. Women who enjoyed secure relationships with men — whether through formal marriage, informal cohabitation, or in some cases, sibling ties — lived differently from women who lived without men (a group that could include some wives as well as many widows and most singlewomen). In other words, a single-woman who lived with her brother might have been, in some ways, more like a wife and less like an archetypal singlewoman.

Despite the differences wrought by marital status and living arrangements, women — especially widows and singlewomen — shared some common experiences. Wiesner tells of how the city fathers of seventeenth-century Württemberg maligned both widows and singlewomen as *Eigenbrötlerinnen* ("women who earn their own bread"). Chojnacka shows how, in sixteenth-century Venice as was also common elsewhere, singlewomen and widows accounted for almost all the women who headed their own households.[45] Moreover, both singlewomen and widows were *femes soles*, allowed to contract debts or sales without the acquiescence of any man; wives, as *femes coverts*, had very restricted contractual powers, although some wives were permitted by their husbands and municipalities to trade as *femes soles*. In other words, singlewomen and widows were often poorer than wives, but they were able to use their meager resources — cash, goods, credit, property — with fewer restrictions. Unlike most wives, they could sell goods, contract debts, loan money, transfer land, and otherwise manage their affairs as they best saw fit.

Because no husbands made sure that singlewomen and widows were well behaved or controlled, these women also shared the anxiety they provoked among their contemporaries, and these anxieties found their fullest expression in the witch craze. Between about 1450 and 1650, many towns and villages in Europe were temporarily gripped by the trauma of witch-hunting; innumerable persons were accused, tested, and tried, and about 100,000 suffered execution. Large-scale persecutions were most common in Scotland, the German states, Switzerland, and parts of France, and somewhat less frequent in England, Scandinavia, the Netherlands, the Iberian peninsula, and Italy.[46] The most likely targets for an accusation of witchcraft were women who lived without men. Of those suspected of communion with the devil, women outnumbered men, the poor outnumbered the rich, the old outnumbered the young, widows outnumbered singlewomen, and singlewomen outnumbered wives. To date we have only vague ideas about why widows and singlewomen were at special risk of accusation, torture, and death at the hands of their neighbors. Perhaps neighbors felt guilty about treating the poorest among them with a lack of charity or petty cruelty; perhaps the women themselves resorted to cunning ways and curses to make a living in desperate situations; perhaps both.[47] In any case, accusations of witchcraft speak in particularly stark terms about the peculiarity and vulnerability of widows and singlewomen.

Despite these similarities, it would be unwise to merge singlewomen and widows into one group of "women alone."[48] As Froide's essay shows, although widows and singlewomen shared the experience of living without husbands in the towns of early modern England, they shared little else. Widows were much more likely to be able to head their own households; widows enjoyed much greater economic security and occupational opportunity; and widows benefited much more often from civic assistance. For example, whereas needy widows were supported by city fathers, needy singlewomen were ignored, maligned, or even expelled. The lives of singlewomen cannot be understood through the lives of widows.

All told, it would be difficult to argue that singlewomen were a different gender from wives or widows in premodern Europe. First, marital status was a fluid category. For life-cycle singlewomen, marriage loomed as a future prospect, as did also the widowhood that followed so many marriages. For lifelong singlewomen, a change in marital status remained possible quite late in life, for even singlewomen in their forties sometimes took husbands. Second, singlewomen did not stand entirely apart, but instead shared with widows both a legal status and a certain measure of social marginality (as Froide's work especially stresses, this marginality was often felt much more strongly by singlewomen). Third, all women — perceived as less able than men and restricted in terms of both political and economic opportunities — shared disabilities peculiar to their sex. Singlewomen's lives were certainly distinct from those of wives and widows, but the distinctions were neither firm nor unchangeable.

To What Extent Were Singlewomen Either "Pioneers" Opening Up New Areas of Activity for All Women or "Victims" Suffering the Worst of Women's Lot in a Patriarchal World?[49]

The essays in this collection offer example after example of the sad circumstances of singlewomen in Europe before 1800. As Stuard shows, singleness and slavery were closely tied in medieval Europe, a tradition echoed in Wiesner's finding that the unmarried daughters of tenants worked as "forced servants" on one Westphalian estate even at the end of the eighteenth century. Prostitution was also linked with singleness. Karras discusses how this connection arose, in part, from the elision of extramarital sexuality with commercial sexuality; a heterosexually active singlewoman, seen as a "whore" in moral terms, was also easily seen as a "whore" in commercial terms. Since heterosexual relations were inherently venal—with singlewomen taking gifts from suitors, or seeking marriage with them—the connections between sex and profit ran very deep indeed. In part, however, prostitution was linked with singlewomen because so many worked at the trade. In cities throughout Europe—examples are found in this volume for thirteenth-century Paris, fourteenth-century Southwark, fifteenth-century German towns, and sixteenth-century Venice—singlewomen sought to support themselves by selling sex, and upright citizens responded by trying to rescue them, regulate them, or expel them.

Most singlewomen, of course, worked neither as slaves nor as prostitutes; most were day-laborers (who lived independently of their employers) or servants (who lived in their employers' homes). Wiesner and Froide demonstrate how singlewomen who supported themselves by day labor prompted considerable anxiety from local governors who opposed singlewomen living on their own. Wiesner observes that the link between service and singleness was so close that *Magd* in German, like "maid" in English, described both a servant and a never-married woman. Some German commentators horribly maligned the singlewomen who cleaned their houses, cooked their meals, and worked in their fields or shops; Philemon Menagius saw serving maids as "nothing but ashes and dirt." Wiesner also describes the other humble employments of singlewomen in Germany: unskilled laboring; working in bathhouses, pesthouses, or hospitals; spinning; weaving; and laundering. Usually excluded from guild-regulated production and commerce, singlewomen also supported themselves by making and selling goods that "no guild bothered to oversee." Wives and widows sometimes worked at the same lowly tasks that occupied singlewomen, but they could also get better employment; for example, some guilds not only allowed wives to assist their husbands in skilled work but also permitted widows to take over the workshops of their deceased husbands. The employment niche that singlewomen occupied was, in short, the most humble niche of all. All women could be found working in these areas, but singlewomen especially made their living from them. In the face of competition from wives or widows, singlewomen sometimes even withdrew from occupations. For example, singlewomen were the first to leave the English brewing industry; long after singlewomen had ceased to brew for profit, wives and widows remained active in the trade.[50]

The living situations of singlewomen were often as difficult as their working lives. If able to live on their own, singlewomen predominated in the poorest and most squalid parts of European towns. Farmer shows how singlewomen often could not survive on their own, needing to band together with other women to support themselves. Singlewomen's sexual options were also fraught with social repercussions, since all sexuality was illicit for them—regardless of whether their lovers were male or female. And their social reception was similarly charged; by the sixteenth and seventeenth centuries, when singlewomen became a more common topic of literary discussion, attitudes towards singlewomen were primarily indifferent or astoundingly hostile (aside from a few positive depictions mostly produced by singlewomen themselves). It is tempting to conclude that singlewomen—especially lifelong singlewomen—were the archetypal female victims of premodern Europe.

Yet this conclusion would be inaccurate. Farmer notes that even among the very poor, singlewomen in thirteenth-century Paris "found practical, economic, and emotional support" in the companionship of women. Chojnacka traces how well-off singlewomen in Venice established and staffed institutions of poor relief for singlewomen less fortunate than themselves. Wiesner observes that some German singlewomen successfully resisted efforts to place them in male-headed households and insisted on "having their own smoke." Froide discusses how middle-class singlewomen in early modern Southampton not only numbered among the town's largest creditors but also owned some of the shops and trades that catered to the town's growing tourist trade. Hunt examines how the prevalence of the single state in eighteenth-century England easily accommodated lesbian love and sexuality. In some ways and at some times, singlewomen—able to live on their own and able to control their own resources—could be seen as the archetypal independent women of premodern Europe.

Moreover, middle-class singlewomen in Europe before 1800 took on increasingly active roles. In eighteenth-century England, it was singlewomen who took advantage of new occupations such as mantua-making (the sewing of ready-made dresses), trading in consumer and luxury goods, and factory work.[51] Other singlewomen, who were financially secure, devoted their time to education (especially female education), charitable causes, and social welfare work.[52] Educated singlewomen also began to speak out on behalf of their sex and their single status. The feminist activity of never-married women in Victorian England might have been more organized and more publicized than before, but it was not a new phenomenon. As Gerda Lerner has shown in her recent history of feminist consciousness, unmarried women in medieval and early modern Europe — nuns, widows, and singlewomen — raised especially loud voices on behalf of their sex.[53] In her essay for this volume, Lanser highlights one particular form of feminist consciousness among singlewomen: their defense of the single state. Singlewomen were important advocates for women, and they pioneered efforts to provide for the educational, economic, social, and legal needs of women. With their voices and pens, they spoke on behalf of all women, and with their lives, they illustrated alternatives for women.

Most of the early feminists or protofeminists known to us today were not only single but also privileged by class and wealth. Yet we should not thereby conclude that middle-class and upper-class singlewomen were fortunate and articulate, whereas ordinary singlewomen were pathetic and silent. The story that Hunt quotes from the diary of the apprentice Roger Lowe — in which he was castigated by a neighbor for maligning women — reminds us that ordinary women could also rise to the defense of their sex, even if privileged women's defenses were better published and preserved. Moreover, although the material benefits of the privileged classes were certainly important, so too was the ability of any singlewoman to manage her own resources, no matter how meager these might have been. Some poor singlewomen had more control over their few goods than did their rich counterparts, and, as we have noted above, they might therefore have been better able to choose the single state and to direct their own lives. We certainly need to investigate more fully how female autonomy and attitudes towards singlewomen varied by class, but it seems likely that poor singlewomen were also — within their more humble and more poorly documented contexts — advocates and examples for women.

How Did Representations of Singlewomen Reflect, Shape, and Diverge from Their Daily Experiences?

In romances, novels, and other fictional narratives, in ballads, lyrics, and songs, and in texts of medical and social commentary, Europeans observed, described, and reflected on the single state. Some authors effusively praised singleness; others condemned and ridiculed the never-married; and others offered deeply ambivalent portraits of singlewomen and their lives. In many cases, any attention — even negative attention — might have been preferable to no attention at all. As Farmer's essay illustrates, serious material consequences could follow from the erasure of singlewomen as a social group. Because the clergy of medieval Paris did not acknowledge singlewomen as a discrete category, they were not deemed worthy of charitable assistance. With their needs unrecognized, singlewomen either managed on their own or masqueraded as widows in order to get some help. Several other essays in this collection similarly suggest that, although invisibility might have been fine for some singlewomen, a lack of social identity was usually more harmful than good.

Representations of singlewomen were so diverse and are, as yet, so little studied that trends are difficult to discern. In medieval literature, only two main genres have been examined for singlewomen per se — Old French courtly narratives and late medieval English songs.[54] Both focused on life-cycle singlewomen, and both offered quite positive assessments. As Krueger demonstrates in her essay for this collection, the twelfth-century *lais* of Marie de France recount the adventures of singlewomen almost as often as those of married women. In some lais singlewomen seem to advocate a new standard of female honor, de-emphasizing chastity and valorizing generosity. These women also rely heavily on female friends and kin, especially those who were, like themselves, not married. Almost all of these fictional singlewomen eventually marry, but beforehand, they actively transform their own lives and the lives of others. In later genres of medieval French literature, singlewomen appear more vulnerable than married women in some respects, but they are also able, competent, and autonomous. Hence, the "maiden's trials" studied by Krueger show singlewomen responding to unhappy circumstances in resourceful and clever ways. Many of these same themes also have been found in late medieval English songs; as Judith Bennett has shown, these songs usually depict young singlewomen as very active participants in courtship and very competent opponents of predatory men.[55]

Representations of singlewomen in early modern literature are only slightly more studied than their medieval counterparts, but it seems possible that later centuries witnessed changes in terms of both which singlewomen were depicted and how. In the sixteenth century, English songs took up a new subject — the *aging* singlewoman — and treated her with more ridicule than sympathy.[56] In the seventeenth century, British authors denounced lifelong singlewomen as sinful and emphasized the undesirability of the single life.[57] And in the eighteenth century, the negative stereotype of the "old maid" came to full fruition, perhaps first in England. This "old maid," the most developed and most negative representation of single-women created in premodern Europe, was depicted as ugly, ill-natured, jealous, nosy, foolish, and simultaneously prudish and lascivious.[58] In her essay for this volume, Lanser argues that Britain was ahead of other countries in its vilification of "old maids," perhaps because singlewomen were perceived as a "national detriment" to mercantile and imperialist expansion (which required a constant reproduction of workers-to-be).

By the eighteenth century, commentators in both England and France (and perhaps elsewhere, as future research might show) focused on the sterility of singlewomen and their lack of social utility.[59] Rather conveniently, writers pursuing such themes did not address how bastard-bearing singlewomen complicated their assumptions. The condemnations of social observers were strengthened by physicians who emphasized the physical and psychological dangers of singleness. Singlewomen, both young and old, were increasingly diagnosed with "greensickness," "melancholy," and various diseases of the womb including "hysteria."[60] Diseased themselves, singlewomen could then infect others; as Lanser shows, metaphors of disease and pollution ran through many discussions of singlewomen in eighteenth-century English writings. As Cécile Dauphin has pointed out for France, a *vieille fille* on her own might be pitied in the eighteenth century, but vieilles filles as a group were to be feared.[61]

Not all depictions of singlewomen in early modern Europe were negative. Female commentators (and a few male ones) entertained the idea of singleness as a choice and outlined the possible roles of singlewomen. In Italy, Moderata Fonte created in *Il Merito delle Donne* the character of Corinna, whose positive rejection of marriage made her a role model for others.[62] In France, authors focused on the services of singlewomen who aided the church, educated the young, and completed other social, moral, and charitable works.[63] In England, authors both advocated singleness and envisioned communities of women who had eschewed marriage. Katherine Phillips's poem "A Married State" portrayed singleness as a haven, an escape from tyrannical husbands as well as the woes of childbearing and childrearing. To her, "A Virgin state is crown'd with much content / It's always happy as it's innocent."[64] Mary Astell and Margaret Cavendish advocated the establishment of retreats for singlewomen where they could immerse themselves in lives of study, creativity, and piety, and Sarah Scott offered a fictional depiction of one such female community in her novel *Millenium*

Hall.[65] These authors and others may well have provided real-life single-women with more self-esteem, new economic options, and expanded social roles. Yet because they directed their attention at women of middling and elite status (women, that is, like themselves), their visions spoke little to singlewomen of the laboring classes.

Whenever numbers of singlewomen began to increase, writers and social commentators seem to have paid more attention to them. This was the case in Renaissance Italy, seventeenth-century England, and eighteenth-century France.[66] Perhaps singlewomen's independence and, in some cases, prosperity mattered more than sheer numbers. This would explain not only why lifelong singlewomen attracted more opprobrium than their younger counterparts, but also why bachelors were never the objects of as much interest (especially, *negative* interest) as were singlewomen. Yet, if commentators were influenced by demographic and social trends, they themselves possibly shaped the trends of the future. As Lanser speculates, the extremely negative depictions of singlewomen that circulated in eighteenth-century England might have helped create a stronger urge to marry. By the end of that century, English people not only married younger but also married in greater numbers than before.

To What Extent Can Lifelong Singleness Be Treated as a "Choice" Made by These Women?

Certainly, for some women, the single state was not a matter of choice. Mental problems, physical disabilities, or illness rendered some women unsuitable for marriage in the eyes of contemporaries; poverty precluded marriage for some; family considerations made it difficult for other women to marry; and the sheer chance of missed opportunities, deceased suitors, or bad timing left some women without husbands. For the single slaves studied by Stuard, singleness was not only unchosen but also compelled; their single state both exemplified and facilitated their enslavement. Yet, just as certainly, some women decided not to marry. For the Middle Ages, opposition to marriage is most readily traced among holy women. Christina of Markyate resisted parents, would-be husband, and even a bishop in her quest to remain single; Catherine of Siena first started to pursue rigorous piety when her parents began to plan for her marriage; and Joan of Arc made much of her status as a never-married maid. In an age that celebrated virginal chastity, piety certainly prompted resistance to marriage, but it also might have been the medium through which resistance could be most acceptably expressed. The distinction between piety-as-motivation and piety-as-explanation might have often blurred in the minds of women who opposed marriage, but it merits more study. For the better-documented and more secular societies of early modern Europe, we have women like Anna Bijns advising "Unyoked is best" and "Happy the woman without a man," and Mary Astell equating marriage with slavery.[67] We might argue about whether these women merely defended a single state in which they found themselves or actively determined not to marry, but they certainly were not at a loss for words.

Motivations are always hard to trace, and the question of whether women were able to choose the single state is especially vexed. For many women, their singleness might have come from a combination of choice, circumstance, and chance. Tangled together in the lives of individual women, these factors should perhaps not be disentangled by historians. Yet it is fair to weigh the balance among them and to see if certain factors facilitated the choice of a single life. Sexuality was one critical factor. As Hunt's essay shows, the same social circumstances that promoted the single state in the eighteenth century also better allowed the expression of lesbian love and sexuality. When many women were single, it was easier for women who preferred the companionship of women to avoid marriage. (As Hunt's essay also emphasizes, however, marriage did not necessarily preclude same-sex love.) Marriage practices were another important factor shaping whether a woman remained single. When and where singleness was less common, women who might have been motivated to avoid marriage — for reasons of sexuality or otherwise — were more likely to take husbands. Female control of property was a third important determinant. Wealth may have allowed some women to remain single if they so wished, for some female authors in early modern England quite explicitly advised privileged women like themselves to choose the single life. Other, less-privileged women might have judged marriage just as harshly and remained single when they were able to do so. Since working women seem to have married less often when they had good employment, perhaps they expressed through their avoidance of marriage what Bijns and Astell expressed in their writings. In influencing the ability of singlewomen to choose their state, economic differences might have been more matters of female prosperity and autonomy than matters of class status. Many women who were privileged by their class status often had no option but to marry or enter a nunnery, whereas some women from more humble class backgrounds were better able to support themselves without husbands.

The delicate balance between chance and choice is very hard to assess, but it seems that some women — those inclined toward lesbian love, those living among large numbers of singlewomen, and those who controlled their own resources — might have been more likely to eschew marriage than others. Sometimes all three factors came together, as they did for Anne Lister in early nineteenth-century Britain.[68] Sometimes one factor might have been enough, as it could have been for the women who earned higher-than-usual wages in seventeenth-century Colyton; they seem to have re-sponded to their relative prosperity by delaying or avoiding marriage.[69] For all women, singleness separated into two discrete issues: did they *want* to remain single, and were they *able* to do so? In negotiating both desire and ability, singlewomen were certainly influenced by sexuality, marriage prac-tices, and their own prosperity. They were also influenced by the normative role of marriage, the association of adulthood with the taking of a spouse, the stories they heard about husbands, children, and married life, and the depictions of singlewomen they found in popular literature and song. For Jane Barker, the decision to remain single was neither easy nor taken lightly. In her poem "A Virgin Life," Barker pleads:

Suffer me not to fall into the Powers,
of Men's almost Omnipotent Amours;
But in this happy Life let me remain,
Fearless of Twenty-five and all its train,
Of slights or scorns, or being called Old Maid.[70]

What Personal Relationships Were Primary to Women Who Lived Without Husbands and, in Many Cases, Without Children? To What Extent Did These Women Live Outside the Emotional and Sexual Norms Set by Heterosexual Marriage?

Singlewomen often forged especially close relationships with parents, sib-lings, nieces, and nephews. These ties were sometimes so close that single-women passed their entire lives in the company of relatives — moving from their parents' household to that of siblings or aunts, and eventually taking other kin into their own households. The kinship networks of singlewomen could be small but intense. Unlike wives or widows, they did not acquire kin through marriage, and they were less likely, of course, to bear or rear children; yet they assiduously cultivated extended kin relations, more so than many married women and men. Cause and effect are hard to determine in this regard; perhaps singlewomen maintained ties with their kin to compensate for their lack of spouse or children, but perhaps, as Adams has suggested, these women remained single precisely because of their strong familial ties.[71] It was not at all uncommon for a singlewoman to share a house with her mother, or to set up household with another single sister, or to live in the home of a married sibling. It was also not at all uncommon for a singlewoman to shower attention, love, and property on nieces or nephews. Close family ties were certainly not enjoyed by all singlewomen, for some lost contact with kin when they migrated away from their original homes. Strong kinship ties were also not unique to singlewomen, for most people in premodern Europe appreciated the importance of parents, siblings, and collateral descendants. Nevertheless, singlewomen seem to have been especially attentive daughters, sisters, and aunts.

Singlewomen were particularly close to their female kin, forming some of their most important relationships with mothers, sisters, and nieces.[72] In early modern Southampton, Froide has found more than fifty pairs of never-married sisters, many of whom lived and worked together throughout their lives, and some of whom left their goods and businesses to nieces (or, more rarely, to nephews). In 1745, for example, the never-married sisters Elizabeth and Joanna Shergold arranged for their brother's daughter Elizabeth to acquire their large tenement on the High Street of Southampton in which they had run a boarding school for girls. In 1756, when the second of the two sisters died, the younger Elizabeth also received her aunts' combined fortune. As she found to her great benefit, singlewomen were often fond aunts — generous in both gifts and bequests.[73]

While blood relatives were important to women without husbands, we should not assume that all singlewomen lacked romantic or sexual relationships. Some singlewomen had lovers — male or female — who were primary sources of emotional, sexual, and sometimes also material support. Some of these couples lived together, and some did not. A Hampshire woman named Joanne Ecton lived with her lover Richard Ecton as his "pretended wife" for seven or eight years and had at least one child with him. When her lover died in 1695 she found that Richard's sister refused to let her inherit Richard's goods since "they had never produced a marriage certificate."[74] In 1680 the singlewoman Arabella Hunt, a musician at the English court, and the widow Amy Poulter, who disguised herself as a man (taking the name James Howard), married each other in a London parish church. They lived together for half a year before Hunt petitioned the local church court for an annulment.[75] Other romantic relationships between singlewomen were more successful. In the eighteenth-century the Anglo-Irish gentlewomen Eleanor Butler and Sarah Ponsonby eloped and set up house together in North Wales. They lived together happily for over forty years.[76]

The homes of singlewomen did not always lack the voices of children. Some singlewomen bore and reared children outside of marriage. Pregnancy was difficult for singlewomen, especially since servants, in particular, were liable for dismissal if pregnant. Mothering was also challenging for singlewomen, who feature prominently among mothers accused of infanticide (it is not clear that single mothers were actually more likely to kill their infants, but it is evident they were more likely to be suspected of the crime).[77] Yet difficult as they were, pregnancy and childrearing were not unmitigated disasters for singlewomen. As Leah Leneman and Rosalind Mitchison have shown particularly well for Scotland, single mothers faced hard times and social criticism, but they were not necessarily subjected to ostracism. Facing a difficult but not uncommon lot, single mothers were able to manage and eventually, in some cases, even to marry.[78]

Other singlewomen lived with children they had not themselves borne. Adoption was not common in Europe before 1800, but at least some singlewomen adopted children — almost always girls — to raise in their homes.[79] Others informally took care of nieces or nephews whose parents had died, disappeared, or fallen into destitution. Coresidence also brought singlewomen into daily contact with children. Young singlewomen who worked as servants in the homes of their employers usually lived with children and sometimes took direct responsibility for their care. Older singlewomen also shared houses with children, for many of them lived with married siblings, shared a home with widowed friends, or lodged with a family.

Relatives, lovers, and children were important to many singlewomen, but so too were friends. Because many of these friends were female — usually other singlewomen or widows — singlewomen provide strong evidence for female support networks and female sociability in past times. Some singlewomen, like those studied by Chojnacka, found support within institutions. The Casa delle Zitelle in Venice sustained not only its inmates but also the women who staffed and administered its services. Other singlewomen combined friendship with commercial arrangements for lodgings. As Farmer shows in her essay, Amelot of Chaumont of thirteenth-century

Paris found to her benefit that landladies could be good friends in hard times; as Hunt shows in her essay, Charlotte Charke in eighteenth-century London turned the same relationship around: for her, a lodger, who may also have been a lover, proved a trustworthy ally in a difficult lawsuit.[80] And still other singlewomen lived together—in beguinages, spinster clusters, and other such arrangements—in order to support themselves better both materially and emotionally. For the singlewomen Farmer studies, the beguinage of Paris was an important refuge, as long as they were willing to observe its many rules. To date, historians have best traced peer support among singlewomen who shared housing, whether in institutions, lodgings, or a common home. Perhaps the relative poverty of singlewomen had a social and emotional benefit; forced to live together to save money, singlewomen might have sometimes found that coresidence offered emotional and social as well as material benefits. Yet we need to explore further how singlewomen drew support and love from people with whom they did not live—neighbors, friends, and kin living in nearby houses or communities. Many singlewomen, for example, found friendship and fellowship in their local churches and religious institutions.[81] Were there other organizations that especially accommodated the singlewoman's social and emotional needs?

Married people and singlewomen did not inhabit radically different social worlds. Some married people had no children; some singlewomen did. Some married people lived without the daily comfort of spouses; some singlewomen cohabited with lovers. Most married people shared housing with servants, lodgers, kin, or friends; most singlewomen did the same. Yet in one respect singlewomen differed markedly from their contemporaries: their emotional lives were often strongly centered on women. Masters, fathers, brothers, and male lovers were certainly important to singlewomen, but for love, support, and shared residence singlewomen turned more often to women—to mothers more than fathers, sisters more than brothers, nieces more than nephews, and female friends more than male ones. This pattern might have been stronger among lifelong singlewomen than among life-cycle singlewomen, and it probably derives in part from social customs that tended to divide the sexes, regardless of marital status. Yet it is certainly intriguing that, of all women, singlewomen were the most woman-focused and perhaps, indeed, the most woman-identified.

This volume is just a beginning. In some respects, these essays present seemingly contradictory findings that can only be resolved through future research. Why, for example, does Chojnacka find such limited employment options for singlewomen in sixteenth-century Venice, whereas Wiesner traces extensive, if humble, possibilities in contemporary German towns? Why, for another example, were singlewomen invisible to the medieval theologians Farmer studies, yet quite obvious to the contemporary authors whose fictional tales are studied by Krueger? In other respects, these essays complement each other, suggesting trends that also demand further investigation. How might female slavery in medieval cities help us better understand singlewomen in domestic service? Was there really a shift, in the sixteenth century, toward more negative representations of singlewomen? Is there a causal connection between the greater prominence of singlewomen in the eighteenth century and the increasingly negative rhetoric directed at them? There is much work yet to be done — theories to test, archives to plunge into, and questions to be asked.

In doing this research, we will learn more about a hitherto neglected group, but there is much more to the history of singlewomen than merely "filling in" an ignored subject. Singlewomen were critical players in the demographic changes of Europe before 1800; their experiences reveal a great deal about adolescence, service, and apprenticeship in the European past; and their lives productively complicate the study of past families and past sexualities. By looking at the lives of singlewomen in premodern Europe, we will learn more about women, gender, and society in premodern Europe. We will uncover more differences — and similarities — among women. We will better understand how women — single, as well as married or widowed — forged familial and social relations with other women. We will more thoroughly reconstruct the social contexts and beginnings of feminist ideas and advocacy. And we will decenter the conjugal family as the essential familial unit of the European past — seeing European society not as it ideally was, but instead as it really existed. Living in a patriarchal culture that praised wives, honored widows, and often ignored or maligned singlewomen, many Europeans between 1250 and 1800 were nevertheless surrounded by large numbers of adult women who had not married. By studying the lives of these women — life-cycle singlewomen as well as lifelong singlewomen — we will construct a more complete and complex picture of the European past.

We would like to thank Sandy Bardsley, Margaret Hunt, Maryanne Kowaleski, and Merry Wiesner for their thoughtful critiques of this essay.

Notes

1. In German *Frau* and *Mann* were used to indicate the words "woman" and "man" as well as "wife" and "husband"; in French *femme* denoted both "woman" and "wife"; in Spanish *mujer* meant both "woman" and "wife."

2. The Oxford English Dictionary gives 1617 as the first use of "spinster" to denote a never-married woman. See also Carol Wiener, "Is a Spinster an Unmarried Woman?" *American Journal of Legal History* 20 (1976): 27–31, and subsequent comments by J. H. Baker and Valerie C. Edwards in *American Journal of Legal History* 21 (1977): 255–65.

3. See Amy M. Froide, "Single Women, Work, and Community in Southampton" (Ph.D. diss., Duke University, 1996), 362–420, for the origins of negative ideas about spinsters in seventeenth-century England. See Susan Lanser's essay in this volume, as well as Katherine Ottaway Kittredge, "'Tabby Cats Lead Apes in Hell': Spinsters in Eighteenth Century Life and Fiction" (Ph.D. diss., SUNY Binghamton, 1991) for eighteenth-century stereotypes of the "old maid." English is not the only European language to have pejorative terms for never-married women. In France these women were neutrally termed *demoiselles* or *femmes célibataires*, but were also called *mademoiselles* or *filles* (terms that became an embarrassment to a woman when she was no longer young), and, more negatively, *vieilles filles* (old maids). In Italian a singlewoman was called a *donna nubile*, a *dimesse* (an adjective meaning meek or humble), or a *zitella* (a term sometimes having negative connotations). In German a singlewoman was termed a *Jungfrau*, more colloquially *Jungfer*, and more pejoratively *alte Jungfer* (old maid). She was also referred to as *Fräulein*, a term associated with youth and perhaps embarrassing to older singlewomen. In Spanish a never-married woman was called a *soltera*, or pejoratively *solterona*. There were no similarly negative terms for bachelors in these languages.

4. For these and other demographic estimates of the presence of singlewomen, see Maryanne Kowaleski's essay in this collection.

5. Singlewomen have generated more interest among historians of the modern era, a fact partly attributable to the availability of sources. In the eighteenth century, the figure of the spinster became a common literary trope, and in the nineteenth century, Europeans and Americans frequently discussed the "problem" of what they called "redundant women" (which they erroneously believed was a new historical dilemma). Interest in modern spinsters also stems from the fact that many middle-class singlewomen were among the first feminists and suffragists, the first women to be educated in colleges, and the first women to enter the professions. Thus, they are hard to miss. For England, see Martha Vicinus, *Independent Women: Work and Community for Single Women, 1850–1920* (Chicago: University of Chicago Press, 1985); Patricia Jalland, "Dutiful Daughters, Desperate Rebels and the Transition to the New Women," in *Exploring Women's Past: Essays in Social History*, ed. Patricia Crawford (Sydney: Allen & Unwin, 1984), 129–70; Ruth Freeman and Patricia Klaus, "Blessed or Not? The New Spinster in England and the United States in the Late Nineteenth and Early Twentieth Centuries," *Journal of Family History* 9, 4 (1984): 394–414; for France, see Arlette Farge and Christiane Klapisch-Zuber, eds., *Madame ou mademoiselle? Itinéraires de la solitude féminine, XVIIIe–XXe siècle* (Paris:

Montalba, 1984); for Europe in general, see Susan Cott Watkins, "Spinsters," *Journal of Family History* 9, 4 (1984): 310–25; Cécile Dauphin, "Single Women," in *A History of Women in the West*, vol. 4, *Emerging Feminism from Revolution to World War*, ed. Geneviève Fraisse and Michelle Perrot (Cambridge, Mass.: Harvard University Press, 1993); for the U.S., see Lee Chambers-Schiller, *Liberty, a Better Husband: Single Women in America: The Generations of 1780–1840* (New Haven, Conn.: Yale University Press, 1984).

6. In its focus on western Europe, for example, this collection reflects the currently imbalanced state of research on the history of women in the various regions of Europe.

7. Demographic historians once focused particularly on death rates as the prime cause of population trends, but in the last few decades they have begun to stress the importance of fertility in determining population growth or decline. See especially E. A. Wrigley and Roger Schofield, *The Population History of England, 1541–1871: A Reconstruction* (London: Edward Arnold, 1981), 255–65; Michael W. Flinn, *The European Demographic System, 1500–1820* (Baltimore: Johns Hopkins University Press, 1981), 19–20.

8. John Hajnal, "European Marriage Patterns in Perspective," in *Population in History: Essays in Historical Demography*, ed. D. V. Glass and D. E. C. Eversley (Chicago: Aldine, 1965), 101–43.

9. See, for example, R. M. Smith, "Some Reflections on the Evidence for the Origins of the 'European Marriage Pattern' in England," in *The Sociology of the Family: New Directions in Britain*, ed. Chris Harris (Totowa, N.J.: Rowman and Littlefield, 1979), 74–112.

10. Watkins has cautioned against overstressing systems of marriage when explaining the singleness of women in the past. In her view, economic circumstances, attempts at population control, and skewed sex ratios also profoundly affected rates of singleness (Watkins, "Spinsters"). For other scholars who emphasize the effect of economic conditions on singleness, see Pamela Sharpe, "Literally Spinsters: A New Interpretation of Local Economy and Demography in Colyton in the Seventeenth and Eighteenth Centuries," *Economic History Review* 44, 1 (1991): 46–65; Olwen Hufton, "Women Without Men: Widows and Spinsters in Britain and France in the Eighteenth Century," *Journal of Family History* 9, 4 (1984): 355–76.

11. Kowaleski's essay; David S. Reber, *Town and Country in Pre-industrial Spain: Cuenca, 1550–1870* (New York: Cambridge University Press, 1990), 75, 80, n. 20; and Hans Johansen, "Never-Married Women in Town and Country in Eighteenth-Century Denmark," in *Poor Women and Children in the European Past*, ed. John Henderson and Richard Wall (New York: Routledge, 1994), 196–206.

12. Vivien Brodsky Elliott, "Single Women in the London Marriage Market: Age, Status, and Mobility, 1598–1619," in *Studies in the Social History of Marriage and Society*, ed. R. B. Outhwaite (New York: St. Martin's Press, 1981), 81–100; Sharpe, "Literally Spinsters."

13. For the connection between spinsterhood and poverty, see especially Sharpe, "Literally Spinsters," 56; and Watkins, "Spinsters," 320, 323. For instances in which elite women were unable to marry, see Klapisch-Zuber, "Female Celibacy and Service in Florence in the Fifteenth Century," in her *Women, Family, and Ritual in Re-*

naissance Italy (Chicago: University of Chicago Press, 1985), 170–72; Virginia Cox, "The Single Self: Feminist Thought and the Marriage Market in Early Modern Venice," *Renaissance Quarterly* 48, 3 (Autumn 1995): 513–81; Hufton, "Women Without Men," 358–59. See also Christine Adams, "A Choice Not to Wed? Unmarried Women in Eighteenth-Century France," *Journal of Social History* 29, 4 (1996): 885.

14. Sharpe, "Literally Spinsters," 62–63; the less well-documented case of fifteenth-century York in P. J. P. Goldberg, *Women, Work, and Life Cycle in a Medieval Economy: Women in York and Yorkshire c.1300–1520* (Oxford: Clarendon Press, 1992), esp. 360–61; and the hypotheses of Richard M. Smith, "Women's Work and Marriage in Pre-industrial England: Some Speculations," in *La donna nell' economia secc. XIII–XVIII*, ed. Simonetta Cavaciocchi (Firenze: Le Monnier, 1990), 31–55. This correlation has only been posited so far by English historians, but they sometimes draw on continental evidence.

15. Elizabeth's own male advisors attributed her lack of desire to marry to her need to be both "king and queen" and believed she stayed single "to govern more absolutely" (Christopher Haigh, *Elizabeth I* [New York: Longman, 1988], 11–16).

16. Adrienne Rich, "Compulsory Heterosexuality and Lesbian Existence," *Signs* 5 (1980): 631–60.

17. Elsa Barkley Brown has argued this point in terms of women of different races in the United States in her "Polyrhythms and Improvisation: Lessons for Women's History," *History Workshop Journal* 31 (1991): 85–91.

18. For similar institutions in other Italian cities see Marina d'Amelia, "Scatole cinesi (chinese boxes): vedove e donne sole in una società d'ancien regime," *Memoria: Revista di Storia Delle Donne* (1986): 49; Daniela Maldini, "Donne sole," *Risorgimento* 33, 2 (1981): 115–38, 56, and again 113; Maura Palazzi, "Abitare da sole," *Memoria* (1986): 50, 95; Maria Vasaio, "Il tessuto della virtu: le zitelle di S. Eufemia e di S. Caterina dei Funari Nella Controriforma," *Memoria* (1984): 51, 71.

19. Hufton, "Women Without Men," 367–72; Adams, "A Choice Not to Wed?" 886–87; Cox, "The Single Self," 546–49, 563–68.

20. Mary Astell, *A Serious Proposal to the Ladies*, 4th ed. (London, 1701); Jane Barker, "A Virgin Life," in *Poetical Recreations* (London, 1688); Moderata Fonte [Modesta Pozzo], *Il Merito delle donne* (Venice, 1600), discussed in Cox, "The Single Self," 558–69.

21. Hufton, "Women Without Men," 363; Johansen, "Never-Married Women."

22. For general studies of adolescence, see especially Philippe Ariès, *Centuries of Childhood: A Social History of Family Life*, English ed. (New York: Vintage Books, 1962); Michael Mitterauer, *A History of Youth* (Cambridge, Mass.: Blackwell, 1993); Paul Griffiths, *Youth and Authority: Formative Experiences in England 1560–1640* (Oxford: Clarendon Press, 1996); Barbara Hanawalt, *Growing Up in Medieval London: The Experience of Childhood in History* (New York: Oxford University Press, 1993); Ilana Krausman Ben-Amos, *Adolescence and Youth in Early Modern England* (New Haven, Conn.: Yale University Press, 1994); Susan Brigden, "Youth and the English Reformation," *Past and Present* 95 (1982): 37–67; Natalie Zemon Davis, "The Reasons for Misrule: Youth Groups and Charivaris in Sixteenth-Century France," *Past and Present* 50 (1971): 41–75; Jacques Rossiaud, "Prostitution, Youth, and Society in the Towns of Southeastern France in the Fifteenth

Century," *Annales, E. S. C.* 31 (March–April 1976): 289–325; Stanley Chojnacki, "Measuring Adulthood: Adolescence and Gender in Renaissance Venice," *Journal of Family History* 17, 4 (1992): 371–96; James A. Schultz, "Medieval Adolescence: The Claims of History and the Silence of German Narrative," *Speculum* 66 (1991): 519–39; Merry E. Wiesner, *"Wandervögel* and Women: Journeymen's Concepts of Masculinity in Early Modern Germany," *Journal of Social History* 24 (1991): 767–82; Roger Thompson, "Adolescent Culture in Colonial Massachusetts," *Journal of Family History* 9, 2 (1984): 127–44.

23. Ben Amos, *Adolescence and Youth*, 133–55. For other examples emphasizing the independence of a young woman's years in service, see Judith M. Bennett, *Women in the Medieval English Countryside* (New York: Oxford University Press, 1987), 65–99; D. A. Kent, "Ubiquitous but Invisible: Female Domestic Servants in Mid-Eighteenth Century London," *History Workshop Journal* 28 (Autumn 1989): 111–28; Marjorie K. McIntosh, "Servants and the Household Unit in an Elizabethan English Community," *Journal of Family History* 9, 1 (1984): 3–23.

24. For many young singlewomen, autonomy was tempered by restriction; they were forced into domestic service, put into houses of correction, and even expelled from communities. See Paul Griffiths, *Youth and Authority: Formative Experiences in England, 1560–1640* (Oxford: Clarendon, 1996), 351–89.

25. For literature on servants in England, see Goldberg, *Women, Work, and Life Cycle*, 158–202; L. R. Poos, *A Rural Society After the Black Death: Essex 1350–1525* (Cambridge: Cambridge University Press, 1991), 183–206; Bridget Hill, *Servants: English Domestics in the Eighteenth Century* (New York: Oxford University Press, 1996); Ann Kussmaul, *Servants in Husbandry in Early Modern England* (New York: Cambridge University Press, 1981). For France, see Cissie Fairchilds, *Domestic Enemies: Servants and Their Masters in Old Regime France* (Baltimore: Johns Hopkins University Press, 1984); Sara Maza, *Servants and Masters in Eighteenth-Century France: The Use of Loyalty* (Princeton, N.J.: Princeton University Press, 1983). For Italy, see Christiane Klapisch-Zuber, "Women Servants in Florence During the Fourteenth and Fifteenth Centuries," in *Women and Work in Preindustrial Europe*, ed. Barbara Hanawalt (Bloomington: Indiana University Press, 1986); Dennis Romano, *Housecraft and Statecraft: Domestic Service in Renaissance Venice, 1400–1600* (Baltimore: Johns Hopkins University Press, 1996). For Germany, see Merry E. Wiesner, *Working Women in Renaissance Germany* (New Brunswick, N.J.: Rutgers University Press, 1986), 75–110; Renate Dürr, *Mägde in der Stadt: Das Beispiel Schwäbisch-Hall in der Frühen Neuzeit* (Frankfurt: Campus, 1995). For the Netherlands, see Marybeth Carlson, "A Trojan Horse of Worldliness? Maidservants in the Burgher Household in Rotterdam at the End of the Seventeenth Century"; Rudolph Dekker, "Maid Servants in the Dutch Republic: Sources and Comparative Perspectives. A Response to Marybeth Carlson," in *Women of the Golden Age: An International Debate on Women in Seventeenth-Century Holland, England, and Italy*, ed. Els Kloek, Nicole Teeuwen, and Marijke Huisman (Hilversum: Verloren, 1994), 87–96, 97–102, respectively.

26. For discussions of the positive possibilities of service for singlewomen, see McIntosh, "Servants and the Household"; Kent, "Ubiquitous but Invisible." See also Wiesner, *Working Women*, 83–92.

27. See Klapisch-Zuber, "Women Servants in Florence"; Hanawalt, *Growing Up in Medieval London*, 173–98; Tim Meldrum, "London Domestic Servants from Depositional Evidence, 1660–1750: Servant-Employer Sexuality in the Patriarchal Household," in *Chronicling Poverty: The Voices and Strategies of the English Poor, 1640–1840*, ed. Tim Hitchcock, Peter King, and Pamela Sharpe (New York: St. Martin's Press, 1997), 47–69; Hill, *Servants*, 44–63, 93–114; Maza, *Servants and Masters*.

28. This link was posited by Hajnal and is critical in the analyses of Smith (see, for example, "Women's Work and Marriage"), Goldberg (see *Women, Work and Life Cycle*, esp. 324–61), and L. R. Poos (see *A Rural Society*, esp. 133–58 and 183–206). All servants were not single; see, for example, Klapisch-Zuber, "Women Servants in Florence," 63, 74, and "Female Celibacy," 172–74.

29. Ilana Krausman Ben-Amos, "Women Apprentices in the Trades and Crafts of Early Modern Bristol," *Continuity and Change* 6, 2 (1991): 229, 236. For some exceptions to this hypothesis of decline before 1800, see K. D. M. Snell, *Annals of the Labouring Poor: Social Change and Agrarian England, 1660–1900* (New York: Cambridge University Press, 1985), 270–319; Claire Crowston, "Women's Work Outside of the (Patriarchal) Family Economy? The Seamstresses of Eighteenth-Century Paris," paper presented at the Third Carleton Conference on the History of the Family, Carleton University, Ottawa, Canada, 15–17 May 1997.

30. Margaret Hunt, *The Middling Sort: Commerce, Gender, and the Family in England, 1680–1780* (Berkeley: University of California Press, 1996), 80, 90–91; Elizabeth C. Sanderson, *Women and Work in Eighteenth-Century Edinburgh* (New York: St. Martin's Press, 1996), 74–107, esp. 79, 84–93; Froide, "Single Women, Work, and Community," 242–302.

31. Pamela Sharpe, "Poor Children as Apprentices in Colyton, 1598–1830," *Continuity and Change* 6, 2 (1991): 253–70; Froide, "Single Women, Work, and Community," 245–46. Pauper apprenticeship is most associated with England, but some poor children in France were fostered out to families who used their labor and sometimes taught them a trade (Carole Loats, "Creating Family and Household Ties Through Adoption, Fostering, Service, and Apprenticeship in Early Modern Paris" and Sylvie Perrier, "The Experience of Orphans Living with Relatives or Strangers in Early Modern France," papers presented at the Third Carleton Conference on the History of the Family, Carleton University, Ottawa, Canada, 15–17 May 1997). In cities on the continent, orphans and poor children were accommodated in institutions; see Brian Pullan, "Orphans and Foundlings in Early Modern Europe," in his *Poverty and Charity: Europe, Italy, Venice, 1400–1700* (Brookfield, Vt.: Variorium, 1994), esp. 7, 9–10, 20–22; Wiesner, *Working Women*, 178, 184.

32. In Renaissance Venice, male adolescence could end before marriage. Women entered adulthood when they married, but men, marrying later in life than did women, achieved adulthood by entering business and government. So it was possible in certain places and times for adolescence to end before marriage — at least, for men (Chojnacki, "Measuring Adulthood").

33. See essays by Froide and Wiesner in this volume; Wiesner, *Working Women*, 83; Olwen Hufton, "Women Without Men"; Carlson, "A Trojan Horse," 92–93; Griffiths, *Youth and Authority*, 33.

34. Amy Froide, "'Old Maids': The Life Cycle of Single Women in Early

Modern England," in *Old Women in England, 1500 to the Present*, ed. Lynn Botelho and Pat Thane (London: Longman, 1999).

35. Richard Wall, "Woman Alone in English Society," *Annales de Démographie Historique* 17 (1981): 310–12; Tamara K. Hareven and Louise A. Tilly, "Solitary Women and Family Mediation in America and French Textile Cities," *Annales de Démographie Historique* 17 (1981): 257–60, 262–65; Maura Palazzi, "Female Solitude and Patrilineage: Unmarried Women and Widows During the Eighteenth and Nineteenth Centuries," *Journal of Family History* 15, 4 (1990): 455; Johansen, "Never-Married Women," 198–99; Hufton, "Women Without Men," 361.

36. See also Johansen, "Never-Married Women."

37. For evidence of the frequency, in certain times and places, of premarital sex (and conception) see Peter Laslett, Karla Oosterveen, and R. M. Smith, *Bastardy and Its Comparative History* (Cambridge, Mass.: Harvard University Press, 1980), 11 and 26; Martin Ingram, *Church Courts, Sex and Marriage in England, 1570–1640* (New York: Cambridge University Press, 1987), 219–81; G. R. Quaife, *Wanton Wenches and Wayward Wives: Peasants and Illicit Sex in Early Seventeenth Century England* (New Brunswick, N.J.: Rutgers University Press, 1979). Also see bibliographies in Olwen Hufton, *The Prospect Before Her: A History of Women in Western Europe*, vol. 1 *1500–1800*, 1st American ed. (New York: Knopf, 1996), 590–92.

38. For England, see Peter Laslett, *Family Life and Illicit Love in Earlier Generations: Essays in Historical Sociology* (New York: Cambridge University Press, 1977); John Gillis, *For Better, For Worse: British Marriages, 1600 to the Present* (New York: Oxford University Press, 1985). For France, see Jean-Louis Flandrin, *Families in Former Times: Kinship, Household, and Sexuality* (New York: Cambridge University Press, 1979). For Scotland, see Leah Leneman and Rosalind Mitchison, "Clandestine Marriage in the Scottish Cities 1660–1780," *Journal of Social History* 26, 4 (Summer 1993): 845–61.

39. For medieval Europe, see Valerie R. Hotchkiss, *Clothes Make the Man: Female Cross Dressing in Medieval Europe* (New York: Garland, 1996); E. Ann Matter, "My Sister, My Spouse: Woman-Identified Women in Medieval Christianity," *Journal of Feminist Studies in Religion* 2, 2 (Fall 1986): 81–93; Jacqueline Murray, "Twice Marginal and Twice Invisible: Lesbians in the Middle Ages," in *Handbook of Medieval Sexuality*, ed. Vern L. Bullough and James A. Brundage (New York: Garland, 1996), 191–222. For early modern Europe, see Judith C. Brown, *Immodest Acts: The Life of a Lesbian Nun in Renaissance Italy* (New York: Oxford University Press, 1986); Emma Donoghue, *Passions Between Women: British Lesbian Culture 1668–1801* (New York: HarperCollins, 1993), esp. 3–4 for early uses of the term "lesbian"; Lillian Faderman, *Surpassing the Love of Men: Romantic Friendship and Love Between Women from the Renaissance to the Present* (New York: Quill, 1981).

40. On migration and delayed marriage, see Brodsky, "Single Women." On migration and prostitution, see Ruth Mazo Karras, *Common Women: Prostitution and Sexuality in Medieval England* (New York: Oxford University Press, 1996), 56–57.

41. Because historians have focused almost exclusively on the experiences of African men in England, it is, as yet, difficult to know how many African women traveled to England and for what purposes. For instance, see Folarin Shyllon, *Black People in Britain 1555–1833* (London: Oxford University Press, 1977); James Walvin,

Black and White: The Negro and English Society 1555–1945 (London: Allen Lane, 1973). For an account that does include the experiences of African women in England, see Peter Fryer, *Staying Power: The History of Black People in Britain* (London: Pluto Press, 1984). Fryer found African women supporting themselves as servants, day-laborers, prostitutes, entertainers, and beggars. For examples of African women in the port town of Southampton, see Douglas F. Vick, ed., *Central Hampshire Lay Subsidy Assessments, 1558–1603* (Farnham, Hants.: D.F. Vick, 1987) ("negro maids" and female "negroes owned" mentioned in 1598–99); Southampton Record Office, D/MC/8/1 ("the Blackwoman" mentioned in 1712), PR 9/15/6 (Sarah Sambo mentioned in 1729).

42. Monastic life seems actually to have precluded single life, for wealthy parents sometimes placed not-married daughters in monasteries rather than accommodating them at home; see Herlihy and Klapisch-Zuber, *Tuscans*, 215. Two factors rendered monasticism less popular in some parts of early modern Europe. First, when the Reformation eliminated monasticism in many parts of northern Europe, the monastery-as-alternative-to-marriage was lost. Second, in some Catholic cities the large dowries demanded by female monasteries seem to have made religious life too expensive, even for daughters of wealthy parents; see Chojnacki, "Measuring Adulthood," 376–77; Cox, "The Single Self." Both circumstances probably worked to create more singlewomen.

43. Cox, "The Single Self," 546–47; Merry E. Wiesner, *Women and Gender in Early Modern Europe* (New York: Cambridge University Press, 1993), 196–97; Mary Elizabeth Perry, *Gender and Disorder in Early Modern Seville* (Princeton, N.J.: Princeton University Press, 1990), 80, 97–98, 103, 108, 116.

44. Stefanie Siegmund, "From Tuscan Households to Urban Ghetto: The Construction of a Jewish Community in Florence, 1570–1611" (Ph.D. diss., Jewish Theological Seminary, 1995), chap. 8; and "La vita nei ghetti," in *Storia d'Italia: Annali 11 gli ebrei in Italia, Part I* (Turin: Einaudi, 1996), 845–92. For estimates of singleness but not ages of marriage among medieval Jews, see Kenneth R. Stow, "The Jewish Family in the Rhineland in the High Middle Ages: Form and Function," *American Historical Review* 92 (1987): 1085–1110, esp. 1087–88.

45. See also Wall, "Woman Alone," 306.

46. For introductions to the burgeoning literature on witchcraft, see Olwen Hufton, *The Prospect Before Her*, 336–62, esp. 340; Wiesner, *Women and Gender*, 218–38.

47. For a recent study of witchcraft that suggests it may have been a career that enabled some women not to marry, see Sally Scully, "Marriage or a Career? Witchcraft as an Alternative in Seventeenth-Century Venice," *Journal of Social History* 28, 4 (Summer 1995): 857–76.

48. To date most studies of singlewomen have come from scholars primarily focused on widows. See Hufton, "Women Without Men"; Amy Erickson, *Women and Property in Early Modern England* (New York: Routledge, 1993), 187–222; Maura Palazzi, "Female Solitude."

49. This question was prompted in part by studies of singlewomen in modern Europe. As the work of Martha Vicinus has particularly shown, never-married women were a powerful force for change in late nineteenth-century and early

twentieth-century England. Yet, as Vicinus has noted, these women were "simultaneously powerful and peripheral" (Vicinus, *Independent Women*, 9). For similar evaluations, see Palazzi, "Female Solitude," 455; Hufton, "Women Without Men," 370–74.

50. Judith M. Bennett, *Ale, Beer, and Brewsters in England: Women's Work in a Changing World, 1300–1600* (New York: Oxford University Press, 1996), esp. 37–59.

51. See also Mary Prior, "Women and the Urban Economy: Oxford 1500–1800," in her *Women in English Society 1500–1800* (London: Methuen, 1985), 108, 110–14; Hunt, *The Middling Sort*, 127 and 132–33; Froide, "Single Women, Work, and Community," 242–302; Eric Richards, "Women in the British Economy Since About 1700: An Interpretation," *History* 59 (1974): 337–57.

52. Hufton, "Women Without Men."

53. Gerda Lerner, *The Creation of Feminist Consciousness: From the Middle Ages to 1870* (New York: Oxford University Press, 1993). As Bridget Hill has discussed in her study of attempts to establish Protestant nunneries in early modern England, single-women were early advocates of women's educational needs (Hill, "A Refuge from Men: The Idea of a Protestant Nunnery," *Past and Present* 117 (1987): 107–30).

54. Without focusing on their single state, other literary studies have, of course, considered never-married women. See, for example, Ann Marie Rasmussen, *Mothers and Daughters in Medieval German Literature* (Syracuse, N.Y.: Syracuse University Press, 1997).

55. Judith M. Bennett, "Maidens and Singlewomen in Late Medieval English Song, c. 1300–1550," Fred Alexander lecture forthcoming from University of Western Australia Press.

56. The first extant English song that ridicules a never-married woman dates from just before 1557; see Thomas Wright, ed., *Songs and Ballads with other short poems chiefly of the reign of Philip and Mary* (London: J. B. Nichols and Sons, 1860), 133–36. Within 50 years, the themes of this song were much multiplied and enlarged.

57. Chambers-Schiller, *Liberty, a Better Husband*, 11; Froide, "Single Women, Work, and Community," 362–420; Cécile Dauphin, "Histoire d'un stéréotype, la vieille fille," in *Madame ou mademoiselle*, 209–12.

58. For discussions of the old maid stereotype, which borrowed much from the older stereotype of the witch, see Lanser's essay in this volume; Kittredge, " 'Tabby Cats Lead Apes in Hell' "; Dauphin, "Histoire d'un stéréotype"; Pierre Darmon and Françoise Thébaud, "Le malheur des femmes célibataires," *L'Histoire* 52 (January 1983): 97–100.

59. Jean Kern, "The Old Maid, or 'to Grow old, and be poor, and laughed at,'" in *Fetter'd or Free? British Women Novelists 1670–1815*, ed. Mary Anne Schofield and Cecilia Macheski (Athens: Ohio University Press, 1986), 205; Darmon and Thébaud, "Le malheur de femmes célibataires"; Dauphin, "Histoire d'un stéréotype."

60. Froide, "Single Women, Work, and Community," 362–420; Dauphin, "Histoire d'un stéréotype," 217–19.

61. Dauphin, "Histoire d'un stéréotype," 217.

62. Cox, "The Single Self," 546–49, 564–67.

63. Dauphin, "Histoire d'un stéréotype," 224–25.

64. Katherine Phillips, *Poems* (London, 1667) cited in *The Cultural Identity of Seventeenth-Century Woman: A Reader*, comp. and ed. N. H. Keeble (New York: Routledge, 1994), 255–56.

65. Hill, "A Refuge from Men." For more on models of female communities in English literature, see Kittredge, " 'Tabby Cats Lead Apes in Hell,' " 82–119.

66. Cox, "The Single Self"; Froide, "Single Women, Work, and Community," 362–420; Lanser's essay.

67. Mary Astell, *Some Reflections upon Marriage* (London, 1706); Anna Bijns, "Unyoked is best! Happy the woman without a man," rpt. in *Women Writers of the Renaissance and Reformation*, ed. Katharina M. Wilson (Athens: University of Georgia Press, 1987), 382.

68. Helena Whitbread, ed., *I Know My Own Heart: the Diaries of Anne Lister, 1791–1840* (New York: New York University Press, 1992).

69. Sharpe, "Literally Spinsters."

70. Barker, "A Virgin's Life."

71. Adams, "A Choice Not to Wed?" 884–85.

72. See Froide, "Single Women, Work, and Community," 162–241; Chambers-Schiller, *Liberty, a Better Husband*, 107–156; Sanderson, *Women and Work*, 98–100; Hufton, "Women Without Men"; John Cashmere, "Sisters Together: Women Without Men in Seventeenth-Century French Village Culture," *Journal of Family History* 21, 1 (1996): 44–62.

73. Froide, "Single Women, Work, and Community," 171, 1–2.

74. Ibid., 225.

75. Patricia Crawford and Sara Mendelson, "Sexual Identities in Early Modern England: The Marriage of Two Women in 1680," *Gender and History* 7, 3 (1995): 362–77. Also see Donoghue for other examples of "female marriages."

76. Eva Mary Hamilton Bell, ed., *The Hamwood Papers of the Ladies of Llangollen and Caroline Hamilton* (London: Macmillan, 1930).

77. The majority of women accused and convicted of infanticide were single-women, and, to a much lesser extent, widows. Pregnant singlewomen who faced social shame and loss of employment often concealed their pregnancies, but con-cealment of birth was one of the proofs of child murder (R. W. Malcolmson, "Infanticide in the Eighteenth Century," in *Crime in England 1550–1800*, ed. J. S. Cockburn [Princeton, N.J.: Princeton University Press, 1977], 192; Hufton, *The Prospect Before Her*, 275–80 and bibliography on 592; Laura Gowing, "Secret Births and Infanticide in Seventeenth-Century England," *Past and Present* 156 [1997]: 87–115).

78. Leah Leneman and Rosalind Mitchison, "Girls in Trouble: Illegitimacy in Early Modern Scotland," *Journal of Social History* (1988): 65; idem., *Sexuality and Social Control, 1660–1780* (New York: Oxford University Press, 1989). See also G. R. Quaife, "The Consenting Spinster," *Journal of Social History* 11, 2 (1977): 228–44. In Italy single mothers were encouraged to give their bastards to foundling institutions so that they "could be restored to their respected position in society," and, thus, presumably, the marriage market (Palazzi, "Female Solitude," 452). In Britain, bastard-bearing women were often able to marry, as were their illegitimate children

(Laslett, Oosterveen, and Smith, *Bastardy and Its Comparative History*, 7, 75–76, 105–7, 217).

79. Kristin Elizabeth Gager, *Blood Ties and Fictive Ties: Adoption and Family Life in Early Modern France* (Princeton, N.J.: Princeton University Press, 1996), esp. 95–99, and 170–71. Most adopting women were widows or independent wives.

80. See essays by Farmer and Hunt.

81. Froide, "Single Women, Work, and Community," 162–241, esp. 194–202; Hufton, "Women Without Men," 368; Adams, "A Choice Not to Wed?" 887–88.

2

Singlewomen in Medieval and Early Modern Europe

The Demographic Perspective

Maryanne Kowaleski

HISTORICAL DEMOGRAPHY, which focuses on the characteristics of earlier populations (such as their age, sex, marital status, and family forms), as well as the processes which helped to shape their size and composition (for example, fertility, nuptiality, mortality, and migration) probably has more to tell us about singlewomen in the European past than any other discipline. Given appropriate sources, historical demographers not only can help us distinguish between life-cycle and lifelong singlewomen, but can also offer us firm data on the actual numbers and proportions of singlewomen in specific places and times. By focusing on entire populations, not just the well-documented and elite members of society, and by generating comparable quantitative data, historical demography allows us to see how proportions of singlewomen varied by region, status, and wealth, as well as across centuries. And because historical demographers study families and households as well as individuals, their analyses offer useful indications of the economic and cultural forces that prompted growth or decline in the numbers of singlewomen in medieval and early modern Europe.

In seeking to summarize the findings of historical demographers, this essay elucidates two major trends in the history of singlewomen: their relatively smaller numbers as one moves from northwestern Europe toward the Mediterranean and their generally growing proportions between 1350 and 1800. To trace these trends, we shall focus especially on the centuries before 1600 when evidence is sparse and historical consensus is, as yet, slim.

The tables cited in this essay may be found in the Appendix, pp. 325–44.

The sources available for the seventeenth and eighteenth centuries are more reliable, more full, and more amenable to quantification. As a result, our view of the numbers of singlewomen in different European regions and societies after 1600 is fairly comprehensive. This later period also provides much of the evidence for the questions addressed at the end of the essay — that is, the influence of such factors as climatic region, migration, wealth, female employment, economic prosperity, and religious culture on the propensities of young women either to delay marriage or never to marry at all.

Historical Demographers and the Study of Singlewomen

Most of what historical demographers tell us about singlewomen arises from their focus on two measures of nuptiality: the timing (age at first marriage) and incidence (proportions married) of marriage. Demographers focus on these measures not because of their interest in singlewomen per se,[1] but because the timing and incidence of marriage are together considered the key determinants of fertility levels (and therefore population growth or decline) in the preindustrial era.[2] These two measures also hold center stage in demographic explanations of family and household formation in past times. Of special interest is the "European marriage pattern," a demographic regime typified by late age at first marriage (at least 23 years for women and over 26 for men) and high proportions of people who never married (around 10–20 percent).[3] Demographers have also recently focused on the interrelationship of this pattern to the "northwestern European household formation system," characterized not only by late age at marriage for both sexes, but also by the establishment of a new household upon marriage (termed "neo-local" by demographers), and by the widespread employment of unmarried young people as servants (called "life-cycle service" by demographers).[4] Most of what we know about the aggregate history of singlewomen in the past derives from demographers' attempts to identify the chronological, geographical, and economic extent of the European marriage pattern and the associated northwestern European household formation system.

   In focusing on when and how many women married, historical demographers have often described singlewomen in problematic ways.[5] In this essay, I employ "singlewomen" or "life-cycle singlewomen" to denote never-married women who have reached reproductive age (generally 12 to 15) and "lifelong singlewomen" to mean adult women who remained permanently unmarried; in this essay, therefore, both terms exclude widows and nuns. Demographers tend to define lifelong singlewomen obliquely as "women who died never married by age 50 or older" (although some researchers use cohorts ranging over the ages of 40–44 or 55–59, depending on when they think menopause occurred). Of course, a never-married woman who died before menopause — at say, age 35 or 40 — should also be considered a lifelong singlewoman in terms of her own life experiences, but demographers' need for rigorously defined comparative data means they exclude these younger singlewomen from their calculations.[6] It should be kept in mind, therefore, that when demographers count lifelong single-women, they almost certainly underestimate the actual numbers of lifelong or permanent singlewomen because their definition of this group is skewed by their greater interest in marriage and reproduction.

While demographers' analyses of the incidence of marriage can offer us a direct (albeit underestimated) count of lifelong singlewomen, it is diffi-cult to find suitable sources for estimates much before the eighteenth cen-tury. For this reason, observations on the age at first marriage provide the bulk of our data on singlewomen in preindustrial Europe. By furnishing a concrete indication of how many years adult women remained single, the "mean age at first marriage" allows us to identify the geographical, eco-nomic, and social distribution of singlewomen in medieval and early mod-ern Europe. For example, during the early modern period (and probably in the late Middle Ages as well), women in most parts of northwestern Eu-rope (British Isles, Low Countries, northern France, Germany, and west-ern Scandinavia) married in their mid- to late-twenties, whereas women in southern Europe married in their late teens or early twenties; thus north-western Europe had many more singlewomen than southern Europe. Vari-ations in the timing of marriage also reflected different life experiences. Women who waited until age 25 to marry, for instance, had generally en-joyed a period of independence while they earned wages and lived outside their parents' home; this independence, in turn, also gave them a greater voice in selecting a marriage partner, a choice perhaps evident in their tendency to marry men only a few years older than themselves.[7] In contrast, women who married at the age of 18 or younger usually went straight from their parents' household to their husband's, thereby experiencing little in-dependence in their short time as an adult singlewoman, while also being subject to more parental influence in their choice of a marriage partner.[8]

The useful data produced by demographers on the timing and inci-dence of marriage have in recent years been increasingly accompanied by greater recognition of the pivotal demographic role played by single-women. David Weir and Roger Schofield argue, for example, that the pro-portion of lifelong singlewomen exercised more influence over variations in the total population size of communities before 1700 than any other single factor.[9] Richard Smith points to domestic service by never-married women as a key determinant of social and demographic structures in western Eu-rope.[10] Keith Snell, Pam Sharpe, and Jeremy Goldberg suggest that changes in female employment and wages could influence whether singlewomen did or did not eventually marry.[11] These new findings expand in exciting ways the many contributions of historical demography to our understand-ing of singlewomen in the European past.

Singlewomen in the Middle Ages

Since no sources offer direct information on singlewomen before the four-teenth century, demographers have not reached any consensus about the proportions of singlewomen in medieval Europe before the Black Death. Efforts to identify the age at marriage of medieval women have generally been stymied by recalcitrant sources and controversial methodologies. Spe-cialists disagree, for example, over how to interpret the census-like estate surveys of the Carolingian polyptyques; some find in them evidence of early marriage for women, around the age of 14 or 15, while others see data indicating that rural women remained single until their late twenties.[12] Similar disagreements center around the issue of the age at marriage of peasant women in pre-plague England. Zvi Razi relies on manorial court rolls to calculate an early age at first marriage for peasant women in the late teens and early twenties, but his methods and assumptions have met with especially harsh criticism.[13] In contrast, H. E. Hallam produces evidence from village genealogies that women delayed marriage in several Lincoln-shire villages until about age 21 before the Black Death and to almost age 25 after the plague; Richard Smith also draws on Hallam's work to argue for a female age at marriage in the early to mid-twenties before the Black Death.[14]

By the late Middle Ages, data improve, especially for the region of Tuscany in northern Italy, where a series of remarkably full fiscal surveys survive. The best is the Florentine catasto of 1427, a thorough census of some 60,000 households in the city and its territories.[15] According to the analyses of David Herlihy and Christiane Klapisch-Zuber, few women in late medieval Tuscany experienced the single life for long since they married around the age of 18 in both town and countryside (Table A1). Lifelong singlewomen were even rarer; in the city of Prato in 1372, for example, only 1.5 percent of laywomen between the ages of 15 and 30 had never married.[16] Their numbers had risen a bit by 1427; at that time, 5.4 percent of women in Prato and 3.8 percent of women in Florence reached the age of 50 without marrying, but only 1.7 percent of women in the Tuscan countryside.

Proportions of lifelong singlewomen remained roughly the same over the course of the fifteenth century (with perhaps some slight decrease in Florence by 1480), but singlewomen became somewhat more common in late fifteenth-century Tuscany as the average age at marriage for women rose to about 21.[17] If the ever-increasing numbers of urban women who became nuns in late fifteenth- and sixteenth-century Italy are added to this figure, however, the percentage of never-married women in Florence might shoot up to roughly 15 percent by 1552.[18] This high proportion of celibate singlewomen was, however, a class-specific phenomenon since few women from peasant or artisanal families would have been able to enter a convent.

Elsewhere in medieval Italy the proportions of singlewomen were roughly similar to those around Florence. In the rural region surrounding Lucca (on the northwestern border of Tuscany), women also married in their teens: only 1.5 percent of adult women were single in the early fifteenth century, while lifelong singlewomen represented less than 0.5 percent; teen marriages seem also to have been the norm for women in late medieval Sicily.[19] In the early fifteenth-century cities of Verona and Vicenza in northeastern Italy, however, women married about two to three years later than their Florentine counterparts, thus increasing the numbers of singlewomen in their twenties in these two towns.[20] Singlewomen in these Veneto cities would have also experienced different patterns of courtship and marital choice since they married men who were usually only six to seven years older than themselves, compared to Florence where husbands were usually some thirteen years older than their brides. These differences, which seem to have been caused more by local traditions than regional economic variations, are significant, but the similarities are even more important.[21] Early and almost universal marriage prevailed in Florence, in the Tuscan countryside, in the Lucchese countryside, and in the cities of Verona and Vicenza; the vast majority of women married by age 20, and lifelong singlewomen represented only a tiny percentage of all women. The secular trend in these regions was also similar; the proportions of singlewomen grew over the course of the fifteenth century, as reflected in the rising age at which women married for the first time.

What accounts for the consistently small percentage of singlewomen in fifteenth-century Italy and the slight increase in their numbers near the end of the century? David Herlihy and Christiane Klapisch-Zuber attribute the early female age at marriage in Tuscany to the mortality crises induced by plague and famine in the fourteenth century; as mortality surged and life expectancy fell, the pressure to marry and reproduce increased, thereby driving down the ages at which people married.[22] The intense competition for husbands also drove down the age at which women married; the substantial spousal age gap, plus the thinning of the age pyramid meant that the number of teenaged girls searching for husbands always outnumbered the number of available husbands. To explain why women's age at marriage then began to rise in the mid-fifteenth century, Herlihy and Klapisch-Zuber point to the effects of the economic and demographic recovery over the course of the fifteenth century; as prosperity increased and life expectancy went up, the ages at which men and women married rose since the imperative to increase fertility and population size had lessened. By 1427, men's average age at marriage had stabilized at about age 30, but women's age at marriage continued to rise by an additional three years over the next fifty years, thereby increasing the proportion of singlewomen, especially in the city of Florence where women usually delayed marriage until age 21 by 1480. The late fifteenth-century rise in women's age at marriage was also propelled by the deterioration of women's ability to negotiate a favorable marriage; as age-specific mortality declined, the cohort of marriageable girls aged over 15 grew, but these girls had to secure husbands from a much smaller cohort of men who were 10–15 years older than their prospective brides. The competition for husbands thus drove up the costs of arranging marriages and the value of the bride's dowry, so inflating dowries that many families took more time to arrange marriages or simply could not afford to marry all of their daughters. To avoid the burden of these expensive dowries, daughters from better-off families were often placed in convents, causing an eight-fold increase of nuns in Florence between the early fifteenth and mid-sixteenth century.[23] Poorer singlewomen, who could not manage even the humbler dowry required to enter the convent, had a harder time. To better their chances of marrying, many entered domestic service in order to augment their dowry, a trend reflected in the increasing numbers of domestic servants in late fifteenth- and early sixteenth-century Florence and

Verona.[24] Presumably entry into domestic service lengthened the period women waited to marry, as did the time it took to build a sufficient dowry.

Other historians find fault with demographic explanations, preferring to place more emphasis on such cultural factors as the increasing tendency for men to avoid marriage, and the vital importance of maintaining family honor and prestige in contracting marriage.[25] Mediterranean notions of honor were so strongly linked to the sexual purity and respectability of women that all women strove to be married. Indeed, spinsters had virtually no place in Mediterranean societies, as borne out both by the early age at marriage and by the extremely small numbers of laywomen who never married.[26] As Anthony Molho persuasively illustrates, the cultural imperative to marry young women soon after they reached sexual maturity even prompted many Florentine fathers to falsify their daughters' ages to give them more time to negotiate a favorable marriage.[27] In such a social climate, it is no wonder that the proportions of singlewomen were extremely small. Interestingly, the role of female choice is almost entirely ignored by all of these scholars, leading to the impression that women were puppets swept along by greater demographic, economic, or cultural forces.[28]

For the rest of late medieval Europe, our knowledge of singlewomen is severely hampered by the absence of appropriate sources. Herlihy argues that all of Europe during the high and late Middle Ages had as few singlewomen as late medieval Tuscany, but his argument leans too heavily on saints' lives and a few other elite-biased sources to justify this conclusion.[29] Some scattered data culled from family genealogies, diaries, and marriage contracts in several northern cities suggest an age at first marriage only slightly later than in Tuscany, but the samples are very small and focus largely on the urban elite, a social group whose dynastic strategies led them to marry at an earlier age than the general population.[30] These northern data show that women from the German nobility married very young, at about age 14, while women from the wealthy urban elite of London, Bristol, and Frankfurt waited longer, marrying around the age of 18; the patriciate women of Zierikzee, however, delayed marriage even longer, waiting until they were about 24 (Table A1).[31]

For the nonelite, direct evidence of the age at which women married is even scarcer and more problematic. For northern England in the late Middle Ages, Jeremy Goldberg cites a small sample of marriage ages to suggest that rural women married in their late teens and early twenties, but urban women waited until their early to mid-twenties.[32] Using a detailed census from the Norman city of Reims in 1422, Pierre Desportes speculates that women married around the ages of 15 or 16 and usually had their first child before age 20, but he offers no firm evidence on these points; in fact, the age pyramid he constructs indicates a very large bulge of single female servants, grouped around the age of 24, who he notes were usually single.[33] In the Burgundian city of Dijon, Jacques Rossiaud finds that women were on the average almost 22 years old when they married in the first fifty years of the sixteenth century, not much older than the age at which Florentine women were marrying in 1480 (Table A1), but his study is also based on a small number of cases that may be biased toward prosperous members of the town's working population.[34] Given the varied nature, scarcity, and bias of the extant data on actual age at marriage in northern regions of late medieval Europe, therefore, we can only draw some cautious conclusions. Singlewomen were rare among the landed elite and urban patriciate because the bulk of them had married by their late teens, but more common among the peasantry because they married sometime between their late teens and very early twenties, and most prevalent among the middling and poorer ranks in towns, where women often waited until their early twenties to marry.

To compensate for the lack of definitive data about medieval singlewomen in northern Europe, historical demographers often approach the problem indirectly by concentrating on how patterns of marriage and household formation provide clues as to the timing and incidence of marriage. Such clues as low proportions of married adults, large numbers of female servants, and frequent neo-local marriage, for example, have encouraged a growing number of scholars to argue that the northwestern European marriage pattern can be traced back to the late fourteenth century, at least for England.[35] In this search for early features of the European marriage pattern in the Middle Ages, the presence of singlewomen has been critical. Although we cannot always correct for the chronic underenumeration of young singlewomen in medieval tax lists, or the medieval scribe's frequent lack of precision in recording exact marital status, demographers have assembled a series of data that reflect the proportions of adult singlewomen and unmarried (widowed and single) women in different medieval populations.[36] These data then suggest other demographic features; for example, John Hajnal argues that societies adhered to the northwestern European marriage pattern of late female age at marriage when at least 45 percent of adult women (aged 15 or older) were unmarried and when at least 30 percent had never (or yet) married.[37]

Calculations of the proportions of unmarried (single and widowed) women in fiscal surveys of England, France, Germany, and Switzerland indicate that late medieval urban populations usually meet Hajnal's criteria while many rural areas of England come close to the standard (Table A1). Singlewomen alone made up over 40 percent of the adult female population in Coventry, Reims, and Zurich, and 31 percent in the German city of Freiburg. In these cases, the figures probably reflect a relatively late age at marriage for women.[38] For rural areas, we have only the evidence from the English poll tax of 1377, a nationwide head tax of all persons over the age of 14. After subtracting probable widows from the group of unmarried women, a recent comprehensive study of this tax has found that around 29.9 percent of the adult female population was single. Since large numbers of singlewomen evaded this tax, this figure represents a minimum estimate.[39]

Although fraught with methodological problems, these estimates strongly suggest that singlewomen were almost as numerous in some late medieval regions and cities as they were in the better-documented early modern period. Our firmest medieval data come from late fourteenth-century England, where poll-tax data suggest that roughly 30 percent of all women aged 14 or older were single, although significant variations were evident, with towns hosting the highest percentage of singlewomen. We have no reliable figures for other rural areas in northwestern Europe, although recent research on Flanders has uncovered convincing evidence of delayed age at marriage (between 20 and 25) among the fifteenth-century peasantry.[40] The extant data on the large numbers of singlewomen in fifteenth-century German, French, and Swiss cities also hint at strong parallels between England and her continental neighbors to the west. Even if the proportions of singlewomen were a bit lower in the continental regions of northwestern Europe than in England, they would still stand in stark contrast to the proportions observed for Italy in the same period, where only 15 percent of adult women were single, half the proportion in late medieval England (Table A1).

New research on medieval servants supports the view that singlewomen were more numerous in northwestern Europe. Medieval demographers have looked hard for evidence of "life-cycle service" (so-called because of its mediating role between leaving home as an adolescent and marrying as an adult), a well-recognized feature of the northwestern European system of household formation in the early modern period. According to Hajnal, this system was characteristic of rural societies in which at least 6–10 percent of the total population were servants; most of these servants were unmarried and young (under 30), resided in their employers' households, usually served for contractually limited periods, and eventually left service when they married.[41] By counting the numbers of servants (especially female servants) in medieval populations, historical demographers can thus discern how closely the medieval situation may have matched patterns observed for early modern European populations. Since young servants, especially women, frequently evaded notice in extant records, this exercise is also burdened with methodological difficulties.[42]

Despite these difficulties, it is clear that the proportions of households containing servants were generally high in late medieval England and in northwestern European towns.[43] According to the English poll-tax returns of the late fourteenth century, servants made up a minimum of 4 to 5 percent of the total rural population and 11 to 17 percent of the total urban population.[44] If these figures are slightly inflated to account for the endemic underenumeration of servants, even the rural proportions might meet the threshold of 6 to 10 percent proposed by Hajnal. Urban censuses provide corroborating evidence on this point; servants comprised 22.7 percent of the population of Reims in 1422, 18.6 percent of the population of Nuremberg in 1449, and 24.8 percent of the population of Coventry in 1523.[45] Historical demographers usually interpret these high proportions of urban servants as evidence of high proportions of singlewomen since female servants were much more common in urban than rural communities, generally outnumbered male servants in cities, and in northwestern Europe were mostly single.[46]

To complement the evidence of life-cycle service found in fiscal surveys, historians also draw on other sources to demonstrate that female servants in late medieval England and northern European towns conformed to a standard profile: they were mostly in their late teens and early twenties, often migrated to towns from rural homes, served for contractually limited periods (normally a year), usually resided in the household of their employer, and were almost always single.[47] Although the evidence for female service is strongest in towns, historians of rural England have also assembled persuasive data on the growing prevalence of life-cycle service in the late medieval countryside.[48] Larry Poos offers a particularly convincing case study, arguing that the changing structure of the late medieval labor market in rural Essex encouraged employers both to hire servants more than occasional laborers and to favor cheaper female over male servants when the situation warranted.[49] Although the scale of rural life-cycle service in England was greater in the early modern than the late medieval period, the fact that we can glimpse the beginnings of the system as early as the fourteenth century provides indirect evidence that a significant number of women residing in the villages of late medieval England may have been single.

Jeremy Goldberg has also argued that an expansion of female employment in the labor-starved decades after the Black Death allowed women to delay marriage, thereby generating increasing numbers of singlewomen.[50] Focusing primarily on the town of York in the late fourteenth and early fifteenth century, he cites rising numbers of women admitted to the urban franchise, falling sex ratios of servants, larger numbers of female-headed households, and many more single female testators as evidence of both the opportunities for working women and the independence that these opportunities brought to women. Many singlewomen were drawn to York where, free from parental control and enjoying a greater degree of economic independence, they exercised considerable choice in selecting marriage partners, usually choosing to marry a man close in age to themselves. In the late fifteenth century, however, these patterns changed as economic recession increasingly pushed women out of craft work and into marginal and poorly paid occupations like domestic service. Goldberg argues that as women suffered a decline in economic opportunity, they married earlier or sought remarriage if widowed. These developments worked, in turn, to raise the birth rate, contributing to the demographic recovery of the sixteenth century. Goldberg's conclusions are often based on very slim samples of data, and many have questioned his key assumptions,[51] but he does offer valuable arguments on the crucial links between female employment and the proportions of singlewomen in medieval populations of northwestern Europe.

In focusing on how changes in servanthood and women's employment affected nuptiality, Goldberg, Poos, and Smith take their cue from demographers of early modern England who emphasize that marriage was the chief determinant of levels of fertility and population growth in the sixteenth through eighteenth centuries. To explain the demographic stagnation of the late Middle Ages, they reason that improved employment opportunities after the Black Death lured greater proportions of young women into the labor market at the same time as employers found more reasons to hire live-in servants on a contractual basis and as opportunities for female work in pastoral farming increased. Since service contracts forbade marriage, the growing prevalence of servanthood delayed marriage and thus drove down the birth rate that, in turn, was responsible for the stagnating population levels of the later Middle Ages. Whether opportunities for work allowed women to stay single longer while they searched for a suitable spouse (Goldberg's view) or whether life-cycle service itself led to later marriages since couples spent years accumulating sufficient resources to marry (Poos's view) is debatable, but most demographers would prefer Poos's interpretation.

Other medievalists have found fault with this fertility-driven model, pointing out that the evidentiary base on which the model rests is not particularly sturdy, and that many of its assumptions about the post-plague economy and the growth of female service are open to question.[52] They also argue, like most historians of continental Europe, that mortality crises played a particularly forceful role in restricting population growth in the late Middle Ages. But the "high-pressure" demographic regime (high fertility and high mortality) advocated by these scholars has quite different implications for singlewomen: the forces of mortality, not the employment choices of singlewomen, played the determining role. In the mortality-driven model, rising death rates from the recurring epidemics of the late Middle Ages opened up inheritance, land, and opportunities for work, thus making it possible for young people to marry earlier.[53] These earlier marriages reduced the number of singlewomen, elevated the birth rate, and led to a surge in population growth in late fifteenth- and early sixteenth-century Europe. Only further research will settle this on-going dispute about the relative importance of mortality and nuptiality in shaping medieval demographic regimes, but it is clear that one path to resolving the conundrum is through analysis of the proportions and experiences of singlewomen.

Given these disagreements about the prevalence of particular demographic regimes, as well as the paucity of direct data about the timing and incidence of marriage in medieval Europe, what conclusions can we reach about the demographic history of medieval singlewomen? Certainly, significantly greater proportions of singlewomen lived in towns and cities than in the countryside (Table A1), probably because towns offered better opportunities for paid employment. This pattern most likely reflected gender-specific migration in which young singlewomen migrated from countryside to town in search of work;[54] it might also have reflected cultural and social differences between town and country, and it certainly reflected the lower sex ratios (that is, more women than men) common in many large medieval towns of northwestern Europe.[55] Although widows might account for some of the feminine surplus in late medieval towns, the high proportions of young, single, female servants in medieval towns strongly suggests both that singlewomen often migrated to towns and that, once there, they married later than their sisters who stayed in the countryside.[56]

We can also point with some assurance to marked contrasts between northwestern and Mediterranean Europe in terms of the opportunities for singlewomen to work and their proportions within the adult population. In both regions female servants predominated in towns and rural women tended to migrate to towns in search of work, but female servants were less numerous in Mediterranean Europe,[57] more likely to reside outside their employers' households, more inclined to work for the same employer for long periods of time, more focused on domestic rather than craft work, and more liable to be very young (under 14) or older, married, or widowed.[58] These characteristics fit the predominance of early and almost universal marriage observed in fifteenth-century Tuscany. Female servants were also especially rare in the Italian countryside.[59] By comparison, the greater availability of craft work and domestic service for women in northwestern Europe seems to have allowed—or forced—more of them to stay single longer.

This disparity between northwestern and southern Europe is also strikingly evident in the known proportions of singlewomen in these two regions (Table A1). In Tuscany, singlewomen rarely represented more than 20 percent of the adult female population while lifelong singlewomen accounted for about 2–5 percent of urban women and 2 percent or less of adult women in rural areas. Although data for Iberia, southern France, and other regions in Italy are less precise than for Tuscany, the surviving evidence points to similarly early ages at marriage for women and a correspondingly low number of singlewomen in these areas. Like the historical demographers of northwestern Europe who compensate for their lack of direct data by focusing on indirect evidence to show the prevalence of the European marriage pattern, so too historians of southern Europe have deduced an early age at first marriage for women from a variety of other types of indirect evidence. In making a strong case for a "Mediterranean" marriage pattern in which few medieval women remained single for long, these historians cite the significant age gap between older husbands and younger wives, a high proportion of married daughters in fathers' wills, a scarcity of nubile daughters in their natal households, the strength of parental influence in the contracting of dowries and marriage, and the prevalence of an honor system that focused on the sexual purity and respectability of women.[60]

In contrast, singlewomen accounted for roughly 30–40 percent of all adult women in many parts of northwestern Europe, including towns and cities, and large areas of rural England. The main point of uncertainty centers on the rural parts of the continent. In northern France, the Low Countries, Germany, and Scandinavia, it is not possible to specify whether singlewomen represented a low (20–30 percent) or high (35–40 percent) proportion of peasant women. Those demographers who favor the lower estimates argue that the "high pressure" mortality-driven demographic regimes of the continent encouraged earlier and more frequent marriage, and thus fewer singlewomen.[61] But in arguing for the higher figures, others emphasize the similarities between the proportions of singlewomen and servants in both English and continental towns of northwestern Europe during the Middle Ages, as well as their strikingly parallel trends in age at marriage during the early modern period (Table A2). Demographers have also singled out the frequency of remarriage among the northwestern European peasantry, the high degree of mobility among young people, and the widespread employment of young women as servants even in rural areas as further evidence of high proportions of singlewomen in northwestern Europe.[62] Although much work remains to be done, it has become increasingly clear that even in medieval Europe, geographical diversity gave rise to strong regional variations in the shape and processes of demographic regimes and proportions of singlewomen.[63]

Singlewomen in Early Modern Europe

From the late sixteenth century on, new sources amenable to better quantitative techniques improve our evidence on singlewomen. Foremost among these sources are parish registers, which survive in long series for many settlements from the late sixteenth and seventeenth centuries. To mine this source, demographers have focused their efforts on "family reconstitution," a technique that links the vital events (baptisms, marriages, and burials) recorded in parish registers to the demographic histories of individuals and their families.[64] Another technique in the arsenal of historical demographers is "back projection," a method of demographic modeling that allows demographers to assess the configuration of past populations (such as the rates of nuptiality upon which we have been focusing) from estimated totals of births, marriages, and deaths stretching backward from a reliable census containing information about age structure.[65] Both family reconstitution and back projection have been criticized on several fronts, but the data these techniques have provided on singlewomen are generally considered sound.[66]

With the aid of these new techniques and sources, historical demographers have produced an impressive array of mean ages at first marriage for women in a variety of early modern European populations at different points in time (Table A2).[67] In the late sixteenth and seventeenth centuries, these figures sharpen patterns familiar from the late medieval evidence; there were more singlewomen in northern Europe, where women usually delayed marriage until their mid-twenties, but fewer singlewomen in the Mediterranean regions of southern France, Italy, Spain, and Portugal where women continued to marry in their teens and early twenties. This regional pattern was not entirely uniform, however, since women in several communities in central France (such as the village of Athis in the Ile-de-France) married in their late teens or very early twenties. Such variations within regions are especially evident in the fuller seventeenth-century data (note in particular some Spanish villages where women married around 22 or 23), but the general trend remains clear: there were more singlewomen in northwestern Europe than in Mediterranean Europe.

Within northwestern Europe, singlewomen were most predominant in Denmark, Sweden, and England, where women in the seventeenth century usually waited until they were 26 or older to marry (Table A2). The picture is more mixed for France, as befitting a country that straddles many different geographical and cultural regions. In northern French regions such as Normandy or the area around Paris, women usually married in their mid-twenties, but the age of marriage generally fell as one traveled south, as exemplified by marriages in the early twenties in the small town of Bourg en Bresse in southern Burgundy or in the late teen years in the Pyrenees village of Saint-Savin. Within southern Europe, the largest regional variations arose in Spain, where historical demographers insist on intrapeninsular diversity and the coexistence of different demographic regimes.[68] In Italy, too, many scholars take exception to classifying all of Italy as subject to a "Mediterranean" demographic regime, noting that a wide variety of marriage patterns and household forms can be found even within the same region.[69] But the evidence for such arguments is drawn almost exclusively from the eighteenth century or later and tends to focus more on household formation than on nuptiality; the few exceptions they note for the late sixteenth and early seventeenth centuries are also hardly enough to contradict the general "Mediterranean" characteristics of the nuptiality patterns.

Significant changes occurred in the eighteenth century, however, when women in Portugal, Spain, and Italy began to wait longer to marry (Table A2), staying single until their early and mid-twenties, with especially long delays in such towns as Venice (where women put off marriage until they were almost 29) and in the Galician region of northern Spain (where women married around the age of 25). As a result, the sharp contrasts between northwestern and Mediterranean Europe became more muted by the mid-eighteenth century. Some marked changes also occurred in northwestern Europe during the eighteenth century as economic and industrial developments provoked some striking divergences from previous patterns. If we focus on countrywide measures, for example, we see that the mean age at first marriage declined in Denmark, Sweden, and England but rose slightly in France. If we focus on smaller settlements or regions, however, contrary movements occurred, as in the Warwickshire village of Alcester, the small Oxfordshire town of Banbury, the cities of Amsterdam and Nördlingen, and the Flemish village of Elversele where women waited even longer to marry in the eighteenth century than they had in the seventeenth century (Table A2).

We can delve more deeply into these chronological and regional variations if we look at the data historical demographers have assembled on lifelong singlewomen, which also show considerable variations within countries and over time (Table A3). Although these figures on the incidence of marriage should be taken only as rough guides,[70] they do offer interesting parallels with the evidence regarding the timing of marriage. In the late fifteenth and sixteenth centuries, scattered data clearly suggest, as do our observations about the age at first marriage, that lifelong singlewomen were more numerous in northwestern Europe (notably England) than in Mediterranean Europe (notably Tuscany). In the seventeenth century, the proportions of lifelong singlewomen generally rose in northwestern Europe, reaching quite startling levels in some periods and places, such as mid-seventeenth-century England where some 20 percent of women who lived until at least age 50 never married at all. Demographers have found similarly high figures of lifelong singlewomen in the late seventeenth-century towns of Rouen (in Normandy) and Geneva, although in France as a whole there were considerably fewer lifelong singlewomen than in England. Whatever the country, however, it appears that lifelong singlewomen were always more prevalent in towns than in villages, a reflection of the very low sex ratios in early modern towns, which in turn stemmed in large part from the abundance of female servants found in premodern towns. These low sex ratios clearly made it difficult for many women to find marriage partners, but some scholars have also argued that female servants in cities such as Rotterdam and London may actually have preferred to remain single because of the security and independence a life in service offered them.[71]

We are much less well informed about lifelong singlewomen in southern Europe during the sixteenth and seventeenth centuries (Table A3). Scattered data from the kingdom of Naples points to the continuing scarcity of permanent singlewomen in southern Italy, although significant differences were beginning to emerge among various agricultural economies.[72] For other areas in Italy and Iberia, we can speculate with some assurance that lifelong singlewomen were markedly fewer than in northern Europe, based on their low numbers in the late fifteenth century and the persistence of early marriages for women in Iberia and Italy into the seventeenth century (Table A2). But the tremendous increase in lifelong singlewomen in these regions by the late eighteenth century suggests that their proportions may have begun to rise even in the seventeenth century. In the eighteenth century, the burgeoning proportions of lifelong singlewomen went hand in hand with a rising age at first marriage (Table A2), although the available data are, admittedly, limited to northern Italy. In Iberia, the story is more mixed since the census of 1787 indicates strong regional differences that do not break down into simple north-south divides. Relatively large numbers of permanent singlewomen (12 to 16 percent of adult women) resided in such northern areas as Galicia and Catalonia, rates that match the figures derived for northern European regions. Their neighboring region of Leon in northern Spain, however, had considerably fewer singlewomen (8 percent). Similar diversity is evident in southern Spain where singlewomen comprised almost 18 percent of adult women in Andalusia, but only 7–9 percent in Castile and Valencia.[73]

What accounts for the rising proportions of life-cycle and lifelong singlewomen in early modern Europe? Many historical demographers focus on the declining incidence of disease-driven mortality; as life expectancy rose, the need for high fertility (and thus early and universal marriage) eased, so women began to marry later.[74] In Spain and Italy, for example, the age at which women married rose most noticeably in the late seventeenth and eighteenth centuries, the same period when plague was becoming rarer. As mortality declined and the population grew, couples increasingly delayed marriage because opportunities for inheritance had narrowed. In seventeenth-century Spain, this trend was aggravated by an economic decline that lowered incomes and reduced opportunities for work, thus further restricting the number of people who had the wherewithal to marry.[75] In highlighting the importance of changes in mortality in determining the timing and incidence of marriage, advocates of this interpretation also place less emphasis on the ability of female employment to influence how long women delayed marriage, thereby according single-women a less active role in determining larger demographic trends. Many early modern historians of continental Europe, like their medieval counterparts, in particular place mortality at center stage in explaining long-term changes in marriage patterns and population.

In contrast, other demographers (especially those who study early modern England) focus more on fertility than mortality to explain population fluctuations, dwelling in particular on how changes in employment opportunities and real wages affected patterns of nuptiality. They attribute the rising age at marriage for women to several factors (including the growing availability of public assistance and contractual retirement, arrangements that lessened the need for high fertility because the value of children as a hedge against insecurity in old age was no longer as great), but they focus primarily on the proliferation of life-cycle service.[76] Early marriage was discouraged by the contractual terms of service, as well as by the massive numbers of young people who entered service to accumulate sufficient savings to marry. The wage-labor context of the early modern English economy also meant that fluctuations in real wages could exercise a potent effect on rates of nuptiality, a relationship set out in some detail by Wrigley and Schofield.[77] For example, during times of economic crisis when wages fell and grain prices soared, couples were compelled to delay marriage until it seemed more feasible to set up a new household and support a family. As a rule, economic changes — such as shifts in wages — seem to have affected rates of nuptiality within a fifteen-to-twenty-year lag.[78] Still open to question is the specific impact of wages earned by singlewomen, or the changing participation of women and men in service in husbandry. More research will also tell us the extent to which this fertility-driven model may explain changes in the age at which continental women first married.

Perhaps the most significant finding about the role of singlewomen in the dynamic relationship between demographic behavior and economic fluctuations is that until the mid-eighteenth century, changes in real wages primarily affected the proportions of lifelong singlewomen rather than the age at which women married.[79] For example, because economic crisis tended to affect the poorer elements of the population to a much greater degree, the poor were as likely to respond to decreased employment opportunities by never marrying at all as they were to delay marriage. It remains unclear, however, whether economic opportunity might have had a similar effect; would, for instance, the rising availability of work in certain towns or regions have produced unequal economic opportunities for men and women, thus leading to sex-specific migration and the unbalanced sex ratios that tended to preclude marriage for a large segment of the population?

Although demographers still debate the relative causal force of mortality and nuptiality in demographic trends, they generally agree that the proportions of singlewomen across Europe grew from the late sixteenth through eighteenth centuries. By the eighteenth century, the essential differences between northwestern and Mediterranean Europe had become much less marked as adult women in southern Europe increasingly delayed marriage until their twenties. The rising urbanization of early modern Europe also appears to have contributed to delays in the timing of marriage. Fast-growing cities stimulated demand for domestic and craft servants, luring more women to urban life (which imposed its own social, economic, and cultural constraints on marriage) and further imbalancing urban sex ratios and the opportunity to marry.[80] Although our evidence on the proportions of permanent singlewomen remains sketchy for many regions in the sixteenth and early seventeenth centuries, it is obvious that their numbers rose significantly over the course of the early modern period. The fact that economic fluctuations exercised an especially strong impact on their proportions before the mid-eighteenth century is a significant area for future research.

Some Factors Influencing the Proportions of Singlewomen

It is possible to single out several factors that in particular affected the proportions of singlewomen in medieval and early modern Europe, although our evidence is, admittedly, far better for the period after the sixteenth century. Geographic location—whether one lived in northwestern or southern Europe—was clearly associated with how many women remained single for how long, although the origins of these distinctive demographic regimes and explanations of why and how they differed remain subject to considerable debate. The climatic differences between northern and southern Europe might be responsible for many of these variations since a particular set of family strategies (such as the early marriage and high fertility of southern Europe) could have evolved to cope with the specific patterns of mortality induced by climate, such as the especially high infant and child mortality in southern Europe where summer-related diseases have a noticeably virulent effect.[81] Others have explained regional variations in marriage patterns by adducing cultural differences in law, kinship, systems of honor, and popular culture.[82] For example, the emphasis in many Mediterranean communities on the sexual purity of women as a reflection of family honor appears to have acted as a spur to early and universal marriage in these cultures.

Geographical influences are also evident in the prevalence of single-women in towns and cities everywhere in western Europe.[83] This urban concentration of singlewomen was reflected in the later mean age at marriage of townswomen, a phenomenon related to the low sex ratios found in so many towns. Many scholars believe that the urban surplus of women produced a particularly competitive "marriage market" that made it difficult if not impossible for some townswomen to marry. Although the skewed sex ratio arose in part from the preponderance of widows in premodern towns,[84] as well as from such factors as heavy male migration out of towns (for warfare or overseas ventures),[85] the consistently large proportions of female servants in towns point to the frequent migration of young countrywomen as perhaps the chief factor behind imbalanced urban sex ratios.[86] Whether female migration was stimulated more by the "push" factor (women left rural regions because of a lack of opportunities for work or inheritance) or "pull" factors (women were attracted to towns by paid work and a different lifestyle) remains open to question. In either case, the link between the opportunities for waged work in towns and the proportions of singlewomen is crucial. Young women who entered domestic or craft service — employment generally more plentiful in towns than in villages — stayed single longer than women who did not seek such steady work.[87] In southern European towns, too, poorer women had to remain in domestic service for long periods in order to save for their dowries, thereby putting off marriage.[88]

When young women migrated to towns, they remained single longer than native-born women (Table A4). Vivien Brodsky Elliott's study of women in late Tudor London, for example, shows that women who migrated to London married almost four years later than women born in the city.[89] Moving to London in their late teens, migrant women usually found employment in domestic service where low wages required them to work for several years before accumulating a sufficient dowry. Because they supported themselves and were freer from parental influence than London-born women (who generally lived with their natal families), migrant women probably enjoyed greater leeway in courtship and more freedom in their choice of a spouse, a freedom perhaps reflected in their tendency to marry men closer in age to themselves. Yet they needed to work for many years to accumulate a dowry, and they also contracted less socially advantageous marriages than did London-born women.

Evidence abounds that migration lengthened the period women remained single throughout Europe (Table A4). In late eighteenth-century Amsterdam, immigrant brides married two to four years later than Amsterdam-born women, with those who married fellow outsiders waiting especially long.[90] Similar delays in marriage awaited women who migrated to Geneva or the Spanish city of Cuenca.[91] Although data on marriage age and migration are less precise for the Middle Ages, there is good reason to believe that medieval singlewomen who migrated to towns also delayed marriage since they faced similar obstacles in terms of saving for a dowry and finding a spouse.[92] The faster pace of rural-urban immigration in the early modern period, however, when urbanization soared and the size of towns grew tremendously, probably enhanced the tendencies of migrant women to delay marriage. More recently demographers have also argued about the critical effect of migration on the rates of permanent singlewomen; English evidence suggests lifelong singlewomen were proportionately greater among those who stayed behind than among those who left, but Dutch evidence points to the disadvantages that women migrating to eighteenth-century Amsterdam faced in contending that migrant women were more likely to remain permanently single than native-born women.[93]

The impact of migration on the timing and incidence of marriage often operated through economic mechanisms. In the Tuscan village of Altopascio, for example, singlewomen who remained in the village married two years earlier than women who married outsiders and left the village, in part because of the extra time they and their families needed to locate a partner outside the village (Table A4).[94] As the local economy declined in the eighteenth century and opportunities to marry within Altopascio contracted, the numbers of women who had to seek husbands from other villages mounted, thereby elevating the overall age at marriage and the length of time women remained single. A study of the "spinster" population of the village of Colyton in east Devon by Pam Sharpe also illustrates how the seventeenth-century rise of employment opportunities for women (such as lace-making, wool-spinning, and dairying) attracted many women to the village, thereby lowering the sex ratio, constraining marriage, and restraining population growth.[95] In this case, changes in female employment prompted female in-migration, thus exercising an especially potent effect on nuptiality.

Sharpe's findings on the demographic effects of changes in employment opportunities for women are very significant. Besides offering a useful corrective to the overwhelming focus of demographers on fluctuations in male wages and male employment, she also questions those demographers who see the development of rural industry as a spur to nuptiality. A number of scholars have argued that "protoindustrialization" encouraged early marriage because earnings from industrial by-occupations eliminated the need to wait for inheritance (especially inheritance of land) to marry. According to this model, women enjoyed a more important role in the industrial workforce than they had in agriculture, which boasted a fairly rigid sexual division of labor.[96] But others question this low estimation of the female agricultural labor force, particularly in England where female servants in husbandry were hardly uncommon. Others, like Sharpe, point to many communities where women's decisions to marry did not operate in the way the model predicts.[97]

There is no denying that economic fluctuations — particularly when they opened up or limited women's options for paid work — could exercise a powerful effect on singlewomen by influencing both when and if women married. For example, Richard Smith argues that when price changes made the marginal returns from pastoral husbandry better than from arable agriculture, employers took steps to hire female labor, which in turn delayed marriage and increased the numbers of singlewomen, developments that occurred in England during the periods 1350–1450 and 1650–1750.[98] In Smith's view, widening demand for female labor explains the rising mean age of marriage for women (Table A2), the very high levels of permanent singlewomen born in the early and mid-seventeenth century (Table A3), and the falling population levels in the second half of the seventeenth century. Although his evidence is firmest for the late seventeenth century, his argument that work opportunities also gave women alternatives to marriage in the late Middle Ages is generally persuasive.[99]

Wealth and social status also exercised a particularly potent effect on the proportions of singlewomen by driving down the age at which women married. In the village of Colyton in Devon, for example, women from the poor and laboring classes generally married later than women from local gentry and craft households, a trend also apparent in a group of eighteenth-century German villages where the daughters of well-off farmers married on the average two years before the daughters of the waged proletariat

(Table A5). The tendency for women from richer families to marry earlier was also evident in the cities of London, Rouen, Geneva, and Florence. The gap was especially large in seventeenth-century Geneva where women from the high and middle bourgeoisie usually married a few months before their twentieth birthdays, but the daughters of the working population delayed marriage until they were almost 27 years old (Table A5). These delays can be explained by the time it took for poorer women, who depended less on family resources, to accumulate enough savings to marry. Since artisanal and laboring women usually married within their own social group, they also had to wait until their future husbands either completed apprenticeships or saved sufficient money.

Not surprisingly, noblewomen, the richest women in Europe, married at the youngest ages, not only because of their value in cementing political alliances, but also because of the need to ensure their sexual purity. In the Middle Ages, noblewomen usually married in their mid- to late teens, but by the late sixteenth and seventeenth centuries they were marrying later, in their late teens and early twenties (yet still considerably younger than commoners: compare Tables A2 and A5). The higher the social group, the earlier the age at marriage, as we see in France where the daughters of dukes and peers married earlier than women from the provincial nobility (Table A5). Interesting variations also occurred across Europe; although women married at roughly the same ages among the French and British peerage, in the eighteenth century the age at marriage rose for British noblewomen while it fell among French noblewomen.

Wealth did not always exercise a parallel effect on the proportions of lifelong singlewomen, a phenomenon that warns us once again not to assume that trends in the rates of life-cycle singlewomen and lifelong singlewomen moved in tandem. Although wealth and social status tended to lower women's age at marriage and reduce the proportions of singlewomen among the landed elite of premodern Europe, economic and social privilege on occasion worked to raise the numbers of permanent singlewomen within the wealthier social groups of town and court. In fifteenth-century Florence, for example, about 10 percent of the wealthier women were still single at age 25 compared to only 3 percent of the women from poorer families.[100] Similar trends are visible in sixteenth- and seventeenth-century Geneva, among the ruling families of Europe, and among the British peerage; aristocratic daughters were more likely to remain permanently single than the daughters of commoners (Table A3). Scholars advance several reasons for the higher proportions of lifelong singlewomen among many of these privileged populations, including the rising costs of dowries and marriage portions for the elite, the social prohibitions against noble and patriciate women marrying out of their class even when the pool of prospective husbands was small, and the growing acceptance of a woman's choice to make a love match.[101]

Also striking are the changes in the proportions of lifelong single-women over time and their different rates among the European nobility. In the British peerage, about 5–9 percent of noblewomen were lifelong single-women in the sixteenth century, but this figure rose to 13–15 percent in the seventeenth century and became as high as 26 percent in the eighteenth century. In contrast, the proportion of lifelong lay singlewomen among the French nobility was always smaller, never going above 5–10 percent and showing little change over the course of the early modern period.[102] These differences between the English and French nobility were due in large part to the many young noble women who became nuns in Catholic France; indeed, if women who joined the convent were added to the number of lay lifelong singlewomen, the proportion of never-marrying women was nota-bly higher among the French than the British.[103] As opportunities for con-vent life declined near the end of the eighteenth century, however, the proportions of lay lifelong singlewomen rose, although not to the same high levels we see for eighteenth-century British noblewomen, more than one-quarter of whom never married (Table A3).

The availability of convent life for singlewomen in France at a time when the Reformation had removed this option for most noblewomen in England and much of Holland, Germany, and Scandinavia points to the role of religious culture in influencing the proportions of singlewomen in medieval and early modern Europe. Scholars of medieval and Renaissance Italy have traced how the wealthier families of Florence and other big cities used convents as sanctuaries (or dumping grounds, depending on the view-point taken) for their unmarried daughters.[104] By the mid-sixteenth cen-tury in Florence, for example, no fewer than 28 percent of the young women whose fathers had enrolled them in the Dowry Fund became nuns, generally taking up the religious life around the age of 17.[105] Yet this alter-native lifestyle was no longer available to English women, which may have been responsible for the growing number of singlewomen and lifelong singlewomen among the country's wealthy elite.[106]

The impact of religious culture on the proportions of singlewomen can also be seen in other spheres. Scattered literary and demographic data sug-gest that Jewish women in late medieval and early modern Europe married at an earlier age, in their mid- to late teens, than did Christian women who resided in the same locale.[107] Lifelong singlewomen were also virtually nonexistent in Jewish communities. Among the Morisco population of early modern Spain, women also married earlier than their Christian neighbors. In early seventeenth-century Valencia, for example, the Christian peasant women of Pedralba had a mean age at first marriage of 20.6 while their Morisco neighbors married around the age of 18.[108] Youthful marriage might have been encouraged by the Islamic practice whereby the bride did not need to bring any substantial dowry to a union since the husband endowed his wife with property.

In most of early modern Europe, however, religious affiliation played little or no role in determining whether or how long women stayed single. A detailed study of Quaker women in Ireland and Britain shows that the elevated socioeconomic standing of Quakers and factors associated with their geographical place of residence exerted more influence than their religious beliefs on the timing and incidence of their marriages. The demographic behavior of Quaker women in Ireland, for example, diverged from the practices of Quaker women in Britain, but closely paralleled that of other well-off Irish women.[109] Considerably more controversy surrounds the question of the effects of Catholicism and Protestantism on the proportions of singlewomen. Some demographers have found evidence that permanent singlewomen were especially numerous in regions of ardent Catholicism, attributing this trend to the Catholic Church's emphasis on virginity and its reliance on the doctrine of consent in marriage.[110] Yet the evidence for this relationship does not adequately distinguish nuns from lifelong lay singlewomen and centers on the late eighteenth and nineteenth centuries. For the sixteenth and seventeenth centuries, moreover, the scattered data are more open to interpretation. In Calvin's Geneva, for example, a drop in prenuptial conceptions might be attributed to puritanical preaching, but changes in the timing and incidence of female marriage owed more to demographic factors (such as a surplus of men) or political and economic causes (such as war and famine) than religious culture.[111] In seventeenth-century Rouen, Catholic women married slightly earlier (27.2 years) than Huguenot women (28.9 years), but the difference is insignificant given that both groups married relatively late.[112] Similar evidence about the correspondence between Protestant and Catholic marriage patterns in the Low Countries and among Anglicans and nonconformists in England also show little difference in the age women married and hence in the proportions of singlewomen.[113] Although some historians dwell on

Protestant encouragement of universal marriage, no firm demographic evidence exists that adherence to the Catholic or Protestant faiths affected the proportions of singlewomen in early modern Europe.

We could add yet more factors to this list of how geographic/climatic region, urban/rural residence, migration, skewed sex ratios, economic fluctuations, the availability of female work, wealth, status, and religious culture influenced the proportions of singlewomen in medieval and early modern Europe. Paramount among these factors are the cultural norms that encouraged certain marriage regimes, especially the strong links among sexual purity, family respectability, and male honor in many Mediterranean cultures that promoted early and universal marriage for young women. Our understanding of the relative importance of these cultural considerations and how they influenced demographic behavior is woefully thin. The influence of inheritance customs has received slightly more consideration. On the face of it, partible inheritance systems in which sons and daughters had equal claim to their parents' property would present few obstacles to early marriage.[114] In contrast, strict primogeniture probably encouraged early marriage of the chief male heir, but dampened his siblings' prospects. It has also been argued that the customary inheritance practices of medieval England provided a particularly favorable climate for independent female economic activity, which in turn may have encouraged women to remain single longer.[115] Dowry systems could also play an important role in determining marriage patterns, as we have seen in late medieval Florence where many fathers coped with dowry inflation by sending their daughters to convents. Individual circumstances, such as being left an orphan or the premature death of one's father could encourage early marriage, while birth order and the number of siblings could also exercise some influence.[116] Changes in the provision of poor relief, such as the expansion of parish welfare and rise of new institutions for the poor in early modern Europe, may also have made it easier for women to remain single.[117] We also need to be aware of how these and other factors may have affected the proportions of singlewomen indirect—by reducing or increasing the likelihood that widows might remarry.

Conclusion

The large and useful body of data produced by historical demographers about singlewomen in preindustrial Europe allows us to make some general observations about their demographic history. Proportions of singlewomen were largest in towns and cities, but varied significantly across Europe. The most marked divide occurred between the Mediterranean regions of Italy, southern France, and Iberia — which until the eighteenth century had relatively few singlewomen and even fewer lifelong single-women — and northwestern Europe, where the later age at marriage and larger percentage of women who never married generated significantly more singlewomen. The reasons behind these variations remain the subject of scholarly debate, but it is clear that cultural systems, perhaps conditioned by climatic variations that stimulated different patterns of mortality, played a major role.

The proportions of singlewomen also varied across the centuries. Al-though the representation of singlewomen in medieval Europe remains subject to some debate, it is unlikely that singlewomen were as numerous in Europe before the fifteenth century as they were afterwards. Only in En-gland, and perhaps in Flanders and some of the larger continental towns, can we definitely see evidence of fairly large concentrations of singlewomen (roughly 30–40 percent of the adult female population) in the later Middle Ages. By the mid-sixteenth century, the proportions of singlewomen in northwestern Europe began to rise, as reflected in the rising age at first marriage. Although subject to significant local and regional variations, the general trend was towards later marriages and more singlewomen into the eighteenth century. The pace of change was slower in Mediterranean Eu-rope, but even there the age at marriage began to creep slowly upward in the late seventeenth century; by the late eighteenth century there were many areas in southern Europe that had as many singlewomen as in north-ern Europe. Scholarly explanations for the increasing numbers of sin-glewomen — both life-cycle and lifelong — vary widely. Some focus on the reduction of mortality crises, arguing that as life expectancy rose, the imper-ative to marry and reproduce eased, thus allowing women to marry later. Others concentrate more on the factors that influenced patterns of nup-tiality, stressing in particular how economic fluctuations influenced deci-sions about when and if to marry. While these differences of opinion arise partly from diverging analytical and methodological perspectives, they also reflect significant contrasts between the demographic regimes of different European regions; for example, the crucial role of nuptiality in the demo-graphic regimes of England and parts of the Netherlands can be explained in large part by the peculiar economic and institutional culture of these regions.

Urban residence, poverty, and migration all raised the age at which women married and prompted higher proportions of singlewomen. Great wealth, high social status, and immobility all tended to lower the age at marriage and depress the number of singlewomen. These factors seemed to operate over all of Europe, despite the striking regional differences noted between northwestern and Mediterranean Europe before the eighteenth century. More open to debate are the effects of economic fluctuations — such as rising or falling standards of living, and the influence of the availability and nature of paid work for women — in part because of the unresolved debates among demographers about the relative importance of mortality, fertility, and nuptiality in determining demographic behavior. We also know far less about the demographic history of singlewomen in the Middle Ages than during the early modern and modern period, although the creative attempts of some medieval demographers to understand the medieval situation by reference to the early modern period are encouraging.

Particularly murky for all periods is the history of lifelong singlewomen, who apparently exercised a crucial effect on overall population trends before the mid-eighteenth century. Unfortunately for our purposes, demographers' greater interest in fertility is evident in their limited definition of lifelong "celibates" since they only count women who died after the age of 50 having never married; they thus underestimate — perhaps to a serious degree — the total pool of lifelong singlewomen in premodern Europe. Yet in drawing on a wide range of sources and devising creative methodologies to measure accurately trends in nuptiality, demographers have also contributed greatly to our understanding of variations in the proportions of life-cycle and lifelong singlewomen. These proportions often moved in the same direction, but on occasion (for example, in the demographic behavior of aristocratic and patriciate women) demographers have also discovered periods and situations when they diverged. As these examples indicate, a full research agenda awaits those who wish to understand the demographic behavior and role of singlewomen in the European past.

I would like to thank Judith Bennett, Mavis Mate, and Steve Rappaport for their comments on an earlier version of this essay.

Notes

1. For feminist complaints about demographers' tendency to focus on processes at the expense of women, see Susan Cotts Watkins, "If All We Knew About Women Was What We Read in *Demography*, What Would We Know?" *Demography*

30 (1993): 551–77; Alison Mackinnon, "Were Women Present at the Demographic Transition? Questions from a Feminist Historian to Historical Demographers," *Gender & History* 7 (1995): 222–40.

2. Only twenty years ago, most historical demographers considered mortality to be the most significant factor influencing population change, but now many (especially in England) have been persuaded that fertility exercised the greatest impact on population fluctuations. Since few births occurred outside marriage in the preindustrial era (illegitimacy rates were usually less than 2 percent of all live births before the mid-eighteenth century) and because birth control was not widely practiced until the early nineteenth century, fertility was largely determined by the age at marriage; the total fertility of a marriage could change by about 7 percent for every year that the age at marriage rose or fell. For a general discussion of these points, see Michael W. Flinn, *The European Demographic System, 1500–1820* (Baltimore: Johns Hopkins University Press, 1981), 19–46. Historical demographers have recently argued that the proportion of women who never married (or, as they are called in this volume "lifelong singlewomen") was more responsible than age at marriage for most variations in fertility before 1700; see David R. Weir, "Rather Never Than Late: Celibacy and Age at Marriage in English Cohort Fertility, 1541–1871," *Journal of Family History* 9 (1994): 340–54, and Roger Schofield, "English Marriage Patterns Revisited," *Journal of Family History* 10 (1985): 2–20.

3. The pattern was identified in John J. Hajnal, "European Marriage Patterns in Perspective," in *Population in History: Essays in Historical Demography*, ed. D. V. Glass and D. E. C. Eversley (Chicago: University of Chicago Press, 1965), 101–43, who thought the pattern was prevalent in the area of Europe west of a line running from Trieste to Leningrad. But under the influence of additional research, Hajnal (n. 4 below) and others have modified the geographical extent of the pattern and now describe it the "northwestern European marriage pattern."

4. Peter Laslett, "Characteristics of the Western Family Considered over Time," in *Family Life and Illicit Love in Earlier Generations: Essays in Historical Sociology* (Cambridge: Cambridge University Press, 1977), 12–49; John Hajnal, "Two Kinds of Pre-Industrial Household Formation System," in *Family Forms in Historic Europe*, ed. Richard Wall, Jean Robin, and Peter Laslett (Cambridge: Cambridge University Press, 1983), 65–104; the literature on this point is now very large.

5. Demographers writing in English usually refer to lifelong singlewomen only obliquely as "proportions never marrying," although several (below, n. 6) prefer the term "spinster." Continental usage tends to be more direct; the French generally employ the term *célibat définitif*, the Spanish prefer *soltería definitiva* or *celibato definitivo femenino*, the Germans use *Junggesellin* or *unverheiratete Frau*, while the Italians use *nubile* (whose connotation of a younger age provides an indirect reflection of the rarity of lifelong singlewomen in the Italian past) and occasionally *zitella* for older women. All these terms carry slightly different connotations from the English usage. Those who focus on household composition rely heavily on the word "solitaries," but this term fails to distinguish between singlewomen and widows.

6. Susan Cotts Watkins ("Spinsters," *Journal of Family History* 9 [1984]: 310, n. 1) also thinks never-married women over age 35 should be considered lifelong

singlewomen (although she prefers the term "spinsters") and draws attention to how different communities may have had different notions of the age at which women entered spinsterhood. Despite this, she is also forced to cite demographic evidence for women at older ages. Olwen Hufton (who also uses "spinster") also remarks on the underestimation of singlewomen by historical demographers in "Women Without Men: Widows and Spinsters in Britain and France in the Eighteenth Century," *Journal of Family History* 9 (1984): 357.

7. The evidence for the different experience of late-marrying singlewomen is particularly good for England; see, for example, Vivien Brodsky Elliott, "Single Women in the London Marriage Market: Age, Status and Mobility, 1598–1619," in *Marriage and Society: Studies in the Social History of Marriage*, ed. R. B. Outhwaite (New York: St. Martin's Press, 1981), 81–100.

8. In such cases, the spousal age gap could be considerable since women tended to marry men significantly older than themselves. For discussions of the greater parental control over women marrying at younger ages, see, for example, Diane Owen Hughes, "Urban Growth and Family Structure in Medieval Genoa," in *Towns in Societies: Essays in Economic History and Historical Sociology*, ed. Philip Abrams and E. A. Wrigley (Cambridge: Cambridge University Press, 1978), 119–29; Anthony Molho, *Marriage Alliance in Late Medieval Florence* (Cambridge, Mass.: Harvard University Press, 1994), 128–43, 221–37.

9. It affects nuptiality, which in turn affects fertility, which many (see n. 2, above) consider the most influential factor in changes in population size; see Weir, "Rather Never Than Late"; Schofield, "English Marriage Patterns Revisited."

10. Richard M. Smith, "Geographical Diversity in the Resort to Marriage in Late Medieval Europe: Work, Reputation, and Unmarried Females in the Household Formation Systems of Northern and Southern Europe," in *Woman Is a Worthy Wight: Women in English Society c. 1200–1500*, ed. P. J. P. Goldberg (Wolfeboro Falls, N.H.: Alan Sutton, 1992), 10, 42–43; see also his "Women's Work and Marriage in Pre-industrial England: Some Speculations," in *La Donna nell'economia secc. XIII–XVIII*, ed. Simonetta Cavaciocchi (Prato: Le Monnier, 1990), 31–55.

11. K. D. M. Snell, *Annals of the Labouring Poor: Social Change and Agrarian England 1660–1900* (Cambridge: Cambridge University Press, 1985); Pamela Sharpe, "Literally Spinsters: A New Interpretation of Local Economy and Demography in Colyton in the Seventeenth and Eighteenth Centuries," *Economic History Review* 2nd ser. 44 (1991): 46–65; P. J. P. Goldberg, *Women, Work, and Life Cycle in a Medieval Economy: Women in York and Yorkshire, c. 1300–1520* (Oxford: Clarendon Press, 1992).

12. For a discussion of scholars who see the high sex ratios (more men than women) in these surveys as evidence of early marriage, see Pierre Toubert, "The Carolingian Moment (Eighth-Tenth Century)," in *A History of the Family*, ed. André Burguière, Christiane Klapisch-Zuber, Martine Segalen, and Françoise Zonabend (Cambridge, Mass.: Harvard University Press, 1996), 385–86, first published in French as *Histoire de la famille* (Paris: Armand Collin, 1986). For how evidence of relatively low proportions of married persons in these surveys indicate a later age at marriage, see C. I. Hammer Jr., "Family and *Familia* in Early-Medieval Bavaria," in *Family Forms in Historic Europe*, ed. Richard Wall, Jean Robin, and Peter Laslett

(Cambridge: Cambridge University Press, 1983), 234–36, 241, 247–48; and David Herlihy, *Medieval Households* (Cambridge, Mass.: Harvard University Press, 1985), 76–78.

13. Zvi Razi, *Life, Marriage and Death in a Medieval Parish: Economy, Society and Demography in Halesowen 1270–1400* (Cambridge: Cambridge University Press, 1980), 60–63. For criticisms of his methods, see the series of articles by Richard M. Smith and L. R. Poos that, along with Razi's responses, first appeared in *Law and History Review* 2 (1984): 128–52; 3 (1985): 191–200, 406–29; 5 (1987): 523–35, and have now been reprinted as "The Population History of Medieval English Villages: A Debate on the Use of Manor Court Records," in *Medieval Society and the Manor Court*, ed. Zvi Razi and Richard M. Smith (Oxford: Oxford University Press, 1996), 298–368. See also Goldberg, *Women, Work, and Life Cycle*, 205–10.

14. H. E. Hallam, "Age at First Marriage and Age at Death in the Lincolnshire Fenland, 1252–1478," *Population Studies* 39 (1985): 55–69. Richard M. Smith, "Some Reflections on the Evidence for the Origins of the 'European Marriage Pattern' in England," in *The Sociology of the Family*, ed. Chris Harris (Keele, 1979), 97, 101; idem, "Hypothèses sur la nuptialité en Angleterre aux XIIIe–XIVe siècles," *Annales: E.S.C.* 38 (1983): 120–24.

15. David Herlihy and Christiane Klapisch-Zuber, *Les Toscans et leur familles: une étude du catasto florentin de 1427* (Paris: Presse de la Fondation Nationale des Sciences Politiques, 1978), published in English as *Tuscans and Their Families: A Study of the Florentine Catasto of 1427* (New Haven, Conn.: Yale University Press, 1985). They use survey data on age and marital status to calculate the mean age at first marriage according to the method developed by John Hajnal ("Age at Marriage and Proportions Marrying," *Population Studies* 7 [1953]: 111–36); see *Tuscans*, 86–88 and 202–11.

16. Herlihy and Klapisch-Zuber, *Tuscans*, 88, for this and the following figures regarding lifelong singlewomen. See also Table A3.

17. Using the 1480 catasto, Molho (*Marriage Alliance in Late Medieval Florence*, 217–18) calculated that only 1.9 percent of women aged 46–55 had never married. Although Herlihy and Klapisch-Zuber (*Tuscans*, 88) note that 3.8 percent of women aged around 50 in 1427 had never married compared to 4.3 percent in 1480, their 1480 figures are based on a sample of one-tenth of the taxed households, so Molho's figure is probably more accurate.

18. In 1552, as many as 11–15 percent of Florentine women were nuns, according to Richard C. Trexler, "Celibacy in the Renaissance: The Nuns of Florence," in *Power and Dependence in Renaissance Florence*, vol. 2, *The Women of Renaissance Florence* (Binghamton, N.Y.: Medieval and Renaissance Texts and Studies, 1993), 15–16, first published in French in *Annales: E.S.C.*, 27 (1972): 1329–50. His findings are reinforced by Molho (*Marriage Alliance*, 306–7) who calculated that the percentage of women who left the Florentine Dowry Fund to become nuns rose most markedly in the early sixteenth century. It is important to note that the Tuscan figures on lifelong singlewomen quoted here (and in Table A3) exclude nuns, who accounted for about 2.3 percent of the adult female population in the catasto population (Herlihy and Klapisch-Zuber, *Tuscans*, 25, 214, n. 16).

19. Franca Leverotti, "La famiglia contadina Lucchese all'inizio del '400," in

Strutture familiari epidemie migrazioni nell'Italia medievale, ed. Rinaldo Comba, Gabriella Piccinni, and Giuliano Pinto (Naples: Edizione Scientifiche Italiane, 1984), 261–63, as in Table A1. Demographic data from medieval Sicily are more indirect and derived largely from wills; see Henri Bresc, *Un monde méditerranéen: Economie et société en Sicile, 1300–1450* (Rome: Ecole Française de Rome, 1986), 77–81, 697–703.

20. David Herlihy, "The Population of Verona in the First Century of Venetian Rule," in *Renaissance Venice*, ed. J. R. Hale (Totowa, N.J.: Rowman and Littlefield, 1973), 114–15; James S. Grubb, *Provincial Families of the Renaissance: Private and Public Life in the Veneto* (Baltimore: Johns Hopkins University Press, 1996), 4–6, 221.

21. Grubb, *Provincial Families*, 6, focuses on the differences more than the similarities.

22. For this and the following, see Herlihy and Klapisch-Zuber, *Tuscans*, 80–92, 223–26; Christiane Klapisch-Zuber, "Female Celibacy and Service in Florence in the Fifteenth Century," in *Women, Family, and Ritual in Renaissance Italy* (Chicago: University of Chicago Press, 1985), 165–77, first published in French in *Annales de Démographie Historique* (1981): 289–302. Herlihy ("Population," 114–15) argues that Verona's late fifteenth-century prosperity drew more migrants and allowed wealthier households to hire more servants, most of them single. His conclusion may be suspect given Klapisch-Zuber's findings about the greater proportion of married and widowed servants in Florence ("Women Servants in Florence During the Fourteenth and Fifteenth Centuries," in *Women and Work in Preindustrial Europe*, ed. Barbara Hanawalt [Bloomington: Indiana University Press, 1986], 63, 74). His assertion that Veronese women were marrying at a younger age in 1502 than in 1425 (p. 114) is also questionable, especially given his more definitive evidence about the significantly higher proportions of singlewomen in the later period.

23. Trexler, "Celibacy," 15–16; R. Burr Litchfield, "Demographic Characteristics of Florentine Patrician Families, Sixteenth to Nineteenth Centuries," *Journal of Economic History* 29 (1969): 197–98, 203. Molho, *Marriage Alliance*, 306, notes that the number of women enrolled in the Dowry Fund of Florence who became nuns rose from about 4 percent in 1425–99 to almost 16 percent in 1500–29, peaking at 28 percent in 1530–60.

24. Herlihy, "Population," 109, 111–12; Klapisch-Zuber, "Female Celibacy," 137–77; idem, "Women Servants," 61, 65. For researchers, the most serious flaw of the catasto of 1427 is that young servants were recorded in their natal home while adult servants submitted a separate declaration, even when they resided with their masters. As several critics point out, this practice would seemingly lead to a marked underestimation of urban servants (and especially singlewomen) since many young servants probably came to the city from the countryside. The high rate of servanthood in Florence by 1552, when a census reveals that 17 percent of the population were servants (70 percent of whom were women; *Tuscans*, 332, n. 73), casts further doubt on the 1427 figures. Herlihy and Klapisch-Zuber downplay the significance of this problem (*Tuscans*, 12–13), but offer few explanations of the vast differences in female servants observed in 1427 and 1552. Richard M. Smith, however, has calculated that the underregistration of female servants would have had to be unre-

alistically massive to bring Florence up to the proportions of singlewomen observed for northern European towns in this period ("The People of Tuscany and Their Families in the Fifteenth Century: Medieval or Mediterranean," *Journal of Family History* 6 [1981]: 118–19; idem, "Geographical Diversity," 29–30). In arguing that the underestimation was not particularly great, Smith also points to the findings of Klapisch-Zuber ("Women Servants") that female servants in Florence were both older and more often married or widowed than single.

25. Molho, *Marriage Alliance*, 219–21; Grubb, *Provincial Families*, 6. Smith ("The People of Tuscany," 112) also notes that demographic factors alone cannot explain the persistence of a large spousal age gap in Tuscany. Klapisch-Zuber has also increasingly focused on cultural traditions to explain the Italian marriage system; see n. 26 below.

26. For example, many of the essays in Klapisch-Zuber's *Women, Family and Ritual in Renaissance Italy* ponder the role of honor, custom, and ritual in shaping women's lives. In order to explain the universal and early marriage patterns prevalent in Italy, historians have focused on the threat that female sexuality unregulated by marriage or the convent posed to men; see Julius Kirshner, *Pursuing Honor While Avoiding Sin: The "Monte delle doti" of Florence* (Milan: A. Giuffre, 1978), 7; Donald E. Queller and Thomas F. Madden, "Father of the Bride: Fathers, Daughters, and Dowries in Late Medieval and Early Renaissance Venice," *Renaissance Quarterly* 46 (1993): 685–711; and below, n. 27. Note, however, that all these studies dwell on the ruling elite or propertied classes.

27. Anthony Molho, "Deception and Marriage Strategy in Renaissance Florence: The Case of Women's Ages," *Renaissance Quarterly* 41 (1988): 193–217.

28. Some social historians of medieval and Renaissance Italy tend to see more of a role for female choice than do historical demographers, but they too focus on the extent to which Italian parents, especially those of the urban elite, limited their daughters' choices; see Stanley Chojnacki, "Measuring Adulthood: Adolescence and Gender in Renaissance Venice," *Journal of Family History* 17 (1992): 371–95.

29. Herlihy, *Medieval Households*, 103–7, 110–11.

30. The marriage contracts studied by Geneviève Laribière ("Le mariage à Toulouse aux XIVe et XVe siècles," *Annales du Midi* 79 [1967]: 350) suggest a marriage age of 15–18, but her age data are haphazard and drawn largely from the propertied classes. The family memoirs examined by Jean-Louis Biget and Jean Tricard ("Livres de raison et démographie familiale en Limousin au XVe siècle," *Annales de Démographie Historique* [1981]: 327) focus on only four elite women, but report a mean marriage age that is older, around 20.6. An average age at marriage of 19.3 is derived from 6 cases drawn from family genealogies in Arras; see Bernard Delmaire, "Le livre de famille des Les Borgne (Arras, 1347–1538). Contribution à la démographie historique médiévale," *Revue du Nord* 65 (1983): 305. For the effect of wealth and status on women's age at first marriage, see below, especially Table A5.

31. The Bristol and London evidence is based on wealthy female orphans who had every reason to marry early; see Table A1. For Germany, see Richard Koebner, "Die Eheauffassung des ausgehenden deutschen Mittelalters," *Archiv für Kulturgeschichte* 9 (1911): 138–40, who draws on the genealogies of the German nobility in 1300–1520. His evidence for the daughters of the urban patriciate indicates they

waited until 18–19 to marry; only 3 of the 28 Frankfurt women in his cohort had married by age 16, but 18 had married by age 18, and 25 by age 20. Of eleven women in the Walther family of Augsburg, none married before the age of 17.

32. Goldberg, *Women, Work, and Life Cycle*, 225–32; note, however, that his data are not without problems. He has less than 30 cases ranging over more than 200 years (1303–1520), and several of these involved marriage before the canonically approved age, while less than 5 can positively be shown to be first marriages. Perhaps more persuasive are his data on 35 female servants (30 urban, 5 rural) who were still single at a certain age; but, as with the data on marriage age, he often knows only the lower limits of the woman's age group rather than her exact age. Despite these problems, Goldberg's data represent some of the best evidence yet found for the age at marriage of nonelite women in northern Europe before the sixteenth century.

33. Philippe Desportes, "La population de Reims au XVe siècle d'après un dénombrement de 1422," *Le Moyen Age* 72 (1966): 487, 498, 501.

34. Jacques Rossiaud, *Medieval Prostitution*, trans. Lydia G. Cochrane (Oxford: Blackwell, 1988), 15; he uses witnesses' declared age at marriage in criminal depositions. While the sample certainly goes further down the social ladder than the evidence for the urban elite, the need to find prudent and trustworthy witnesses probably slants the relatively small sample (32 cases) towards the better-off members of the community.

35. The list of scholars who now accept that the European marriage pattern and household formation system operated in this region during the late Middle Ages is a growing one and includes Richard M. Smith (nn. 10, 14, 24, above); Alan MacFarlane, *Marriage and Love in England 1300–1840* (Oxford: Blackwell, 1986); L. R. Poos, *A Rural Society After the Black Death: Essex 1350–1525* (Cambridge: Cambridge University Press, 1991); Goldberg, *Women, Work, and Life Cycle*, esp. 232 and 272–79; and Jan de Vries, "Population," in *Handbook of European History 1400–1600, vol. I*, ed. Thomas A. Brady, Heiko A. Oberman, and James D. Tracy (Grand Rapids, Mich.: Eerdmans, 1994), 36–40.

36. Methods to correct for these flaws have become increasingly sophisticated; see, for example, Herlihy and Klapisch-Zuber, *Tuscans*, 203–21; Smith, "Hypothèses"; Poos, *Rural Society*, 149–56, 294–99.

37. Hajnal, "European Marriage Patterns," 119, 136; widows are included in the "unmarried" group.

38. Although some widows were probably included in the "single" group, urban censuses were generally more careful to record marital status than national taxes; see Hajnal, "European Marriage Patterns," 117; Charles Phythian-Adams, *Desolation of a City: Coventry and the Urban Crisis of the Late Middle Ages* (Cambridge: Cambridge University Press, 1979), 91–92, 155, 201–3, 306–7; Desportes, "Reims," 486–87, 502.

39. Caroline Fenwick ("The English Poll Taxes of 1377, 1379, and 1381: A Critical Examination of the Returns" [Ph.D. thesis, University of London, 1983], 179) calculated that unmarried women comprised 16.8 percent of the total taxpaying population, or 33.6 percent of adult women if we assume that there were equal numbers of men and women in the taxpaying population; after subtracting known

and probable widows and widowers (people of unknown marital status who resided with children or who headed households comprising 2 or more people), she
calculated that 29.9 percent of the total adult population was single in 1377. Since
there were more male than female taxpayers, the actual proportion of singlewomen
would theoretically be less than 29.9 percent, but the underenumeration of singlewomen in the tax would more than make up the difference. Singlewomen escaped
enumeration for several reasons: because of their poverty (Fenwick, 179–96, convincingly argues that most of those who escaped the tax were actually considered
not liable to pay because of their poverty) and because it was easier to hide a young
singlewoman than a young bachelor from the tax collectors, or to claim she had not
reached the taxable age of 14 or 15. Scholars have also shown that servants, many of
them young singlewomen, were also frequently underenumerated in the tax. On
these points, see also Poos, *Rural Society*, 149–57 and 294–99; P. J. P. Goldberg,
"Urban Identity and the Poll Taxes of 1377, 1379, and 1381," *Economic History Review*
2nd ser. 43 (1990): 197–208. Estimates of the total degree of evasion/exclusion
range from 5–25 percent, but recent research favors the lower end of this range, with
perhaps 5–10 percent of the adult population escaping enumeration; see Poos,
Rural Society, 296 and 299.

40. Erik Thoen, "Historical Demography in Late Medieval Rural Flanders:
Recent Results and Hypotheses," in *Peasants and Townsmen in Medieval Europe:
Studia in Honorem Adriaan Verhulst*, ed. Jean-Marie Duvosquel and Erik Thoen
(Ghent: Snoeck-Ducaju, 1995), 580–81.

41. Hajnal, "Two Kinds," 96–97. The most thorough study of this system is
Ann Kussmaul, *Servants in Husbandry in Early Modern England* (Cambridge: Cambridge University Press, 1981).

42. Tax evasion was especially marked in the poll-tax returns of 1379 and 1381
(R. H. Hilton, *The English Peasantry in the Later Middle Ages* [Oxford: Clarendon
Press, 1975], 31–35; Poos, *Rural Society*, 149–51, 187–88, 297–98; Goldberg, "Ur-
ban Identity," 197–208).

43. The evidence is best for England (both rural and urban areas) and for
continental towns since little work has been done on medieval rural regions on the
continent. Smith ("Some Reflections," 100) notes that 20 percent of the rural
households in the English county of Rutland kept servants in 1377, a figure that
compares well with the 14–25 percent of households that had servants in a large
sample of early modern villages (see Richard Wall, "Regional and Temporal Variations in English Household Structure from 1650," in *Regional Demographic Development*, ed. John Hobcraft and Philip Rees [London: Croom Helm, 1980], 89–113).
For the high proportions of servants in other English poll-tax populations, especially in towns, see Goldberg, *Women, Work, and Life Cycle*, 159–67. In Ypres in
1506, 30.5 percent of households in the Poorterie quarter had servants (Henri
Pirenne, "Les dénombrements de la population d'Ypres au XVe siècle [1412–
1506]," *Vierteljahrschrift für Social- und Wirtschaftsgeschichte* 1 [1903]: 13, 15, 19). In
Reims in 1422, 47.3 percent of the households in two parishes had servants (Desportes, "Reims," 489). In Coventry in 1523, 24.8 percent of the households had
servants (Phythian-Adams, *Coventry*, 204).

44. The English poll-tax evidence reveals that servants comprised about 7–10

percent of the rural taxpaying population and 20–30 percent in towns (Goldberg, *Women, Work, and Life Cycle*, 159–67, 370–71). If we use a multiplier of 1.75 (midway between the range of 1.5 and 1.9 adopted by various historians) to account for those excluded from the tax (because of poverty or youth), roughly 4–5 percent of the total rural population and 11–17 percent of the urban population were servants. Yet these figures almost certainly underestimate the proportions of servants, since they often escaped enumeration in the poll taxes (see n. 42, above).

45. Desportes, "Reims," 489, 491; Phythian-Adams, *Coventry*, 204, 221, 306–7.

46. For the low servant sex ratios (more women than men) in towns, see Roger Mols, *Introduction à la démographie historique des villes d'Europe* (Louvain: Gembloux, J. Duculot, 1954–56), 2:180–81; Peter Ketsch, *Frauen im Mittelalter*, ed. Annette Kuhn (Düsseldorf: Schwann, 1983), 1:54–55; Goldberg, *Women, Work, and Life Cycle*, 159–62, 165–67. Indeed, the surplus of female servants in towns was largely responsible for the low sex ratios in many late medieval northern European towns; see Goldberg, "Urban Identity," 198–201; and Smith, "The People of Tuscany," 116. For convincing evidence that female servants in late medieval England were young and single, see Poos, *Rural Society*, 189–95; P. J. P. Goldberg, "Marriage, Migration, Servanthood and Life-Cycle in Yorkshire Towns of the Later Middle Ages: Some York Cause Paper Evidence," *Continuity and Change* 1 (1986): 141–69; idem, *Women, Work, and Life Cycle*, 168–72, 180–86. For France, see Mols, *Introduction*, 2:180; Desportes, "Reims," 487, 501. For Germany, see Ketsch, *Frauen im Mittelalter*, 1:51–78.

47. The evidence consists of urban censuses that record household members by age and marital status (Desportes, "Reims," 487–92, 498–501; Phythian-Adams, *Coventry*, 84–85, 204–11), as well as depositions in ecclesiastical court cases, wills, manorial and borough court rolls, and proof-of-age inquests; see Poos, *Rural Society*, 188–206; Goldberg, *Women, Work, and Life Cycle*, 158–201; idem, "Marriage, Migration and Servanthood."

48. Poos, *Rural Society*, 183–227; Marjorie K. McIntosh, "Local Change and Community Control in England, 1465–1500," *Huntingdon Library Quarterly* 12 (1986): 224; H. S. A. Fox, "Servants, Cottagers and Tied Cottages during the Later Middle Ages: Towards a Regional Dimension," *Rural History* 6 (1995): 125–54; idem, "Exploitation of the Landless by Lords and Tenants in Early Medieval England," in *Medieval Society and the Manor Court*, 518–68. For indirect evidence of the earning power of rural singlewomen which might reflect their participation in life-cycle service, see Judith Bennett, "Medieval Peasant Marriage: An Examination of Marriage License Fines in the *Liber Gersumarum*," in *Pathways to Medieval Peasants*, ed. J. A. Raftis (Toronto: Pontifical Institute of Mediaeval Studies, 1981), 193–246. For seasonal peaks in medieval marriages that Ann Kussmaul (*Servants in Husbandry*, 97–100, and *A General View of the Rural Economy of England, 1538–1840* [Cambridge: Cambridge University Press, 1990], 1–43) interprets as evidence of rural life-cycle service, see Razi, *Life, Marriage, and Death*, 154–55; and Bennett, "Medieval Peasant Marriage," 230–31.

49. Poos, *Rural Society*, 181–230.

50. See especially Goldberg, *Women, Work, and Life Cycle*.

51. See, for example, the reviews of Goldberg's book by Judith M. Bennett in

Albion 25 (1993): 676–78 and F. Pederson in *Continuity and Change* 9 (1994): 349–54; Mark Bailey, "Demographic Decline in Late Medieval England: Some Thoughts on Recent Research," *Economic History Review* 2nd ser. 49 (1996): 1–19. Mavis Mate, *Daughters, Wives, and Widows After the Black Death: Women in Sussex, 1350–1535* (Rochester, N.Y.: Boydell, 1998), 21–31 has also recently argued that many women delayed marriage not out of choice as Goldberg contends, but out of necessity, given the surplus of women over men in towns and the limited opportunities for singlewomen to make a decent living.

52. Bailey, "Demographic Decline"; some of his criticisms are well taken, but the evidence for a rise in life-cycle service by singlewomen in the later Middle Ages is stronger than he admits. Moreover, although he complains about the narrowness of the evidentiary base and typicality of the Yorkshire and Essex regions studied by Goldberg and Poos, his observations do not disprove their arguments, since further research could well allow us to extend their findings to other regions. Bailey also does not adequately counteract the persuasive arguments by Poos (*A Rural Society*, esp. 111–29) against the existence of a mortality-driven demographic regime in late medieval England.

53. Demographers, who often use the term "homeostatic" to describe how fertility responded to levels of mortality, note how high death rates accelerated inheritance and made more land available, thus allowing young people to find the means to marry at an earlier age. Continental historians who adhere to this model for the Middle Ages include Guy Bois, *The Crisis of Feudalism: Economy and Society in Eastern Normandy c. 1300–1550* (Cambridge: Cambridge University Press, 1984), 266–67, 355–56; and Bresc, *Un monde méditerranéen*. Besides Bailey (n. 51 above) the other English historians who favor the mortality model include John Hatcher, *Plague, Population and the English Economy, 1348–1530* (London: Macmillan, 1977); Robert S. Gottfried, *Epidemic Disease in Fifteenth-Century England: The Medical Response and Demographic Consequences* (New Brunswick, N.J.: Rutgers University Press, 1978); Barbara Harvey, *Living and Dying in England, 1100–1540: The Monastic Experience* (Oxford: Clarendon Press, 1993).

54. For female migration to medieval towns, see Grethe Jacobsen, "Female Migration and the Late Medieval Towns," in *Migration in der Feudalgesellschaft*, ed. Gerhard Jaritz and Albert Müller (Frankfurt and New York: Campus Verlag, 1988): 43–55; Goldberg, "Marriage, Migration, Servanthood"; and Paul Bishoff, "From Village to Town: Gender Variation in Migration Patterns of the East Midlands," unpublished paper, Mid-America Medieval Association Conference, July 1996.

55. These ratios are especially striking in the face of the chronic underenumeration of women in fiscal surveys and censuses. One of the first to point out the surplus of women in many late medieval towns was Karl Bücher, *Die Frauenfrage im Mittelalter*, 2nd ed. (Tübingen, 1919), although his conclusions have been somewhat modified in light of findings about the underenumeration of young men who had temporarily left cities like Nuremberg to avoid military conscription; see Kurt Wesoly, "Der weibliche Bevölkerungsanteil in spätmittelalterlichen und frühneuzeitlichen Städten und die Betätigung von Frauen im züftigen Handwerk (inbesondere an Mittel- und Oberrhein)" *Zeitschrift für Geschichte des Oberrheins* 128 n.s. 89

(1980): 69–117. On the skewed sex ratio in northern European towns, see also Mols, *Introduction*, 2:183–87; Josiah Cox Russell, *British Medieval Population* (Albuquerque: University of New Mexico Press, 1948), 150–54; Goldberg, "Urban Identity," 198–208.

56. See below and Table A4 for further discussion of the impact of migration on age at marriage.

57. This observation is, however, subject to conflicting evidence; see n. 24 above. In Verona, 7 percent of the population were servants in 1425 and 12.3 percent in 1502; see Herlihy, "Population," 109.

58. For the characteristics of female service in medieval Italy, see Herlihy, "Population," 108–15; Klapisch-Zuber and Herlihy, *Tuscans*, 112, 136–37, 332; Klapisch-Zuber, "Women Servants"; idem, "Female Celibacy"; Marzio Barbagli, *Sotto lo stesso tetto: Mutamenti della famiglia in Italia dal XV al XX secolo* (Bologna: Il Mulino, 1984), 234–36. Note, however, that there is some conflicting evidence regarding the numbers of female servants in Florence (see n. 24 above) and Verona, where Herlihy ("Population," 109) notes that 7 percent of the population were servants in 1425 and 12.3 percent in 1502.

59. Barbagli, *Sotto lo stesso*, 234–36. Hajnal ("Two Kinds," 97–98) treats the characteristics of urban service rather indirectly, but Richard M. Smith ("Geographical Diversity") usefully expands on his comments by comparing late medieval English servanthood to that described by Klapisch-Zuber for Florence. Note that although there were variations over time in the sex ratio of servants, male servants appear to have been more numerous in Florence in 1427.

60. See, for example, Andrée Courtemanche, *La richesse des femmes: patrimoines et gestion à Manosque au XIVe siècle* (Paris: Vrin, 1993), 210–13, 223–27; Bresc, *Un monde méditerranéen*, 1:77–81, 702–5; Annie Molinié-Bertrand, *Au siècle d'or: l'Espagne et ses hommes: la population du royaume de Castille au XVIe siècle* (Paris: Economica, 1985), 331–34; Emmanuel Le Roy Ladurie, *Montaillou: The Promised Land of Error*, trans. Barbara Bray (New York: Vintage, 1978), 190–91; Arlette Higounet-Nadal, *Périgueux aux XIVe et XVe siècles: étude de démographie historique* (Bordeaux: Fédération Historique du Sud-ouest, 1978), 282–95.

61. The consensus of French historians is that women married fairly young in medieval France, in their late teens and occasionally in their early twenties; see, for example, Henri Dubois, "L'essor médiéval," in *Histoire de la population française*, vol. 1, *Des origines à la Renaissance*, ed. Jacques Dupâquier et al. (Paris: Presses Universitaires de France, 1988, 348–53, and the items in notes 53 and 60 above. For a long-range analysis of the differing demographic regimes of western Europe that describes the persistence of a high-pressure demographic regime in France, see Vicente Perez-Moreda and David S. Reher, "Demographic Mechanisms and Long-Term Swings in Population in Europe, 1200–1850," *International Population Conference, 1985, Florence* 4:313–29.

62. Richard M. Smith has assembled the most impressive data on these points, aided by his students, L. R. Poos and P. J. P. Goldberg. For a list of other works (often not demographic in scope) that provide support for these trends in England, see Smith, "Geographical Diversity," 50–51, n. 45. Thoen ("Historical Demogra-

phy," 581, n. 23) says little about singlewomen, but believes he has found evidence of a relatively late age at marriage (20–25) among peasant women in fifteenth-century Flanders.

63. For sustained discussions of variations in the demographic regimes of medieval Europe, see in particular, Alan MacFarlane, "Demographic Structures and Cultural Regions in Europe," *Cambridge Anthropology* 6 (1981): 1–17; Smith, "Marriage Processes in the English Past: Some Continuities," in *The World We Have Gained: Histories of Population and Social Structure, Essays Presented to Peter Laslett on his Seventieth Birthday*, ed. Lloyd Bonfield, Richard M. Smith, and Keith Wrightson (Oxford: Blackwell, 1986), 69–98; idem, "The People of Tuscany"; idem, "Geographical Diversity," and L. R. Poos, "The Pre-History of Demographic Regions in Traditional Europe," *Sociologia Ruralis* 26 (1986): 228–47.

64. Family reconstitution was developed in France and provides a large range of demographic measures; for the most recent and sophisticated work in family reconstitution, see E. A. Wrigley, R. S. Davies, J. E. Oeppen, and R. S. Schofield, *English Population History from Family Reconstitution, 1580–1837* (Cambridge: Cambridge University Press, 1997). Note that family reconstitution methods are also applied to the *stati d'animi* (lists of communicants) of Italy and village genealogies of Germany.

65. For a description of back projection, see E. A. Wrigley and Roger S. Schofield, *The Population History of England, 1541–1871: A Reconstruction* (Cambridge: Cambridge University Press, 1981), 192–99, and 257–65 for its application to the problem of proportions ever marrying within the English population. The technique has now been superseded by "general inverse projection"; see below, n. 66.

66. The effectiveness of family reconstitution is limited by the laborious nature of the process and the necessity for a good continuous series of surviving registers, as well as by the relatively small yield of observable families once such difficulties as underregistration and migration are taken into account. Demographers are continually working to develop a set of assumptions and statistical adjustments to correct for most of these problems. To address some of the problems of back projection, demographers now favor a technique called "inverse back projection." On these recent developments, see Wrigley et al., *English Population History*, chaps. 3, 4, 8, and appendices.

67. Note too that much of the southern European data in Table A2 were derived via Hajnal's method of calculating the singulate mean age at marriage, a method also used by Herlihy and Klapisch-Zuber for the Florentine catasto data; see n. 15 above. For recent discussions and modifications of this method, see Robert Rowland, "Sistemas matrimoniales en la Península Ibérica (siglos XVI–XIX). Una perspectiva regional," in Vicente Peréz-Moreda and David S. Reher, *Demografía histórica en España* (Madrid: 1988), 133–37, and K. Schurer, "A Note Concerning the Calculation of the Singulate Mean Age at Marriage," *Local Population Studies* 43 (1989): 67–70.

68. Rowland, "Sistemas matrimoniales," 72–137.

69. Francisco Benigno, "The Southern Italian Family in the Early Modern Period: A Discussion of Co-Residence Patterns," *Continuity and Change* 4 (1989): 165–87. Others also make this complaint for Italy and Iberia; see, for example,

William A. Douglass, "The South Italian Family: A Critique," *Journal of Family History* 5 (1980): 338–59; idem, "Iberian Family History," *Journal of Family History* 13 (1988): 1–12; and item in n. 68 above.

70. The methodological problems in calculating the proportions of lifelong singlewomen should not be underestimated, particularly the frequent failure of parish clerks to record marital status in death registers before the eighteenth century; French clerks were particularly remiss about this, which accounts for the minimum estimates represented by a + in Table A3, as well as the absence of countrywide data before the late seventeenth century. The figures in Table A3 should also be considered minimum estimates because of the age parameters at which demographers considered women permanently single (usually 50 or above). It is also dangerous to make too much of the national differences discussed here since the rates have been calculated by slightly different means, obscure significant regional differences within each country, and have been derived from sources that have many difficulties and lacunae. The representativeness of the national samples is also questionable since they are based on a relatively small proportion of the total number of parishes in each country; the English figures derived from back projection, for example, are based on 404 of a total of more than 10,000 parishes in the country (albeit chosen to provide a good geographical cross-section of the country). For France, this problem is even more severe. The methodology used to calculate the English figures, moreover, makes it impossible to distinguish the proportions by sex. On the problems that demographers face in calculating the rate of "permanent celibacy," see also Weir, "Rather Never than Late"; Schofield, "English Marriage Patterns Revisited."

71. D. A. Kent, "Ubiquitous but Invisible: Female Domestic Servants in Mid-Eighteenth Century London," *History Workshop Journal* 28 (1989): 111–28; Marybeth Carlson, "A Trojan Horse of Worldliness? Maidservants in the Burgher households in Rotterdam at the End of the Seventeenth Century," in *Women of the Golden Age: An International Debate on Women in Seventeenth-Century Holland, England, and Italy*, ed. Els Kloek, Nicole Teeuwen, and Marijke Huisman (Hilversum: Verloren, 1994), 86–96.

72. Gérard Delille, *Famille et propriété dans le royaume de Naples (XVe–XIXe siècle)* (Rome: Ecole Française de Rome, 1985), 188–97; and see Tables A2 and A3 for Apulia and Campania in Italy.

73. For longer discussions of these regional differences, see Rowland, "Sistemas matrimoniales"; and David Sven Reher, *Town and Country in Pre-Industrial Spain: Cuenca, 1550–1870* (Cambridge: Cambridge University Press, 1990), 69–149.

74. For examples, see Flinn, *European Demographic System*, esp. 47–64; A. Perrnoud and D. Zumkeller, "Caractères originaux de la démographie genevoise du XVIe siècle, structure ou conjoncture," *Annales de Démographie Historique* (1980): 125–41; and the essays in Jacques Dupâquier et al., eds., *Histoire de la population française*, vol. 2, *De la Renaissance à 1789* (Paris: Presses Universitaires de France, 1988); David R. Weir, "Life Under Pressure: France and England, 1670–1870," *Journal of Economic History* 44 (1984): 27–47.

75. For the complex interaction of demographic processes and economic fluctuations in early modern Spain, see especially Reher, *Town and Country*, 123–49,

245–79, although his consideration of gender is largely placed in the context of rural-urban migration.

76. The literature on these points is very large, but see especially Kussmaul, *Servants in Husbandry*; Richard M. Smith, "Fertility, Economy and Household Formation in England over Three Centuries," *Population and Development Review* 7 (1981): 595–622; Snell, *Annals of the Labouring Poor*.

77. Wrigley and Schofield, *Population History of England*, 402–84. The exceptions were mainly in the late sixteenth century when wages fell but marriage age also fell; see Schofield, "English Marriage Patterns Revisited," 16.

78. Wrigley and Schofield originally thought that nuptiality responded with a generation-long delay to changes in the economy, but they have now modified their position in the light of new evidence from J. A. Goldstone, "The Demographic Revolution in England: A Re-Examination," *Population Studies* 49 (1986): 5–33. See also E. A. Wrigley and Roger S. Schofield, Introductory Note to the paperback edition of *The Population History of England, 1541–1871: A Reconstruction* (Cambridge: Cambridge University Press, 1989), xx–xxv.

79. Weir, "Rather Never Than Late"; Schofield, "English Marriage Patterns Revisited."

80. The effect of urbanization and migration is also treated at greater length below. See also Katherine Lynch, "The European Marriage Pattern in the Cities: Variations on a Theme by Hajnal," *Journal of Family History* 16 (1991): 79–96.

81. Perez-Moreda and Reher, "Demographic Mechanisms," 320–22.

82. See the items in n. 26 above, and MacFarlane, "Demographic Structures"; Smith, "The People of Tuscany"; Poos. "The Pre-History of Demographic Regions."

83. Several studies suggest that by the eighteenth century women in some Scottish and German towns were marrying earlier than their rural counterparts, which would have reduced the usually high proportions of singlewomen in towns (although the absence of permanent singlewomen in these studies as well as their inability to account fully for immigrants makes their results tentative); see Houston, "Age at Marriage"; Heide Wunder, *"Er ist die Sonn', sie ist der Mond": Frauen in der Frühen Neuzeit* (Munich: Beck, 1992), 48–49, 158 (who cites the work of such historical demographers as Arthur Imhof). I thank Merry Wiesner for bringing this work to my attention.

84. Almost all urban surveys show a preponderance of widows, in large part because the wide age gap between husband and wife (especially noticeable in southern Europe) meant most husbands predeceased their wives. Remarriage was also often discouraged (especially in southern Europe) because it was perceived as disadvantageous to heirs, as well as dishonorable. Remarriage could also be difficult when an older or poorer widow faced competition from a large pool of younger singlewomen. For an introduction to the very large literature on these points, see the essays in Jacques Dupâquier, Etienne Hélin, Peter Laslett, Massimo Livi-Bacci and Solvi Sogner, eds., *Marriage and Remarriage in Populations of the Past* (London: Academic Press, 1981); Herlihy and Klapisch-Zuber, *Tuscans*, 143–44, 216–22, 301, 305; Isabelle Chabot, "Widowhood and Poverty in Late Medieval Florence," *Continuity and Change* 3 (1988): 291–311.

85. For example, male migration overseas was especially important in Iberia

from the sixteenth century on and Britain from the late seventeenth century onward. Intense male migration from the towns of the Low Countries to the East Indies, and from the Swiss cantons to serve as mercenaries were also responsible for skewing sex ratios in many communities; see de Vries, "Population," 17–18.

86. Elliott, "Single Women in the London Marriage Market"; Reher, *Town and Country*, 250–79. For evidence on the migration of young women to towns, see also n. 54 above.

87. They stayed single longer for a variety of reasons: because the terms of their contract prohibited marriage while in service, because they were poor and needed to save for a dowry, or because they favored the independence and security a life in service gave them (see n. 71 above). On these points see also Lotte C. Van de Pol, "The Lure of the Big City: Female Migration to Amsterdam," in *Women of the Golden Age*, 73–81; Renate Dürr, *Mägde in der Stadt: Das Beispiel Schwäbisch Hall in der Frühen Neuzeit* (Frankfurt: Campus Verlag, 1995), 174–75.

88. Klapisch-Zuber, "Female Celibacy," 172–77; idem, "Women Servants in Florence," 68, 72.

89. Elliott, "Single Women in the London Marriage Market."

90. Jan de Vries, *European Urbanization 1500–1800* (Cambridge, Mass.: Harvard University Press, 1984), 190–92.

91. Alfred Perrenoud, "Croissance ou déclin? les mécanismes du non-renouvellement des populations urbaines," *Histoire, Economie et Société* 4 (1982): 581–601; Reher, *Town and Country*, 81–83.

92. Goldberg makes this argument; see above, n. 46.

93. E. A. Wrigley, "The Effect of Migration on the Estimation of Marriage Age in Family Reconstitution Studies," *Population Studies* 48 (1994): 81–97; but Van der Pol, "The Lure of the Big City," 79, argues that the disadvantages facing eighteenth-century female migrants to Amsterdam meant more of them remained permanently single.

94. Frank McArdle, *Altopascio: A Study in Tuscan Rural Society 1587–1784* (Cambridge: Cambridge University Press, 1978), 62–64.

95. Sharpe, "Literally Spinsters."

96. The literature on the topic is now immense (see also n. 97 below), but see the seminal contribution by Hans Medick, "The Proto-industrial Family Economy: The Structural Function of Household and Family during the Transition from Peasant to Industrial Capitalism," *Social History* 1 (1976): 291–315. For important modifications of these views, see, for example, David Levine, *Family Formation in an Age of Nascent Capitalism* (New York: Academic Press, 1977); and Gay L. Gullickson, *Spinners and Weavers of Auffay: Rural Industry and the Sexual Division of Labour in a French Village, 1750–1850* (Cambridge: Cambridge University Press, 1986); Peter Kriedte, Hans Medick, and Jürgen Schlumbohm, "Proto-Industrialization Revisited: Demography, Social Structure, and Modern Domestic Industry," *Continuity and Change* 8 (1993): 217–52, along with the other articles in this special issue.

97. R. A. Houston and Keith Snell, "Proto-Industrialisation? Cottage Industry, Social Change, and Industrial Revolution," *Historical Journal* 27 (1984): 473–92; Snell, *Annals of the Labouring Poor*, esp. 344–51.

98. Smith, "Women's Work and Marriage." His arguments draw heavily on the

work of Snell (*Annals of the Labouring Poor*, chap. 1) and Kussmaul (*Servants in Husbandry*).

99. Smith, "Women's Work and Marriage," 49–55. He supports his medieval arguments with evidence drawn from Goldberg (above, nn. 11, 46) and Poos (above, n. 35).

100. Klapisch-Zuber, "Female Celibacy and Service," 170–72. For the continuation of this trend into the early modern period, see Litchfield, "Demographic Characteristics," 197–99, 202–3.

101. See the discussion in Hufton, "Women Without Men," 358–59.

102. Although no firm figures on rates of celibacy among the women of the French peerage can be calculated because the age at which women died cannot be firmly established in the family genealogies that demographers employ (Louis Henry and C. Levy, "Ducs et pairs sous l'Ancien Régime, caractéristiques démographiques d'une caste," *Population* [1960]: 812), a larger study of the provincial nobility (Jacques Houdaille, "La noblesse française, 1600–1900," *Population* [1989]: 503–4) found the following rates of singlewomen at age 25: 8–9 percent for generations born in the seventeenth century, 3–7 percent for those born in the eighteenth century, but rising to 12–18 percent for those born after 1790.

103. About 30–48 percent of the female nobility had joined a convent by age 25; see Houdaille, "La noblesse," 503.

104. See above, n. 23, and D. Zanetti, *La demografia del patriziato milanese* (Pavia: Università, 1972), 84.

105. Molho, *Marriage Alliance*, 306.

106. On this point see also Barbara Harris, "A New Look at the Reformation: Aristocratic Women and Nunneries, 1450–1540," *Journal of British Studies* 32 (1993): 89–113.

107. Jacob Katz, "Family, Kinship and Marriage among Ashkenazim in the Sixteenth to Eighteenth Centuries," *Jewish Journal of Sociology* 1 (1959): 4–22; Steven M. Lowenstein, "Ashkenazic Jewry and the European Marriage Pattern: A Preliminary Survey of Jewish Marriage Age," *Jewish History* 8 (1984): 155–75. By the eighteenth century, however, late marriage was becoming more common for Jewish brides.

108. James Casey, *The Kingdom of Valencia in the Seventeenth Century* (Cambridge: Cambridge University Press, 1977), 18–19, 25–26 for this and the following. Morisco women in Extramadura also married around age 18 in the sixteenth century; see Bernard Vincent, "Les morisques d'Estrémadure au XVIe siècle," *Annales de Démographie Historique* (1974): 438–40.

109. Richard T. Vann and David C. Eversley, *Friends in Life and Death: The British and Irish Quakers in the Demographic Transition, 1650–1900* (Cambridge: Cambridge University Press, 1992), 83–127; see also R. A. Houston, *The Population History of Britain and Ireland 1550–1750* (Cambridge: Cambridge University Press, 1992), 26–27; and Tables A2 and A3.

110. Watkins, "Spinsters," 321–22; Hufton, "Women Without Men," 368–71.

111. E. William Monter, "Historical Demography and Religious History in Sixteenth-Century Geneva," *Journal of Interdisciplinary History* 9 (1979): 414–26.

112. See Jean-Pierre Bardet, *Rouen aux XVIIe et XVIIIe siècles: les mutations d'un*

espace social (Paris: Société d'Edition d'Enseignement Supérieur, 1983), 25. The marginally larger spousal age difference for Protestant couples (2.8 years) compared to Catholics (1.5 years) has also been interpreted as a reflection of the higher socioeconomic standing of the Huguenot.

113. Jan De Vries, "The Population and Economy of the Preindustrial Nether-lands," in *Population and Economy: Population and History from the Traditional to the Modern World*, ed. Robert I. Rotberg and Theodore K. Rabb (Cambridge: Cambridge University Press, 1986), 105; Pamela Sharpe, "Locating the 'Missing Marryers' in Colyton, 1660–1750," *Local Population Studies* 48 (1992): 49–59.

114. For example, see Reher, *Town and Country*, 76, 83, 192–93.

115. On this point see Richard M. Smith, "Women's Property Rights Under Customary Law: Some Developments in the Thirteenth and Fourteenth Centuries," *Transactions of the Royal Historical Society* 5th ser. 36 (1986): 165–94; idem, "Coping with Uncertainty: Women's Tenure of Customary Land in England c. 1370–1430," in *Enterprise and Individualism in the Fifteenth Century*, ed. Jenny Kermode (Wolfe-boro Falls, N.H.: Alan Sutton, 1991), 43–67, although his examples focus more on married women and widows.

116. David B. Rheubottom, "'Sisters First': Betrothal Order and Age at Marriage in Fifteenth-Century Ragusa," *Journal of Family History* 13 (1988): 359–76, argues that sisters had to become betrothed before their brothers and siblings of the same sex married in order of their birth, although these traditions exercised a greater impact on male than on female age at marriage.

117. A suggestion made by Smith, "Women's Work and Marriage," 48.

3

"It Is Not Good That [Wo]man Should Be Alone"

Elite Responses to Singlewomen in High Medieval Paris

Sharon Farmer

I AM INCLINED TO BELIEVE that late thirteenth- and early fourteenth-century Paris had a substantial population of women who never married and who stood outside of any formal religious life. However, as Maryanne Kowaleski indicates in this volume, we have very little trustworthy demographic information on singlewomen for the period before 1348. Indeed, such women are extremely difficult to find, or to differentiate from other women, in the Parisian sources for this period. As I suggest in the first section of this essay, this obscurity was due, in part, to the way in which records were kept, and to the fact that people at the lower end of the economy often left no traces in the sources. However, as I argue in the second part of this essay, ideological factors also contributed to the invisibility of singlewomen. Medieval Christian clerical elites believed that all women should be subordinated to the authority of men, and thus they often failed to acknowledge many of the women who were neither married nor members of formal religious institutions. As I argue in the third section of this essay, this ideological discomfort with singlewomen had important economic consequences. In their charitable giving, the lay elites of Paris responded to the presence of unattached women in their city, but their responses tended to favor unattached women who fit the marriage paradigm or who could be ushered into domestic and institutional settings where they were safely under male control.

One reason for singlewomen's invisibility in the sources of high medieval Paris is the fact that the Parisian tax assessments of this period did not list simple wage earners and other people at the bottom of the economic ladder. Such people constituted about half of the 200,000 inhabitants of Paris in 1292.[1] Another reason for singlewomen's invisibility has to do with inconsistent naming practices: many married and widowed women were identified in the sources as "so-and-so, the wife of so-and-so"; however, many other women — both married and single — were identified with place names, professional names, or descriptive names.[2] Thus, it is often impossible to distinguish a singlewoman from a widow or married woman. Still, if we look hard enough, we can find some of the singlewomen of Paris. They earned their livings in various sectors of the economy and worked out strategies of survival either on their own or in partnership with other women.

The form of identification that most indisputably points to a singlewoman is that in which she is identified as someone's daughter, sister, or niece, when the relative in question is clearly absent from, and irrelevant to, the document in question.[3] The problem here, of course, is that we often cannot identify the age of these daughters, sisters, and nieces, so we do not know whether they were nubile girls or older singlewomen. Moreover, there is no way to determine whether these women married at some later date.

As was the case in late medieval and Renaissance Italy, most Parisian women who neither married nor entered a convent were from artisan or laboring families: those noblewomen and women from the merchant elite who did not marry usually found their way into formal religious institutions.[4] Many elite Parisian girls were placed in such institutions at a very young age by parents who had apparently already decided that these daughters would never marry.[5]

Some of the independent singlewomen of Paris were members of female guilds. Paris was one of only three cities in medieval Europe that had female guilds. The *Livre des métiers* of Etienne Boileau, which was compiled between 1261 and 1271, included five such guilds, and another two were established toward the end of the thirteenth century.[6] There were also a number of guilds that had a high percentage of female members. One of those, the poulterer's guild, was explicit about singlewomen's rights to full membership status.[7] The few membership lists that we have also indicate that these guilds included singlewomen. Jehanne the daughter of Giles the mercer, Marie the daughter of Stephen the furrier, Belon the daughter of Michael the convert, Denise the daughter of Jacques the cobbler, and Amelot Marote the daughter of Adam the bathhouse-keeper, all members of the embroiderers' guild, were evidently single. Members of the silk almspurse-makers' guild who were apparently single included Alice the niece of brother Richard, Jehannete the daughter of John the physician, and Sedile the daughter of Richard the tanner.[8]

Other singlewomen worked outside the guild structure, at the lower levels of the cloth-making industry. Orenge of Fontenay, for instance, an immigrant to Paris from the diocese of Bayeux, lived for well over thirty years in the home of Maurice the Weaver, for whom she worked as a wool comber. When a paralysis prevented Orenge from working for four years, Maurice and his wife continued to care for her. When Orenge recovered, she resumed her work within Maurice's household.[9]

Still other singlewomen—perhaps the largest number—worked as domestic servants. Some of these servants probably fit the pattern that P. J. P. Goldberg found in fourteenth- and fifteenth-century Yorkshire, where domestic service was almost exclusively an occupation for adolescents and young men and women in their early twenties. Goldberg assumed that this was a pattern of life-cycle service for those who would later marry.[10] However, the Dominican Master General, Humbert of Romans (†1277), who trained in Paris and drew much of his preaching material from French society, did not describe servants as women who were preparing for marriage. Indeed, his description of female servants suggests that they were women who took a path that differed from that of married women: "Among the many types of women there are some who are not rich and do not dwell in their own houses. That is to say, they do not have their own households to manage; rather, they remain in the service of the rich."[11]

Both the female and the male servants from the Parisian region whose ages I can determine also point to a pattern that was apparently different from that of late medieval York. Amelot of Chaumont, for instance, was twenty-eight when she immigrated in 1277 from Chaumont in the Vexin (the region between Normandy and the Ile-de-France) to the town of Saint-Denis just outside of Paris. After a brief illness, Amelot went to work as a domestic servant for a prominent bourgeois of Saint-Denis. Two years later she fell seriously ill, was placed in a public hospital, and died.[12] Agnes of Pontoise—a town in the diocese of Paris—worked in several bourgeois households in Pontoise until she was more than thirty years old. Then, in 1271, she fell victim to an eye disease that rendered her blind and compelled her to beg for a living. When she recovered her sight about four years later, she took up residence in the house of a bourgeois named Guillaume de Villierlande, for whom she spun wool.[13] Henry the Englishman was apparently in his mid-twenties when he became a servant in the household of Luce of Rémilly-sur-Lozon and her husband, who lived in Saint-Denis.

Henry continued to work for Luce and her first and second husbands for at least another ten years.[14]

Some Parisian singlewomen, like Perrenele the laundress, apparently supplemented their meager incomes through prostitution. In 1300 Perrenele was banished from the lands of the abbey of Sainte-Geneviève, on the left bank of Paris, for pandering and prostituting.[15] Prostitutes were sometimes threatened with capital punishment if they returned to a given juridical territory after being banished. However, the more common threat, and practice, was branding with a hot iron.[16]

Singlewomen sometimes found practical, economic, and emotional support in their companionships with other unattached women.[17] When Amelot of Chaumont immigrated to Saint-Denis she did so with two other women from Chaumont. The three women sought lodgings at the house of Marguerite of Rocigny, with whom, it seems, they had some prior connection.[18] Marguerite could not accommodate the women, but she recommended the house of her neighbor, Emmeline, where the three women took up lodging and where Amelot shared a bed with one of her two companions from Chaumont.

Several nights after Amelot arrived in Saint-Denis one of her legs became paralyzed. The next day Emmeline, Amelot's hostess, carried Amelot on a stretcher to the tomb of the not yet canonized King Louis IX, in the nearby basilica of Saint-Denis, in the hopes that she would be cured by the saint. Emmeline was assisted by three women, including one, or possibly two, of Amelot's companions from Chaumont. Amelot was not cured on that first day, but she did receive a pair of crutches, which enabled her to return to Emmeline's hostel by her own power. During the next two months she visited the tomb often. And in the meantime she apparently moved to Marguerite of Rocigny's house. Marguerite was with Amelot at Saint Louis's tomb on the day she was finally cured, and she comforted her when sharp pains signaled the beginning of the end of her paralysis.[19]

We know something about Amelot's network of support because it is described for us in Guillaume de St.-Pathus's *Miracles of Saint Louis*, which was based on an ecclesiastical inquest held in Saint-Denis in 1282–83 to determine whether miracles were taking place at the tomb of King Louis IX. The Parisian tax records support this anecdotal evidence of female companionship by offering us glimpses of women — singlewomen and widows — who lived and worked together for years. Ameline Agace and her companion Marie, for instance, were assessed together in 1292, 1296, and 1297; Aalis of Saint-Joce (who was identified in various years as a beguine, a silkworker, and a maker of almspurses) was assessed with a companion named Philippote in 1296 and 1297 and with an unnamed companion, quite possibly Philippote, in 1313.[20] Some of these female companions identified themselves as beguines — semireligious women who took no formal vows — congregating not in the formal beguinage that King Louis IX had founded on the right bank of Paris, in the Parish of Saint-Paul, but in the streets around the Franciscan convent on the left bank.[21] There was a similar relationship between settlements of semireligious women and the local Franciscan convent in Florence, Italy, as well.[22]

Once we focus our attention on the question of singlewomen's presence in medieval Paris they begin to enter our field of vision. However, such was not the case for thirteenth-century clerical elites, whose conceptual framework often caused them to deny the existence of these living, sweating, struggling women. When they did recognize the presence of such women, clerics responded by trying to place them under male control. In order to understand why singlewomen violated the clerics' conceptual framework, we must examine the clerics' understanding of women's purpose and place in the social order. That understanding began with male Christian exegesis of the Yahwist account of the creation and fall, in the second and third chapters of Genesis.

According to Genesis 2:18, God initiated the creation of Eve with the following observation and promise: "It is not good that man should be alone; let us make him a helper resembling him" (translated from the Vulgate). Unlike many of their Jewish counterparts, ancient and medieval male Christian commentators interpreted this passage to mean that women were secondary, and thus hierarchically inferior, to men, that they were created *for* men, and that their principal raison d'être was procreation.[23] As Thomas Aquinas put it in a passage borrowed neatly from Augustine, "It was necessary for woman to be made, as the scripture says, as a helper to man not, indeed, as a helpmate in other works, as some say, since man can be more efficiently helped by another man in other works; but as a helper in the work of generation."[24]

The account of the fall in the third chapter of Genesis only served to underscore this reading. As a result of her rebellion Eve was condemned to pain in childbirth and to subordination to her husband, "who shall rule over you."[25] Thus, medieval Christian commentators assumed, woman in general was defined by reproduction, by her relationship to man, and by her subordination to male authority.[26]

Because ancient and medieval male Christian authors took this explanation for women's existence seriously, they had difficulty incorporating singlewomen into their descriptions of the social world.[27] It might have been otherwise. After all, Christianity was unique in the ancient world for providing women with a lasting alternative to marriage: the celibate life. A number of recent scholars have argued convincingly that many early Christian women celibates interpreted their sexual abstinence as a ticket to freedom from subordination. However, the male hierarchy answered back with the message that these women were wrong.[28] As Tertullian put it, "If the man is the head of the woman, of course [he is the head] of the virgin too, from whom comes the *woman* who has married."[29]

According to Christian symbolism, ascetic women — both virgins and consecrated widows — were "married," for they were brides of Christ. Organized in the early Church into orders of widows and virgins, and cloistered in the Middle Ages as nuns, these women were considered safe by male clerics both because they were subject to Christ's authority and because the church assumed the paternal role of protecting them until the celestial marriage feast could take place.[30] However, uncloistered, semi-religious women, like the beguines of the left bank of Paris, were often viewed as a threat because they eluded clear lines of male authority. Thus they ran into repeated opposition and condemnation from the church in the high Middle Ages. As Bishop Bruno of Olomouc made clear in the report that he prepared for the Council of Lyons that took place in 1274, clerics perceived uncloistered beguines as "fleeing obedience both to priests and to husbands."[31]

The pervasiveness of the Genesis paradigm, which suggested to Christian clerics that all women should be subordinated to male authority and thus rendered singlewomen both a threat to the social order and a logical contradiction, is evident in the ways in which thirteenth-century clerics classified the social order in their sermon literature. The division of punishments in the third chapter of Genesis — between manual labor for Adam and sexual/reproductive labor for Eve — apparently provided clerics with a grid for classifying men and women. In their ad status sermons — sermons, that is, that were addressed to people of various walks of life — these authors usually categorized men according to their occupations or social status, and women according to their sexual or married status: nuns and virgins (either consecrated virgins or young girls), widows, and married women.[32] Moreover, despite the fact that married women were considered the lowest of the three categories because they did not practice chastity, marriage, in this system of classification, was the prism through which all women were viewed.

As I argue below, even those authors who discussed certain categories of singlewomen (servants and prostitutes) viewed them through the sexual paradigm. They were only comfortable with these women, moreover, when they were encompassed within a legitimate household, and were thus subject to male authority. Those authors who strictly adhered to the tripartite categorization of women seemed to suggest that there was no such thing as a singlewoman, and even those who considered *certain* categories of singlewomen ignored the existence of many others.

All three of the most influential thirteenth-century authors of ad status sermons—Humbert of Romans, Jacques de Vitry, and Gilbert of Tournai—composed sermons for one category of working women: servants. Humbert, moreover, went even further. In his manual of advice for preachers, Humbert classified women sometimes by social status, sometimes by profession, and sometimes by age. Thus, he offered preaching topics for those who might find themselves preaching to noblewomen, rich urban women, female servants, peasant women, prostitutes, and girls.[33]

Humbert was also willing to discuss some women without even bringing up the issue of sexuality, and for all women he considered a variety of sins. Regarding rich urban women, for instance, Humbert was most concerned with the ways in which they conspired in the sins of their husbands, often approving their usury and illicit gain. He also discussed the ways in which these women neglected their own spiritual welfare as well as that of their children and husbands, their inclination to use excessive ornament, and the fact that some of them neglected their charitable obligations.[34] Regarding poor village women, Humbert was most preoccupied with the practice of sorcery, although he also discussed illicit sex among peasant women.[35]

What we find, then, is that Humbert sometimes discussed and categorized women through a prism other than the sexual one. Nevertheless, if we divide Humbert's sermon literature along lines of social status, what emerges is a clear pattern: he virtually ignored the issue of sexuality in his discussions of elite women, both noble and urban, but in his discussion of poor women—servants, prostitutes, and peasants—he dwelt on the subject, although not always exclusively.

Two of Humbert's three categories of poor women—servants and prostitutes—were also assumed to be single. In his discussion of these women, Humbert emphasized sexuality even more than he did in his discussion of poor peasant women. Moreover, he emphasized not only the sexual transgressions of prostitutes and female servants, but also the threat that those women posed to the social order. Thus, the promiscuity of female servants threatened the married household and its progeny:

Oh how many sons of families and youths who would have been ashamed to go to women in the streets lost their virginity with these [servant] women. And thus woe to such women, for they are guilty of all the subsequent sins that those young men later commit.[36]

The promiscuity of prostitutes, Humbert claimed, threatened the spiritual well-being of men of every social and moral status. Through them the devil snared many men. Prostitutes, he asserted, "are the incendiaries of the world."[37]

There are two points that I want to highlight about Humbert: first, he limited his discussion of singlewomen to two categories, servants and prostitutes, emphasizing that these women posed a seductive and Eve-like threat to the married household and the social order; second, he considered only one of those categories — that of maidservants — morally acceptable.[38] Like Jacques de Vitry and Gilbert of Tournai, Humbert found it possible to include servant women within the acceptable gendered universe because they constituted a part of an extended household; thus, they were subject, at least indirectly, to the authority of the male head of household. In other words, in his discussion of singlewomen, Humbert did not stray very far from the story in the second and third chapters of Genesis, with its emphasis on women's sexual relations to men and on the need to subordinate women to male authority.[39]

Although their system of classification for women was otherwise that of the three sexual orders of virgins, wives, and widows,[40] Jacques de Vitry (†1240) and the Franciscan Gilbert of Tournai (†1284) both composed several sermons for male and female servants, and Gilbert discussed the supervision of maidservants in one of his sermons for wives.[41] Because female servants stood outside Jacques's and Gilbert's general system of classification, they constituted a special case that was almost an exception to the category "women." Like men, and unlike all other women, they were identified primarily by their occupation. Unlike most other women, they did not easily fit into a single sexual status: most were unmarried, but many were suspected of promiscuity. In other words, the classification of "women" into three sexual categories begins to break down, for Jacques de Vitry and Gilbert of Tournai, when they discuss nonelite women.

Unlike Humbert of Romans, Jacques de Vitry and Gilbert of Tournai structured their sermons in such a way that they appeared, at first, to give

equal weight to the sexual dangers that both male and female servants posed
to the households they served.[42] Jacques and Gilbert each warned more
than once that masters and mistresses needed to exercise great diligence in
guarding the chastity of both their male and their female servants, especially
if men and women resided in the same house, ate together, and slept in
proximity to one another.[43]

Nevertheless, these two clerical authors did not consider male and
female servants to be equal in the sexual dangers that they posed. All of the
examples and *exempla* stories that Jacques drew on in order to illustrate his
points about the sexual dangers of male and female servants were about
sexually transgressive women. Moreover, he associated such women with
animals, and he did not hesitate to recommend the most brutal of punishments for them. For instance, in warning masters that they ought to give
their male and female servants burdensome tasks so that they would not
have the occasion for wandering and lusting, Jacques quoted Hosea 4:16:
"Like a lusting cow she digressed."[44] He went on to explain that "cow"
signified "a lascivious woman" who "stimulated by diabolic frenzies follows
bulls in order to satiate her desires."[45] Such women, he asserted, should be
treated like a certain female cat who had wandered through various houses
looking for male cats until her master burned her beautiful tail and removed
most of her beautiful hair. "In this way," Jacques concluded, "a ragged
servant woman, vile and dejected, ought to be returned to the house."[46]

Jacques de Vitry clearly thought that maidservants threatened the sta-
bility of the household in ways that male servants did not. Thus he wrote of
the "intolerable evil" that occurred when maidservants supplanted their
mistresses, stealing the affections of their masters and thus gaining control
of the houses that they were supposed to serve. "Certain miserable men," he
wrote, "are exceedingly infected with this crime," and thus they placed their
maids before their wives, even though their wives were more beautiful.[47]

Unlike Jacques de Vitry, Gilbert of Tournai did not draw on exempla
stories to elaborate his discussions of the need to control male and female
servants; therefore his discussion of that topic had a degree of gendered
symmetry. Nevertheless, Gilbert did write about "vile" women servants
who supplanted their mistresses by entering the beds of their masters.[48]
Moreover, he claimed that maidservants posed a special threat to the households in another way, since, through their vain words about the attentions
of certain men, they were capable of inciting lust in their mistresses or in the
daughters of their mistresses. Gilbert then praised a certain mistress who,
according to an exemplum, whipped such a maidservant in front of her

other female servants, then threw her out the window into the river below.[49] Despite minor differences, then, Humbert of Romans, Jacques de Vitry, and Gilbert of Tournai shared the perspective that because of their sexuality female servants threatened the households in which they served in ways that male servants did not.

Clerical authors clearly perceived lower-status men as more susceptible to bodily temptation and less informed about spiritual matters than elite men.[50] Moreover, according to Humbert of Romans, all laypersons should marry early because of the threat of incontinence.[51] Nevertheless, since they classified men by their social or occupational status and not by their sexual status, clerical authors did not really address whether men of various walks of life were married. Nor, as Humbert's, Jacques's, and Gilbert's sermons to male and female servants make clear, did they dwell on the lasciviousness of male servants within the household in the same way that they dwelt on the lasciviousness of female servants.

Because they defined women — especially lower-status women — through their sexuality and because they assumed that all women should be subordinated to men, Parisian clerics tended to ignore the existence of a large number of working singlewomen in the cities: singlewomen who were neither household servants nor prostitutes. Moreover, in their discussions of household servants and prostitutes, Parisian clerics stressed the ways in which the sexuality of these singlewomen threatened the domestic and social order.

When we turn from clerical conceptions of singlewomen to the behavior of Parisian laypeople, it seems at first glance that lay elites, unlike clerical elites, were willing to consider and to respond to the needs of singlewomen. Archival evidence, especially that of testaments, indicates that Parisian elites worried about the city's unattached women.[52] However, a close examination of this evidence reveals that most of the charitable assistance that lay elites directed toward unattached women benefited widows, nubile girls, or women who were willing to submit to some form of male authority.[53]

Parisian elites addressed the "problem" of unattached women in two ways: by founding institutions to either shelter or cloister such women, and by donating money to certain categories of girls and women. The principal institutions that were created for unattached women fell into three categories: shelters for older widows, convents for reformed prostitutes, and the beguinage of Paris, an institution for semireligious women.

The earliest known Parisian shelter for widows, which came to be known as Sainte-Avoye, was founded in 1283 on the rue du Temple by the treasurer of the parish church of Saint-Merry, Jean Sequens, and a widow named Constance. The founders specified that the shelter was to house forty poor widows aged fifty or older.[54] In 1306 the wealthy draper Stephen Haudry and his wife Jehanne founded another shelter near the Place de la Grève, which was to house thirty-two widows. That shelter came to be known as the Haudriettes.[55]

A Parisian register from 1342 lists ten shelters for women, including Sainte-Avoye and the Haudriettes.[56] One of those shelters — the hospital of Pierre Larrent — had benefited from a bequest in the will of a Parisian bourgeois in 1332. A second — the hospital of Andry Marcel — may have been the same as the shelter that housed fourteen "poor women in the house of Agnès la Martelle," which benefited from a bequest from a Parisian bourgeois woman in 1313.[57] The bourgeois wills of 1313 and 1332 referred to Sainte-Avoye, the Haudriettes, the hospital of Pierre Larrent and that of Agnès la Martelle as shelters for "poor women"; the 1342 register referred to all ten shelters as institutions for "good women": thus, the evidence does not permit us to determine if the eight institutions other than Sainte-Avoye and the Haudriettes were intended to help all poor unattached women, or just widows. Nevertheless, charitable bequests to Sainte-Avoye and the Haudriettes — the two institutions that were definitely intended to benefit widows alone — far outnumbered the bequests to the other institutions, and Sainte-Avoye and the Haudriettes were probably the largest, or two of the three largest, of the hospices for women in Paris.[58]

Once they entered a hospice for women, single or widowed women probably gave up a great deal of their independence. The statutes of the Haudriettes, which were established by the founders, stipulated that women who entered the hospice could never leave it, that they were under the authority of Stephen Haudry and his male heirs, that they could not give away any of their personal property without the permission of the founders and their successors, and that they must designate the hostel and its residents as their heirs. The women were required to pray three times a day for the founders and their successors and to make confession and receive communion four times a year. Finally, each resident risked expulsion — and the loss of her personal property — if she told a lie, slandered, stole, drank to excess, sinned "with her body," or harbored any outsider, especially a man. Sainte-Avoye had similar rules in the sixteenth century, but we do not know anything about the statutes of that house for the thirteenth and fourteenth centuries.[59] Although we catch only a passing

glimpse of the other eight hospices that were listed in 1342, it seems reasonable to assume that every hospice had a set of rules and an authority figure
to whom the residents had to answer.

Thirteenth-century Paris had two institutions that were originally
intended to house reformed prostitutes: the convent of Saint-Antoine,
founded in 1198 by the charismatic preacher Foulques de Neuilly, and the
Filles Dieu, founded in the first quarter of the thirteenth century by William
of Auvergne.[60] Saint-Antoine was given over to the Cistercian order in 1204
and soon became a popular choice for noble and prosperous bourgeois girls
and women who wished or were compelled to enter the monastic life. Thus
it seems that the Filles Dieu became the only convent for reformed prostitutes. In both cases, the intent of the original founders was to help prostitutes by getting them off the streets and cloistering them — ushering them,
in a sense, into the category of "consecrated widows," loosely defined.
Saint-Antoine, in its early years, and the Filles Dieu helped "single" women
by turning them into nuns, thus rendering them "not single."

The Parisian beguinage, which was founded by King Louis IX sometime before November 1264, may have housed as many as four hundred
women — young and old, rich and poor, widowed and never married.[61]
Wealthier women, most of them probably widows, bought their own
houses at the beguinage. The poorest women were given free lodgings and
were apparently expected to work for a living: Alès Malachine, who "fre-
quented" and worked at the beguinage, was a wool comber. When a disability prevented Alès from working she had to beg for a living.[62] Guillemete la Grande was a silk spinner and a resident of the beguinage. In 1330
Jehanne Du Faut, a wealthy bourgeois who may herself have been a beguine, gave Guillemete the use of a house in the beguinage for the rest of
her life.[63]

Beguines were not required to take vows, so they could cease living at
the Parisian beguinage at any time. As long as they stayed there, however,
they were subject to its rules and to the authority of the mistress, who was
herself under the authority of the Dominicans of Paris. Hence, each beguine
at the beguinage was under the authority of the male clerical hierarchy.

According to the earliest statutes (1341), women residing at the Parisian beguinage could not entertain men in their houses, sleep or eat away
from the beguinage, or bathe in the public baths without permission from
the mistress. Those beguines who resided at the beguinage, as opposed to
those who lived on their own and in small groups throughout the city, were
thus safely under the authority of the male hierarchy, although they were

sometimes suspected of disobeying its rules: in 1354 one beguine was expelled from the Parisian beguinage after being accused of having sexual
relations with a man.[64] Singlewomen benefited from this institution if and
only if they submitted to its yoke.

While some singlewomen clearly received material assistance from the
Filles Dieu and the beguinage of Paris, the institutional arrangements of
both institutions fit within the Genesis paradigm: unattached women in
thirteenth- and early fourteenth-century Paris received institutional support only if they fit the prism of marriage — as widows did — or were willing
to submit to male clerical authority.

When we turn from institutionalized charity to individual charity, we
find a few exceptions to the Genesis model: some testators designated small
amounts of money to be given to women and girls in the Hôtel Dieu or to
poor women in childbirth.[65] Clearly such bequests benefited singlewomen,
widows, and married women. However, the most popular form of testamentary charity for singlewomen was the establishment of dowries for poor
nubile girls, with the express purpose of making them "not single."[66]

Many testators, both male and female, also gave gifts to their maidservants.[67] On one level, this suggests that the testators were breaking with the
clerics' representations of female domestic servants — for it seems unlikely
that elite *women* would have given gifts to maidservants who seduced their
husbands, or who otherwise violated the rules of sexual conduct that they
wished to impose within their households. On another level, however,
these donations to female domestic servants are perfectly consistent with
the categories of singlewomen that the clerics were willing to consider and
condone: the only safe singlewoman was a domestic servant, one who was
encompassed by, and under the authority of, the elite household. Such
women could be the objects of both the imagination and the charitable
purse.

A large number of singlewomen — those who lived on their own and
worked outside of the elite household structure, as almspurse-makers, embroiderers, laundresses, poulterers, hucksters, or whatever — were excluded
both from the system of classification that clerics created for women and
from the predominant forms of charity that we find in elite wills. Some of
these women may have benefited from guild charity, especially if they were
themselves members of a guild. However, the six Parisian guilds in the
thirteenth century that made explicit provision for poor members or their
children had very few female members.[68] Other singlewomen would have
benefited from informal charity and from the various hospitals that were

intended for an undifferentiated population of poor people. Finally, it is possible that some of the institutions for "good women" included both widows and lifelong singlewomen, or that after a certain age no one cared whether a woman was a widow, and that older singlewomen thus slipped into the hospices that had originally been founded for widows. Once they entered those hospices, however, these women had to submit to their rules.

The prevailing cultural constructs of the thirteenth and fourteenth centuries rendered most singlewomen invisible or undesirable, and those cultural constructs had material consequences. Clerics were willing to acknowledge the existence of singlewomen only insofar as they could press them into the mold of Eve the seductress, whose existence could be tolerated only if she was clearly under the authority of a man. Clerics were unwilling to acknowledge the existence of the many other single-women—spinsters, combers, embroiderers, laundresses, companions living together—who did not fit this mold. Rendering the women in this second group a nonexistent conceptual category had important material consequences. Thirteenth- and early fourteenth-century Parisians expressed their concern for the unattached women in their midst primarily by making them "not single": either helping them to marry or placing them in institutions where they were safely under the control of the male hierarchy. Domestic servants were the major exception to this rule, but they were acceptable because they lived within the bourgeois or artisan household, and were thus subject to the control of the master and mistress. Because they did not fit into the predominant social categories, women who eluded male control—at least in their domestic arrangements—did not, for the most part, benefit from elite charity.

I wish to thank Judith Bennett and Amy Froide for their extremely helpful comments on earlier drafts of this essay.

Notes

1. See notes 20 and 21 below for references to the tax assessments. On the exclusion of simple wage earners see Janice Archer, "Working Women in Thirteenth-Century Paris" (Ph.D. diss., University of Arizona, 1995), 83–84, 152–53. See also her argument on pp. 20 and 56ff. that "chambrière" and "ouvrier/ouvrière" referred to individuals working in the putting-out system rather than as domestic servants or wage laborers. On the size of the population of Paris, see Raymond Cazelles, "La population de Paris avant la peste noire," *Académie des Inscriptions et Belles Lettres: Comptes Rendus* (1966): 539–54; Cazelles, "Le parisien au

temps de Saint Louis," *Septième centenaire de la mort de Saint Louis: Actes des Colloques de Royaumont et de Paris (21–27 mai 1970)* (Paris: Société d'Edition Les Belles Lettres, 1976), 98; idem, *Nouvelle histoire de Paris: de la fin du règne de Philippe Auguste à la mort de Charles V, 1223–1380* (Paris: Hachette, 1972).

2. On naming patterns in the Parisian tax assessments see Caroline Bourlet, "L'anthroponymie à Paris à la fin du xiiieme siècle d'après les rôles de la taille du règne de Philippe le Bel," *Genèse médiévale de l'anthroponymie moderne*, vol. 2-2, ed. Monique Bourin and Pascal Chareille (Tours: Publications de l'Université de Tours, 1992), 9–44.

3. Thus, for instance, the statutes of the predominantly female embroiderers' and silk almspurse-makers' guilds identified a number of women as the daughters or nieces of men who had nothing to do with the guild. I am assuming that these were singlewomen: if they had been married, the preferred form of identification would have been "wife of so-in-so," rather than "daughter" or "niece" of so-and-so. Women in the same statutes who were identified as relatives (daughter, niece, sister) of other women in the guild *may* have been married (one, in fact, was mentioned both as the sister of another guild member and as someone's wife), but the context dictated a preference for identifying them as relatives of other women in the guilds (G.-B. Depping, *Réglemens sur les arts et métiers de Paris* [Paris: 1837], 379–86).

4. Elite bourgeois Parisian families placed their daughters in a variety of religious institutions in and around Paris. Two Cistercian houses—Saint-Antoine, which was originally founded just outside Paris in 1198 and was handed over to the Cistercians in 1204; and Maubuisson, founded near Pontoise by Blanche of Castille in 1236—were among the favorites, as was the Hôtel Dieu of Paris. Others included Jarcy, Gis, Chelles, Yerres, and Longchamps (Anne Terroine, "Recherches sur la bourgeoisie Parisienne au xiiie siècle" [unpublished thèse, Ecole des Chartes, 1940], 2: 133ff.). On Saint-Antoine see Constance Berman, "Cistercian Nuns and the Development of the Order: the Abbey of Saint-Antoine-des-Champs Outside Paris," in *The Joy of Learning: Studies in Honor of Jean Leclercq*, ed. E. Rozanne Elder (Kalamazoo, Mich.: Cistercian Publications, 1995), 121–56. On elite practices in Italy see Stanley Chojnacki, "Measuring Adulthood: Adolescence and Gender in Renaissance Venice," *Journal of Family History* 17 (1992): 376–77. Chojnacki notes that in the fifteenth century a more accepting attitude toward single women living at home began to emerge among Italian urban elites.

5. Terroine, "Recherches," 2: 148ff.; Adolphe Dutilleux and Joseph Depoin, *Cartulaire de l'abbaye de Maubuisson (Notre-Dame la Royale)*, 2 vols. (Pontoise: Société Historique du Vexin, 1890–1913), 2: 164, no. 604 (Tiphaine Savore was thirteen when she professed at Maubuisson, where she had been raised with a younger sister); A. de Dion, *Cartulaire de l'abbaye de Porrois au diocèse de Paris*, vol. 1 (Paris: Alphonse Picard et fils, 1903), 299–301, no. 305 (Marie and Agnes, daughters of the Parisian goldsmith Jean de Lagny, were less than twelve years old when they were placed in the abbey in 1266; they would decide whether to profess when they reached the age of twelve); Auguste Molinier, *Obituaires de la province de Sens*, 2 vols. (Paris: Imprimerie Nationale, 1902), vol. 1, pt. 2, pp. 673, 675, 676 (Blanche des Essarts was seven years old when she was vested at the abbey of Longchamps in 1326, Marguerite la Flamenge was eight when she was vested in 1355, Yolent des

Essars was about ten when she was vested in 1349, and Jehanne des Essars was ten when she was vested in 1351).

6. *Le livre des métiers d'Etienne Boileau*, ed. René de Lespinasse and François Bonnardot (Paris: Imprimerie Nationale, 1879), nos. 35, 36, 38, 44, 95; pp. 68–72, 74–75, 83–84, 207–8 (silk spinners using large spindles, silk spinners using small spindles, silk weavers, silk handkerchief weavers, milliners); *Les réglemens*, ed. Depping, 379–86 (embroiderers, silk almspurse-makers). Only 15.96% (15 out of 94) of the listed members of the embroiderers' guild were men at the time that its statutes were drawn up. However, men constituted 74% of the listed taxpayers practicing that craft in the 1297–1300 tax assessments (Depping, *Les réglemens*, 379–80; Archer, "Working Women," 258). For a general discussion of women in the *Livre des métiers* see E. Dixon, "Craftswomen in the *Livre des métiers*," *Economic Journal* 5, 2 (1895): 209–28; Diane Frappier-Bigras, "La famille dans l'artisanat parisien du xiiie siècle," *Le Moyen Age* 95 (1989): 56–62. For broader discussion of women and craft guilds see Maryanne Kowaleski and Judith Bennett, "Crafts, Gilds, and Women in the Middle Ages: Fifty Years After Marian K. Dale," *Signs: Journal of Women in Culture and Society* 14 (1984): 474–88. For background on the *Livre des métiers* see B. Mahieu, "Le *livre des métiers* d'Etienne Boileau," *Le siècle de Saint Louis* (Paris: Hachette, 1970), 64–74. For a general discussion of the occupations of women in the Parisian tax assessments see Archer, "Working Women."

7. The small purse-makers' guild (*crespiniers de fil et de soie*) and the linen merchants' guild apparently had a majority of women (*Livre des métiers* nos. 37 and 57, pp. 72–73 and 117–20; Archer, "Working Women," 259, 254). The poulterers', bathhouse-keepers', and mercers' guilds were among the guilds with large numbers of women members and no restrictions on their membership (*Livre des métiers*, nos. 70, 73, and 75, pp. 147–49, 154–55, and 157–59; Archer, "Working Women," 257, 269, 254). On singlewomen's rights in the poulterers' guild, see *Livre des métiers*, no. 70.7, p. 148.

8. Depping, *Les réglemens*, 379–86.

9. Guillaume de St.-Pathus, Confesseur de la reine Marguerite, *Les miracles de Saint Louis*, ed. Percival B. Fay (Paris: Champion, 1931), no. 58, pp. 177–79.

10. P. J. P. Goldberg, "Marriage, Migration, and Servanthood: The York Cause Paper Evidence," *Woman Is a Worthy Wight: Women in English Society, c. 1200–1500* (Wolfeboro Falls, N.H.: Alan Sutton, 1992), 4–5.

11. "Inter multa genera mulierum, quaedam sunt, quae nec sunt divites, nec secum morantur, idest non habent propriam domesticam curam, sed consueverunt in servitiis divitum commorari," Humbert of Romans, "Ad famulas divitum," ed. Carla Casagrande, *Prediche alle donne del secolo xiii* (Milan: Valentino Bompiani, 1978), 50. On Humbert's background and his tendency to draw his examples from French society see Alexander Murray, "Religion Among the Poor in Thirteenth-Century France," *Traditio* 30 (1974): 285–324.

12. Guillaume de St.-Pathus, *Les miracles*, no. 2, pp. 7–12.

13. Ibid., no. 59, pp. 179–84.

14. H.-François Delaborde, "Fragments de l'enquête faite à Saint-Denis en vue de la canonisation de Saint Louis," *Mémoires de la Société de l'Histoire de Paris et de l'Ile de France* 23 (1896): 64–66. Henry was fifty at the time of the inquest, and he said he

had first met Luce twenty-four years earlier. He was still working for Luce fourteen years before the inquest, when Luce lost her sight.

15. "Registre criminel de Ste.-Geneviève," in L. Tanon, *Histoire des justices de Paris* (Paris, 1883), 350. On the discrepancies between men's and women's salaries see Bronislaw Geremek, *Le salariat parisien au xiiie–xive siècles*, trans. Anna Posner and Christiane Klapisch-Zuber (Paris: Mouton, 1982), 89–91; Archer, "Working Women," 158, 168–69. For a general discussion of prostitution as a supplement for inadequate wages see Ruth Mazo Karras, *Common Women: Prostitution and Sexuality in Medieval England* (New York: Oxford University Press, 1996), 48–55.

16. "Registre criminel de Ste.-Geneviève," in *Histoire*, ed. Tanon, 347, 348, 350; "Registre criminel de Saint-Germain-des-Prés," in *Histoire*, ed. Tanon, 412. See Tanon, ed., *Histoire*, 29, 32, for an explanation of *brulée* ("branded") and *sus la besche* (the threat of capital punishment).

17. For an argument concerning female companionship in late medieval England see P. J. P. Goldberg, *Women, Work, and Life Cycle in a Medieval Economy: Women in York and Yorkshire, c. 1300–1520* (Oxford: Clarendon Press, 1992), 305–23. Goldberg found evidence for "spinster clustering" (unattached women clustering in certain neighborhoods) and for women migrating together, but he could only surmise that such women must have assisted each other through hard times.

18. My hypothesis that Amelot and her companions knew, or knew of, Marguerite of Rosigny is based on the role Marguerite plays in the narrative: the three women went first to Marguerite's hostel, Amelot later moved to her hostel, and Marguerite was with Amelot on the day that she was cured. If indeed the immigrant women had a contact in the town, they fit a broader pattern of migration from the countryside to the metropolis; see Goldberg, *Women, Work, and Life Cycle*, 301–2; Cissie Fairchilds, *Domestic Enemies: Servants and Their Masters in Old Regime France* (Baltimore: Johns Hopkins University Press, 1984), 66–67; Émilie Carles, *Soupe aux herbes sauvages*, trans. Avriel Goldberger, *A Life of Her Own: A Country-woman in Twentieth-Century France* (New Brunswick, N.J.: Rutgers University Press, 1991), 65.

Claude Gauvard's discussion of links between city and countryside indirectly supports the idea that migrants to the city often had contacts there ("Violence citadine et reseaux de solidarité: l'exemple français au xive et xve siècles," *Annales: Economies, Sociétés, Civilisations* 48, 5 [September–October 1993]: 1113–26). The concentration of people from certain regions of France on certain streets and parishes of Paris also points to a pattern of migration through contacts; see, for instance, Hercule Géraud, *Paris sous Philippe le Bel*, new ed., with intro. and index by Caroline Bourlet and Lucie Fossier (Tübingen: Max Niemeyer, 1991), 104–14 (concentration of people designated as "Normans" in the Parish Saint-Gervais).

19. "Consultation du Cardinal Pietro Colonna sur le IIe miracle de Saint Louis," ed. Louis Carolus-Barré, *Bibliothèque de l'Ecole des Chartes* 117 (1959): 72; Guillaume de St.-Pathus, *Les miracles*, no. 2, p. 11.

20. In 1296 Aalis of Saint-Joce and Philippote jointly paid a relatively large tax of 18 s. In 1313 Aaliz of Saint-Joce and her unnamed companion paid a tax of 30 s. (Karl Michaëlsson, *Le livre de la taille de Paris, l'an 1296* [Göteborg: Almquist & Wiksell, 1958], 20, 167; Michaëlsson, *Le livre de la taille de Paris, l'an 1297* [Göte-

borg: Almquist & Wiksell, 1962], 151; Géraud, *Paris sous Philippe-le-Bel*, 130; Mi-chaëlsson, *Le livre de la taille de Paris, l'an de grace 1313* [Göteborg: Wettergren & Kerbers Förlag, 1951], 11; Archer, "Working Women," 299, 300). Archer argues convincingly (104, 129) that nearly all the women in the Parisian tax rolls were either widows or single. I am grateful to Caroline Bourlet of the Institute de Re-cherche et d'Histoire des Textes for providing me with a list of female companions and beguines from the Institute's computerized data base of the Parisian tax assess-ments of 1292, 1296–1300, and 1313. Only the lists of 1292, 1296, 1297, and 1313 have been published. The assessments of 1296 to 1300 are in register KK283 of the Archives Nationale. Those of 1292 and 1313 are in the Bibliothèque Nationale, ms. fr. 6220 and 6736.

21. The minimum tax in 1292 was one sou. Maheut the beguine and Dame Aalès des Cordèles each paid a tax of 16 s.; Jehanne the embroiderer and Martine her companion (later identified as a beguine) paid 20 s. together; Gile the daughter of Jehan de Compiagne paid 36 s.; Ermengar the deaf paid 12 s.; and Marguerite the beguine and her sister Denise paid 16 s. together (Géraud, *Paris sous Philippe-le-Bel*, 159 and 160). Jehanne and Martine were still together in the 1296, 1297, 1299, and 1300 assessments (Archer, "Working Women," 303).

22. Anna Benvenuti Papi, "Mendicant Friars and Female Pinzochere in Tus-cany," in *Women and Religion in Medieval and Renaissance Italy*, ed. Daniel Bornstein and Roberto Rusconi, trans. Margery J. Schneider (Chicago: University of Chicago Press, 1996), 91.

23. On Jewish readings of Genesis 1–3, which stressed marriage for *both* men and women and were less negative about women and sexuality, see Daniel Boyarin, *Carnal Israel: Reading Sex in Talmudic Culture* (Berkeley: University of California Press, 1993), 77–106.

24. Aquinas, *Summa theologicae*, part 1, question 92, art. 1, response, ed. Black-friars (New York: McGraw-Hill, 1963), 13: 34, trans. Elizabeth Clark and Herbert Richardson, *Women and Religion: A Feminist Sourcebook of Christian Thought* (New York: Harper and Row, 1977), 86. See Kari Elisabeth Børresen, *Subordination and Equivalence: The Nature and Role of Women in Augustine and Thomas Aquinas*, trans. Charles H. Talbot (Washington, D.C.: University Press of America, 1981), 17–18, 157, for a discussion of Aquinas's reliance on Augustine.

25. Some scholars have suggested that the Genesis text was not, in its original form, asymmetrical concerning the governance of one partner over the other. They argue that a phrase now found in Genesis 4: 7 ("and unto you [shall be] his desire and you shall rule over him,"), which makes little sense in its present context, was originally part of Yahweh's speech to Eve, and thus created a reciprocal relationship between Adam and Eve. See Mieke Bal, *Lethal Love: Feminist Literary Readings of Biblical Love Stories* (Bloomington: Indiana University Press, 1987), 126–27, citing Jarich Oosten and David Moyer, "De mythische omkering: een analyse van de sociale code van de scheppingsmythen van Genesis 2–11," *Anthropologische Verkin-ningen* 1 (1982): 83.

26. On wives' obedience to their husbands see Jacques de Vitry, "Sermo [primus] ad coniugatos," Paris, Bibliothèque Nationale, ms. lat. 3284, fol. 177v. Jacques told several exempla stories about disobedient and litigious wives. As a

result of their quarrelsome and disobedient behavior, one wife had her tongue cut out, another drowned, and a third was pierced by a sharp nail (Thomas Frederick Crane, *The Exempla or Illustrative Stories for the Sermones Vulgares of Jacques de Vitry*, nos. 221, 222, 227, 228 [Rpt. ed., New York: Burt Franklin, 1971], 92, 94–95). To a certain extent, Jacques tempered his stress on women's necessary obedience with a critical discussion of men who mistreated their wives.

27. See, for instance, the numerous discussions of Eve's creation from Adam's rib, which emphasized that women should thus neither dominate their husbands nor be their servants (Hugh of St. Victor, "Adnotationes Elucidatoriae in Pentateuchon," chap. 7, ed. J. P. Migne, *Patrologiae cursus completus, Series latina* (Rpt. ed., Turnhout: Brepols, 1968), 175:40; Humbert of Romans, "Ad omnes mulieres," ed. Casagrande, *Prediche*, 43). See Casagrande, ed., *Prediche*, 6, n. 2 for other examples. See also R. Howard Bloch, *Medieval Misogyny and the Invention of Western Romantic Love* (Chicago: University of Chicago Press, 1991), 24ff.

28. Jo Ann McNamara, *A New Song: Celibate Women in the First Three Christian Centuries*, Women and History 6/7 (New York: Haworth Press, 1983), esp. 107ff.; Elizabeth Castelli, "Virginity and Its Meaning for Women's Sexuality in Early Christianity," *Journal of Feminist Studies in Religion* 2(1986): 61–88; Dyan Elliott, *Spiritual Marriage: Sexual Abstinence in Medieval Wedlock* (Princeton: Princeton University Press, 1993), 25–50; Ross Shepard Kraemer, *Her Share of the Blessings: Women's Religions Among Pagans, Jews, and Christians in the Greco-Roman World* (New York: Oxford University Press, 1992), 128–56, 191–98; Joyce Salisbury, *Church Fathers, Independent Virgins* (London: Verso, 1991).

29. "On the Veiling of Virgins," *Fathers of the Third Century*, ed. A. Cleveland Coxe, Ante Nicene Fathers 4 (Rpt. ed., Grand Rapids, Mich.: Eerdmans, 1976), 31, cited in Bloch, *Medieval Misogyny*, 35.

30. See, on this paternal role of the church, Edith Pasztor, "I Papi del Duecento e Trecento di fronte alla vita religiosa femminile," *Il movimento religioso femminile in Umbria nei secoli xiii–xiv*, ed. Roberto Rusconi (Florence: Nuova Italia, 1984), 29–67.

31. "Relatio de statu ecclesiae in regno Alemaniae," *Monumenta Germaniae Historica, Legum, Sectio IV*, vol. 3 (Hannover: Hahn, 1904–6), 593. See Jean-Claude Schmitt, *Mort d'une heresie: l'église et les clercs face aux béguines et béghards du Rhin supérieure du xive au xve siècle* (Paris: Mouton, 1978), 58.

32. Geneviève Hasenohr, "La vie quotidienne de la femme vue par l'église: l'enseignement des 'Journées chrétiennes' de la fin du moyen-âge," *Frau und spätmittelalterlicher Alltag* (Vienna: Österreichischen Akademie der Wissenschaften, 1986), 19–101; Carla Casagrande, "The Protected Woman," trans. Clarissa Botsford, in *A History of Women in the West II: Silences of the Middle Ages*, ed. Christiane Klapisch-Zuber (Cambridge, Mass.: Belknap Press of Harvard University Press, 1992), 70–104. For a general introduction to ad status sermons, and to Humbert of Romans, Jacques de Vitry, and Gilbert of Tournai see D. L. D'Avray and M. Tausche, "Marriage Sermons in *ad status* Collections of the Central Middle Ages," *Archives d'Histoire Doctrinale et Littéraire du Moyen Age* 47 (1980): 71–119.

33. Humbert of Romans, *De eruditione religiosorum praedicatorum*, ed. Casagrande, *Prediche*, 43–56. Casagrande published all of Humbert's sermon material for

laywomen, but she left out a number of his discussions of sermon materials for various categories of nuns. See her list of Humbert's sermon topics on 142–44 and the seventeenth-century edition: *De eruditione religiosorum praedicatorum*, Liber II, tractatus 1, ed. Margarin de la Bigne, *Maxima Bibliotheca Veterum Patrum* (Lyons: Anissonii, 1677), 25:416–506.

34. Humbert of Romans, "Ad mulieres burgenses divites," ed. Casagrande, *Prediche*, 47–78.

35. Humbert of Romans, "Ad mulieres pauperes in villulis," ed. Casagrande, *Prediche*, 52–53.

36. "O quot filii familias, et juvenculi, qui verecundabantur ire ad publicas mulieres, cum istis mulieribus amiserunt Virginitatem suam. Ed ideo vae talibus mulieribus, quia sunt culpabiles omnium peccatorum, quae postea committuntur per istos" (Humbert, "Ad famulas divitum," ed. Casagrande, *Prediche*, 50).

37. ". . . istae enim sunt incendiariae mundi. . . . per hoc peccatum nocetur animabus, quod pejus est. . . . non solum paucos, sed plurimos recipiunt hujusmodi mulieres, modo corruptos, modo virgines, modo solutos, modo uxoratos, modo Clericos, modo laicos, modo consanguineos, modo etiam Religiosos. . . . ita diabolus per hujusmodi mulieres capit magnos viros" (Humbert, "Ad mulieres malas corpore, sive meretrices," ed. Casagrande, *Prediche*, 54–55).

38. He said of prostitutes, "detestabiles sunt, quae in hujusmodi peccatis perseverant" (ibid., 54).

39. See Casagrande, "The Protected Woman," for a similar argument.

40. Actually, Jacques composed sermons for virgins, widows, and "married persons." See the list of his ad status sermons in Joannes Baptista Cardinalis Pitra, *Analecta Novissima Spicilegii Solesmensis*, 2 vols. (Paris: 1885–1888; Rpt., Farnborough, England: Gregg Press, 1967), 2:346.

41. Jean Longère, ed. and introduction, "Deux sermons de Jacques de Vitry (†1240) Ad Servos et Ancillas," in *La femme au moyen-âge*, ed. Michel Rouche and Jean Heuclin (Maubeuge: Publications de la Ville de Maubeuge, 1990), 261–96; Gilbert of Tournai, "Ad ancillas et servos [sermons] primus . . . secundus . . . tertius," Paris, Bibliothèque Nationale, ms. lat. 15943, fol. 175–180v; Gilbert of Tournai, "Ad coniugatas, Sermo tertius," ed. Casagrande, *Prediche*, 93–97.
Susan Mosher Stuard has argued, drawing primarily on Mediterranean sources, that the word *ancilla* refers to female slaves ("Ancillary Evidence for the Decline of Medieval Slavery," *Past and Present* 149 [November 1995]: 3–28). This was not exclusively the case for Jacques de Vitry and Gilbert of Tournai, whose word choice was determined by the language of the Vulgate (Psalm 122: 2, Proverbs 30: 23), and who employed this word to distinguish female from male persons in serving/servile positions; see Jacques de Vitry, ed. Longère, 271, 283; and Gilbert of Tournai, "Ad ancillas . . . sermo primus," fol. 175–175v. Jacques attempted to define various categories of "servus" in his second sermon "ad servos et ancillas." His definitions included slaves, serfs, and hired servants, suggesting that he considered all of these to be potential auditors for these sermons ("LXV, Sermo ad eosdem," ed. Longère, 285–86). I have found no evidence of domestic slaves in thirteenth- and early fourteenth-century Paris.

42. Humbert addressed sexuality extensively in his chapter on sermons for

female servants, but he alluded only briefly, in his chapter on sermons for both male and female servants, to the "unclean sins" that could result from "evil familiarity" among comrades: "Quandoque vero mala familiaritate coniuncti [the context suggests that this should be translated as 'comrades' rather than 'spouses'] iuuant se inuicem, et zelant in peccatis immunditiae." Humbert seemed to be more concerned about thefts, quarrelsomeness, laziness, and fighting among male servants than he was about sexual sins — and in his reference to "unclean sins" he said nothing about the threat that such sins posed to the household in which the servants were working (*De eruditione*, 2:1:76, "Ad familiam diuitum in ciuitatibus," ed. de la Bigne, *Maxima*, 25: 493–94).

43. Jacques de Vitry, "LXIV, Sermo ad servos et ancillas," ed. Longère, "Deux sermons," 11a, 11d, pp. 278, 279–80; Gilbert of Tournai, "Ad ancillas et servos sermo primus," Paris, Bibliothèque Nationale, ms. lat. 15943, fol. 175–77; Gilbert of Tournai, "Ad coniugatas sermo tercius," ed. Casagrande, *Prediche*, 94–95.

44. "Sicut uacca lasciuiens declinauit," Jacques de Vitry, "LXIV, Sermo ad servos et ancillas," ed. Longère, "Deux sermons," 11a, p. 279.

45. "*Vacca* enim, id est mulier lasciuia oestro dyaboli stimulata, tauros sequitur, ut suam libidinem adimpleat" (ibid.).

46. "Ita huiusmodi ancilla pannosa, uilis et abiecta, in domo debet retineri" (ibid., 11b, p. 279).

47. "intollerabilis malicia. . . . Hoc crimine ualde infecti sunt quidam miseri qui ancillas suas licet turpiores uxoribus preponunt, quamuis sint pulchriores" (Jacques de Vitry, "LXV, Sermo ad eosdem," ed. Longère, "Deux sermons," 294).

48. Gilbert of Tournai, "Ad ancillas et servos sermo primus," Bibliothèque Nationale ms. lat. 15943, fol. 175v.

49. Gilbert of Tournai, "Ad coniugatas sermo tercius," ed. Casagrande, *Prediche*, 95.

50. In addition to the discussions of male servants detailed above, see Humbert of Romans's discussion of hired laborers. He says that many of them are ignorant of spiritual matters and that some drink too much — an issue that he never raises in his discussions of elite men (*De eruditione*, 2:1:88, "Ad operarios conductivos," ed. de la Bigne, *Maxima*, 25:500). According to Claude Gauvard, marriage was also part of a man's "good reputation" in the secular sphere. In the criminal register of the Châtelet of Paris, men declared themselves married in order to avoid torture (Gauvard, *"De grace especial": Crime, état et société en France à la fin du moyen âge*, 2 vols. [Paris: Publications de la Sorbonne, 1991], 1: 384).

51. *De eruditione*, 2:1:71, "Ad omnes laicos," ed. de la Bigne, *Maxima*, 25:490.

52. I am not the first to observe that women were sometimes singled out as special objects of charity. See, for instance, John Henderson, *Piety and Charity in Late Medieval Florence* (Oxford: Clarendon Press, 1994); Henderson, "Women, Children and Poverty in Florence at the Time of the Black Death," in *Poor Women and Children in the European Past*, ed. Henderson and Richard Wall (London: Routledge, 1994), 160–79; Brian Pullan, "Support and Redeem: Charity and Poor Relief in Italian Cities from the Fourteenth to the Seventeenth Century," in *Charity and the Poor in Medieval and Renaissance Europe*, ed. Henderson, *Continuity and Change* 3, 2 (1988): 188–89; Stephen Epstein, *Wills and Wealth in Medieval Genoa*,

1150–1250 (Cambridge, Mass.: Harvard University Press, 1984), 171–72, 185–86; Elizabeth Rothrauff, "Charity in a Medieval Community: Politics, Piety, and Poor-Relief in Pisa, 1257–1312" (Ph.D. diss., University of California, Berkeley, 1994), 99, 193; Jacques Chiffoleau, *La comptabilité de l'au-delà: les hommes, la mort et la religion dans la région d'Avignon à la fin du moyen âge (vers 1320–vers 1480)* (Rome: Ecole Française de Rome, 1980), 135–36, 304, 307; Suzanne F. Roberts, "Les consulats du Rouergue et l'assistance urbaine au xiiiᵉ et au début du xivᵉ siècles," *Cahiers de Fanjeaux* 13 (1978): 135, 137.

53. The following discussion is based on an examination of thirty-two Parisian bourgeois wills from the mid-thirteenth to the mid-fourteenth century. These constitute all the Parisian wills that I have located thus far, in the archival sources for numerous Parisian religious institutions. There was no central repository for Parisian private documents, thus we are dependent on the recordkeeping whims of individual religious institutions, which often chose to make authenticated copies of extracted clauses from original documents rather than copying the entire documents. Thus we know about the existence of many Parisian wills that are no longer extant. Only complete originals or complete copies of originals provide the information for which I am looking.

54. Gérard Dubois, *Historia ecclesiae parisiensis* (Paris: F. Muguet, 1690–1710), 2: 510–11. Dubois gives the date of 1288 in his printed version of the foundation document; however, a fifteenth-century vidimus of the same document gives the date of 1283 (Archives Nationales [henceforth AN] L 1078, nos. 1 and 2). See also Léon Le Grand, "Les béguines de Paris," *Mémoires de la Société de l'Histoire de Paris et de l'Ile-de-France* 20 (1893): 334–41 and 354–57.

There were similar shelters for widows in Italian towns. See Richard Trexler, "A Widows' Asylum of the Renaissance: The Orbatello of Florence," *Old Age in Preindustrial Society*, ed. Peter N. Stearns (New York: Holmes and Meier, 1982), 119–49; F. Semi, *Gli "ospizi" di Venezia* (Venice: Helvitia, 1983), 40–43, 87–95, 161–62; Rothrauff, "Charity in a Medieval Commune," 99.

55. AN L 1043, nos. 18, 20, 21, 22, and 24. Jehanne Haudry's testament (no. 24) specified that the residents were widows. See also Le Grand, "Les béguines," 354–57, 349–55.

56. They were Ste.-Avoye ("Bonnes fames de la porte du Temple"), the Haudriettes ("Bonnes fames de lospital Estienne Haudry"), "Bonnes fames de lospital Andry Marcel," "Bonnes fames de la rue aux Fauconniers," "Bonnes fames de lospital Jehan Gensan," "Bonnes fames de lospital Denys de St. Just," "Bonnes fames de lospital Gieffroy de Flory," "Bonnes fames de lospital Mestri P. Larrent," "Bonnes femmes du pont parvum," and "Bonnes femmes Mestrie Jehanne Mignon" (AN KK 5, fol. 368–368v).

Another hospital, founded by Ymbert of Lyons in 1316, had evolved, by the end of the fifteenth century, into a hospice providing temporary shelter for female beggars, many of whom were probably single. Some historians have assumed that the original foundation provided temporary shelter for female beggars. However, none of the original foundation documents make any mention of this function. Indeed, neither the foundation documents nor the early fourteenth-century testaments that make reference to Ymbert of Lyon's hospital indicate that it provided services only to women (AN LL 7, fol. 57v–60 [copies of foundation documents of 1316 in the Grande Cartulaire de l'Archevêché de Paris]; AN L 1053, no. 12 [1348 vidimus of Ymbert of Lyon's testament of 1316]; Archives de l'Assistance Publique, Fonds St.-Jacques (henceforth, AAP, S.-J.), first chartrier, no. 14 [Testament of Jehanne Du Faut, 1330, gift to "hospitali defuncti Ymberti de Lugduno"]). The 1483 document describing the shelter provided for female beggars is printed in Jacques Du Breul, *Le théâtre des antiquitez de Paris* (Paris: Société des Imprimeurs, 1639), 662–63.

57. AN L 938 no. 46 (Testament of Jehanne la Fouacière, 1313), AAP, S.-J., first chartrier, no. 17 (Testament of Jehan de Troyes, 1332).

58. In the 1342 register, the largest disbursements to hospices for "bonnes fames" went to the Haudriettes (16 livres), Ste.-Avoye (8 livres), and the hospice of Andry Marcel (8 livres) (AN KK 5, fol. 368–368v).

Testamentary gifts to both Ste.-Avoye and the Haudriettes by testators other than the original founders and their descendants include AN L 938, no. 46 (Jehanne la Fouacière, 1313); AN L 938 no. 58 (Margaret, wife of Pierre Loisel, 1330), AAP, S.-J., first chartrier, no. 17 (Jehan de Troyes, 1332); and probably "Inventaire de Galeran le Breton et Testament de Jeanne de Malaunay," ed. Arthur Goldmann *Bulletin de la Société de l'Histoire de Paris et de l'Ile-de-France* 19 (1892): 168 (Jeanne de Malaunay, 1311: she gives 5 [sous] each to "pauperibus hospitalibus pauperum mulierum viduarum Parisiensis"). Testators giving gifts only to Ste.-Avoye include *Chartes et Documents de l'Abbaye de St.-Magloire*, ed. Anne Terroine and Lucie Fossier (Paris: Editions du Centre National de la Recherche Scientifique, 1966), 2: 150, no. 108 (Pierre la Pie, 1302); "Testament d'une bourgeoise de Paris," ed. L. Le Grand, *Bulletin de la Société de l'Histoire de Paris et de l'Ile-de-France* (1887): 43 (Sédile de Laon, 1316); AN L 1043, no. 24 (Jehanne, wife of Stephen Haudry, 1309; Jehanne gave both to the Haudriettes and to Ste.-Avoye). Testators giving only to the Haudriettes include AN L 938 no. 61 (Guillaume de Mailly, 1327).

59. Le Grand, "Les béguines," 349ff.

60. On the Filles Dieu see Paul and Marie-Louise Biver, *Abbayes, monastères, couvents de femmes à Paris des origines à la fin du xviiie siècle* (Paris: Presses Universitaires de France, 1975), 67–71. On St.-Antoine, see Berman, "Cistercian Nuns."

61. The following discussion of the beguines of Paris draws on Le Grand, "Les béguines," 295–357.

62. Guillaume de St.-Pathus, *Les miracles*, no. 44, 135–37. It is unclear if Alès actually resided at the beguinage.

63. AAP, S.-J., first chartrier, no. 14 (Testament of Jehanne Du Faut). In her testament Jehanne never indicated that she was a beguine, and in fact she was currently residing in another house that she owned, on the Rue Trousse-vache, in the Parish of St.-Merry. However, a later document concerning the disposition of Jehanne's former property in the beguinage (she had designated that it was to devolve to her daughter after Guillemete's death, and the leaders of the beguinage apparently opposed this arrangement), calls Jehanne "condam dicti loci beguine" (AN Xia7, fol. 89v, quoted by Le Grand, "Les béguines," 328, n. 4). Le Grand was not aware of Jehanne's testament.

64. Le Grand, "Les béguines," 324–25. The episcopal court declared that the

woman was innocent, but she was expelled nevertheless because of the ill fame that she now carried.

65. AAP, S.-J., first chartrier, no. 14 (Jehanne Du Faut, 1330); AAP, S.-J., first chartrier, no. 17 (Jehan de Troyes, 1332); AN L 938, no. 46 (Jehanne la Fouacière, 1313).

66. Archives des Quinze-Vingts, ms. 5848, f. 213 (Jean Le Grand, 1310); AN L 938, no. 46 (Jehanne la Fouacière, 1313), AN L 840 no. 99, copied by Terroine, "Recherches," 4:127 (Robert Evrout, 1306); AN L 1021 no. 18, copied by Terroine, "Recherches," 4: 166 (Robert le Vinetier, 1311); *Archives de l'Hôtel Dieu de Paris*, ed. Léon Brièle (Paris: Imprimerie Nationale, 1894), 550 (Tiphaine la Commine, 1295); "Testament de Simon Piz d'Oue, Chanoine de Saint-Gérmain-L'Auxerrois (3 Octobre, 1307)," ed. Henry Martin, *Bulletin de la Société de l'Histoire de Paris et de l'Ile-de-France* 3 (1909): 37.

67. Archives des Quinze-Vingts, ms. 5848, fol. 213ff. (Jean le Grand, 1310); AAP, S.-J., first chartrier, no. 17 (Jehan de Troyes, 1332); AN L 840 no. 99, copied by Terroine, "Recherches," 4:126 (Robert Evrout, 1306); AN L 840, no. 100, copied by Terroine, "Recherches," 4:133–36 (Marie, widow of Robert Evrout, 1307); AN L 1043, no. 24 (Jehanne, wife of Stephen Haudry, 1309); AN S 896, no. 17 (Guillaume Fresnel, 1293); AN LL 387, fol. 73v (Adam Le Panetier, 1271); "Testament d'une bourgeoise" (Sédile of Laons, 1316); *Recueil de chartes et documents de Saint-Martin-des-Champs Monastère Parisien*, vol. 5, ed. J. Depoin (Paris: A. Picard et Fils, 1921), 98 (Jeanne Argence, 1273). A number of these bequests may have been settlements for back wages, but that was not the case with Sédile of Laon, who settled her debts with her servants at the beginning of her will, then went on to give gifts of money and clothing to her own servants, the daughter-in-law of one of her servants, and to servants of two other people. It is also unlikely that the gifts of clothing from Jehanne, the wife of Stephen Haudry, Adam le Panetier, and Jeanne Argence were paying off debts. None of these bequests specifically mentions that the gift constituted a dowry, but the gifts of bedding from Guillaume Fresnel and Jean Le Grand may have been intended as dowries.

68. *Livre des métiers*, ed. Lespinasse and Bonnardot, nos. 21:5–6, 56:5, 69:14, 84:12, 87:7, 88:13, pp. 49, 116, 146, 184, 189, 195; Janice Archer, "Working Women," 258, 263, 264, 266, and 267. See also my discussion in "Down and Out and Female in Thirteenth-Century Paris," *American Historical Review* 103 (April 1998): 361–62.

4

Single by Law and Custom

Susan Mosher Stuard

WESTERN EUROPE HAS SEEN more lifelong singlewomen in its midst than any other part of the world, at least in documented centuries.[1] Of course singlewomen differed in their reasons for remaining single, and an entire continuum from preference to coercion dictated the terms under which women negotiated the critical decision about marriage or no marriage in their lives. A woman referred to as *ancilla*, the Roman term for female chattel slave that remained in use through the medieval centuries, stands at the extreme end of the continuum. Women slaves negotiated no decision about remaining single — custom and law dictated a single state — nor were they able to exert control over their sexual activity. As a result they bore offspring who suffered under the same "error of condition" (church law's grimly descriptive phrase for a slave's legal state) as did their mothers.[2] While slaves' numbers do not appear to have been great, the Mediterranean world saw an increase in their numbers in the late Middle Ages when singlewomen slaves were traded to European households to serve as domestics. Whatever their numbers, slaves were a familiar feature of life in most cities in the western Mediterranean region. To an important extent ancillae's continued presence helped ensure the persistence of the institution of slavery itself in Europe. In that sense a single state mattered more than just to the ancilla herself; it is quite possible that the survival of slavery, that "peculiar" institution, rests at least in part on the female slave's being single by law and custom through the medieval centuries.

By the late thirteenth century the number and wealth of great households had risen substantially in European cities, creating a demand for domestic labor that was filled at least in part by slaves in the Mediterranean South. Active efforts to import slaves from the East answered this increased demand and imported female slaves served in affluent commercial households from Dalmatia to Barcelona and often beyond. Some boys and men were sold into slavery as well, but nearly 90 percent of the slaves mentioned in the notarial charters that documented the slave trade were young girls and women.[3]

Slavery was an old institution tolerated by the church and sanctioned in canon law; it was recognized in the laws of virtually all European polities. Charles Verlinden, in an exhaustive archive-to-archive investigation of medieval slavery's revival in the later Middle Ages, found that slaves were overwhelmingly female and young. These women or, more likely, young girls anywhere from nine or ten through their teenage years, were destined to serve in domestic households and they would likely remain single unless manumitted; their offspring were unfree and they would be sold along with their mothers, although of course they could be manumitted as well.[4] Slave women became a common sight in Europe, especially in the Mediterranean region; they would become an even more common sight on the streets of towns and on plantations in the New World after 1500.

Men had every good reason to avoid marriage with one of these single female slaves — because ancillae passed on unfree status to offspring. From about 1200 when some unfree men (the category generally meant serfs under obligation to lords, but "unfree" was an encompassing term in canon law including many degrees of unfreedom) were gaining a few rights through canon law — rights that were commensurate with establishing stable families and rights over children born to them — an enslaved condition for ancillae persisted. These women and girls lacked rights even if they contracted a valid and sacralized marriage. Of course the church could not deny a sacrament like marriage to Christian slaves; thus, marriage was not expressly forbidden to them.[5] Unfortunately this had tragic consequences for a female slave: marriage did not change the fact that she and her offspring belonged to the master; hence any man wishing to marry her learned his rights as husband and father were null. This fact was a legal dilemma that medieval canon law simply could not resolve: after the thirteenth century, accordingly, ancillae might cohabit with husbands, but the principle of slave descent from an enslaved mother did not change. An ancilla's incapacity, her "error of condition," appears to have been unmoderated in the law whether she found a man to marry her or not. In practice that meant a wedded female slave was treated as if she were single, and thus slavery was passed on to a new generation of individuals who were her offspring, keeping the institution very much alive.

Canon law appears to have been caught between the logic of a slave owner's property rights and the logic of the church's own initiative in extending marital rights and obligations to ever greater numbers of peasant families, where certainly the father and probably the entire family were bound in some degree to a lord. These partially bound families actually gained recognition and rights in canon law after 1200 because fathers' rights were strengthened in some cases.[6] But this would not necessarily help female slaves. Complicating the issue was the practice among ecclesiastics of owning slaves themselves. No churchman could alienate church property, and that extended to slaves within their possession. Also, devout Christians everywhere understood that the church did not condemn slavery as an institution. Underlying all these factors stood the principle of law that a child followed the condition of the mother. This was a very old premise adopted by the church from Roman law, and medieval people did not show much interest in relinquishing this time-sanctioned principle of law that often worked to their benefit.

Orenetta

A greater incentive to resolve this inconsistency in canon law might have existed if slavery had not proved to be an effective way to fill the need for domestic labor in cities. A market niche developed for imported slaves destined to work alternatively in domestic tasks, commerce, and production. Francesco de Marco Datini of Prato instructed his partner Andrea de Bonnano, resident of Genoa:

> Pray buy me a little slave-girl, young, and rustic, between eight and ten years old, and she must be of good stock and strong enough to bear much hard work, and of good health and temper, so that I may bring her up in my own way. I would have her only to wash the dishes and carry wood and bread to the oven, and work of that sort . . . for I have another here who is a good slave, and can cook and sew well.[7]

With typical clarity Datini defined the niche occupied by a newly enslaved child in a complex commercial household. Iris Origo has noted in a list of 357 slaves, 34 girls under twelve and 85 under eighteen, in a Florentine register of 1363.[8] Origo also noted that the rest of the slaves listed were young; the few males among them were boys and likely offspring of ancillae. Study of the Adriatic trade in slaves reveals a similar market preference for mere children.[9] Verlinden's archival researches stress that extreme youth characterized slaves imported from the Crimea as well as from the

Balkans with, later, Moorish or African slaves fitting the same narrowly conceived market niche in the fifteenth century. While James II of Aragon and the citizens of Barcelona expressed scruples about selling enslaved Greeks in the market in 1314 on the grounds that those Greeks were found to be Christian, the trade may have been rendered doubly repugnant to them because many of those slaves were Christian children.[10]

Nevertheless, the advantage in purchasing very young female slaves was significant. Foreign merchants, traveling agents, factors, and porters were not always fed or housed on the town but rather in the commercial household. Goods arrived seasonally or when the fleet came in, lending commercial establishments a rhythm of intense work interrupted by inactivity that did not lend itself to hiring wage labor.[11] Datini's eight- to ten-year-old child would then supplant hired male servants in a reascribing of tasks — a reassigned sexual division of labor. The new ancilla would indeed tend the ovens, haul the wood, and wash up the pots and cauldrons; whether she would be trusted with the good plate is another question. She would also haul loads, sew commercial goods into bales, sort, fetch, and carry.[12]

Female workers were considered more tractable than male workers, and housed with other servants, subordinate to the "good" slave Datini mentioned, they found scant opportunity to act otherwise. Extreme youth, separation from kin and friends, and a wholly foreign environment cut off most paths of rebellion. Also the mistress of the house might prefer to take on the challenge of directing female rather than male slaves.[13] This medieval system of household slavery was enforced largely by lack of alternatives in distinction to the beatings that had "motivated" male slaves in earlier times. Affluent householders seldom judged such domestic arrangements inhumane. When Ragusans outlawed the slave trade in 1416, it was the export of slaves overseas they labeled inhumane and illegal. What they did in their own households escaped censure.[14]

To return to Datini of Prato: Genoa did not supply Datini a suitable slave so he turned to the market at Venice, where he bought a child named Orenetta. She was very likely a Bosnian and therefore a Christian child imported from across the Adriatic Sea,[15] and she pleased the household. On New Year's Day in 1395 Francesco noted in his private accountbook "2 *soldi* to Orenetta, the little slave who comes from Venice."[16] Datini's tip or bonus suggests the little slave had begun her ascent through the complex layers of servitude in a great commercial household.

For the child Orenetta in the Datini household an incentive system led in time to more skilled, more woman-identified, and less exhausting tasks, provided she pleased the household. Nonetheless, Orenetta's assimilation occurred in the years when she passed through puberty and a child born to her in slavery was not out of the question. In the childless Datini household Mona Marguerita Datini had already agreed to raise as her own Lucia, the child of a household slave. Lucia had been fathered by Datini and became a daughter of the household. This child was remarkably fortunate, as was the Florentine storyteller Franco Sacchetti, the child of a slave, when his father's young Italian bride accepted him into her household.[17]

A snide bit of doggerel from Florence noted how householders "married off" their locally recruited rural servants with dowries once they became pregnant by a man of the *casa*. On balance this seems a far kinder fate than that of the child-bearing female slave.[18] Rural girls serving great households for a contract gained the legal recourse of marriage with dowry. The pregnant slave girl produced a child who belonged to a household. Her masters could recognize, pamper, free, or disregard the child at will. Even the happy outcomes for Lucia Datini and Franco Sacchetti may relate stories of violated motherhood; neither slave mother called her child her own.[19] A system of assimilation that left the definition of a "good" slave entirely to the whim of the household exerted enormous power over a female slave. Harriet Beecher Stowe, who placed domestic relations at the top of the list of slavery's outrages in nineteenth-century America, might have commented similarly on late medieval domestic slavery that took a child from a mother even if the mother qualified as a "good" slave.[20]

Over time a compliant slave learned skills. Datini's older "good" slave could both cook and sew, skills she supplied alternately at the command of her owners. In 1400, a ship from Venice to Majorca listed "nine Turkish heads" worth 360 lire on its ship's lading. One of these slaves was a woman who could "sew and do everything." The agent found her too good for the Majorcans so she traveled on with the ship to be sold in Valencia.[21] Any woman with skills, particularly cooking, spinning, weaving, and sewing, would exact a high price. And slaves were expensive. In Italy, a ten-year-old might cost as little as 20 florins in the fourteenth century; a skilled woman in her late teens cost 80 florins or even more.[22] In fact an earlier thirteenth-century slave girl's market price increase from about 5 ducats in Ragusa to 30, 40, or 50 ducats once she was transported to Venice, demonstrates the strong demand for female slave labor in Italian port cities. Slaves traded after reaching the age of thirty brought lower prices, unless they possessed specialized skills.[23] On top of the market price Italian cities taxed slave sales.

The Supply of Ancillae

It is valuable to compare this household of Datini in Prato to comparable wealthy households in port cities. In Ragusa/Dubrovnik, merchant citizen's homes were scattered all over the city, with a concentration in the oldest *sexteria* on the high perch of Castellum. Commercial goods, firewood, and foodstuffs moved up steps from the two city gates and the harbor to these homes. While men, a few of them also enslaved, might be used to haul, cart, or ship outside the city walls, within town loads were often packed on the backs of women or girls for the trek up the steps.[24] A clear advantage lay in the fact that this was not a specialized labor force of men but a squad of unfree women who could be redirected to work inside the household when the commercial needs of the establishment had been satisfied. In this community even the fifteenth-century Renaissance palaces newly built outside the town continued to house commercial functions on the ground floor and family functions on the first floor and above. Domestic architecture in most port cities favored similar solutions. Venice, whose trunk, arterial, and neighborhood canals most closely approximated our modern highway systems (down to the attached boathouse equivalent to our garages), gives the clearest visual evidence of this efficient urban deployment of labor. Gondolas were, literally speaking, manned, while women often hefted commercial goods once they were delivered to the household.[25]

A division of labor into public and private components assigned to men and women respectively suited urban commercial households. Where cost efficiency lay in keeping down overhead, a multipurpose labor force of tractable individuals was a sufficiently powerful incentive to alter the sexual division of labor and employ numbers of enslaved women and girls in private households. As a matter of fact, Italian merchants may have observed the use of slave labor when trading in the eastern Adriatic and Black Sea regions and brought the solution back home. In the markets of Ragusa, where slaves had traditionally served households, seasonal variation in the price of slaves emerged by the late thirteenth century, at just the time when urban household slavery had begun to spread more widely in Italy. When Venetian ships lay in port in the late summer sales increased quite dramatically. Venetians would buy virtually any slave they could find, including the personal or "dowry" slaves of noble households. It was entirely probable that Italian merchants used the stop at Ragusa, on the Levantine fleet's return voyage, to secure themselves slaves for their own households.[26]

Slaves like Orenetta were available from a number of port cities with whom Christian merchants from the West maintained close contacts. Additionally, the frontiers over which single women were transported to augment the supply of those of inherited servile status never completely closed. On Europe's various frontiers — in Scandinavia, in the Balkans, in Castile — slave women were a reasonably easily obtained resource.[27] Heath Dillard noted in *Daughters of the Reconquest* that slave traders worked both sides of the frontier, supplying Christian ancillae to Muslim households, and Muslim ancillae to Christians. The *fueros* (laws) were aimed at curtailing that traffic — at least when it preyed upon the Christian community — but slavery of Muslims in Christian homes was a tolerated institution; presumably enslaved Christian women were tolerated as well in affluent Muslim households.[28] More problematically in Scandinavia, as in England and France, the domiciled slave remained a feature of rural life even after the unfree agricultural worker "hutted" separately disappeared.[29]

As for the Balkans and the Adriatic region, the probable homeland of little Orenetta, there does not appear to have been an era when the slave trade died down or slavery fell into disuse, so a full apparatus was in place when the demand for slaves intensified in the thirteenth century. The West Balkans had been a region where towns had survived from ancient times, maintaining some continuity of practice with Late Antiquity. The traders at the mouth of the Narenta (Neretva) and in Dalmatian cities continued to buy and sell at least some slaves from the countryside into coastal towns. In 985 Prince Crnomir of Bosnia had deplored the conditions that prevailed in nearby rural Bosnia, where people had no defense against foreign traders capturing and enslaving them.[30] But slavery persisted, in matter of fact at the very court of the Ban of Bosnia, well into the thirteenth century, while traders from the coast bought or captured slaves from Bosnian villages.[31]

The fourteenth-century Code of Dušan (Kingdom of Serbia) prohibited the sale of Christians to unbelievers or heretics on pain of the vendor having his hands cut off and his tongue cut out. The true faith was Orthodoxy, and the fearsome slave vendor a Roman Christian from the coast.[32] Nevertheless slavery was practiced in Old Serbia (Rascia). In Catar (Kotor), the kingdom's urban window on the Adriatic, Dobroslava and two small slaves, almost certainly her infant sons, brought 30 *hyperperi* (about 15 ducats) in 1326, while the slave Calia gained freedom through manumission at Catar in 1332.[33] Both rural Serbs and Greeks were enslaved and reached Venice in the later Middle Ages.[34] Domestic slaves never truly disappeared; they remained close at hand, that is to say, localities practicing slavery were never very distant from those lands where slavery was revived in the later Middle Ages.

Indeed, single and unfree women called ancillae — the term possessed a precise, restricted meaning in charters and in law — appear to have fallen into a different category from married and "hutted" laborers, even if those laborers were in some degree unfree through being bound to a lord. Single female slaves were identified in the law as ancillae, they did not marry although they may very well have borne children, and they were domiciled workers set at labor-intensive and tedious chores by their masters' orders.[35]

Ancillae as Mothers

How had this come to pass? Orenetta had her predecessors in Europe, that is, other singlewomen called ancillae who by custom and law were not free, and they had passed on their status to their offspring. The later Middle Ages did not see a revival of slavery as an institution as much as an increased market demand for female slaves. Slavery itself was a traditional institution; it was an inherited system accepted within the three great religions of Europe: Christianity, Judaism, and Islam. Within the Christian tradition slavery had elicited a fair amount of commentary over the centuries, but that is an issue I have addressed more fully elsewhere.[36] On the practical level one stream of church commentary, the canon law debate over priest's hearthmates or wives and the status of their offspring, kept the issue of slavery a matter of concern for society at large. In early church councils hearthmates of priests had been equated with ancillae and the *Decretum* of Gratian incorporated this opinion into canon law in the twelfth century. It remained part of the canon through the great era of codification of church law in the later Middle Ages.

In one regard this canon law tradition may have changed attitudes toward female slaves. In the much earlier Penitential literature the culpability of slaves, the state of their souls or sinfulness, had not been an issue. With the pronouncements of church councils and the promulgation of canon law in the twelfth century, the ancilla's own sinfulness came to the attention of the law, when she was a hearthmate of a cleric. A Biblical justification was offered by canon lawyers to declare her offspring slaves: *"Unde illi dicuntur servi et filii ancillae, pertinentes ad Ismahel: isti dicuntur liberi et filii liberae, pertinentes ad Ysaac"* [From which it follows that the condition of Ismahel extends to those referred to as slaves or the offspring of slaves, while the condition of Isaac pertains to the free and the offspring of the free].[37] The offspring of a priest or cleric and his hearthmate (now termed ancilla) was a slave, and as such property of the church, not of the parents; in canon law such children had become *res ecclesia*.

Three texts in the canon law of the twelfth and thirteenth centuries, commonly referred to as the *Decretum*, discuss clerics' intimate associations with ancillae. The first, *Distinctio* 34, c. 15, forbids deacons to wed women slaves. The slave's culpability is implied in that cohabiting with a slave was described as equally odious as cohabitation with a prostitute.[38] In *Distinctio* 81, c. 30, the law provided for the sale of a woman slave serving as a consort or sexual companion of a cleric. This provision stood in sharp contrast to the earlier Penitential that had provided for freeing a slave who consorted with a master and while doing so bore offspring.[39] The third instance is the most telling: *Causa* 15, q. 8, c. 3, specified that offspring of an ancilla cohabiting with a cleric were themselves slaves. They were of "polluted" birth and were not to be counted as heirs. By implication such offspring were property of the church.[40] Taken together these three opinions confirmed that a slave woman cohabiting with a cleric would continue in her enslaved state and so would her offspring. If some serfs saw their marriages confirmed in canon law, modifying to an extent their unfree condition, domestic slaves, at least those called ancillae who lived in a cleric's household, benefited from no such softening of the law. While the law's intent was to condemn clerics cohabiting with domestic servants as part of a general enforcement of clerical celibacy, the provisions of the law enforced the conditions of chattel slavery as Roman law defined it on another party, that is, on the woman with whom the cleric cohabited. Such condemnations bore more heavily on the unfree woman and her offspring than on the cleric himself.

Not all female slaves were attached to the households of clerics, however, and their lay owners had the legal right to free ancillae. When in 1050 the Holy Roman Emperor Henry III struck a coin from the hand of Sigena, the "female serf" of a nobleman named Richolf, a woman escaped from chattel servitude. The charter specified that her status was now that of serf, so that she no longer passed on chattel status to her children, but "assumed the same liberty and legal status as all the other female serfs who have been freed in the same way by kings and emperors."[41] The question remains, how many women had access to the emperor and his grant of manumission? Equal numbers to men? Where offspring were concerned this was an important issue. Fathers did not pass their status to offspring; mothers did. If women found it difficult to change their status from chattel servitude, their children's condition would be affected as well.[42] While freeing a female slave had the capacity to bring about the demise of the institution itself were it repeated with great frequency, a tendency to free male slaves while women slaves remained unfree had no such effect, suggesting one way in which slavery might maintain a presence as an institution in medieval Europe.[43]

Since neither medieval law nor custom treated slavery as the same institution for women as for men, both ecclesiastical and secular laws governing the sexual unions of slaves and free persons indicate that slavery brought different outcomes to women than to men. In secular law a free woman's union with a male slave, a rare occurrence under any circumstance, was treated as analogous to bestiality from the era of Roman law through the barbarian law codes; not until the ninth century, complicated by servile status that created half-free conditions, did non-slave women marry *servi*, and then only in rural areas where custom condoned the practice.[44] While penalties often fell on this potential union of a free woman and a slave, neither severe penalties nor opprobrium fell on the sexual union of a free man and a slave woman in secular law, since in those cases no ambiguity about the status of offspring existed. Medieval law tended to punish a free man only when he copulated with a female slave who did not belong to him, and conditions pertained even then: in cases of mistreatment (of another owner's possessions) or if the union occurred in the house of the master of the ancilla.

So when Marino Ranina, noble citizen of Ragusa, brought charges against a fellow nobleman for assaulting his two *famulae* who were working in his vineyard outside the town walls, he was protecting his property interests. The defendant, Marino de Getaldi, need only restrict his attentions to his own slaves to avoid prosecution.[45] Michel Balard noted of medieval Genoa that a free man who impregnated another's slave owed the master twenty-five lire — fifty if the woman died in childbirth.[46] Having interfered with another man's property, most likely diminishing the slave's market value, such a man faced a stiff fine.

As a result of the law's tolerance of sexual liaisons with owned slave women, a wide range of legal initiatives were available that a free man, who was both master and father of a slave's child, might adopt in the day-to-day practice of slavery. A woman's slave status need not stand in the way of her master freeing her, marrying her, and legitimating her offspring (unless he was a priest). Short of that her child might be acknowledged and any

number of provisions in wills attest to the widespread acceptance of slave
offspring into the households of masters. It was a pious act to free slaves and
provide them bequests in last wills and testaments. Pasque de Goce had an
illegitimate child from a union with a household slave, and his noble parent,
rather than he, left that child a testamentary bequest.[47] In great households
that assumed responsibility for the offspring of their inmates, free or unfree,
such a solution ameliorated the bleak terms of unfree birth.

Such alternatives created freedom of action for owners of female
slaves, and, as a result, masters held vastly greater power over female slaves
and their offspring than a man might wield over his offspring in an out-of-
wedlock union with a free woman. Options ranged from turning the ancilla
out; punishing her; selling her or her offspring; acknowledging the issue;
freeing the mother and child immediately or at a later time; freeing them
and finding another man to marry the former slave; settling mother and
children in the household or far away; to marrying the former slave and
legitimating the offspring. In sum an extraordinary range of choices existed,
all of which may be found in the "documents of practice," as notarial charters are sometimes known. Orenetta might have faced any of these possibilities over her lifetime as a slave.

Intentionally or not great medieval households employing domestic
slaves produced a renewable substratum of persons, primarily girls and
women, but some unfree sons as well, all laboring at the will of their
masters.[48] They faced a wide diversity of future prospects. In a world of
rights and obligations shaded hierarchically from the most to the least
privileged, domiciled slaves were useful precisely because they stood below
all others; that is, they were virtually rightless, allowing maximum options
to their owners, a fact well illustrated by reference to the ancilla's sexuality
and child-bearing capacities.[49] Furthermore this condition of standing below all others was inherited and of long-standing, so householders did not
need to impose new forms of servitude or coercion as they so often attempted to do in rural environments in the later Middle Ages.[50]

Canon law weighed and debated the condition of children born to an
unfree woman from the thirteenth century onward, a sign that they were
common enough in society to attract the attention of the law. The *Decretales*
considered one case of a son whose mother was not free. If such a son has
fled his mother's servile condition for ten years, that is, he has followed his
father's free condition successfully for those years, he shall remain free.[51]
Despite this concession canon law generally remained true to the principle
that "he who is in the power of another cannot have another in his power,"

and applied that principle to those referred to as *originarii* (unfree persons in regard to birth and probably bound to the land) and servi. The controversy over parental rights of the unfree remained a discourse about very different groups of persons. For the legal authority known as Paucapalea an originarius has the right to give his daughter in marriage; however, a famulus (another category of unfree servants) has not.[52]

This was a complex discourse on rights won only piecemeal and for specific groups rather than for the general condition of all the unfree. In general men — that is, fathers and sons — were the focus of the discussion of enhanced rights, so the law's definition of "error of condition" for female slaves did not change. Orenetta, or any female slave like her, did not gain the rights of a parent over offspring.

Ancillae as Potential Wives

If slavery survived because it was sanctioned by law and custom and because of its utility to great householders, there was still an arena where the absolute conditions of chattel slavery might be challenged. That arena lay in canon law itself, within the debate about the right of Christians to marry.[53] This issue became a topic of some importance around the year 1200 when marriage rites came to be considered sacraments in the church. Within the Christian community slaves had the right to be baptized, so there was no question that a slave might receive a sacrament. Indeed, slaves from the Black Sea region who reached Genoa, Florence, Barcelona, or Majorca were often baptized on the grounds that they were heathen, and no self-respecting Christian householders wanted to harbor heathens within their homes. If one sacrament, baptism, was awarded to slaves, then why not another — the sacrament of marriage? So the traditional single status of slaves like Orenetta was opened to discussion within the larger issue of debate over the right of all Christians to marry. This debate was in turn premised on giving consent to marry. Since no sacrament was valid without proper consent, as soon as canon lawyers raised the question of consent to marry the related question of whether slaves had the freedom to give their consent to marry arose as a possible impediment to marriage. This issue was, of course, discussed in canon law under the heading of "error of condition."

Scholars today are generally convinced that the marital rights of the unfree were established in the century between Gratian's *Decretum* and the

compilation of church canons known as the *Decretales* issued by Gregory IX
in 1234. They are also generally in agreement that based on the text *Dignum
est* of Pope Hadrian IV, the ideas of the legist Walter of Mortagne came to be
included in subsequent compilations of papal letters and in the compiler
Bernard of Pavia's *Breviarium extravagantium*, thus making their way into
the *Decretales* as the right for the unfree to true marriage, regardless of a
master's consent.[54] A married couple were not to be kept from living together as man and wife even where their right to do so conflicted with the
master's rights to service from either spouse, although both still owed that
service as before.[55] Whether a master's right to a slave's services outweighed
the marital right to cohabit was a continued source of disagreement among
scholars of the law; the theologian Thomas of Chobham took the extreme
position in the thirteenth century that an ancilla was entitled to escape if
kept from living with her spouse, but few were willing to follow Thomas's
daring lead.[56] Canon law did come to recognize that unfree persons were
capable of moral acts, and the law set up the expectation that servile couples
would contract valid marriages even while the precise nature of a valid
marriage and its relationship to the master's consent remained matters of
debate.[57] If this was true a slave like Orenetta could marry, assuming she
knew her rights in church law.

   Dignum est was widely published and some of its provisions made their
way into secular law codes. For example, *Las Siete Partidas* of King Alfonso
the Learned of Castile, codified about 1265, included the provision that
slaves may marry. "Slaves can marry one another and although their masters
oppose it, the marriage will be valid," stated the law; "They must still serve
their masters but they cannot be sold, one in one country and one in
another, or they become free."[58] On this still-contested issue Alfonso's
provisions took a firm stand in favor of the rights of the unfree. It was this
stand in particular that prompted Frank Tannenbaum to argue that slavery
practiced by Iberian societies settled in the New World had been modified
and was therefore milder than North American slavery, where the laws of
slavery were taken directly from Roman law precedent.[59] Tannenbaum has
been sharply criticized for this — not on his reading of Iberian law, but
rather on the grounds that slavery on Brazilian and Spanish plantations in
the New World was every bit as harsh as on French and English ones.[60]
Nevertheless the moderating influence of the canon law of marriage on the
institution of chattel slavery had long-term implications. In Catholic South
and Central American towns — that is, wherever practicable — slaves took

advantage of the right to cohabit as it was explained to them by priests, and they lived outside the households of their masters, remarrying almost immediately on the loss of a spouse in order to perpetuate their privilege. This well-known deviation from the general practice of slavery in the New World was a strictly limited right that too stemmed from the later medieval discourse about the unfree in canon law. Living as man and wife did not imply parental rights over offspring, at least when the unfree wife was an ancilla; her children belonged to her master.

Commentary in the law and confessional literature continued to employ the term ancilla for female slave, and this was true in both civil and canon law. In the instance of a valid marriage (recognized in canon law) contracted by a servus with an ancilla, or for that matter a marriage contracted by a poor man of a greater degree of freedom with an ancilla, the condition of the offspring still followed that of the mother. Very possibly canon lawyers hesitated before compromising a master's property rights over his ancilla. This fact was likely the reason for the failure of a positive ruling on parental rights for female slaves — that is, a ruling more in keeping with the church's general understanding of rights in a valid marriage.

As a result the rights of a free man married to an unfree woman had not changed significantly over time. If the free party — that is, the husband — understood and consented to marriage with an unfree woman, the marriage was valid. However, legal opinion in canon law, in later penitentials, in secular law codes, and in *repertorium* (reference books) that served as guides for students of both ecclesiastical and secular law the old principle remained: children followed the condition of their mother. A man, unfree or free, marrying an ancilla, gained the limited right of cohabiting with his wife; he did not gain full parental rights over his children any more than did his enslaved wife. Under these circumstances, would any man wish to marry an ancilla?

It is useful at this juncture to turn to one of the great legal repertorium of the later Middle Ages, Giovanni Bertachini's *Repertorium Iuris Utriusque* in three volumes, which was composed and dedicated to Pope Sixtus IV in 1481.[61] Bertachini's definitions were precise: *Servuus meum est qui natus est de ancilla mea* [whoever is born of my female slave is my slave] or by the same principle, *Servuus ascriptitius & censitus sequuntur conditionem matris* [both *ascriptitius* and *censitus* servants follow the condition of the mother]. Rights won by any designated group like these would then pertain to that group only by a principle of descent. As for an ancilla, children born to her still belonged to her master. Neither the phrasing nor the principle of descent had deviated significantly over the long centuries of the medieval era on this issue; therefore an ancilla gained no parental rights through marriage.

Conclusion

In law, in custom, in daily routine, and over a life's course a single condition determined life for the ancilla. An irony of slavery for women in the later Middle Ages was that even valid, but qualified, marriage did not alter these conditions.

Orenetta lived out her life as a slave of the household in the fourteenth century. Insofar as the record shows no priest explained the right to valid marriage to Orenetta, although the Datini household had a spiritual advisor in Fra Giovanni Dominici. Francesco de Marco Datini left a bequest to doctors of theology and canon law in his will, so he knew something about church law himself.[62] And if priests had advised Orenetta, would it have made a difference? Who would want to marry her? Perhaps a male slave could profit from marrying, especially if he could find a free woman who would marry him. Then, his offspring would not suffer the "taint" of slavery. But Orenetta's offspring belonged to her owners whether she learned of her right to marry or not. To move ahead in the story to 1410, Francesco Datini freed all his slaves at his death "in whatever part of the world they may be, restoring them to their original freedom."[63] Because she was not too old or infirm to enjoy it, Orenetta may have had some years of freedom in her later life, but it required a specific act of manumission for her to gain this right. As an older illiterate woman, her story is simply missing from the records of history.

Singlewomen slaves have left only a faint trace in our histories. Aside from a few Tartar, Greek, and Slavic names and a few verses in *linguaggio di schiave*, slaves working in Italy's households left almost no mark.[64] The same is true of other port cities like Barcelona and Valencia, and the islands of the Mediterranean. In matter of fact, historians' neglect of the institution's survival through the Middle Ages may be attributed to the fact that the traces left are few and difficult to find. But these female slaves are largely responsible for changing the name of the institution itself to "slavery."[65] And while society remained firm in its conviction that singlewomen slaves passed on their servile status to their offspring, slavery, as an institution, might persist.

The seaborne migration of singlewoman slaves into western Europe anticipated the larger seaborne migration of the sixteenth century across the Atlantic Ocean. In fact Mediterranean slaves, men and women alike, were employed on the plantations of Crete and other islands, a dress rehearsal, so to speak, for their introduction onto the plantations of the New World.[66] And domestic slavery in medieval households played its own instructive role for the early modern spread of slavery. Slaves in medieval households were rendered compliant through effective controls: they served cheaply and well. Thus this slave corps, composed chiefly of singlewomen, provided a compelling model for others who later used the plantation household as the locus of both commerce and production.

Notes

1. Susan Cotts Watkins, "Spinsters," *Journal of Family History* 9, 4 (1984): 310–25.

2. Error of condition was defined in canon law and generally referred to an unfree condition that stood as an impediment to marriage or ordination. See *Corpus juris civilis*, ed. Emil Friedberg (Leipzig: Tauschnitz, 1922), vol. 1, col. 1093, C. 29, q. 2, c. 2; vol. 1, col. 1123, C. 32, q. 2, q. 11–12.

3. Charles Verlinden, *L'esclavage dans l'Europe médiévale*, 2 vols. (Bruges and Ghent: De Tempel, 1955–77).

4. Verlinden, *L'esclavage dans l'Europe médiévale*, vol. 1. See also Stuard, "Urban Domestic Slavery," *Journal of Medieval History* 9 (1983): 160–67.

5. If slaves were not Christian, their new masters were obligated to have them baptized.

6. John Gilchrist, "The Medieval Canon Law of Unfree Persons," *Studia Gratiana* 19–20 (1976): 278, n. 11. See also Peter Landau, "Hadrianus IV: Decretale '*Dignum est*' (X. 4.9.1) und die Eheschliessung Unfreier in der Diskussion von Kanonisten und Theologen des 12. und 13. Jahrhunderts," *Studia Gratiana* 12 (1967): 511–63.

7. Iris Origo, *The Merchant of Prato* (New York: Knopf, 1957), 206. Origo noted it was not unusual for slaves to be this young. She turned attention to the issue of domestic slavery well before others recognized its importance, and was pleased to see it "addressed again" before her death in the 1980s (personal correspondence, Iris Origo, April 1984). The following useful example from her research in the Datini archives is included to honor her foresight.

8. *Archivio di Stato, Firenze*, Classe XI, Distr. 8, no. 81, cited in Origo, *The Merchant of Prato*, 206 n. 4.

9. Stuard, "Urban Domestic Slavery in Medieval Ragusa," 155–71. Important studies of slavery in the Adriatic are Gregor Čremošnik, "Pravni položaj našeg robilja u sredjem veku" [Legal Position of Our Laborers in the Middle Ages], *Zemaljiski Muzej u Bosni i Hercegovini Glasnik* n.s. 2 (1947): 69–73, and "Izvori za

istoriju robilja i servijalnih odnosa u našim zemljama sr. vijeka" [Evidence for the History of Laborers and Servants in the Medieval World], *Istoriski Pravni Zbornik* 1 (1949): 146–52. See also A. Teja, "La schiavitu domestica ed il traffico degli schiavi," *Rivista Dalmatica* 22 (1941): 33–44; and A. Tenenti, "Gli schiavi di Venezia alla fine del cinquecento," *Rivista Storica Italiana* 67 (1955): 52–69.

10. Charles Verlinden, "Orthodoxie et esclavage au bas moyen âge," *Melanges Eugene Tiserant, Studi e Testi* 235 (1964): 428.

11. As a system for rendering labor, slavery differs from wage labor. An owner pays for a slave "up front" and must recover that cost through labor over a lifetime. Also, slaves must be fed, clothed, and housed regardless of productivity. For these reasons the challenge in making slave labor economically profitable lies in using it as intensively as possible. For domestic slaves that meant using slaves in piecework for production or domestic work in an alternate pattern depending on need. By contrast if one hires day wage laborers and there is not enough work to fill the day, one still needs to pay them; hence, the investment is not profitable.

12. This argument follows the line established in studies of great noble households where retinues of men served at table and prepared food. Women assigned such tasks constitutes a shift that may be dated to the later Middle Ages, although of course regional differences in sexual division of labor exist. See Joseph and Frances Gies, *Life in a Medieval Castle* (New York: Crowell, 1974), 95–124. See also Pierre Riché, *Daily Life in the World of Charlemagne*, trans. JoAnn McNamara (Philadelphia: University of Pennsylvania Press, 1978), 100.

13. Cf. Drew Gilpin Faust, "'Trying to Do a Man's Business': Slavery, Violence, and Gender in the American Civil War," *Gender and History* 4 (1992): 197–214, which covers the experience of Lizzie Neblett during the Civil War when she was left to manage a farm and male slaves for two years.

14. Stuard, "Urban Domestic Slavery in Medieval Ragusa," 170. But punishment of slaves could be harsh and include beating, maiming, and assignment to harder labor.

15. At Genoa, Tartar or Black Sea slaves were often baptized before they were allowed to serve in Christian households. In Adriatic towns this was far less common, suggesting that slaves imported from the West Balkans were understood to be Christian in at least some formal sense.

16. Origo, *The Merchant of Prato*, 206.

17. Ignacij Voye, "Bencius del Buono," *Istorijski Časopis* 19 (1971): 189–99.

18. Christiane Klapisch-Zuber, "Childhood in Tuscany," in *Women, Family and Ritual in Renaissance Florence*, trans. Lydia Cochrane (Chicago: University of Chicago Press, 1985), 107; also "Female Celibacy and Service in Florence in the Fifteenth Century," 165–77. See also Klapisch-Zuber, "Women Servants in Florence during the Fourteenth and Fifteenth Centuries," trans. Nancy Elizabeth Mitchell, in *Women and Work in Preindustrial Europe*, ed. Barbara Hanawalt (Bloomington: Indiana University Press, 1986), 56–80.

19. Gilchrist, "The Medieval Canon Law on Unfree Persons," 289–94. A serf (*originarius*) has right over a daughter in contrast to a *famulus*, or a slave who does not. Here, as elsewhere, the terminology is not consistent.

20. Cited by Elizabeth Fox-Genovese, "Ghosts and Memories, The Legacy of Slavery in Women's Imaginings," Anna Howard Shaw Symposium, Bryn Mawr College, February 16, 1991.

21. Origo, "The Domestic Enemy," *Speculum* 30 (1955): 326–44. Origo cites (Prato) *Archivio Datini*, File 1142, but the date, September 1400, is supplied by another letter about the same goods.

22. Origo, "The Domestic Enemy," 336–40.

23. Clifford R. Backman, *The Decline and Fall of Medieval Sicily* (Cambridge: Cambridge University Press, 1995), 255–56.

24. While almost 90% of local slave sales specified women, there were always some males within the urban slave population. Servi ran away more often than ancillae. Over half the fugitive slaves advertised for capture in early fourteenth-century Ragusa were male, whereas the great preponderance of the enslaved were female (Stuard, "Urban Domestic Slavery," 155–58).

25. See Dennis Romano, "The Gondola as a Marker of Station in Venetian Society," *Renaissance Studies* 8, 4 (1994): 359–74.

26. Stuard, "Urban Domestic Slavery," 165–66.

27. See Richard Hoffman, "Outsiders by Birth and Blood: Racist Ideologies and Realities Around the Periphery of Medieval Culture," *Studies in Medieval and Renaissance History* n.s. 6 (1983): 14–20. It is perhaps more than a coincidence that these same "frontiers" practiced slavery and understood that inheritance conveyed unfree status.

28. Heath Dillard, *Daughters of the Reconquest* (Cambridge: Cambridge University Press, 1984), 98, 154, and 207–8.

29. Ruth Karras, *Slavery and Society in Medieval Scandinavia* (New Haven, Conn.: Yale University Press, 1983), 21, 26, 31–32, 70, 91, 94, 129, and 146–47.

30. *Fr. 985, Pismo Kneza crnomira Knezu i Opcini Dubrovačkoj*, Dubrovnik State Archives [Fragment 985, Letter of Prince Crnomir to the Ruler and Community of Dubrovnik], published in L. Stojanović, *Acta srpske opovelje i pisma* (Serbian Charters and Letters) (Belgrade: SAN, 1929), doc. 25, pp. 23–24.

31. Stuard, "Urban Domestic Slavery," 157.

32. Malcolm Burr, "The Code of Stefan Dušan," *Slavonic and East European Review* 28 (1949–50): 380–81. Serbs as well as Greeks were enslaved, however; see Verlinden, "Orthodoxie et esclavage," 427–56, and "Recruitment des esclaves à Venise aux XIV et XV siècles," *Institut Historique Belge de Rome* 34 (1968): 83–202.

33. *Kotorski spomenici, god. 1326–35* (Commemoration Volume for Kotor for 1326–35), ed. Antun Mayer (Zagreb: JAZU, 1951), doc. 171, p. 72; doc. 1019, p. 343.

34. A. Tenenti, "Gli schiavi di Venezia alla fine de cinquecento," *Rivista Storica Italiana* 67 (1955): 52–69.

35. David Herlihy, *Opera Muliebria: Women and Work in Medieval Europe* (Philadelphia: Temple University Press, 1990), 80–94, emphasizes the reputation for licentiousness that surrounded *gynaecea*. Herlihy believed this reputation rested on the fact that gynaecea contained the only concentration of adult unmarried women outside convents in the early and central Middle Ages. Georges Duby

strikes the same chord in discussing humble women servants in great feudal households who provided a sexual outlet for "youth," that is, nobly born bachelors (Georges Duby, *Love and Marriage in the Middle Ages*, trans. Jane Dunnett [Chicago: University of Chicago Press, 1994], 22–35, 59–60). See also Michael Goodich, "*Ancilla Dei*: The Servant as Saint in the Late Middle Ages," in *Women of the Medieval World*, ed. Suzanne Wemple and Julius Kirschner (Oxford: Blackwell, 1985), 122–23.

36. Susan Mosher Stuard, "Ancillary Evidence for the Decline of Medieval Slavery," *Past and Present* 149 (1995): 3–28.

37. John Gilchrist, "The Medieval Canon Law on Unfree Persons," 283 and n. 38, citing *Gl. Palat.* (fol. 51 vb.) ad C. 12, q. 2, c. 68.

38. *"Aut meretriccem, aut ancillam, vel aliquam de his"* (*Corpus Iuris canonici*, ed. Emil Freidberg, 2 vols. [Leipzig: Tauschnitz, 1911] vol. 1, col. 129; *Decretum* pt. 1, *dist.* 34, c. 15).

39. Ibid., vol. 1, col. 288, dist. 81, c. 30, *"ancillarum suarum."*

40. Ibid., vol. 1, col. 760, causa 15, q. 8, c. 3, *"vel ex ancillae."*

41. *Monumenta Germaniae Historica, Diplomatum Regum et Imperatorum Germaniae*, V, pt. 2, ed. P. Kehr (Berlin: Weidmann, 1931), doc. 253, pp. 336–37, 16 July 1050; trans. O. J. Thatcher and E. H. McNeal, *A Source Book for Medieval History* (New York: Charles Scribners, 1905), 547–48.

42. For example, on royal manumissions in France see Pierre Bonnassie, *From Slavery to Feudalism* (Cambridge: Cambridge University Press, 1991), 56–57. Bonnassie cites the researches of Veronique Sablayrolles, "De l'esclavage au servage, de Louis le Pieux à Philippe Ier. d'après les actes royaux," University of Toulouse-Le Mirail, *Mémoire de maîtrise*, 1982, for the table he presents here. Marc Bloch, "How and Why Ancient Slavery Came to an End," in *Slavery and Serfdom in the Middle Ages*, trans. and ed. William R. Beer (Berkeley: University of California Press, 1975), 1–31, casts the issue in the masculine, as indeed do Pierre Bonnassie and the authors of many regional studies. For canon law favoring the manumission of unfree persons marrying outside a lord's holdings, see Gilchrist, "The Medieval Canon Law on Unfree Persons," 285, 290–93.

43. Compare the evidence offered in Paul Freedman, *The Origins of Peasant Servitude in Medieval Catalonia* (Cambridge: Cambridge University Press, 1991), app. 4, pp. 227–30. This series of redemptions from serfdom in the Diocese of Girona between 1200–1282 favors women over men. However, a number of these are nominal sums for redemption to marry outside the lord's jurisdiction (ibid., 132–33). Presumably a lord gained as well as lost in this kind of transaction.

44. For example, *Die Gesetz der Langobarden*, 3, c. 221; trans. Katherine Fischer Drew, *The Lombard Laws* (Philadelphia: University of Pennsylvania Press, 1973), no. 221, p. 95. See also Gilchrist, "The Medieval Canon Law on Unfree Persons," 276–92, for examples from the central Middle Ages and later times.

45. Dubrovnik State Archives, *Lamenta de Intus*, 1404–7, 4/15/1406, f. 181v. Famulae were slaves in most instances in Ragusa/Dubrovnik, but the term is imprecise and it may cover free and unfree servants in other contexts. It means, simply, family servant.

46. Michel Balard, "La femme-esclave à Gênes à la fin du Moyen Age," in *La femme au Moyen-âge*, ed. Michel Rouché and Jean Heuclin (Ville de Maubeuge, 1990), 306.

47. Dubrovnik State Archives, *Testamenta* [Wills], V, f. 41v.

48. In Ragusa/Dubrovnik while enslaved persons were overwhelmingly female, the majority of fugitives or runaways were male suggesting that enslaved males escaped slavery more successfully than female slaves (Stuard, "Urban Domestic Slavery," 163).

49. Some evidence of property owning exists where slaves "purchased" their own freedom (Stuard, "Urban Domestic Slavery," 168; Michel Balard, "La femme-esclave à Gênes," 306–8; and Origo, "Domestic Enemies: Eastern Slaves in Tuscany in the Fourteenth and Fifteenth Centuries," *Speculum* 30 (1955): 351).

50. See Paul Freedman, "The German and Catalan Peasant Revolts," *American Historical Review* 98, 1 (1993): 39–53.

51. *Decretales* X.4.9.3 in *Corpus Juris Canonici*, vol. 2, col. 691–93.

52. See Gilchrist, "Medieval Canon Law on Unfree Persons," 294, for a full discussion. Gilchrist interpreted the *Glossa Ordinaria*'s impact to bring rights to serfs: "in the matter of marriage, times have changed, the serf now has freedom to marry without the consent of his lord, thus only the father and no one else may exercise authority over the daughter." This refers to a serf, however, not a slave.

53. See Charles Verlinden, "Le 'mariage' des esclaves," in *Il matrimonio nella società altro medievale* (Spoleto: Centro Italiano di Studi sull'Altro Medioevo, 1977) 2: 569–601.

54. Michael Sheehan, "Marriage of the Unfree and the Poor," *Mediaeval Studies* 50 (1988): 477.

55. Gregory IX, *Decretales* X.4.c.9 in *Corpus Juris Canonici*, vol. 2, col. 691–93.

56. Thomas of Chobham, *Summa confessorum*, ed. F. Broomfield (Louvain: Editions Nauwelaers, 1968) 7.2.16; 177.

57. James Brundage, *Law, Sex, and Christian Society* (Chicago: University of Chicago Press, 1987), 360–61. See also Landau, "Hadrianus IV," 511–53.

58. *Las siete partidas*, trans. S. P. Scott (Chicago: American Bar Association, 1931), Tit. 5, 1, in pt. 2, p. 901.

59. Frank Tannenbaum, *Slave and Citizen* (New York: Knopf, 1946), 48.

60. Carl Degler, *Neither Black Nor White* (New York: Macmillan, 1971); G. R. Andrews, *Blacks and Whites in Sao Paulo, Brazil, 1888–1988* (Madison: University of Wisconsin Press, 1991); Orlando Patterson, *Slavery and Social Death* (Cambridge: Cambridge University Press, 1982).

61. Giovanni Bertachini, *Repertorium Iuris Utriusque* (Venice: Arrivabene, 1494) III, fol. 183v, ra 1.

62. Origo, *The Merchant of Prato*, 386.

63. Ibid.

64. Mario Ferrara, "Linguaggio di schiave nel quattrocento," *Studi di Fiologia Italiana, Bullettino Accademia della Crusca* 8 (1950): 320–28. Tartar female names used in Italy: Cotlu, Jamanzach, Tholon, Charactas, Aycholu, Bollaza.

65. Ragusa/Dubrovnik, *Liber statutorum*, ed. V. Bogišić and C. Jireček (Za-

greb: JAZU, 1909) 1, c. 14. There are German counterclaims to the first use of *slavi* as slave; however, this thirteenth-century example from the Adriatic region made the precise designation of slavi as slave because it was used in statute law defining slave status.

66. Charles Verlinden, "La Crête débouché et plague tournante de la traité des esclaves au XIV^c et XV^c siècles," in *Studi in onore di Amintore Fanfani* (Milan: Guiffre, 1962), 594–699.

5

Sex and the Singlewoman

Ruth Mazo Karras

IN HER 1962 CLASSIC *Sex and the Single Girl*, Helen Gurley Brown, later editor of *Cosmopolitan* and creator of the "Cosmo Girl," urged unmarried women to have not just jobs but careers, on the grounds that "a married woman already *is* something. . . . Whatever hardships she endures in marriage, one of them is *not* that she doesn't have a place in life."[1] This theme — the lack of social space or social identity for the singlewoman — has been taken up for the medieval and early modern periods by many of the other essays in this volume. In explaining that women could be happy while single, however, Brown also had to face the scandalous issue of sexuality. She wrote that "theoretically, a 'nice' single woman has no sex life."[2] Brown went on to dispute that claim in an eloquent, albeit hardly protofeminist, plea for the advantages (at least temporary) of the unmarried state to a woman and the enjoyable nature of sex unconstrained by the bounds of matrimony.

Like her statement about women's social identity, Brown's observation about society's expectations of singlewomen's sexuality could apply equally well to medieval Europe as to postwar United States. In medieval Europe with its strict classification of women as virgins, wives, and widows, any woman who did not fit into one of the three categories risked being equated with members of the only identifiable, demarcated group that did not fit: prostitutes. Was there in practice any cultural space in the Middle Ages, as Brown claimed there was in practice in the 1960s, for the sexual activity of singlewomen other than prostitutes? The short answer is undoubtedly yes. But it is not possible to know very much more than that, for we have only rare traces of singlewomen as sexual subjects rather than objects.[3]

Medieval singlewomen certainly did have sex just as Helen Gurley Brown urged her readers to do. Like Brown's readers, they did so despite —

or in resistance against—the social norms they were taught. Also like the Cosmo Girls, they did so in part because of their own desires and in part because of what they hoped to gain from men (in many cases, marriage). However, both medieval and modern commentators have been at pains to suppress the fact of medieval singlewomen's heterosexual activity by limiting it to sex for money. Medieval writers emphasized the seriousness of the singlewomen's sin by attributing it to greed as well as lust, while modern authors emphasize the singlewomen's agency and respectability by treating their sexual activity as work. While modern historians' views of medieval singlewomen and their sexuality have an effect only on modern readers, the views of medieval commentators had serious consequences for the singlewomen themselves. The confusion of all heterosexual activity by singlewomen with prostitution has left a gap in the historical record, preventing us from knowing much about their noncommercial sexual activity.

The erasure of women's sexuality from the historical record has already been remarked on with regard to same-sex relations. As Ann Matter has noted, we have many medieval examples of passionate friendships among women (most often within a monastic context), but these were not considered to be sexually problematic. Moral theologians did not pay much attention to the question of what we would today call lesbian sex, perhaps because anything that did not involve a phallus did not fall within the bounds of their understanding of the sexual. They were concerned mainly with the usurpation of masculine roles.[4] Some legislation against lesbian relations can be adduced for the period, but there are remarkably few cases of its enforcement, and in any case it mainly involves the use of "instruments," in other words dildoes.[5] There are other clues to the existence of same-sex erotic practices—for example, in discussions of midwives palpating the genital region[6]—but these were not discussed by moralists focusing on sexual behavior. Lesbian sex simply did not count.

Nor did voluntary, noncommercial heterosexual activity on the part of singlewomen count; it had to be reclassified as prostitution. Where same-sex activity was irrelevant to men's control over women, independent heterosexual activity threatened that control. Rather than simply ignoring it, medieval men had to explain it away. Or rather, they had to define it away, by using language that placed it in a received category of sexual sin. Any sex act involving a woman and a man not her husband might put her at risk for identification; simple fornication, especially as a prelude to marriage, might not be regarded as severely in practice as it was in theory, but popular medieval conceptual schemes still equated it with prostitution.

Pastoral literature, which flourished all over Europe in the thirteenth through fifteenth centuries, analyzed sexual sin extensively. It translated the views of the moral theologians into terms intended for the laity. Most of the treatises, whether organized around the Ten Commandments, the Seven Deadly Sins, or some other scheme, listed sexual offenses and ranked them in order of seriousness. "Simple fornication" was generally the least of the sins, and where it was defined it was said to be sexual relations between an unmarried man and an unmarried woman. This definition implies some degree of recognition of singlewomen (and widows) as sexual beings, but within this context of a catalog of sins, it is not surprising that the recognition was an exclusively negative one.

Where the texts went into more detail about fornication, listing the possible partners with whom the sin might be committed, it becomes clear that the sexually active singlewoman was viewed in quite narrow terms — indeed, defined as a prostitute. The *Fasciculus Morum*, for example, a fourteenth-century English compendium of exempla and other pastoralia, defined fornication as follows: "[W]hile fornication is any forbidden sexual intercourse, it particularly refers to intercourse with widows, prostitutes, or concubines. But the term 'prostitute' must be applied only to those women who give themselves to anyone and will refuse none, and that for monetary gain."[7] The translator has rendered the term *meretrix* here as "prostitute" because of the specification about commerce. It had a more generalized meaning, closer to the semantic field of the contemporary "whore."[8] Here, though, the author makes clear that he has a commercial prostitute in mind. The *Fasciculus* also includes categories for adultery and the defloration of a virgin, but there is no place for a singlewoman who is no longer a virgin.[9] The only category for her is either concubine, a term that indicates the domestic partner of a priest, or meretrix, which would conflate her with the commercial prostitute.

Whereas pastoral literature concentrates on the moral implications of singlewomen's heterosexual activity, other sources treat it less judgmentally. Unmarried women of unfree status who became pregnant, for example, had to pay a fine to their lord, and the prevalence of these fines can be read as an indication of the practical acceptability of sex outside of marriage.[10] The fines were levied as a fiscal mechanism for the lords rather than as a penalty for sin. The fact that such sexual activity took place frequently, however, does not mean that it was acceptable. One might think of more modern contexts in which heterosexual activity is common, and acceptable for the men engaged in it, but considered to reflect poorly on the moral character or the psychological makeup of the women.[11] Within particular communities or subcultures nonmarital sexual activity might be acceptable — "sexual nonconformism" and "bastardy prone sub-society" are terms early modern historians have used — but even within those communities sexually active women might be suspect. As the demographer Peter Laslett put it, "breaches of social rules do not necessarily weaken those rules, and under certain circumstances can even serve to strengthen them."[12]

Singlewomen, and the communities around them, may well have rejected the normative teachings of church and society about their sexual behavior. It is this nonconformity that allows us occasional glimpses of sexual activity that was not denigrated as commercial or sinful or both. However, such understandings went against the dominant currents in medieval culture. Even when laypeople considered fornication so routine as to be only a venial sin (a position the church vehemently rejected), the prevalent sexual double standard made it far less serious for men than for women.[13] Manorial courts levied leyrwite, a fine for fornication, on women rather than on men, in part because it was often a pregnancy that called it to the courts' attention, but it still shows that women's fornication was considered more significant than men's.

Was the conflation of heterosexually active singlewomen with prostitutes just a way of slandering women whose behavior did not meet society's standard, or was it evidence of a real lack of conceptual distinction within the culture? It cannot have been entirely the latter: people would have been able to say who were practicing commercial prostitutes and who were not, and there were practical if not theoretical consequences to the distinction. Nor, however, was it entirely the former. The verbal equation was based on a fundamental denial of independent, noncommercial sexual activity on the part of singlewomen.

The conflation of heterosexually active singlewomen with prostitutes is not unique to the Middle Ages. The word "whore" today is used to mean both "prostitute" and "promiscuous woman," and indicates a conceptual overlap between the two, but we also have the more technical term "prostitute" to use when we wish specifically to denote one who engages in commercial sex. The Latin term meretrix, with approximately the same semantic field as "whore," was the most technical term available, demonstrating how language used for any sexually active woman in the Middle Ages overlapped with that used for commercial prostitutes. The distinction made today (although not always consistently) between "pros" and amateurs was not made in the Middle Ages. The church courts of the diocese of

London in the fifteenth century illustrate the fuzziness of the categories. A woman could be presented either for fornication or for being a meretrix; a clear distinction existed between the two. But the distinction was not based on the presence of financial exchange. Payment could be taken as evidence that a woman was a meretrix, as with a case in which Margaret Weston was accused "by the token that she received a penny for her labor." But other women were accused as meretrices for having sex with priests. A number of those accused as meretrices had borne children whose fathers were named, unlikely if they were really commercial prostitutes with numerous customers.[14] The term meretrix meant a woman engaged in some sort of sexual behavior that was considered especially scandalous, and any unmarried woman could fall into that category whether or not she sought or took money for the sexual activity. The conceptual overlap between any heterosexual activity by a singlewoman and commercial activity was thus considerable.

Indeed, by the sixteenth century in England, "singlewoman" could be used as a semantic equivalent for "prostitute." In Southwark, just across the Thames from the City of London, where legally condoned prostitution continued until 1547, a fifteenth-century set of customs proclaimed that the lack of regulation had led to "the great multiplication of horrible sin upon the single women."[15] Sixteenth-century legal records accuse men of committing adultery "with a certain singlewoman" in one of the Southwark brothels, refer to a "common woman of her body" whose by-name was "Singlewoman," and report the dunking in the Thames of two women for being "singlewomen." John Stow's late Tudor chronicle of London refers to the prostitutes of the Stews as "single women" and describes the "single womans churchyard" where they were buried. A sixteenth-century ordinance about prostitutes was recorded in the Repertory Book of the London Court of Aldermen with the marginal notation "Singlewomen."[16] "Single woman" was also used in these same records to refer to never-married women when their sexual behavior was not in question; it was not always a euphemism for "prostitute." It was used to refer to them frequently enough, however, to demonstrate a clear linkage.

The linkage between heterosexually active singlewomen generally and commercial prostitutes did not mean that all singlewomen were prostitutes, nor that none of them were. Commercial prostitution did exist, practiced by wives and widows as well as singlewomen. Many towns in medieval Europe had licensed brothels, where prostitution was condoned.[17] In this situation, an official list of prostitutes would be created, and there can be no question to a historian of the validity of classifying as a prostitute a woman who was employed as such in a municipal brothel. One might expect that the existence of a class of official prostitutes would lead to a clear understanding of who did and who did not fall into the category, as was the goal with nineteenth-century registration movements.[18] However, the existence of some official prostitutes did not mean the disappearance of "clandestine prostitutes"—that is, commercial prostitutes practicing on their own rather than in officially recognized brothels. And it is for these women that the lines blur. It is difficult to know how many of the women thus labeled in the extant sources were full-time professionals, how many were occasional prostitutes, and how many were simply heterosexually active women with no commercial involvement. We must not lose sight of the fact that a number of singlewomen did in fact practice prostitution at least occasionally.

In many respects, widows occupied the same social position as singlewomen, and if heterosexually active were referred to as meretrices (whores) in the same way as singlewomen. Yet the confusion of categories does not seem to have affected them as significantly. The widow was not as problematic as the singlewoman; medieval society recognized her existence and allowed her a space, even if not always an entirely respectable one.[19] Even the *Fasciculus Morum* allows for the possibility of heterosexually active widows who are not meretrices. Whereas singlewomen were out of place for not marrying, widows had performed that obligation—indeed, the church frowned upon, though it did not prohibit, their remarriage.[20] Their independence and their morals might be suspect like those of singlewomen, but they were not as anomalous.

The anomalousness of singlewomen put them in a position where their heterosexual activity could easily—sometimes deliberately—be confused with prostitution. The legend of the sacristan, a popular miracle of the Virgin that appears in many European vernaculars, reflects the failure to draw a sharp line. In this legend, a nun leaves her convent out of lust for a lover; he later abandons her. In several versions of the story, she is described as living an evil life, or more specifically as living with a lover and bearing him children. In other texts, however, she is described as turning to prostitution in order to support herself after her lover abandons her.[21] In English texts at least, later texts have the second version of the story.[22] There is a certain plausibility in this shift: a former nun, abandoned by the man she hoped would support her, would be unlikely to have the skills or connections she would need to earn a living in another way. Yet we also see here a slippage between the categories of unchaste woman and prostitute: if she was no longer a nun, but was not married, there was no other way to think about her. The contrast between the nun and the prostitute certainly created a dramatic contrast to emphasize the moral message, but it was also indicative of a pervasive way of thinking about women.

The stories of saints who were former prostitutes, so popular in the Middle Ages, illustrate this same slippage. There were a number of these saints, and their stories were popular in both Latin and vernacular versions: Mary of Egypt, Mary the Harlot, Pelagia, Thaïs.[23] The preeminent repentant saint, of course, was Mary Magdalen. The Magdalen became the patron saint of repentant prostitutes; shelters for them took her name. The medieval stories about her all identify her with the "sinful woman" of Luke 7:37, and all assume that her unnamed sin was sexual, although it is very rare that they represent her as a prostitute in the commercial sense. In the fifteenth-century Arras Passion, for example, she explicitly repudiates financial gain:

Here is my body which I present
To anyone who wants to have it.
I don't want to sell it,
I don't want to have gold or silver,
Let each one do his will with it.[24]

Many of the texts also stress the Magdalen's social standing: she is a woman of good birth and of riches, needing no money from her lovers. Yet because there was no conceptual space for a singlewoman who was heterosexually active, she became identified with prostitutes.

This suspicion of singlewomen, especially heterosexually active ones, is illustrated for a very different social group — working women — in a fifteenth-century German text, "Stepmother and Daughter," also known in some manuscripts as "How a Mother Teaches her Daughter Whoring."[25] The story describes an older woman training a younger one in the entrapment of men. The terms of the account do not envision commercial prostitution of the sort practiced in fifteenth-century German towns with their official brothels,[26] but clearly a financial element is involved: the younger woman is to expect gifts of cash or apparel, or long-term maintenance, in return for her sexual activity. As Ann Marie Rasmussen points out, the women in the story are presented as typical working singlewomen of the town, who were always viewed with suspicion by the town fathers; indeed, Beate Schuster argues that in Germany by the end of the fifteenth century "the boundaries between prostitutes and unmarried, independent women had been obscured."[27] The poem is misogynous in the sense that it implies a sexual and financial greed on the part of all women (or at least all single-women), but on the other hand it also presents some element of women's redefinition of themselves. The older woman speaks of her daughter's "honor"; this might be ironic to someone who considered such a woman dishonored by definition, but it could indeed reflect such women's actual evaluation of their own activity. Both the character of the older woman and the advice to extract wealth from the lover are reminiscent of La Vieille in the *Roman de la Rose* and indeed a whole lineage of similar representation of older women, from Aphrodisia to La Celestina.[28]

These representations emphasize, indeed, the venality of all feminine sexuality, not only that of singlewomen. The message was that any woman could be bought: any unchaste woman was the equivalent of a prostitute. The effect was greater, however, for a singlewoman. Lacking a wifely iden-tity, she was more obviously in need of categorization. Further, a wife (or a nun) was subject to clear lines of authority: there was a man or a rule who was supposed to be in control, even if the woman had managed to escape that control. The singlewoman who was no longer living in her father's home lacked such an authority and was therefore a greater threat to social order; conflating her with a prostitute at least gave her a familiar identity and, depending on local regulations and their enforcement, a means for controlling her. If a singlewoman living in her father's or master's home was accused of prostitution, he was assumed to be in control, and could be accused of procuring or of brothelkeeping.

The venality of singlewomen as represented in literature had its roots in reality. Singlewomen needed money. As other chapters in this book indicate, they worked in poorly paid crafts and it was only the exceptions who became wealthy. Thus, it is only to be expected that they would seek gifts from lovers. Kathy Peiss's work on "charity girls" and treating in the late nineteenth-century and early twentieth-century United States provides a model of what may have been going on. Working-class women commonly accepted gifts and treats from men they dated. This was the only way, given their wages and expenses, that they could afford the luxuries and amuse-ments offered in the nascent consumer society. When they had sex with the men, in more or less explicit return for the treating, they were known as "charity girls," and reformers considered them not much different from "occasional prostitutes" who accepted cash. For the women themselves, however, the meaning was quite different.[29] Joanne Meyerowitz notes, for the same time period, that among singlewomen in Chicago, "The higher wages of men, plus the social sanction given to a courtship in which a man plied a woman with gifts, encouraged forms of dependence that fell somewhere between professional prostitution and marriage."[30]

Medieval singlewomen, of course, did not have available to them the same range of luxuries and amusements as did modern ones, but gift exchange was still an important part of courtship. Indeed, material considerations were a major part of medieval marriage generally, and both men and women seeking to marry could well be considered venal. The exchange of gifts — if not the property arrangements that would be part of a marriage contract among the better-off — risked confusion with prostitution. In one case brought before the bishop of London's Consistory Court in 1470, a woman testified that she and her sexual partner had exchanged gifts, which she had understood as being signs of betrothal. He, on the other hand, acknowledged having given her gifts of knives, gloves, and cash, but said that they were given not with the intent of marriage but "so she would continue with him in sin."[31] Perhaps he was indeed deliberately misleading her, but the case indicates that the same sorts of gifts were used as steps towards marriage and as the price of sex with a prostitute. These circumstances reinforced the association of heterosexually active singlewomen or widows with prostitution. Even in the case of a relationship apparently leading to marriage, the association might be made.

The confusion between courting gifts and prostitutes' fees did not happen among the aristocracy. As one would expect, the conflation of the heterosexually active singlewoman with the prostitute operated more strongly at lower than at higher social levels. Poorer women were more likely to turn to prostitution for economic reasons. In addition, the definition of sexual categories was, in medieval European society as in so many others, one of the tools used by those in power to control others. Geoffrey Chaucer might have one of his pilgrims (the Manciple) note that the only difference between a woman "of high degree" who sins and a poor woman is one of terminology: he reminds the reader that "Men lay the one as low as lies the other,"[32] but in practice aristocratic women were less likely to be equated with prostitutes. This fact is not simply because such an equation would have been ludicrous for a wealthy woman; a real suspicion of commercial activity need not have been present for her to have been called a whore. Rather, it has to do with the reasons independent feminine sexual activity was suspect. The higher one looks in medieval society, the more closely monitored was the sexual activity of unmarried daughters, who could be an important commodity in the marriage market. Even when they

were not — when finding a dowry for yet another daughter could become a
drag on even a large fortune — the sexuality of daughters reflected on the
honor of fathers and brothers, and stigmatization of the woman took a back
seat to the seeking of revenge against her "seducer."[33]

This is not to say that aristocratic women's heterosexual activity was
not an issue in the Middle Ages. It certainly was, and indeed its extent
remains hotly debated today, but it did not mainly involve singlewomen.
Adultery was the sexual transgression commonly associated with aristocratic women, and most commonly represented in literature (even if scholars have questioned its acceptability in reality).[34] Where we do see heterosexually active aristocratic singlewomen, in literature or in documents
closer to actual practice, their transgression was not in wrongly using their
independence (of which they had a good deal less than women of other
social groups) but rather, in effect, in stealing one man's property in them
by transferring it to another man.[35]

Male aristocrats, in late medieval and Renaissance Italy at least, also
created a demand and hence an opportunity for one type of sexually active
singlewomen, who did to some extent operate on a commercial basis. The
courtesan was mainly an Italian phenomenon. Aristocratic men elsewhere
in medieval Europe were certainly involved in sexual liaisons, but the social
position of an Alice Perrers (the mistress of Edward III) or Katherine
Swynford (the mistress of John of Gaunt, mother of his Beaufort children
and ancestor of Henry VII) at the English court in the fourteenth century
was not the same as those of the famous courtesans of the seventeenth and
eighteenth centuries. The Italian courtesans were distinguished from common prostitutes largely through their selectivity: they were automatically
choosy because their price was high, but they also developed a reputation
for culture and preferring men of cultivated tastes.[36] Here too, however, a
sort of conflation might have been going on: a singlewoman who was the
lover of a particular aristocratic man would be considered a courtesan simply because the courtesans were a recognized class of women (a class that
could, if necessary, be denigrated as whores).

At higher as well as lower levels of society sexual practices were at odds
with the dominant moral code. Heterosexual relations outside of marriage
persisted despite anything the church — or individuals within the church —
the law, or secular literature said or did. Lawmakers or authors, within the
church or without, and their legal enactments and textual productions
could, however, deeply affect, if not control, the way society viewed the
women involved in those relations. That view was extremely negative, plac-

ing all the opprobrium on the woman. In addition to the consequences to those women, they also created consequences for modern historians in terms of the evidence they left us.

Modern scholars have collaborated with medieval sources in blurring the distinction between heterosexually active singlewomen and prostitutes.[37] Victorian attitudes tended to attribute prostitution to a moral defect common to all working-class women.[38] Even a relatively enlightened reformer like Abraham Flexner, who believed it was circumstances rather than innate defects that drove women to prostitution, wrote that "the seduced servant or shopgirl, or the pregnant country lass" may turn to prostitution because "in point of character, the girl has no longer anything to lose; meanwhile need presses."[39] Any heterosexually active singlewoman thus risked crossing the line. By the twentieth century, too, the medicalization of prostitution had proceeded far enough that prostitutes were seen as having psychological problems that brought them into the trade; this, too, they shared with other sexually active singlewomen.[40]

Historians long accepted these attitudes, whether they came from medieval sources or from modern reform movements. W. W. Sanger's influential *History of Prostitution*, for example, amounted to a history of what he termed "vice." In his chapters on medieval France and Britain, he discussed not only commercial prostitution but also *gynecaea*, concubinage, lewd manuscript illumination, the sodomy of the Templars, the *Roman de la Rose*, incubi and succubi, flagellation, bridal chambers, women's property ownership, incest, rape of nuns, brideprices, and royal mistresses.[41] He found prostitution in any sexual activity by women; like the fourteenth-century author of the *Fasciculus Morum*, he had no other category for the heterosexually active singlewoman. Nor was he the only historian to group singlewomen with prostitutes. Paul LaCroix, who published his massive *History of Prostitution* in 1852–54 under the name of Pierre Dufour, was a bit more careful in his scholarship but even so made similar assumptions: he claimed that a number of women named in the Paris *taille* of 1292 were prostitutes even though they are not labeled as such and "the majority of them were scattered among various kinds of trades." He apparently assumed this on the basis of their nicknames, which are not in fact unusual among working men and women, and on the basis that independent women must have been sexually immoral.[42]

These views more or less conflating all heterosexual activity outside marriage with prostitution grow from an attitude that lumps all such behavior together as immoral. But one can observe the same process occurring with historians who have very different sorts of agendas. In the case of historians who pioneered the study of the history of sexuality in the Middle Ages as a serious academic subject, for example, the inclusion of information on sexually active women generally in a discussion of prostitutes stemmed from a desire for comprehensiveness in the study: all pertinent evidence was to be included.[43] Other, less academic, historians have lumped all feminine sexuality together because they see women as having a robust heterosexual desire expressed both through prostitution and otherwise.[44]

The same conflation of heterosexually active singlewomen with prostitutes appears in the work of feminist historians. These historians begin from a position of not wanting to make moral judgments about women's sexual behavior in the past, and from a position of respect for women workers and their work. This respect occasionally leads them, however, to treat all nonmarital sex as work. In line with the strand of feminist thought that calls prostitutes "sex workers," attempting to eliminate judgmental language and treat their work like any other,[45] historians of several societies have examined prostitution from the point of view of women's agency. Asking why the women involved chose prostitution and what they got out of it, they focus on prostitution as one of a number of possible career choices for a singlewoman.[46] Feminist medievalists, too, have tended to emphasize the agency of female workers, including prostitutes. The conjunction of this respect for women's work and willingness to accept prostitutes as workers rather than as moral transgressors puts us at some risk for conflating heterosexually active singlewomen generally with prostitutes.

If a singlewoman was labeled a meretrix — or even if she was accused of fornication with multiple partners — we have tended to accept that she was a commercial prostitute, so that we may include her in an analysis of female workers. In my own *Common Women* I treated many women as prostitutes even though there were problems (noted in the book) with this identification. For example, in the records from York, I interpreted repeated accusations of fornication and adultery as pointing to prostitutes, and elsewhere I interpreted meretrices as prostitutes although the term meretrix did not always mean a prostitute in the modern sense.[47] Maryanne Kowaleski, in an important article on women's work in medieval Exeter, treats prostitutes as one of the occupational groups.[48] "Prostitute" here is a translation of "meretrix" in the Exeter records. Kowaleski assumes that women so labeled were commercial prostitutes, and that their inclusion along with other commercial offenses means that the fines for prostitution were de facto licensing fees like the fines for brewing and baking; I used this insight of hers in my work. Yet, we should be aware that this is simply an assumption. Fines for other, noncommercial offenses, such as assault or quarreling, are also found in the same records. Many of the meretrices were cited for sex with a specific man, although others were called *communes*. Are they commercial prostitutes, or are they unmarried women whose sexual activity posed a threat to the orderliness of the town? The likely answer is that they are both, but this hypothesis is by no means proven. Since Kowaleski's treatment of prostitutes is only a few paragraphs in a larger context of women's work, one could hardly expect her to go more deeply into the question, but it still remains.

Jeremy Goldberg, whose knowledge of the records of medieval Yorkshire and their application to women's history is unparalleled, has made similar assumptions. A main theme implicit in Goldberg's work is women's agency: that is, he assumes that when women married early or late, when they went into one job or another, they were making a choice. Prostitution was one of those choices, constrained of course by the range of other opportunities available. When Goldberg states in his chapter on "Women and Work" that from 1403 to 1432 Isabella Wakefield was "regularly presented as a prostitute, procuress, and brothelkeeper,"[49] he relies on sources that never use the word "meretrix." Rather, he deems repeated accusations of adultery and fornication the equivalent of accusations of prostitution.[50] Goldberg is quite probably right about Isabella Wakefield.[51] But the evidence is not unambiguous, and it is difficult for a historian to draw the line. We may deem Wakefield a prostitute because of repeated accusations of fornication and adultery; yet she also had a long-term lover, the priest Peter Byrde. Might that not be what got the authorities so upset about her? What about the singlewoman accused only one or two times: can we safely conclude either that she was a prostitute or that she was not?

These examples, taken from the work of historians that I respect greatly, illustrate the readiness of thoughtful, careful feminist historians to assume or accept that singlewomen's heterosexual activity is paid work. When historians focus on marriage and work, the heterosexually active singlewoman who is not seeking remuneration has disappeared. If we are too ready to equate heterosexually active singlewomen with prostitutes, we fall into the trap set for the singlewomen themselves by medieval moralists and municipal authorities.

If the heterosexual activity of singlewomen were only a taxonomic problem for historians, it might seem unimportant. People behaved as they behaved regardless of what historians choose to call it. However, if we wish to understand medieval culture, it matters a great deal whether we believe women were engaging in sexual behavior for economic, affective, or libidinous reasons. Not all singlewomen who had sex with men were rape victims or prostitutes (though of course some were). Given the nature of the sources that describe the sexuality and sexual behavior of singlewomen, we must treat any given incident or representation as falling within a range of options, rather than assuming from the language used that we can automatically know or categorize it.

While the medieval sources' conflation of heterosexual activity by singlewomen with prostitution creates problems for historians, it created the greatest problems, of course, for medieval singlewomen themselves. The association with prostitution worked to undercut the possibility of sexual independence. We must reckon with the possibility, however, that singlewomen rejected that association.[52] We know that there were many heterosexually active singlewomen who were not professional prostitutes. Some of them may have internalized the rhetoric about feminine sinfulness. Surely, however, not all of them did. Some singlewomen, as we know, carried on long-term relationships with men whom they did not marry — because the men were clerics, because they were married to other women with whom they no longer lived, or simply because the couple did not feel formal marriage was necessary.[53] Such women were subject to opprobrium from their communities — the appellation of "whore," in their neighbors' comments if not in formal court accusations, applied to them.[54] But we should not forget that despite the efforts of medieval society to deny to women other than the most degraded the possibility of sexual activity outside of marriage, women were still making choices for themselves, and those choices could include sexual activity.

Notes

1. Helen Gurley Brown, *Sex and the Single Girl* (New York: Pocket Books, 1963), 80.

2. Ibid., 4.

3. Heloise is probably the best-known example, but the letters in which she describes her premarital sexual feelings about Abelard were, of course, written after both her marriage and her profession as a nun. The most up-to-date account of authorship of these letters is Barbara Newman, "Authority, Authenticity, and the Repression of Heloise," in her *From Virile Woman to WomanChrist: Studies in Medieval Religion and Literature* (Philadelphia: University of Pennsylvania Press, 1995), 46–75.

4. E. Ann Matter, "My Sister, My Spouse: Woman-Identified Women in Medieval Christianity," *Journal of Feminist Studies in Religion* 2 (1986): esp. 88–93; Judith Brown, *Immodest Acts: The Life of a Lesbian Nun in Renaissance Italy* (New York: Oxford University Press, 1986), 6. See now Jacqueline Murray, "Twice Marginal and Twice Invisible: Lesbians in the Middle Ages," in *Handbook of Medieval Sexuality*, ed. Vern L. Bullough and James A. Brundage (New York: Garland, 1996), 191–222.

5. Brown, *Immodest Acts*, 14. Louis Crompton, "The Myth of Lesbian Impunity: Capital laws from 1270 to 1791," in *Historical Perspectives on Homosexuality*, ed. Salvatore J. Licata and Robert P. Petersen (New York: Haworth Press, 1981), 11–25, provides no medieval examples where the woman was not taking what was considered a masculine role. Similarly, female masturbation was not considered problematic.

6. Murray, "Twice Marginal," 201.

7. Siegfried Wenzel, ed. and trans., *Fasciculus Morum: A Fourteenth-Century Preacher's Handbook* (University Park: Pennsylvania State University Press, 1989), 7:7, 669.

8. For a discussion of the terminology of prostitution in the Middle Ages, especially England, see Ruth Mazo Karras, *Common Women: Prostitution and Sexuality in Medieval England* (New York: Oxford University Press, 1996), 10–12. The first part of this essay draws heavily from my previously published work; citing that work has seemed preferable to repeating in detail arguments developed elsewhere.

9. The term "concubina" in Latin pastoral literature from England meant a woman who had sex with a priest. Some of them were apparently prostitutes whom the priest visited regularly; others may have been supported financially by an individual priest; but most seem to have been in quasi-marital relationships for which the contemporary language of domestic partnerships seems appropriate and nonjudgmental. See Karras, *Common Women*, 108–9.

10. Tim North, "Legerwite in the Thirteenth and Fourteenth Centuries," *Past and Present* 110 (February 1986): 3–16; E. D. Jones, "The Medieval Leyrwite: A Historical Note on Female Fornication," *English Historical Review* 107 (1992): 945–53.

11. See, e.g., Rickie Solinger, *Wake Up Little Susie: Single Pregnancy and Race Before Roe v. Wade* (New York: Routledge, 1992). The double standard in premarital sex — with the blame placed on women — is by no means the main point of this work, but is amply illustrated there.

12. Peter Laslett, "Introduction," in *Bastardy and Its Comparative History*, ed. Peter Laslett, Karla Osterveen, and Richard M. Smith (Cambridge, Mass.: Harvard University Press, 1980), 3.

13. Ruth Mazo Karras, "Two Models, Two Standards: Moral Teaching and Sexual Mores," in *Bodies and Disciplines: Intersections of Literature and History in Fifteenth-Century England*, ed. Barbara A. Hanawalt and David Wallace (Minneapolis: University of Minnesota Press, 1996), 123–38.

14. Karras, *Common Women*, 25–30; quotation from Guildhall Library, MS 9064/1, fol. 82r.

15. J. B. Post, "A Fifteenth-Century Customary of the Southwark Stews,"

Journal of the Society of Archivists (1977): 423; Ruth Mazo Karras, "The Regulation of Brothels in Later Medieval England," *Signs: Journal of Women in Culture and Society* 19 (1989): 427.

16. Corporation of London Records Office, Repertory Book 5, fol. 103v; London, Guildhall Library, MS 9064/6, fol. 70r; CLRO, Rep. 9, fol. 256v; John Stow, *A Survey of London*, ed. C. L. Kingsford (Oxford: Clarendon Press, 1908), 2: 54; CLRO, Rep. 12, fol. 27r.

17. These are discussed in Karras, *Common Women*, 32–43.

18. Judith Walkowitz, *Prostitution and Victorian Society: Women, Class, and the State* (Cambridge: Cambridge University Press, 1980), 69–89, 202–4; Alain Corbin, *Women for Hire: Prostitution and Sexuality in France After 1850*, trans. Alan Sheridan (Cambridge, Mass.: Harvard University Press, 1990), 30–36, 84–86; Jill Harsin, *Policing Prostitution in Nineteenth-Century Paris* (Princeton, N.J.: Princeton University Press, 1985), 19–32, 212–15; and Mary Gibson, *Prostitution and the State in Italy 1860–1915* (New Brunswick, N.J.: Rutgers University Press, 1986), 32–37.

19. Joel T. Rosenthal, "Fifteenth-Century Widows and Widowhood: Bereavement, Reintegration, and Life Choices," and Barbara A. Hanawalt, "Remarriage as an Option for Urban and Rural Widows in Late Medieval England," in *Wife and Widow in Medieval England*, ed. Sue Sheridan Walker (Ann Arbor: University of Michigan Press, 1993), 33–58, 141–64. See also Christiane Klapisch-Zuber, *Women, Family, and Ritual in Renaissance Italy* (Chicago: University of Chicago Press, 1985), 119–20; Louise Mirrer, ed., *Upon My Husband's Death: Widows in the Literature and Histories of Medieval Europe* (Ann Arbor: University of Michigan Press, 1992), esp. Heather M. Arden, "Grief, Widowhood, and Women's Sexuality in Medieval French Literature," 305–19; Caroline M. Barron and Anne F. Sutton, eds., *Medieval London Widows, 1300–1500* (London: Hambledon Press, 1994).

20. James A. Brundage, "Widows and Remarriage: Moral Conflicts and Their Resolution in Classical Canon Law," in *Wife and Widow*, ed. Walker, 17–31.

21. Robert Guiette, *La légende de la sacristine: étude de littérature comparée* (Paris: Honoré Champion, 1927; rpt. Geneva: Slatkine, 1981).

22. Karras, *Common Women*, 115–17.

23. The legends of these saints are discussed in Ruth Mazo Karras, "Holy Harlots: Prostitute Saints in Medieval Legend," *Journal of the History of Sexuality* 1 (1990): 3–32; extensive references to different versions of their stories may be found there. The following discussion of Mary Magdalene is also based on "Holy Harlots."

24. *Le mystère de la passion joué à Arras*, ed. Jules-Marie Richard (Arras: Société du Pas-de-Calais, 1891; rpt. Geneva: Slatkine, 1976), 117, ll. 9981–86.

25. This discussion relies heavily on Anne Marie Rasmussen, "'How a Mother Teaches her Daughter Whoring': The Rhymed Couplet Text 'Stepmother and Daughter,'" chap. 7 of *Mothers and Daughters in Medieval German Literature, 1185–1557* (Syracuse, N.Y.: Syracuse University Press, 1997). I am grateful to Professor Rasmussen for allowing me to see this work in advance of publication.

26. Peter Schuster, *Das Frauenhaus: Städtische Bordelle in Deutschland (1350–1600)* (Paderborn: Ferdinand Schöningh, 1992).

27. Beate Schuster, *Die freien Frauen: Dirnen und Frauenhäuser im 15. Und 16. Jahrhundert* (Frankfurt: Campus, 1995), 216.

28. Karras, *Common Women*, 62, 90–91.

29. Kathy Peiss, "'Charity Girls' and City Pleasures: Historical Notes on Working-Class Sexuality, 1880–1920," in *Powers of Desire: The Politics of Sexuality*, ed. Ann Snitow, Christine Stansell, and Sharon Thompson (New York: Monthly Review Press, 1983), 74–87.

30. Joanne J. Meyerowitz, *Women Adrift: Independent Wage Earners in Chicago, 1880–1930* (Chicago: University of Chicago Press, 1988), 101.

31. Greater London Record Office, DL/C/1, fol. 55v. Cf. the case translated by Shannon McSheffrey in *Love and Marriage in Late Medieval London* (Kalamazoo, Mich.: TEAMS, 1995), 42–43.

32. Geoffrey Chaucer, *The Riverside Chaucer*, ed. Larry Benson, 3rd ed. (New York: Houghton Mifflin, 1987), 285, ll. 221–22. This passage — and the theme of the relation between social difference and sexuality in the Middle Ages — is discussed in Ruth Mazo Karras, "'Since the Other is a Poor Woman, She Shall be Called His Wench': Gender, Sexuality, and Social Status in Late Medieval England," *Difference and Genders in the Middle Ages*, ed. Sharon Farmer and Carol Braun Pasternack, (forthcoming).

33. Guido Ruggiero, *The Boundaries of Eros: Sex Crime and Sexuality in Renaissance Venice* (Oxford: Oxford University Press, 1985), 17–18.

34. John F. Benton, "Clio and Venus: An Historical View of Medieval Love," in *The Meaning of Courtly Love*, ed. F. X. Newman (Albany: State University of New York Press, 1969), 19–42, is still a classic. See now Peggy McCracken, *The Romance of Adultery: Queenship and Sexual Transgression in Medieval French Narrative* (Philadelphia: University of Pennsylvania Press, 1998).

35. Paul Strohm, *Hochon's Arrow: The Social Imagination of Fourteenth-Century Texts* (Princeton, N.J.: Princeton University Press, 1992), 121–44, discusses this issue with regard to married women; for the unmarried it was the father's rather than the husband's property that was at stake.

36. The courtesan became an established and recognized status in Italy in the sixteenth century. See Guido Ruggiero, *Binding Passions: Tales of Magic, Marriage, and Power at the End of the Renaissance* (Oxford: Oxford University Press, 1993), 33–48; Cathy Santore, "Julia Lombardo, 'Somtuosa Meretrize': A Portrait by Property," *Renaissance Quarterly* 41 (1988): 44–83; Margaret F. Rosenthal, *The Honest Courtesan: Veronica Franco, Citizen and Writer in Sixteenth-Century Venice* (Chicago: University of Chicago Press, 1992); Lynne Lawner, *Lives of the Courtesans: Portraits of the Renaissance* (New York: Rizzoli, 1987).

37. I am far from the first to point this out: Iwan Bloch — the M.D. who was a pioneer of what he termed *Sexualwissenschaft*, or the scientific study of sexuality — offered in his two-volume study of prostitution, published in 1912, a trenchant critique of those who, "in accordance with canon law, have identified prostitution with any illegitimate sexual satisfaction, and thereby unacceptably blurred the boundaries between prostitution and other forms of extramarital sexual relations" (Iwan Bloch, *Die Prostitution*, vol. 1, Handbuch der gesamten Sexualwissenschaft in

Einzeldarstellungen, 1 [Berlin: Louis Marcus, 1912], 25). Bloch himself was not always consistent in drawing the distinction: see, e.g., p. 787, where he finds prostitutes in the Prose Edda.

38. Henry Mayhew and Bracebridge Hemyng, "The Prostitute Class Generally," in Mayhew, *London Labour and the London Poor*, vol. 4, *Those That Will Not Work* (1862 ed., rpt. New York: A. M. Kelley, 1967), 35, classified any woman living with a man to whom she was not married a "cohabitant prostitute."

39. Abraham Flexner, *Prostitution in Europe* (New York: The Century Co., 1914; rpt., Patterson Smith Reprint Series in Criminology, Law Enforcement, and Social Problems, 30, Montclair, N.J.: Patterson Smith, 1969), 80.

40. Barbara Meil Hobson, *Uneasy Virtue: The Politics of Prostitution and the American Reform Tradition* (New York: Basic Books, 1987), 184–99.

41. William W. Sanger, *The History of Prostitution: Its Extent, Causes, and Effects Throughout the World* (New York: Medical Publishing, 1897, rpt. New York: AMS Press, 1974), 93–108 and 282–94. The point of all this was that vice was rampant in medieval society, encouraged by the church (except among the "hardy, vigorous race" [283] of Anglo-Saxons).

42. Paul LaCroix, *History of Prostitution Among All the Peoples of the World, from the Most Remote Antiquity to the Present Day*, trans. Samuel Putnam (Chicago: Pascal Covici, 1926), 2:410. I thank Janice Archer for suggesting some of the details about this source that confirmed my hunch that these women are not likely to have been prostitutes.

43. Historians who discuss other heterosexually active women along with prostitutes out of a concern for inclusiveness or context include Vern Bullough and Bonnie Bullough, *Prostitution: An Illustrated Social History* (New York: Crown, 1978), 106–29.

44. E. J. Burford, *The Orrible Synne: A Look at London Lechery from Roman to Cromwellian Times* (London: Calder and Boyars, 1973), 10; Andrew McCall, *The Medieval Underworld* (London: Hamish Hamilton, 1979), 189, 182. See also Burford, *Bawds and Lodgings: A History of the London Bankside Brothels c. 1000–1675* (London: Peter Owen, 1976).

45. The other strand in feminist thought calls them "prostituted women" or "women used in systems of prostitution," emphasizing their victim status. This position is especially prominent among feminists who have worked with women whom all would agree are exploited — that is, where race, class and the global economy enter the picture (as with child prostitutes in southeast Asia) — but it is by no means limited to these situations: a study of prostitution in a socialized and relatively ethnically homogeneous European nation notes that "prostitution's destruction of emotional life, self-image, and self-respect is so massive that the comparison with typical waged work grows thin." See, e.g., Asia Watch and The Women's Rights Project, *A Modern Form of Slavery: Trafficking of Burmese Women and Girls into Brothels in Thailand* (New York: Human Rights Watch, 1993); Cecile Høigård and Liv Finstad, *Backstreets: Prostitution, Money, and Love*, trans. Katherine Hanson, Nancy Sipe, and Barbara Wilson (University Park: Pennsylvania State University Press, 1992), quote at p. 183; Kathleen Barry, *The Prostitution of Sexuality* (New York: New York University Press, 1995). See also Shannon Bell, *Reading, Writing,*

and Rewriting the Prostitute Body (Bloomington: Indiana University Press, 1994), 49–54. The prostitution-as-work perspective comes out of the prostitutes' rights movement in the U.S. and Europe, in which prostitutes themselves (though usually the more independent and better educated ones) agitate for good working conditions, civil and legal rights, and respect. See Valerie Jenness, *Making It Work: The Prostitutes' Rights Movement in Perspective* (New York: de Gruyter, 1993); Gail Pheterson, ed., *A Vindication of the Rights of Whores* (Seattle: Seal Press, 1989); Bell, *Reading*, 99–123; Laurie Bell, ed., *Good Girls/Bad Girls: Sex Trade Workers and Feminists Face to Face* (Seattle: Seal Press, 1987). Anne McClintock, "Screwing the System: Sexwork, Race, and the Law," *boundary 2* 19, 2 (1992): 70–95, reconciles the two positions I have identified by arguing that prostitution is exploitative under male control, but when free of that control it is well-paid work that allows women's independence.

46. Examples include Marilynn Wood Hill, *Their Sisters' Keepers: Prostitution in New York City, 1830–1870* (Berkeley: University of California Press, 1993); Veena Oldenberg, "Lifestyle as Resistance: The Case of the Courtesans of Lucknow," in *Contesting Power: Resistance and Everyday Social Relations in South Asia*, ed. Douglas Haynes and Gyan Prakash (Delhi: Oxford University Press, 1992), 23–61; and especially Luise White, *The Comforts of Home: Prostitution in Colonial Nairobi* (Chicago: University of Chicago Press, 1990), who presents the sexual behavior of the prostitutes as incidental to the work aspect.

47. Karras, *Common Women*, 27–28.

48. Maryanne Kowaleski, "Women's Work in a Market Town: Exeter in the Late Fourteenth Century," in *Women and Work in Preindustrial Europe*, ed. Barbara Hanawalt (Bloomington: Indiana University Press, 1986), 154.

49. Goldberg, *Women, Work, and Life Cycle*, 155.

50. Similarly, of the other terms used for Wakefield, "pronuba" could mean a number of things besides procuress, and "keeps *scortum* in her house" did not necessarily mean keeping a brothel (Ruth Mazo Karras, "The Latin Vocabulary of Illicit Sexuality in English Ecclesiastical Court Records," *Journal of Medieval Latin* 2 [1992]: 1–17).

51. Indeed, I used her as a case study: Karras, *Common Women*, 66–67, citing Goldberg's work as well as the relevant court records.

52. Jones's suggestion (in "Medieval Leyrwite," 949) that the fact that most women paid their own leyrwite instead of having a man pay it for them indicates women's independence may be a trifle optimistic. They were considered "individuals in their own right, able to, and expected to, take responsibility for their own actions," but here the responsibility is blame rather than credit.

53. Michael Sheehan, "Theory and Practice: The Marriage of the Unfree and Poor in Medieval Society," *Mediaeval Studies* 50 (1988): 457–87, shows how some people who simply chose not to marry were forced to marry or simply defined as married by the church courts.

54. Karras, *Common Women*, 29–30.

6

Transforming Maidens

Singlewomen's Stories in Marie de France's *Lais* and Later French Courtly Narratives

Roberta L. Krueger

IN A CELEBRATED MOMENT in Heldris de Cornuälle's *Roman de Silence*, the eponymous heroine, who has been brought up as a boy in order to protect her birthright, wonders at the onset of puberty — age twelve — whether she should continue to enjoy the social privileges of a boy who rides and hunts or whether she should assume her "natural" female role, which includes sewing and playing amorous games (*Silence*, 2496–2688).[1] Underscoring the social import of this question, the allegorical characters, Nature, Nurture, and Reason participate in the debate. Silence decides to remain "on top" by maintaining her disguise as a male, but she eventually adopts a persona that allows her to revert to being a woman, should the need or occasion arise. Transforming herself into a minstrel, she darkens her face, takes up a *viele*, and learns to play and sing so well that she is acclaimed at the English royal court. But her male cover fails to protect Silence from the threat of female sexuality, which she meets in the disturbing form of Queen Eufeme, who attempts to seduce her and then banishes her to die in France. The spunky heroine is spared, thanks to the French king's wise counselors, and she performs valiantly as a knight. After the narrator has explored at length the ambiguities of gender and language, his androgynous character is finally exposed as female, after which she rather perfunctorily marries the king of England, whose wicked wife has been fatally punished.

Although the romance terminates in a royal marriage, Heldris de Cornuälle lavishes most of his attention on his heroine's activity as an autonomous female cross-dressed as male. By raising explicitly the matter of whether Silence's female role is natural or socially acquired, and by demonstrating the skill and courage with which its unmarried heroine undertakes hunting, singing, jousting, and life at court, the romance raises questions about young women that other twelfth- and thirteenth-century romances pose implicitly: What are the possibilities for and the limitations on an adolescent girl's social activities? What is the fate of a young, single woman who has left home? What does Nature permit that Nurture will not allow (and vice versa)? As the critical controversy surrounding this text attests, the romance's answers are ambiguous, and perhaps expressly so.[2] Clever and resourceful as she may be, the heroine expresses doubts about her ability to assume the roles appropriate for either gender and thus reveals how difficult the transition to adulthood can be. By focusing on the inner conflicts and social tensions of a virtuous *mescine* [girl], the *Roman de Silence* participates in an investigation of the promise and perils of maidenhood that links it to numerous other fictions of medieval France.

Amazons in the *romans d'antiquité*;[3] virgin martyrs in hagiographies;[4] harassed shepherdesses in the *pastourelle*;[5] naive but amorous girls in fabliaux such as the "Demoiselle qui ne pouvait entendre parler de foutre" . . . ;[6] Nicolette in the *chantefable*, *Aucassin et Nicolette*; *trobairitz* [female troubadours] debating the pros and cons of marriage;[7] the voice of a female clerk who subverts her suitor's rhetoric in the *Response au Bestiare d'amour*;[8] fairy ladies, distressed damsels, or resourceful maidens in romance; the old prostitute La Vieille (and her fabliau counterparts) who defends free love in the *Roman de la Rose*;[9] exemplary or transgressive young women depicted in conduct books of the late Middle Ages;[10] the writings of the mystic Marguerite Porete, who was burned for heresy in 1310;[11] or the legend and texts surrounding the warrior maiden, Joan of Arc:[12] Old French vernacular literature tells the stories of singlewomen in a polyphony of voices that reflect its culture's conflicted attitudes toward female autonomy—desire, fascination, fear, wonder. Following Heldris's lead in *Silence*, I propose to explore some scenarios for unmarried women that are present in selected twelfth- and thirteenth-century Old French courtly fictions, beginning with Marie de France (fl. 1170–90), who perfected the brief narrative *lai*, and Chrétien de Troyes (fl. 1160–90), who launched Arthurian romance on its course, and then moving on to some of their twelfth- and thirteenth-century continuators and successors. As they mapped out their distinct, complex fictional terrains, Marie and Chrétien traced different paths for the life stories of singlewomen that later romancers would explore.

Before embarking on a quest for singlewomen in Marie, Chrétien, and some of their successors, a few words of caution are in order. Old French romance comprises more than two hundred richly diverse works produced from the mid-twelfth century onward and arising from different literary, regional, and social contexts;[13] the unmarried women in our modest sampling of twelfth- and thirteenth-century romances have numerous sisters elsewhere. Romances' representations of men and women are set within intricate and often self-reflexive narrative patterns whose meanings reveal themselves only gradually to the reader. To extract unmarried women, or any literary type, from their specific literary contexts risks oversimplifying romance's gender relationships as well as literary and moral complexities in individual works.

As characters who are frequently anonymous, dispersed, marginalized, or eventually wed, singlewomen defy easy location and categorization. One is hard-pressed to find a leading lady in romance who is not defined in relationship to marriage, as the object of a quest or a courtship (*Floire et Blancheflor, Partonopeu de Blois, Cleomadés*); as a partner in adultery, as in the many narratives featuring Iseut or Guinevere, or in the *Roman du Castelain de Coucy et de la Dame de Fayel*; or as a wife whose virtue, obedience, or patience is tested (*Erec et Enide, Yvain, Le Roman du Comte de Poitiers, La Fille du Comte de Pontieu, La Manekine*, to name but a few examples). Numerous young women who assert a strong degree of autonomy and resourcefulness as maidens, such as Silence, are refashioned in the end as wives. Many damsels yearn to wed. If we focus on where the major protagonists of courtly romances eventually "end up" (or where they might wish to end up), we find that many *damoiseles* and *puceles* become — or might still become — *dames*. Even romance characters who are renowned for their independence in numerous episodes, such as Morgan or the Dame du Lac, may be assigned a mate in a later episode or subsequent version. Lifelong singlewomen as defined by this volume (never married and beyond reproductive age) are anomalous, and, in many ways, antithetical to romance's feminine ideal.

However, a shift in focus from romances' concluding nuptials to events within their stories reveals a large population of singlewomen, most of marriageable age.[14] In some romances, particularly those in the Arthurian tradition that begins with Chrétien, the knightly protagonist encounters maidens and young ladies without husbands, sometimes in profusion, at nearly every turn of the tale; otherworldly women like Morgan or the Lady of the Lake exert the power they do precisely because they act autonomously.[15] In other romances, especially among those dubbed as *"romans réalistes*," closer in spirit to Marie's *Lais*, the heroine sets forth into the "real" social world on her own before her eventual marriage. If we allow our gaze to linger either on those moments of a chivalric narrative where secondary female characters appear alone or in groups, or on those narratives that explore the period of a maiden's autonomy before marriage, we may piece together a fuller portrait of unmarried women than previous studies have offered.[16]

Such an approach may yield useful insights into how these texts may have engaged the young women in its mixed, noble audience, which surely included many adolescent girls and unmarried women.[17] Few would dispute that romances served to educate boys into knighthood: Chrétien's *Perceval*, Robert de Blois's *Beaudous*, and the *Prose Lancelot*, for example, portray the instruction of young men.[18] If the story of women's education is less explicitly the focus of most romances, the fears and desires of unmarried women loom large on the periphery and some texts, such as *Silence*, explore a maiden's coming of age directly. The young *pucele* who reads a romance in the garden of Pesme Aventure in Chrétien's *Yvain* (ll. 5354–63) and whose father attempts to marry her to the reluctant hero is a fictional instance of an unmarried reader facing an uncertain future. Adolescent noblewomen in the historical audience may have shared the maiden's uncertainty as they contemplated her plight and the fate of other romance maidens.

A word must be said about the terminology for singlewomen in Marie's *Lais* and the later romances. Although Marie often uses the terms "pucele," "meschine," and "dameisele" in a single lai to denote unmarried status (one finds instances of the three words applied at different moments to the maidens in *Frêne*, *Deux Amants*, and *Eliduc*, for example), each word also has a more specific connotation that she sometimes exploits. Thus, the word *meschine*, which according to Godefroy means "jeune fille" and "femme ou fille de noble extraction, dame, damoiselle," has as its third meaning "fille ou femme attachée au service d'une autre, servante."[19] Marie clearly intends this meaning in *Frêne* when she names the lady-in-waiting who advises Frêne's mother to put her baby up for adoption ("La dame aveit une meschine, / ki mult esteit de franche orine," 99–100). Deriving from the Arab word for poor, "meschine" can also designate someone in an unfortunate position, deserving of sympathy;[20] it can also denote a concubine.[21] Marie's use of this term to emphasize Frêne's role as servant and former mistress in her husband's household on his wedding day (375) heightens our sense of her servile status, of her misfortune, and of the mother's fears about her history with Gurun. "Pucele" also has a more precise resonance: the word may be applied to any unmarried woman without regard to rank, but it more particularly designates a virgin; this is clearly illustrated in Enide's passage from "pucele" to "dame" on her wedding night in Chrétien's *Erec et Enide* (2048–54). Marie's choice of the term pucele to describe the fairy lady who loves Lanval emphasizes her youthfulness and her sincerity when she first appears before Lanval (108). Even when she is presumably no longer a virgin, the narrator continues to call her a "pucele" (555), perhaps to underscore her otherworldly youth and beauty, which cannot be tarnished by sexual relations, in contrast to Guinevere's corruption. The term *dameisele* denotes a "fille noble"; in later romances, this term can also be used to denote a married lady of lesser rank in service.[22] Finally, *dame* can refer in general to any "femme noble" (and it is used in this sense in *Lanval*, 508), although it is usually used in the *Lais* and elsewhere to designate a noble "femme mariée"; it may also designate a lady who is beloved, whether she is married or not. *Dameisele* and *dame* are more class-specific than the terms *fille* [daughter], *amie* [girlfriend or beloved], or *femme*, which can denote generically either "woman" or "wife" and which Marie also uses for lexical variety and for rhyme (as in "'Veiz tu,' fet ele, 'cest *femme*, / ki de belté resemble une *gemme*?'" applied to Guilliadon by Guildeluec in *Eliduc*, 1021–22; emphasis mine). Although Marie generally uses the terms *pucele*, *meschine*, *dameisele*, and *dame* with precision, the slippage of meanings can sometimes lead to confusion about the marital status of a particular female figure. This is the case for the "dame" of *Chaitivel*, for whom no husband is mentioned, but whose relative maturity (or cynicism) do not qualify her for the title of "pucele" or "dameisele." Such imprecision recurs in later courtly fiction and makes our quest for bona fide singlewomen trickier.[23]

As we have said, singlewomen who have reached "a certain age" without being married or widowed, or without having entered a convent, and with no connection to the Other World, are rare. Most major characters whom we first meet as puceles and damoiseles eventually marry. Many secondary characters who remain damoiseles within a story are young enough to be marriage candidates. Others are depicted as fairies and sustain their power and autonomy by means of enchantment or by association with the Other World. But among the unmarried damsels who eventually marry and the fairies who live apart from social constraints, there are provocative, resourceful, and accomplished young women who use their temporary or supernatural status to remarkable ends. In many narratives recounting a quest or courtship, the trials or transformation of the heroine before her nuptials receive far more attention than the marriage itself. If we extend our search beyond major characters to include auxiliary characters who assist the primary female character or who are instrumental (or obstructive) in the hero's exploits, our sense of romance's social landscape is considerably enriched. Although unmarried women do not have formal ties to a social institution, as do young men through knighthood, and they cannot always be located with geographic precision, centered in a court or attached to land holdings, and even if they are frequently anonymous, singlewomen and networks of women living out of marriage (widows and nuns) are a constitutive feature of romance, as integral to the literary landscape as married women or married or single knights. This phenomenon is evident from the start, in the seminal works of Marie de France and Chrétien de Troyes.

Translatio *and Transformation: Maidens in the* 'Lais' *of Marie de France*

The *Lais* of Marie de France (c. 1170) are narrated by a woman who stands alone, boldly, risking presumption, to present an unusual collection of stories to the king (probably Henry II of England), as the author tells us in the Prologue (42–56).[24] Whether Marie was or had been married or whether she was a member of a religious order,[25] the narrator of the *Lais* writes as an independent woman who strives to distinguish herself from male clerks by choosing to tell stories from the Breton oral tradition rather than to translate from Latin texts, as her contemporaries have done; such is the innovative program announced in the Prologue.[26] Michelle Freeman has demonstrated that Marie enacts a feminine *translatio studii*, modeled on the traditional carrying over of studies into a new domain, by recasting her enigmatic stories with an androgynous voice that highlights female virtue, silence, and poetic creation.[27] Others have shown how Marie's *Lais* explore emotional and sexual maturation, which are underscored by poetic transformations.[28] Her brief, complex fictions can also be read as family histories that offer deft analyses of courtship, marriage and adultery, pregnancy, birth, paternity, motherhood, childhood, and death, in which unmarried women play a central role. The social displacements and moral transformations of maidens and singlewomen are constitutive features of the *Lais*. As she transmits moral knowledge and translates stories, Marie portrays the process of human *translatio* involved in crossing from childhood to adulthood, a passage described as especially poignant for young women. The author of a later collection of moral *Fables*, written for a nobleman but with evident instructional value for both sexes, Marie may have been especially aware of the concerns of youth.[29]

Of the twelve lais included in Harley manuscript 978, which is the only manuscript that includes all the lais attributed to Marie, seven lais recount the adventures of young women who are married, each unhappily or inappropriately in her own way (they are thus *mal mariées*), and six tell of girls or young women who are not attached to a husband for at least an important portion of the story. In the order of the Harley collection, these are: *Le Frêne*; *Lanval*; *Deux Amants*; *Milun*; *Chaitivel*, which recounts the story of a "dame" whose husband, if she has had one, is never mentioned and who appears to live alone; and *Eliduc*, which presents both a maiden and a married lady. Striking in Marie's collection is the variety of singlewomen whose situations are represented. They include a foundling who is prevented by her uncertain birth from marrying her chosen knight (*Frêne*); a fairy who loves a forgotten knight at Arthur's court (*Lanval*); a motherless adolescent prevented by her jealous and possibly amorous father from marrying her suitor (*Deux Amants*); a young woman who conceives a child out of wedlock (*Milun*); a haughty lady who refuses four suitors because she cannot decide between them (*Chaitivel*); and a young maiden, daughter of a king, who falls innocently in love with a married man who has concealed his status from her (*Eliduc*). With the exception of *Chaitivel*, these lais treat a young woman in love whose desires are thwarted by familial or social constraints; the sexual and emotional maturation of the maiden on the cusp of adulthood often triggers a crisis — and transformation — in those around her. *Frêne*, *Milun*, and *Eliduc* terminate in the heroine's marriage, albeit in each case routed through another marriage. *Deux Amants* ends with the heroine's tragic death out of sorrow for her expired lover; *Lanval* concludes with the lady's elopement with Lanval to Avalon, her fairy kingdom. Only *Chaitivel* allows the heroine to retain her single status in the "real" social world and in life, although her failure to love results in the death of three knights and the impotence of a fourth; thus, her self-imposed solitude comes at a price to those around her.

If none of these lais presents a heroine who achieves social honor and fulfills emotional longings as a singlewoman in the long term, all focus on young women's transitions and transformations as they travel from maidenhood to adulthood. Marie depicts the social and internal obstacles to the maidens' happiness; their desire or longings; the fragmentation of their social and familial identities, often accompanied by physical displacement (for all but Frêne there is no mention of a mother; all but *Chaitivel*'s lady physically depart from their childhood home); the ways they intervene in the social processes that constrain them; and the assistance they receive from others. Finally, Marie portrays the often startling transformations that occur in the lives of maidens and those around them as they attain maturity. Acting alone or in concert with other women or men, the unmarried women in these lais often work to construct a sense of autonomous female honor that has no equal in the Arthurian romances of Marie's near-contemporaries.

Deux Amants, a lai whose title and central placement give it an exemplary quality within the collection, presents a paradigm of a maiden's difficult *translatio* from childhood to adulthood that emblematizes the concerns of other lais. The narrator's presentation emphasizes obstacles to the maiden's happiness; the dameisele's resourcefulness; the assistance of another woman; the girl's physical displacement as she is literally carried to another level; her courageous, but tragically inefficacious actions; and the final transformation of the maiden and those around her.[30]

Deux Amants recasts within a local legend the story of two young lovers' tragic deaths in Piramus and Thisbé from Ovid's *Metamorphoses*.[31] The obstacle impeding the union of a *dameisele* and her *damisel* is a jealous father, the King of Pistre, whose excessive attachment to his beautiful daughter after his wife's death verges on incest, since Marie tells us that the father "pres de li esteit nuit et jur" [was close to her night and day, 30]. The king has imposed an impossible trial that concretizes the perversity and excess of his love: each potential suitor must climb a high mountain with the girl in his arms. The daughter is a model of filial obedience, one who loves her *ami* in part because the king esteems him (67–68) and who does not wish to cause the father pain by eloping with her lover (96–100). Yet despite the father's jealous guard and the daughter's devotion, the girl emerges as a strong protagonist. It is she who initiates the action by speaking first to the young man, as is often the case with the women in Marie's lais.[32] She sends her lover, armed with a letter that she has written, to seek counsel from her aunt in Salerno, who provides the young man with a "beivre" (potion) that will provide the "vertu" that will enable him to climb the mountainside while holding his beloved.

With characteristic economy, Marie presents the aunt as a strong, accomplished person: she is a "riche femme" who has a significant income from lands ("mult a grant rente") and who is skilled in the art of medicine (103–12). Although the aunt's marital status is not described, the narrator's use of the term "femme" as opposed to "dame" allows us to imagine her independent existence as a healer.[33] But the maiden's efforts and the aunt's medical knowledge are not enough to prevent a tragic outcome. Lacking *mesure* in his love, the young man fails to heed the advice of the maiden who urges him to drink his potion. The rhyme "mescine"/"meschine" [medi- cine/damsel] underscores simultaneously the promise of happiness for the maiden, her special efforts to secure a marriage with her intended, and the tragic failure of her plan: "Sovent li prie la meschine: / 'Amis, bevez vostre mescine'" [The maiden often begs him, "Friend, drink your potion"] (209–10). He dies of exhaustion and she expires out of sorrow, stretched out at his side and embracing him with passion. The narrator's use of the term "enfanz" twice in the final verses to describe the couple emphasizes their youthful innocence and, by contrast, the cruelty of the adult world represented by the father.

As it recounts the story of two children who die for love, *Deux Amants* might seem to emphasize the powerlessness of young women to free them- selves from filial obligations and social constraints. Yet, even if the girl does not overcome the father's tyranny in her own life, the narrator valorizes the maiden's virtuous actions. As the hero dies, the maiden flings the un- used potion against the mountainside, where it miraculously flowers into "meinte bone herbe" [many good plants] that enhance the countryside and the entire region ("mult en a esté amendez / tuz li païs et la cuntree," 226– 27). This profusion of good plants echoes the flowering of "gran biens" in the narrator's Prologue (5–8). Marie's narrator thus poetically allies her- self with the maiden, who is, significantly, also a writer of "letres."[34] The "meinte bone herbe" link the girl's actions to other images of flowering and generation in the lais. Tragically, the girl and her lover pass from life to death (a negative *translatio*), but a final, positive transformation occurs. Moved by the lovers' tragic demise, the king and onlookers sanction the love that was formerly forbidden: girl and boy are buried together, and the mountain is named "Deux Amants" in their memory. The mountain in bloom, the bodies conjoined in death, and the new name stand as enduring symbols of the power of maidenhood to transform a hostile social land- scape, even if it does not alter the underlying social structure.

Milun and *Frêne* also depict the plight of young women whose loyal love for a knight is thwarted by family-imposed obstacles. Both lais portray maidens who act on their desires and consummate their love before mar- riage; thanks to the heroines' constancy in love and their resourcefulness, each maiden is eventually able to incorporate her "transgressive" sexuality into marriage with her beloved. Significantly, the maiden's honor is ultimately not compromised by her extramarital affair, although the stakes are especially high for the damsel in *Milun*, who bears a child out of wedlock. The life story of each maiden entails an initial fragmentation of identity and physical displacement, which subsequently provoke radical moral and social transformations that alter the very configuration of family life.

The period of maidenhood occupies a little less than a third of the story in *Milun* (where the heroine endures an arranged marriage for twenty years before being married to her lover, father of the child the couple gave up for adoption). Yet this important narrative segment conveys the young woman's desire, her sexual autonomy, and her vulnerability as a result of her passion. As in *Yonec*, *Lanval*, and *Eliduc*, the woman takes the initiative in desiring the hero and in calling him to her: "Par sun message li manda / que, se li plaist, el l'amera" [By her messenger she offered, / if it pleased him, to love him] (27–28). But when she finds herself pregnant, her joy turns quickly to woe, as the rhyme of "enceinte"/"pleinte" emphasizes: "Quant aparçut qu'ele est enceinte, / Milun manda, si fist sa pleinte" [When she realized that she was pregnant, / she called Milun, and lamented to him] (55–56). The maiden fears "granz justise" [a stern punishment] (60), that she will be tormented at the point of a sword ("a glaive sera turmentee") (61), or that she will be sold into another country ("u vendue en altre cuntree") (62). The narrator hastens to note that such were the punishments meted out to unwed mothers in earlier times, which is when her story took place: "Ceo fu custume as anciëns / e s'i teneient en cel tens" (63–64). When the young girl later contemplates her arranged marriage to another man, she worries that her husband will discover her lack of virginity and enslave her, as she laments at the beginning of a lengthy *plainte*: "Ja ne sui jeo mie pucele / A tuz jurs mes serai ancele!" [I am not a virgin any longer / I will now always be a slave!] (135–36).

As in *Deux Amants*, the girl initiates the rescue plan, which involves sending the baby to her sister and conveying her story in a letter, concealed in a silk purse that accompanies a coverlet. The ring she attaches to the baby's neck will allow him to be recognized, years later, by his father. The letter, the cloth, and the ring evoke a realm of feminine activity, set within a network of female relations. (The helping lady in *Milun* is married, presumably to provide a proper cover for the child's illegitimacy.) When the girl is "given" to another man as his bride and Milun departs, displacement and fragmentation ensue. But for twenty years, the now married lady and her *ami* communicate by means of a swan, a sort of surrogate child that they train to convey the messages that they attach to its neck. The lady's resourcefulness and the couple's constancy allow for the lai's final act of transformation, when the couple are reunited with their son and a new, legitimate family is formed.

The narrator Marie places her signature on this marvelous outcome when she tells how the son "assembla" [brought together] (527) his parents in marriage (the husband having conveniently died); such a reunion recalls the way that Marie has "assembled" her lais ("m'entremis des lais assembler"), which recount a "grant bien." In the final lines of *Milun*, the couple lives "en grant bien" for the rest of their days and nights (529). As in many thirteenth-century *chansons de toile* — "sewing songs" written in a female voice — the predicament of a young maiden in distress is happily resolved, with no loss of honor.[35]

The maiden's vulnerability, displacement, and the fragmentation of her identity are acute in *Frêne*, which recounts the story of a female twin who has been abandoned by her mother as a baby. (The mother fears incurring dishonor after having borne twins, since she has recently accused a neighbor's wife of having given birth to twins as a result of infidelity — a mistaken notion.) A network of singlewomen — the ladies-in-waiting, a meschine, the porter's widowed daughter, and an abbess, all of them acting outside the confines of marriage — ensure the survival of the child (whom the mother intended initially to kill) and arrange for Frêne to be "found" in an ash tree, from whence the heroine derives her name.[36] The beautiful, courtly, and learned maiden has a difficult journey to maturity, one that entails two subsequent displacements or separations: first, because of her sexual relationship with Gurun, she flees the convent where she has been raised; and second, because Gurun has become engaged to a woman of higher rank (her sister, Codre, as it turns out), she cedes her role as Gurun's mistress and begins to prepare his bed for the new wife. But, in so doing, Frêne performs an act of generosity that will transform the moral climate of the lai. Upon the marriage bed she lays the *paile roé*, or coverlet, in which her mother had wrapped her as a baby and thus sets the stage for the mother's recognition of her daughter and her contrition for her earlier misapprehension and calumny.

Although this lai ends in a double marriage (that of Frêne to Gurun and of Codre to another knight) and reveals a secret within a long-standing conjugal union, it is also a lai about sexual and emotional maturation that valorizes the desire of an unmarried woman and allows her to find an honorable solution. Like other lais in the collection, *Frêne* contrasts a conventional sense of honor, conceived of strictly as chastity for maidens or as sexual fidelity for married women, with a transformed sense of female honor forged by the generous actions of women acting on their own. We shall see how the thirteenth-century *Galeran de Bretagne* expands the realm of Frêne's autonomy.

If *Le Frêne* anticipates the resourceful heroine of the "roman réaliste," then *Lanval* explores the power and desire of fairies who will play a preponderant role in later romance, particularly in Arthurian fictions. Lanval's lady can be read both as the answer to a landless knight's dreams and as the agent of her own desire. As the lai begins, Arthur has failed to provide Lanval either a woman or possessions during the last distribution of royal gifts, but the lady satisfies him on both counts. Like the maidens in *Milun* and *Eliduc*, she initiates the relationship. She explains to the knight that she has come from a faraway land in search of him, and she promises to give him great happiness "kar jo vus aim sur tute rien" [for I love you above all others] (116). Emanating from a marvelous realm whose material riches and sensual pleasures seem limitless, Lanval's "pucele" possesses power, wealth, and freedom that contrast strikingly with those of Marie's real-world maidens. She is aided by female companions who are almost as beautiful as she is.

But even as it explores a realm of female pleasure and power, *Lanval* locates these freedoms for women in an Other World domain. The fairy warns Lanval that he will lose her if he ever mentions her existence to anyone — an interdiction typical of fairy legends.[37] After the young woman forgives the knight for having defied her orders (which he does to rebuff Guinevere's advances), she appears at the Arthurian court to vindicate the hero's honor by proving the superiority of her beauty to that of the queen. In contrast to the inequality, scarcity, corruption, and injustice of Arthur's court, the alternative world of the fairy is characterized by generosity, reciprocity, and erotic and material fulfillment. The singlewoman in *Lanval* is the most autonomous and powerful pucele of the collection, and yet she is also the most elusive, for she does not remain in the "real" world. Lanval's fairy carries him off on horseback to Avalon, from whence the couple never returns. In marvelous defiance of Arthurian conventions, the only rescue on horseback in the *Lais* is performed not by a man to save a damsel in distress, but by a fairy pucele to rescue a knight from a hostile court. Combining as she does both elements of the "Melusinian" and the "Morganian" fairies whose apparitions Harf-Lancner has analyzed, Lanval's lady prefigures the young women with magic powers who appear in future idealized landscapes where female power, desire, and autonomy are elevated to marvelous heights.[38] Her well-timed appearance with a retinue of damsels to resolve a judicial crisis also prepares the way for Lïenor's arrival at Conrad's court in *Le Roman de la Rose ou de Guillaume de Dole.*

By contrast, *Chaitivel*'s lady derives no happiness from her self-imposed autonomy, which is portrayed in the end as a state of lack. Having chosen to court four men in order to maximize her gains, the lady ends up with nothing. Three of the four die while fighting in a tournament to win her favors, and a fourth is wounded in the thigh. No female friendship or familial bond sustains her in her loss, and she cannot love the one wounded knight who survives her test. Her composition of a lai to celebrate her own sorrows is a solipsistic activity. The lai demonstrates the absence of social benefits for either men or women of a system in which knights compete for the favors of the most beautiful lady, who will love only the "best." Marie thus critiques, in advance, the chivalry topos that plays itself out in numerous courtly romances. As one who is both arrogant and disappointed, this unhappy singlewoman prefigures both the proud or discerning damsels of romances such as *Ipomedon* and *Partenopeu de Blois* and the ultimately disappointed (because rejected) ladies who repeatedly populate Arthurian romances, as we shall see.

Finally, the maiden's vulnerability, her displacement, her troubled passage to sexual and emotional maturity, her reliance on a mature woman, and her final transformation are recast in *Eliduc*, which is the longest and final lai in the Harley manuscript. This densely woven tale about a married lady and a maiden should be entitled "Guildeluec et Guilliadon" and not "Eliduc," as the narrator tells us, for the "aventure" has come about because of the ladies — "car des dames est avenu / l'aventure dunt li lais fu" (25–26).[39] By conjoining a wife's and a damsel's stories, Marie signals the complementarity and intertextuality of her "married" and "unmarried" lais. By conjoining a knight's tale with a women's tale — and by insisting on the primacy of the women's tale in her final lai — Marie signals the importance of women's voices in her enterprise and *names*/designates a space for women's stories that some of her successors will explore.

Guildeluec and Guilliadon, dame and dameisele, wife and amie, share a common fate: they both love, and are deceived by, the same man. Marie's final representation of heterosexual love is highly ambivalent, since both the "loyal" marriage and the "loyal" (extramarital) love are tainted by Eliduc's duplicity. Like the dameiseles in *Milun* and *Lanval* (and the mal mariée of *Yonec*), the damsel boldly desires and cautiously seeks out Eliduc. The maiden's lament in lines 387–400 emphasizes her fundamental inability to *know* this "hum d'altre païs" who has swept her off her feet. Eventually, the maiden is carried off by Eliduc on a ship that sails back to his country; once again, the maiden's maturation involves physical displacement and *dépaysement*. When she finally learns that he has betrayed her by concealing the truth about his marriage, Guilliadon falls into a shock-induced coma; her temporary death echoes the permanent demise for love of the maiden in *Deux Amants* and maiden's fear of violent punishment in *Milun*.[40] Yet, as in *Deux Amants*, where the sight of the two lovers' bodies effected a new understanding among the citizens of Pistre, so here the body of a maiden will be the catalyst for a series of remarkable moral and social transformations. These transformations echo the endings of *Lanval*, *Le Frêne*, and *Milun*, which also construct alternate social worlds.

When Guildeluec discovers the recumbent maiden in the church where Eliduc has sequestered her, she is moved by her very beauty to feel not jealousy and hatred (as did Iseut of the White Hands when she discovered Tristan's love for Iseut the Blond), but understanding for her husband's predicament and sorrow for the girl's loss. By using a magic flower with which a weasel in the church has healed its companion (who was struck by a boy), Guildeluec revives the girl. Marie thus glosses, in a final instance, the images of generation, rhetorical flowering, and generosity that have run throughout the collection. Guildeluec's deep compassion for a "meschine" is an affective blend of pity and love that "summarizes" and completes the earlier acts of generosity and support we have seen by women for singlewomen. As she says, "Tant par pitié, tant par amur, / Ja mes n'avrai joie nul jur" [As much for pity as for love, I will never be joyful any day again] (1027–28). For Guildeluec, as for the narrator and perhaps for her readers, the plight of a maiden moves the spectator beyond "pité" to "amur," engendering an inner metamorphosis.

Marie's conclusion does not leave us with the maiden in despair. The narrator transforms the triangle of two women loved and then betrayed by the same man into a new social arrangement. First, the wise wife, Guildeluec, "corrects" Guilliadon's misreading of Eliduc's baseness (evoked in her outburst against men's follies in ll. 1071–84) and explains how much her husband has suffered for his amie. Then, in the penultimate reversal in a collection of moral transformations and social rearrangements, Guildeluec herself becomes a "single woman," and changes places with Guilliadon so that the maiden becomes the married lady, and the married lady establishes a religious order with thirty nuns. After many years, Eliduc and Guilliadon also enter religious life. The final "don" [gift] in a collection of poems where gifts and presents figure so importantly, is Eliduc's bestowal of his second wife, GuilliaDON (my emphasis), upon his first wife, Guildeluec (whose name contains his).[41]

The *Lais*'s last couple are the "sisters," Guilliadon and Guildeluec, two women who have forged a new kind of *enor* outside feudal marriage, as underscored by the rhyme of "serur" and "honur"; "El la receut cum sa serur / et mult li porta grant honur" [She received her like a sister / and showed her great honor] (1167–68). Solitary maidenhood and profane marriage are transcended in spiritual sisterhood, the *Lais*'s final transformation.

With the exception of *Chaitivel*'s lady, the maidens of the *Lais* all display boldness in loving. Except for Lanval's lady, each maiden experiences serious psychological or social constraints. Her perils are overcome not by the violent intercession of a knight on horseback (as will be true for the *puceles desconseillies* of Arthurian romance), but by her inner resources — courage, fortitude, patience, generosity, forbearance, and trust, as it may be. But no maiden succeeds by her efforts alone, unless she hails from Avalon. All depend upon others, particularly on other women.

Although Marie's direct influence is traced to relatively few fictions, her early collection of stories maps out, with almost uncanny prescience, the scenarios for maidens that later romances will revisit. Future romances will take up the tales of maidens who are victims of incest,[42] maidens who undergo adventures before marrying their beloved,[43] fairy ladies who seek out an Arthurian knight, and proud and rejected maidens, as we shall see. In contrast to many subsequent fictions where the tales of singlewomen will be fragmented and dispersed, Marie casts a steady gaze on the life stories of singlewomen. Marie's real-world maidens work within tight familial and social constraints; they do not set forth for extended periods of autonomy, as do later heroines who more actively shape their fate. But Marie's poetic enterprise in the *Lais* explicitly invites those who will add to her subtly subversive tales the "surplus de leur sens" [the addition of their understanding]. Her poignant tales of the subtle strategies through which young women may subvert the plot of the mal mariée sow the grain for future fictions. From *Le Frêne* to *Eliduc*, Marie's female clerkly narrator explores the capacity of young women to transform social relationships as they face opposition to their choice in love. Standing apart from her contemporaries and offering a collection that honors the king, Marie redefines female *enor* and sets the stage for future transformations of maiden's tales.

The Enigma of (Single)women in Chrétien de Troyes

If Marie de France's *Lais* offer glimpses of alternative social worlds that maidens have helped to shape, the works of Chrétien de Troyes depict worlds that are more threatening to female identity. In an Ovidian tale often attributed to Chrétien, the narrator offers a chilling account of how a victimized maiden seeks to tell her story by weaving a tapestry after her rapist has cut out her tongue and how she conspires with her sister to punish the rapist, her brother-in-law, by feeding him his son. *Philomena* takes the complicity of sisterhood using the feminine arts of weaving and cooking to subvert the patriarchal stronghold to an extreme and disturbing end.[44] *Philomena* illustrates two opposing truths about damoiseles that will apply to the representation of singlewomen in many Arthurian fictions: first, that unmarried women are frequently figured as objects of male desire or victims of male aggression; and second, that singlewomen often threaten male honor or integrity by virtue of their desires, their speech, or their powerful knowledge.

Within the Arthurian courts of Chrétien's five full-length romances, women play more attenuated, but no less troubling, roles. Chrétien's complex female figures have elicited a range of critical assessments, including views that the romancer portrays powerful women,[45] that his work traces the "degradation" of female characters from first romance to last,[46] that his romances aestheticize and thus normalize rape in the motif of the *pucele esforciée* [raped maiden],[47] or that his heroines can use female speech to "disrupt" patriarchal discourse.[48] As I have argued, Chrétien's problematic representation of women as both privileged and displaced, subject and object, sets up a fundamental gender tension that future romancers will not cease to explore.[49] Such tensions are exacerbated for Chrétien's unmarried women. Even as their plots depend upon a steady supply of "puceles" and "damoiseles" as a proving ground for male honor, Chrétien's romances project a realm of autonomous female pleasure and desire that threatens that very honor. His chivalric plots attempt to contain or diminish singlewomen's considerable power, either by converting them to married ladies or by marginalizing their activities to the periphery. But, as if the existence of singlewomen — and the reality of their pleasures and activities — could never be fully controlled or understood, the damsels of the Arthurian landscape disappear only to reappear.

Maidens are never the primary subject of Chrétien's Arthurian ro-

mances, as they are in Marie de France's *Lais*. Chrétien's leading ladies —
Enide, Fenice, Laudine, and Guinevere — are married. But none of Chrétien's stories could be told without the unmarried women who fulfill a
range of functions — from helpless damsel to resourceful entrepreneur,
from threatening *amie* to helpful assistant — and whose numbers proliferate
from the first romance to last.[50] As Marie-Luce Chênerie has shown, the
chivalric honor and social accomplishments of Arthurian heroes depend on
the existence of women who are all "belles, libres, nobles" [beautiful, free,
noble] — either so that they may be won as brides, defended against other
knights, or so that their amorous advances may be rejected, in all cases for
the greater glory of the knights.[51] The types that Chênerie identifies — the
fairy-mistress, the damsels at tournaments, the proud damsel, the damsel
escorted by another knight, and the damsel (or lady) at risk — all find early
incarnations within Chrétien's romances.[52] Just as Marie's resourceful heroines establish roles that future singlewomen will flesh out, so do Chrétien's
puceles and *damoiseles* inhabit spaces that will be occupied by unmarried
girls and women in future Arthurian romances.

That singlewomen are both peripheral and central to the "sens" of
Arthurian narrative is evident in Chrétien's first romance, *Erec et Enide*,
which establishes heterosexual marriage as the courtly norm. Enide is a
lovely "pucele," daughter of an impoverished vavasor, whose hand Erec
wins when he emerges victorious from a sparrowhawk contest. Although
she speaks not a word to Erec before her wedding (it is only afterwards that
she will perform her troublesome speech acts), we are told that she views
with joy her eventual union with Erec and the social elevation it will bring
to her and her family (681–90).[53] From rags to riches, from lowly pucele to
noble wife and, finally, to powerful queen: Enide's trajectory will be that
desired by numerous puceles in Arthurian romance.

In contrast, Enide's cousin remains a *dameisele* and her autonomy is
clearly threatening.[54] She has entrapped her "ami," Maboagrain, for her
own pleasure inside her magic garden, where he remains until Erec defeats
him and releases him from the girl's hold. Erec breaks the perverse "custom" of female power and reestablishes "courtly," masculine norms. Like so
many unmarried "puceles" and "amies" who cannot be absorbed into the
Arthurian world through marriage, Enide's cousin disappears from the narrative, which turns to focus on the magnificent coronation of the married
couple, the romance's ultimate *molt bele conjointure*. Arthurian romance, in
this founding instance, abhors the singlewoman. But, at the same time, by
refusing to be delighted by Erec's victory and by telling her own story,

Enide's cousin has provided an important counternarrative of female plea-sure and control.[55] The figure of the desiring female who attempts to "en-trap" or otherwise test the knight will recur in numerous guises in Ar-thurian fictions—a memorable instance being the Pucele del Gaut Destroit in *La Vengeance Raguidel*,[56] and, in a different guise, in the fairy Morgan.

Other singlewomen may exploit their autonomy to advance, rather than to impede, the honorable cause of knights or ladies. Among the many servant women in supporting roles in medieval French literature, surely one of the most enterprising is *Yvain*'s Lunete, lady-in-waiting to Laudine. She supplies Yvain with a magic ring so that he can escape the wrath of those seeking to punish him for having murdered Esclados le Ros, and she cleverly convinces Laudine, Esclados's widow, to marry the man who killed her husband. In the end, it is she who tricks Laudine into reconciling with the Knight of the Lion, a.k.a. Yvain, after he has broken his promise to return to her within a year. Lunete's insights into human nature and her clever verbal manipulation allow her to exert considerable influence on political and sentimental life in Brocéliande; she shares obvious traits with the clerkly narrator who similarly delights in character observation and verbal wit.[57] Lunete's loyal, resourceful service recalls, as it contrasts with, the faithful service of another famous lady-in-waiting, Brangien, in the Tristan legend, who furthers the cause not of marriage but of adultery, as she takes Iseut's place in the marriage bed with King Mark and repeatedly assists the lovers. Chrétien has more directly recast the figure of Brangien in *Cligés*'s Thessala, the heroine's nurse or *mestre* (2962), who uses her knowl-edge of magic potions—in complicated maneuvers that we cannot discuss here—to promote the eventual legitimate marriage of Fenice and Cligés.[58] In all these examples, the unmarried status of servants allows them to play powerful roles as go-between, peacemaker, or negotiator for men and women in couples, and to soften the tensions that attend marriage. The singlewoman as helper will be recast by Chrétien in the figure of Melea-gant's sister, who frees Lancelot from prison,[59] and in numerous auxiliary "damoiseles" throughout Arthurian fiction—foremost among them, as we shall see, in the Lady of the Lake. Lunete and her benevolent sisters suggest that even the best knight profits from association with a smart maiden or clever fairy to rescue him from the trouble in which he will find himself one day.

However, for all her power and access to magic, Lunete's status is precarious. Charged by Laudine's barons with treason after Yvain's betrayal of his wife, Lunete would have met death at the stake or by hanging if Yvain had not shown up to champion her cause. The "helping" damsel is also, at some level, helpless. Lunete's crisis in the second half of the romance is intercalated within a chain of episodes that focus on maidens or unmarried ladies at risk, all of whom the hero saves as part of his redemption. One by one, the hero rescues women who lack a husband or other male relative to protect them: the besieged dame of Norison and her dameisele;[60] the pucele whom the giant Harpin de la Montagne wants to hand over to his filthy "garçons" for their sexual pleasure;[61] the younger sister of Noire Espine, who has been stripped of her inheritance by an older sister; and finally, the three hundred silk workers from the Isle as puceles who are constrained by the "custom" of Pesme Aventure and the young pucele, daughter of the lord of Pesme Aventure, who reads in the garden. Yvain rescues all from peril, but he fails to satisfy the desires of the Dame de Norison and the pucele of Pesme Aventure, who wish to take Yvain as their lord and husband. If a few singlewomen in Chrétien are extraordinarily powerful, a much greater number are puceles desconseillies.

The contingent status of maidens within the Arthurian kingdom is expressed as a curious law or "custom" in the *Chevalier de la Charrete* (1293ff.), which a maiden in love with Lancelot invokes for her own self-interest. The *costume* of Logres dictates that a knight who comes upon a maiden traveling alone would incur shame if he dishonored her, but that any knight who wins a damsel from another knight may do what he will without shame or blame.[62] While this law might offer some solace to maidens who have a valiant champion or who never meet a dishonest man, it also inscribes all but the luckiest of maidens as prizes of chivalric competitions and objects of male "volenté" [will or pleasure]. As Kathryn Gravdal has noted, this law authorizes rape.[63]

Yet, by having the damsel explain the Logrian custom, Chrétien inscribes (once again) the paradox of singlewomen's status, for the damsel who attempts to apply this law to her own case is both a "helping" and "obstructive" damsel: she offered Lancelot lodging in exchange for having the knight in her bed and then staged a mock rape (in an attempt to rouse his passion?) from which Lancelot rescued her. In the amorous maiden, the designing damsel and the damsel in distress are conflated and confused. The maiden eventually disappears from the narrative, when she realizes that she cannot compete with Guinevere. She remains a mysterious character who seems to figure the enigma of female desire that subtends this romance. Unlike Guinevere, who is bound by different obligations to her husband, her abductor and his father, and her lover, the "amorous damsel" pays homage to no lord and literally rules the men in her household. Her sexual and social demands impede Lancelot's quest and threaten to compromise his honor. She joins Maboagrain's amie as an obstructive force, and the narrative ultimately eliminates her in favor of a benign damsel, Meleagant's sister, who desires nothing more than to serve Lancelot's "enor" and "bien" [honor and well-being] (*Charrete*, 6696–99).

From *Erec et Enide* to *Perceval*, Chrétien's singlewomen become increasingly numerous and their meanings ever more inscrutable. *Li Contes del Graal*, or *Perceval* (1190?), the earliest romance to stage a quest for the Grail, presents a world overpopulated with women who are not married, including Perceval's mother, a widow; Blanchefleur, an orphan; as well as a succession of damsels in distress or maidens who seek to assist, or impede, the progress of Perceval and Gauvain. The ostensible program of the romance — what the young man learns from his mother — is that the knight must defend and protect each "dame" in need and every "pucele desconseillie" [afflicted maiden] that he meets (533–40); so, too, must he treat young women courteously, never forcing his will or asking for "le sorplus" [sexual consummation] (544–49). But Perceval mistreats women almost immediately: first, by leaving his mother without saying goodbye and, shortly thereafter, by forcing a kiss upon a damsel in a tent, who later suffers at the hands of her jealous knight. After he leaves the Grail Castle, Perceval learns from the Hideous Damsel that his failure to have asked the crucial questions about the Grail (a failure linked to his treatment of his mother) will result in the permanent solitude and misfortune of all the singlewomen in the Terre Gaste. As she tells him, "dames" will lose their husbands and "puceles" will become "desconseillies" [afflicted] and will remain "orphelines" [orphans] (4678–83). Later, in the section recounting Gauvain's adventures, we learn that the ladies and orphaned maidens at the Castle of Champguin Rock await a knight to return their inheritances to dispossessed widows and to bestow husbands on maidens (7532–47). The predominance of widows, orphans, and puceles desconseillies in this romance is thus portrayed as a blight, a feminine corollary to the sterility of the maimed king of the Grail Castle. Ultimately, the maidens' tenuous status points up the inadequacy of knights who have failed to protect them or, worse, whose actions have caused them harm.[64]

Perceval's and Gauvain's interlaced adventures are both punctuated by the regular appearance of puceles desconseillies. But, as Lefay-Toury has noted, the trajectories of their encounters with women are different.[65] After his initial brusque kiss of the damsel in the tent, and his amorous embrace of Blanchefleur, Perceval gradually rises above physical love and focuses on the mysteries displayed by the puceles who hold the Grail and serving dish; after five years of wandering alone, he encounters not his ladylove but a hermit who preaches confession. Gauvain, on the other hand, implicates himself in a series of adventures where he is surrounded, indeed encumbered, by feminine attentions. These culminate in the profusion of admiring damsels who observe him at Ygerne's castle. In *Perceval*, Gauvain rehearses his role as chivalric spectacle in future romances that conflate his chivalry and his amorous prowess displayed before the admiring, and sometimes judgmental, gaze of puceles.[66]

As has often been noted, the bifurcation of Perceval's spiritual voyage and Gauvain's worldly journey articulates a division between spiritual and worldly chivalry that will be played out in successive histories, most notably in the Prose Vulgate cycle (as we shall see). What these two paths mean for the singlewomen who frequently cross them, however, is not so very different. The puceles and dameiseles of *Perceval* exist less as individuals in their own right than as projections of masculine desires and fears. Their numbers have multiplied, but their ability to lead the game, as did Lunete, has diminished. Although the credo of the knight is to protect the interests of widows and orphans, the damsels themselves loom as ambivalent signs of male desire or inadequacy — or, as with the Grail maiden, as bearers of inscrutable truths.

Chrétien's final romance trails off incompletely (after more than 9,000 verses), and we never learn the final fate of its singlewomen. As with other "disappearing" maidens, readers might wonder whether their desire for husbands will be fulfilled or continually frustrated. Among all of Chrétien's singlewomen, only Lunete seems to have attained a completely satisfactory "conclusion" to her project, as evoked in the narrator's Epilogue, "et Lunete rest molt a eise" [and Lunete remains very happy] (6799).[67] Her self-sufficient autonomy may derive from her association with fairyland.[68] The uncertain future of other singlewomen is comically evoked by Chrétien at the end of the tournament at Noauz, where the damsels who are disappointed that they cannot take Lancelot as their husband (for he intends to marry no one) vow not to marry at all that year (6047–56). Leaving the question of the damsels' future open, Chrétien allows his readers to imagine them and other puceles in his romances as potential brides or as eternal singlewomen.

The Passing of Damsels: Singlewomen in the Vulgate Cycle

Chrétien's most monumental legacy lies arguably in the thirteenth-century production of the conjoined *Prose Lancelot*, the *Queste del Saint Graal*, and *La Mort le Roi Artu*.[69] The Vulgate cycle recasts the stories of Lancelot and Guinevere's adultery, Gawain's worldly chivalric adventures, and Perceval's Grail quest within a vast, intricate narrative conjoining Arthurian and Christian history, which makes Arthur and his knights players in an unfolding drama that ends with the destruction of his kingdom. Among the many themes, motifs, and textual practices that the Vulgate "architect" or authors have inherited from Chrétien must be counted their extensive population of demoiseles, puceles, and dames who appear to have no spouse. The damsels — enchanting, helpful, needy, obstructive, malevolent, benevolent as they may be — who vanished from Chrétien's texts reappear in other guises throughout *Prose Lancelot*, *Queste*, and *La Mort le Roi Artu*. Our necessarily limited discussion of a few key characters will emphasize some of the questions about singlewomen's autonomy raised by these enigmatic figures.

Foremost among the Vulgate's singlewomen are two characters who emanate from the land of fairies or are associated with the arts of magic: the Lady of the Lake, who abducted Lancelot when he was a baby, raised him, sent him to Arthur's court after imparting the code of chivalry to him, and who seeks to assist him at every turn; and Morgan, Arthur's sister, who harbors resentment against Guinevere and seeks, on several occasions, to imprison Lancelot. As Laurence Harf-Lancner has described it, these two women act as competing forces of Good and Evil, alternately attempting to assist or impede the hero in his pursuit of the queen and, later, of the Grail.[70] Morgan and the Lady of the Lake are also complementary representations of powerful singlewomen, women not linked through marriage to a powerful court or kingdom but who operate, in the main, as autonomous agents.

The Lady of the Lake represents the benevolent mother from whom sexual desire has been purged. The existence of her ami, a sketchy figure whom she marries at a belated point in the text, seems to rule out any incestuous connection between her and Lancelot.[71] In the *Prose Lancelot*, she is assimilated to Ninianne, who learned the arts of magic from Merlin to put the enchanter to sleep so that she may avoid his advances (Micha, ed., *Lancelot*, 7: VIa, 1–10). Although she carries the boy into her kingdom and raises him to adulthood, her aim is to return him, strengthened and enriched, to the land of mortals. Her own erotic desires are sublimated to the maternal attentions that she lavishes on Lancelot; she wisely seeks to influence him within the realm of the court, but not to contain him in her own watery, distant world. This singlewoman is constructed as a sublimated support rather than a sexual threat to the knight. Thanks to the intercession of Saraïde and other damsel emissaries, the Lady of the Lake's influence directs Lancelot's story at every turn, but her power is ultimately "socialized" and "rationalized," in Harf-Lancner's terms. Seen this way, it is not surprising that she eventually marries a *chevalier* who has been endowed with land in the "real" world by Bors (Micha, 6: CIV, 52).

By contrast, Morgan is a singlewoman whose sexual desires have been openly expressed and who suffers shame, sorrow, and unfulfilled lust. Morgan's appearance in earlier texts, such as Geoffrey of Monmouth's *Vita Merlini*, is as a wise, helpful fairy, one of nine sisters on the Isle of Apples.[72] In the *Prose Lancelot*, her characterization is more "human," since she is Arthur's half-sister. Her powers are more extensive (thanks to the art of magic she, too, has learned from Merlin), and her character is darker. From her father, the Duke of Tintagel, she inherits her ugliness; and when she reaches maturity, she becomes more "chaude" [literally hot, meaning lustful] and "luxuriose" [wanton] than any woman: "et quant ele vint an aage, si fu si chaude et luxuriose que plus chaude feme ne convint a querre" [and when she came of age, she was more lustful and wanton than any woman could be found] (Micha, 1: XXIV, 39).

The narrative and its characters approach Morgan's adolescent sexuality without sympathy. The young woman is discovered in bed with Guiomar by Guinevere, who convinces her cousin to give up Morgan, for whom he does not care much (Micha, 1: XXIV, 40–41). Distressed that Guinevere has chased away her lover, and distressingly pregnant, Morgan learns "enchantemens" from Merlin so that she can use them to harm Lancelot and, by extension, Guinevere, whom she now hates. She avenges her frustration and anger in repeated attempts to manipulate knights whom she would entrap in her domain. Ultimately, Morgan's elaborate schemes fail to capture Lancelot, since he escapes three times from her prison. As Harf-Lancner says, "Les pouvoirs surnaturels de la fée s'amoindrissent devant la valeur du héros" (272). The *Prose Lancelot* and subsequent romances transform Morgan from a wise, healing maiden into an ugly, lascivious, spurned, and vengeful figure.[73] (In the Post-Vulgate, Morgan marries.) Although she is clearly negatively valued within the narrative, her opposition to Arthur's greatest knight and her fierce independence from Guinevere's retinue endow her with what Maureen Fries has called a "counter-cultural" power.[74] It is perhaps the potential threat of such a singlewoman's power that *Lancelot* and later narratives seek to contain as they marginalize Morgan.[75]

Beyond these two powerful singlewomen whose influence permeates the Vulgate cycle, the *Prose Lancelot* alone abounds with unmarried female characters. In addition to those who are named (usually by association with a toponym) and who may enter the limelight for extended or recurrent appearances,[76] Micha's edition lists 101 "damoiseles" (plus three figures listed as "puceles") who aid the heroes, or seek their love or assistance, during the eight volumes of this sprawling fiction.[77] Some of these maidens are sent by the Lady of the Lake or by Morgan, but many others appear and act in their own right, either as victims of an atrocity that must be punished by one of Arthur's knights; as admiring and desiring maidens who seek the attentions of Lancelot, Bors, or another; or as women who provide information, or carry weapons or messages.

The role of these damoiseles and amies has been variously interpreted. Jane Burns has suggested that the maidens who lead the heroes along and astray, meandering via indirect paths through the forest of story, are allied with a narrative voice who seeks to explore fictional terrain rather than arrive directly at an end.[78] Anne Berthelot has shown how Lancelot's encounters with two "demoiselles" in seemingly minor scenes enact important stages of the hero's "sentimental education" and prefigure his more significant union at Corbenic with the Fisher King's daughter, with whom he engenders Galahad.[79] Another scholar, who refrains from a "lecture totalisante" of what she calls the "masse d'occurrences" of female characters in the opening chapters of the *Lancelot en prose*, focuses on two damoiseles sent by the Lady of the Lake to help Lancelot at the Dolorous Guard who are instrumental in Lancelot's quest for his identity and, as such, carry on the maternal functions of Helaine and the Lady of the Lake.[80] In her study of Hector's truncated relationship with two women who eventually "disappear" from the *Prose Lancelot*, Carol Chase notes the failure of Vulgate cycle heroes to marry and observes the prevalence of unmarried ladies, some of whom are rescued from marrying against their will by the bachelor knights. The preponderance of unmarried men and women may say as much about the cycle's fraternal, religious conception of chivalry as it does about the medieval marriage market.[81] The propensity of these puceles and damoiseles to surface without extensive explanation or motivation, to seemingly blend into one another, and "disappear" from the narrative confounds the reader's attempts to understand them.

Can we read these proliferating damsels, at once central and peripheral, alternately helpful and threatening, as evidence of the role that young
women in service may have played in courts and noble households? Do the
frustrated desires of those who seek to wed reflect the aspirations of young
ladies in the aristocratic audience?[82] Or, should we read these elusive, enigmatic figures as aspects of a "feminine" textual function that subverts as
much as it "supports" the "straight" chivalric narrative? Whatever else they
may signify in specific contexts, the alternately helpless, maternal, amorous,
and obstructive damsels in Arthurian legend represent contradictory attitudes about female autonomy and reflect medieval culture's fascination
with and fears of women who wander on their own. The *Prose Lancelot*
repeatedly attempts to foreclose on a female narrative space that beckons
continually on the horizon. But, in the end, the final acts of the *Queste del
Saint Graal* and the *La Mort le Roi Artu* subordinate the stories of singlewomen to the spiritual and profane stories of their male heroes.

Within the strongly religious register of the *Queste*, female characters
are dichotomized by clerical misogyny and idealization into temptresses,
following Eve, or redemptive mothers, like Mary.[83] So, too, the *Queste*'s
singlewomen are cast as vehicles for male spiritual peril or redemption, as
exemplified in a final positive instance by Perceval's sister. This *pucele* leads
Bors, Perceval, and Galahad to the marvelous *nef* [ship] constructed by
Solomon on the advice of his wife, that will lead the heroes to see the Grail
(Pauphilet, ed., 198–202). In order that the male companions may continue, Perceval's sister gives her own blood to cure a leprous woman; sym-
bolically, her blood washes away the sins of the others. She is a figure of
Christian sacrifice and also of Mary, who redeems Eve's sins by bearing
Christ. Her spiritual support stands in opposition to the nefarious powers
of Morgan and completes the maternal function of the Lady of the Lake;
her intercession is essential to the quest. Ultimately, however, Perceval's
sister is excluded from the ultimate Eucharistic communion: she dies so
that her brother and his companions may attain the Grail.[84]

At the story's end, the *La Mort le Roi Artu* recounts another maiden's
death, that of the lady of Escalot, whom Lancelot refuses because of Guinevere. As a kind of living *summa* of all the lovelorn and rejected maidens of
the cycle (a motif we glimpsed first in *Eliduc*), the girl enacts a familiar
drama: she actively seeks the hero's love, coerces his favor (he wears her
sleeve and thereby incites Guinevere's jealousy), and becomes disconsolate
when he later refuses to love her.[85] Other rejected maidens in the cycle
vanish into the wilderness of the text; this damsel actively stages her death:

"Tout en ceste maniere devisa la damoisele sa mort" [In that very way the damsel devised her death] (39). She writes a letter explaining that she has died "por le plus preudome del monde et por le plus vilain" [for the most noble and most vile man in the world] (72) and sets herself adrift, bearing the letter in a lavish purse, on a richly decked funereal *nacele* [boat]. When the boat floats up to Arthur's court, Gauvain and the king are moved to pity by the sight of the "damoisele morte nouvelement" [recently deceased damsel] (71) whose beauty and youth are still apparent. The damsel's young corpse and pointed words accuse Lancelot of moral corruption and underscore the failure of the Arthurian world in its demise. Her passing not only concretely embodies the refusal of Arthur's knights to marry and form families; it also leaves us with a haunting image of the fragmented or incomplete lives of singlewomen in Arthurian legends.

The Singlewoman Sets Forth: Resourceful Maidens in L'Escoufle, Le Roman de la Rose ou de Guillaume de Dole, *and* Galeran de Bretagne

In contrast to narratives where singlewomen proliferate or pass by in the margins, another vein of romance after Marie de France and Chrétien de Troyes places a woman at the center of the story, sometimes as a virtuous wife, at other times as a resourceful maiden.[86] Among the most intriguing thirteenth-century romances are those within the tradition of the so-called "roman réaliste" in which a young woman leaves home and sets forth on her own adventure before marrying.[87] Drawing their inspiration either directly or indirectly from Marie's *Lais*, or from other popular traditions, these stories portray maidens who display extraordinary virtue and industry to surmount overwhelming obstacles before they marry. Within the extended framework of a full-length romance, the maidens experience more autonomy than did Marie's; they venture at greater distance and for longer periods into new social spaces, which are often "real" cities. Several of these romances describe the maiden's activities as an embroiderer and depict the young woman working for pay away from home as she struggles to regain her status.[88] Furthermore, the heroines who work ally themselves with other women; female friendship, a budding motif in Marie, develops into an intense bond in some of these texts. As heroines travel back and forth between domestic, urban, and courtly spaces, they test the categories of class as well as gender.

Three romances selected from this rich tradition — Jean Renart's *L'Es-coufle* (c. 1202) and *Le Roman de la Rose ou de Guillaume de Dole* (c. 1210) and Renaut's *Galeran de Bretagne* (c. 1216) — provide striking instances of singlewomen at work; these romances contain among the most fully real-ized portraits of active women in Old French literature. Aélis, Liénor, and Frêne all eventually marry the man of their choice and achieve, or regain, high noble status. But before she weds, each maiden sets forth from her habitual space to cross social boundaries, transform her identity, and, in the process, amend the lives of those around her. As did Marie's maidens, the heroines of these romances command their readers' attention as agents of sentimental and social transformation.

In each romance, the maiden's trials are embedded within an overarch-ing *conjointure* that tells the story of a couple and concomitantly portrays a crisis of male identity. As in *Aucassin et Nicolette*, where Nicolette's activity rouses the hero from passivity, in each romance the heroine takes the initia-tive in a way that points up the inadequacy of male actions. In *L'Escoufle*, Guillaume strays away from his sleeping lover in search of a purse stolen by a bird (an *escoufle*, or kite); it takes him years to wander, as a rather pathetic, bumbling figure, to the spot where Aélis's adventures as a seamstress began. In the meantime, Aélis has actively forged a series of friendships with women that replace the support and affection her father and Guillaume have failed to provide, and she has earned fame and fortune as an embroi-derer. In the *Roman de la Rose*, Liénor moves assertively and inventively to counter the charge that she has lost her virginity, while her disappointed suitor, the Emperor Conrad, laments in lyric poetry. She stages a literal "trial" that not only refutes the slander but also critiques the very represen-tation of woman as object. Finally, while Galeran submits passively to marry a woman he does not love (because she reminds him of his beloved Frêne), Frêne deploys her own needlework and singing to test the sincerity of Galeran's love for her. Each romance portrays its maiden in opposition to the passive *pucele desconseillie* of Arthurian romance. These damsels in distress save *themselves* and, as they do so, their virtue and intelligence redeem their social worlds. The transformative capacities and qualities of embroidering maidens are the brightest thread in these romances' narrative design.

In the central section of *L'Escoufle*, the heroine, Aélis, undergoes a series of ruptures, displacements, and transformations. Bonds with women replace the failed support of family and love; she moves from court to city, from leisure to work, from heterosexual love to female friendship. Dismayed by her father's broken promise that she may marry Guillaume, son of Count Richard of Montivilliers, she boldly plans her elopement. Like Nicolette in the chantefable, she uses a rope made of linens to scale down the castle wall; she provisions herself with a purse and a ring (tokens that she bestows on Guillaume) and a good amount of money, on which she depends after Guillaume wanders off. After Aélis wakes to find herself alone, feeling that Guillaume has abandoned her, her grief soon turns to activity; she befriends a singlewoman in a city. Isabelle, the "meschine," lives with her mother, a "vieille" who makes wimples. (We do not know whether the mother has ever been married.) Aélis leaves court, feudal politics, family, wealth, and men for a new liminal space marked by private domesticity, variable economic status, ties with women, and urban settings.

The "realistic" detail of this section of the narrative contrasts with the heroic and idyllic register of the sections that have preceded it, which have told of Count Richard's exploits and of the young lovers. Mother and daughter live in the "grange" and "pressoir" (barn and press) of a rich bourgeois who lets them use his space in return for their protection of his equipment (4964–74). Their room has no bed, except for a straw pad, and only a small table and skimpy cloth; the women have no money to buy food until Aélis supplies it; and the narrator contrasts their simple wooden drinking cup, or *hanap*, to the silver one that Aélis carries in her sack (5222–26). This gynaceum is the most primitive female space we will encounter.[89]

Jean Renart opens a window here on the lives of singlewomen who may have made their living by sewing at home, living alone or in limited family groups, with no hope of social advancement. As Nancy Jones points out, Jean Renart does not choose to portray women who are members of prosperous female-dominated guilds.[90] Instead, *L'Escoufle* portrays an old woman and her daughter living in near-poverty who are acutely aware of their lowly status and of Aélis's high standing.

The relationship between the emperor's daughter and lower-class women quickly becomes more than an exchange of money and services. Isabelle replaces Guillaume as protector, confidant, and bedmate. Because Aélis believes that Guillaume has failed her ("K'ele voit bien c'or maintenant / a ele a Guilliaumes *failli*," 5286–87), she emplores the initially reluctant Isabelle to lie with her, promises her all the riches and wealth she has, snuggles up next to her, and kisses and embraces her. This intriguing scene transfers the language of heterosexual courtly coupling onto a same-sex bond that the narrator portrays as mutually beneficial (5264–93).[91] Their friendship forms the base of a partnership in which Isabelle assists

Aélis, who provides the impoverished girl with the material sustenance she has lacked.

Failing to find Guillaume in Normandy (after a two-year search), Aélis and Isabelle venture to Montpellier, where they set up a household that becomes a favorite meeting place for bourgeois and knights. As Isabelle makes wimples and towels, Aélis displays her talent in creating luxury objects — embroidered belts and fasteners — that please clients of both classes. As Jones has pointed out, the romance encodes "social differences through the language of textiles" (32); Isabel's lower-level wimple-making contrasts with Aélis's aristocratic embroidery. The narrator remarks that Aélis's "grans gentelise" [nobility, courtesy] increases the value of her goods (5490–95). On feast days, Aélis re-creates the atmosphere of a court, amusing her guests by telling "romans et contes" and offering chess and other games. In the economy described by this story, Isabelle's work alone would not have lifted these women above poverty, and Aélis's high birth, without her virtue and industry, would have been worthless.

Although Aélis proves her ability to support herself, her goal is not to become self-sufficient but to regain noble status. Upset that the lady of Montpellier has ignored her, she seeks and wins the lady's favor by making a purse with her husband's arms; just as Aélis earlier "seduced" Isabelle into companionship, so the lady here seeks Aélis's physical presence — the narrator tells us that she would happily have shared her bed with Aélis (5750–54).[92] When the lady gives the purse to her paramour, the count of Saint-Gilles, it becomes coveted by that knight's wife, who transfers her suppressed sexual jealousy to Aélis's handiwork. Eventually, Aélis's friendship with the lady of Saint-Gilles compensates for her husband's infidelity. This alliance echoes the one that Aélis formed with Isabelle when Guillaume "abandoned" her; from this point forward, sustained by female friendships and especially by Isabelle — with whom she is "one body and one soul" — Aélis forgets Guillaume (6166–71). For a time, female bonds replace the void created by a father's death (Guillaume's), an emperor's broken promise, a lover's absent-minded zeal, and a husband's infidelity.

The ease with which Aélis finds Isabelle and her mother and then establishes a household of singlewomen in Toul and Montpellier suggests that spheres of female-dominated economic activity were not uncommon. But, as Jones points out, the romance "makes no serious attempt to represent an urban workshop whose goal would be to perpetuate itself" (32). Rather, the romance portrays the benefits of female friendship and idealizes the service of life-cycle singlewomen.[93] It shows how poor women can elevate themselves by association with wealthy women or noble households. At the end of the romance, when Aélis and Guillaume are reunited and married, ready to assume their positions first as count and countess of Rouen and then as emperor and empress of Rome, Aélis takes twenty puceles into her service. The girls are quickly transformed from poor women, some even lacking good shoes, into ladies who have new dresses, saddles, and bridles, "autel comme leur dame" [just like their lady] (8669). Although their mothers cry at being separated from their daughters, readers learn that the girls will be compensated with riches, as soon as Guillaume becomes emperor (8688–93).

Compared to fragmented tales of vanishing puceles desconseillies in Arthurian romance, Aélis's story is remarkable. She breaks out of the mold of the woman who waits to be rescued, turns away from dependence on men, forms strong affective relationships with women, and transforms the lives of poor women around her. In the end, heterosexual love, the feudal family, and imperial politics assert their primacy. But the narrative offers a tantalizing glimpse of a liminal space beyond court and marriage where bonds with other women replace failed relationships with fathers, lovers, and husbands and where women working together can transform their lives.

The transformations wrought by the maiden Lïenor in Jean Renart's *Le Roman de la Rose ou de Guillaume de Dole* are both more subtle and more profound. Lïenor does not set forth to a city to go to work, like Aélis; nor does she form an alternate community, however temporary, with other women. But, like Aélis, Lïenor refuses to be the victim of the forces that conspire against her. (She has been defamed by a jealous seneschal who has learned from her mother about the rose on her thigh and who has claimed to have deflowered her, thus disqualifying her for her projected imperial marriage.) Unlike the Emperor Conrad and her brother Guillaume, who lament passively, Lïenor acts astutely and assertively to subvert the very system that constructs female *enor* as chaste property for men by turning the ruse against her accuser. She plants objects, including an embroidered belt, on the body of the seneschal, who is forced to deny that he has ever seen her in order to clear himself of the rape charge. Renart's description of Lïenor's arrival at Conrad's court, which consciously replays the spectacular arrival of Lanval's fairy, heightens the boldness and originality of her move.[94] Like Lanval's lady, Lïenor's "truth" reveals the court's corruption but, in contrast to the fairy, Lïenor has no supernatural power. Her solution is not otherworldly, but eminently sensible. As the narrator points out, Lïenor could not have done a better job defending herself if she had studied law for five years (*GD*, 4768–73).

Furthermore, as Helen Solterer has observed, Lïenor's manipulation of the seneschal's body, which is first tightly bound in the belt and then disrobed before the court, effects first a "mock defloration" of a man and then a "delicious parody of the ritualized inspection of the virgin's body."[95] Lïenor's clever moves allow her not only to assert uncontestably her own chastity, but also to call into question the processes by which the "rose" (the female body) is represented. As she rewrites the plot against her, she redefines female *enor* — "li enor" — on her own terms, which comes to entail not only chastity but her own sense of worth, defended forcefully before those who would not believe her.

Like Aélis, Lïenor strives not for autonomy, but for an imperial marriage. The lavish ceremony with which the romance concludes celebrates her transformation from *pucele* to *dame* and empress. This romance, like *L'Escoufle*, holds forth the tantalizing possibility that maidens who surmount the painful trials of adolescence on their own may gain the ultimate "prize": marriage to a social superior.[96]

These summary remarks can only hint at the complexities of an extremely elaborate literary creation in which forty-eight lyric fragments are intercalated into the narrative as an embellishment and as a metacritical device.[97] Lïenor, like other heroines who use their wits, allows the narrator to critique conventional courtly behaviors and systems of representation. Lïenor's brilliant performance as a feisty young woman and the narrator's ingenious manipulation of his character have made the conclusion of the *Roman de la Rose* the focus of pointed debate about the representation of women in romance. Does Lïenor's successful marriage feed "the wildest dreams of countless knights and ladies of the lower levels of the French aristocracy," as argued by John Baldwin?[98] Does the narrator celebrate female agency in his creation of Lïenor, or does he ultimately undermine the power and autonomy of women's work, particularly textile work?[99] Is Lïenor a figure for the artifice of language?[100] Or does the narrator convey through her very complexity the failure of earlier courtly romances to "represent" women?[101] The ongoing scholarly debate attests to this spunky maiden's enduring capacity to generate critical reflection, in Conrad's court and in our own scholarly venues.

For the purposes of the present essay, what Lïenor demonstrates most persuasively is the power of a fictional singlewoman (allied with an astute narrator) to critique and transform social relations. Lïenor embodies the capacity of romance maidens to generate sympathy for their plight, admiration for their resolve, and reflection about the social changes they effect. The complex, composite character of Lïenor combines the spectacular appearance of Lanval's fairy, the verbal agility of Lunete, and the determined action of the damoiseles who decide their fate in the chansons de toile. Lïenor's appearance at Conrad's court to set her own story straight epitomizes the boldness of other maidens who rewrite the plots in which they are embedded.

Our final encounter with a singlewoman reveals one who actively devises her own story, deploys her artistry, and quite self-consciously stages the final moral transformations that lead to the romance's happy conclusion. Frêne's story in Renaut's *Galeran de Bretagne* expands and embellishes the story of the orphaned twin in Marie de France's *Frêne*. The narrator extends the 546-line lai into a nearly 8,000-line romance by conjoining tales of a knight's and a maiden's education, that of Galeran and Frêne, who, like Floire and Blancheflor, have fallen in love as youths and are separated by hostile families. In ways that we can only sketch out here, Renaut enhances the creative activity of Marie's heroine, who in his version becomes richly accomplished as an embroiderer of beautiful objects and singer of a variety of songs in many languages (1157–73). Just as the maiden Frêne sings "notes sarrasinoises, / chançons gascoignes et françoises, Loerraines, et lais bretons" (1169–71), so does Jean Renart weave together elements of maiden's tales from many sources — not only from *Frêne* and *Floire et Blancheflor*, but also from *Aucassin et Nicolette*, *L'Escoufle*, *Milun*, and *Eliduc*.[102] As he embroiders a sophisticated text that interlaces motifs of twinning, reflection, needlework, and song,[103] Renaut stresses his heroine's capacity to script her own story and to transform those around her.

Renaut spins the tale of the knight's and damsel's education in two interlacing threads; as in *Escoufle*, *Aucassin*, and the *Roman de la Rose*, the heroine's independence contrasts with the relative passivity of the hero. Frêne does not leave the abbess's domain out of fear that she may be found pregnant (as did Marie's heroine) or to live with Galeran (Gurun's counterpart). When the abbess accuses her of wanton behavior and blames her foolishness in hoping to marry her noble nephew, Frêne proclaims the "gentillesse" of her heart — attested by her love of reading, singing, and sewing — and defiantly criticizes and rejects convent life. Then she sets off on her own, by choice.

Like Aélis and Nicolette before her, Frêne rejects the unhappy destiny that others have designed for her and moves to amend her fate. With her

harp, the precious embroidered materials her mother had left with her as a
baby, and a generous quantity of money (left by her late mentor), she
ventures into a liminal space and fashions a new identity as "Mahaut," a
talented seamstress and singer. Like Aélis, Frêne trades the circumscribed
roles of court or convent for new social space in the city (Rouen). She also
enters into a partnership with other women (here, a wealthy bourgeois
widow, Blanche, and her daughter, Rose) whose lives she materially im-
proves. Her creativity, industry, and autonomous self-advancement in the
central episodes of the narrative contrast with the sentimental confusion of
Galeran, who like Gurun before him (and like Eliduc), enters into a relationship with a second woman; he agrees to marry Floire, Frêne twin sister,
not out of love, but for her resemblance to the portrait Frêne has embroidered for him.

Like Marie's heroine, Frêne finds herself triply displaced: from home,
from convent, from love. But, as in *Frêne* and other lais, the maiden's
displacement is prefatory to a greater social transformation, a transformation that Renart's heroine brilliantly enacts when she learns of Galeran's
impending marriage. Rather than accept her fate or expire in sorrow, she
intervenes to turn her own trial of misfortunes into a trial of *truth* that she
designs. She decides to test her lover's fidelity by appearing at his wedding, to see how his heart will "prove" itself: "La je pourray moult bien
apprendre / Comment cuers se prouve d'amer" [There I will be able to
learn / How a heart proves its love] (6564–65).

In Renart's story, the transformative episode wherein Marie's heroine
lays her mother's *paile* on the nuptial bed, thus triggering the mother's recognition, is itself transformed into an embellished, amplified episode, which
portrays the heroine's artful refashioning of identity and her integration of
a fragmented self. Allying herself with Rose and with a "veuve qui file"
[widow who spins], sequestered in humble quarters, Frêne sets to work.
Fragmentation precedes transformation: first, Frêne cuts up the "chier
drap" [precious cloth] into which her mother had embroidered the stories
of Floire et Blancheflor, Paris and Helen, and in which she had wrapped her
abandoned baby. Then, Frêne fashions a cloak so skillfully that it seems to
have been made for her; the "ymages" [designs] sewn by her mother remain
intact, yet seem new (6744–68). Decked in magnificent garb, carrying her
harp and her mother's marvelous pillow, plaintively singing "Je voiz aux
noces mon amy" [I'm off to my lover's wedding] (6976), Frêne stages an
entrance that is as spectacular as that of Lanval's fairy or Lïenor.

In the episode where Frêne appears before her lover and mother in her newly stitched cloak, Renaut threads together motifs of maiden's stories in Marie's *Lais* (especially *Frêne*, *Lanval*, *Milun*, and *Eliduc*) with motifs from *Aucassin* (the heroine's performance in song before her lover) and Jean Renart's *Roman de la Rose* (Lïenor's trial). As this maiden undergoes the perilous *translatio* of adolescence, carrying a harp and her mother's textiles, Renaut demonstrates how the spectacle of his composite figure (carried over from his predecessors) can also transform those who gaze upon her or hear her story. Her singing and harping render the minstrels speechless; her accusatory, haunting words stun Galeran into remembrance of Frêne and incite his refusal to marry. Frêne's words and beauty move her mother, Gente, to rekindle "vraie amour" in her heart (7256–68); his wife's confession elicits the pardon of her husband Brundoré, Frêne's father. Later, even the spiteful abbess repents of her harsh treatment of Frêne, who graciously forgives her in repayment for the "doulce nourreture" [kind upbringing] she has received. In the end, Frêne's displacement as a single-woman into a liminal space where she can forge a new identity has proved to be her greatest fortune. Arranging her own marriage (and a noble marriage for Rose), she avoids the plot of the mal mariée or the reluctant nun. By contrast, her forlorn sister takes the veil.

L'Escoufle, *Le Roman de la Rose ou de Guillaume de Dole*, and *Galeran de Bretagne* thus join *Le Roman de Silence* in exploring the perils and challenges of adolescence. In each case, parental protection is absent or parental authority has broken down; as the maidens venture forth from home, they encounter discomfort, separation, loss, and crisis. These romances do not advocate the single life for women as a necessary step in growing up. But the maiden's period of autonomy allows her to explore other identities and to penetrate other social spaces — the forest, the city, a new court, even the battlefield. Her intellectual or artistic skills, and her inner virtues, allow her to survive and to succeed in the task to which she has set herself. In *L'Escoufle* and *Galeran de Bretagne*, maidens quickly establish sentimental and economic bonds with women (widows and their adolescent daughters) that replace failed relationships at court or in the convent. Starting from the premise introduced by Marie de France that an "aventure de femmes" — a women's story — deserves to be remembered and may well be the *force motrice* of a fiction, these romances set their heroines free to wander on their own within the frame of a marriage plot so that they may participate in the fabrication of their own fate.

The popularity of the plot of what we might call "the maiden's trials" in thirteenth-century romance suggests that these stories had appeal for new audiences in lower aristocratic and high bourgeois households, beyond the courts of kings and counts. For some readers, these stories may have provided a welcome demonstration of what young women might accomplish, if given half a chance. For others, these tales might have offered an idealized representation of a "trial" period that many young women may have undergone, by dint of necessity. The readiness with which maidens such as Aélis and Frêne insert themselves into communities of female workers corroborates historical findings that the world outside the court or the convent might provide opportunities for young women who found themselves alone either as orphans, as rebellious daughters, or as abandoned fiancées. The emphasis on differences of social standing and on the importance of noble birth in all these romances (in complex ways that we cannot explore here) reminds us that the destiny of a singlewoman was determined especially by her class. A singlewoman with the polished demeanor and skills that result from a courtly education, to say nothing of an ample supply of money, has a better chance of prospering than does a poor maiden or widow. If an estranged noblewoman can attach herself to an industrious worker or wealthy bourgeoise from an urban setting, the two may become a happy and prosperous "couple" in a city until each makes a successful "high" marriage.

Our journey through the vast forest of twelfth- and thirteenth-century verse and prose romance has revealed diverse ways in which the stories of singlewomen are told and transformed. Portrayed through the inflections of their narrators' voices, embedded within the distinct registers of romance's subgenres, the puceles, damoiseles, meschines, and unmarried dames of romance beckon readers down different paths to confront the question of their significance for medieval singlewomen. What these (and many other) fictional accounts may contribute to a historical understanding of singlewomen is perhaps, above all, a sense of the prevalence, complexity, diversity, and incompleteness of their stories. Marie de France's *Lais* commemorate the "granz biens" of maidens who, as they undergo the *translatio* from childhood to adulthood, transform their limited social worlds; her subtle voicing of singlewomen's stories was heard by some later romances and, whether her influence is explicit or not, her treatment of singlewomen is prophetic of later fictional developments. Chrétien and his Arthurian successors celebrate the valor of the knights who save puceles desconseillies and confront the enchantments of fairies. Try as these romancers may to marginalize secondary female characters — as if to contain female autonomy through dispersion, fragmentation, or eradication — the powerful figures of Morgan and the Lady of the Lake reappear in many guises, revealing, at every turn, a culture's desire for and fears about a separate female domain. The romans réalistes and romances like *Silence* offer by far the most extensive narrative development of female autonomy in the "real" world; the maidens' freedom to explore new mixes of class and gender in an urban setting encourages readers to imagine social scenarios that depart from courtly, heterosexual, married norms. Each fictional transformation of a singlewoman's story, partial as it may be, gives voice to the perils and the possibilities of life outside the bonds of medieval marriage and sustains a cultural discourse about female autonomy and honor. At the end of the Middle Ages, female honor will be reconfigured with female clerkly authority by the most prolific "seulette" of late medieval France, Christine de Pizan, who will not fail, in her final work, to celebrate the transformative powers of a maiden — Joan of Arc, la pucele.[104] How Christine's and Joan's stories transform the narratives of their fictional predecessors is another tale, of course, but we can surmise that their stories might have been told differently without the "aventures" of earlier singlewomen, as commemorated in the deeds of lais and romance.

I would like to thank Matilda Bruckner, Jane Burns, Carol Chase, Peggy McCracken, Nancy Jones, and Nancy Rabinowitz for reading and commenting on drafts of this paper.

Appendix

EDITIONS

Aucassin et Nicolette. Ed. Jean Dufournet. Paris: Flammarion, 1984.

Chrétien de Troyes. *Philomena. Conte raconté d'après Ovide*. Ed. C. de Boer. Paris: Paul Geuthner, 1909.

——. *Erec et Enide*. Ed. Mario Roques. Paris: Champion, 1978.

——. *Cligés*. Ed. Alexandre Micha. Paris: Champion, 1965.

——. *Le Chevalier de la Charrete*. Ed. Mario Roques. Paris: Champion, 1972.

——. *Le Chevalier au Lion (Yvain)*. Ed. Mario Roques. Paris: Champion, 1971.

——. *The Story of the Grail (Li Contes del Graal), Or Perceval*. Ed. Rupert T. Pickens. Trans. William W. Kibler. New York: Garland, 1990.

Floire et Blancheflor. Ed. Jean-Luc Leclanche. Paris: Champion, 1980.

Heldris de Cornuälle. *Le Roman de Silence: A Thirteenth-Century Arthurian Verse Romance*. Ed. Lewis Thorpe. Cambridge: Heffer, 1972.

Jehan Maillart. *Le Roman du Comte d'Anjou*. Ed. Mario Roques. Paris: Champion, 1931.

Jean Renart. *Le Roman de la Rose ou de Guillaume de Dole*. Ed. Félix Lecoy. Paris: Champion, 1979.

Jean Renart. *L'Escoufle: roman d'aventure*. Ed. Franklin Sweetser. Paris: Droz, 1974.

Lancelot: roman en prose du XIIIe siècle. Ed. Alexandre Micha. 9 vols. Vols. 1–8. Geneva: Droz, 1978–83.

Marie de France. *Les Lais de Marie de France*. Ed. Karl Warnke. Trans. Laurence Harf-Lancner. "Lettres gothiques." Paris: Librairie Générale Française, 1990.

La Mort le Roi Artu: roman du XIIIe siècle. Ed. Jean Frappier. Geneva: Droz, 1964.

Partonopeu de Blois. Ed. Joseph Gildea. 2 vols. Villanova, Pa.: Villanova University Press, 1967–70.

Philippe de Remi's La Manekine. Text, Translation, Commentary. Ed. Irene Gnarra. New York: Garland, 1988.

La Queste del Saint Graal. Ed. Albert Pauphilet. Paris: Champion, 1921.

Raoul de Houdenc. *La Vengeance Raguidel*. In *Raoul von Houdenc. Sämtliche Werke*. Ed. Mathias Friedwanger. 2 vols. Halle: Niemeyer, 1909. Vol. 2.

Renart (Jean Renart). *Galeran de Bretagne: roman du XIIIe siècle*. Ed. Lucien Foulet. Paris: Champion, 1925.

Renaut de Beaujeu. *Le Bel Inconnu: roman d'aventures*. Ed. G. Perrie Williams. Paris: Champion, 1929.

Tristan et Iseut. Les poèmes français. La saga norroise. Ed. and trans. Daniel Lacroix and Philippe Walter. Lettres gothiques. Paris: Librairie Générale Française, 1989.

TRANSLATIONS

Chrétien de Troyes. *The Complete Romances of Chrétien de Troyes*. Trans. David Staines. Bloomington: Indiana University Press, 1993.

Heldris de Cornuälle. *Silence: A Thirteenth-Century Romance*. Trans. Sarah Roche-Mahdi. East Lansing, Mich.: Colleagues Press, 1992.

Jean Renart. *The Romance of the Rose, or, Guillaume de Dole*. Trans. Nancy Vine Durling. Philadelphia: University of Pennsylvania Press, 1993.

——. *L'Escoufle: Roman d'aventures*. Trans. Alexandre Micha. Paris: Champion, 1992.

Lancelot-Grail. The Old French Arthurian Vulgate and Post-Vulgate in Translation. Ed. Norris J. Lacy. 5 vols. New York: Garland, 1993–1996.

Marie de France. *The Lais of Marie de France*. Trans. Robert Hanning and Joan Ferrante. New York: Dutton, 1978.

Renaut. *Galeran de Bretagne*. Trans. Jean Dufournet. Paris: Champion, 1996.

Notes

1. Old French editions will be cited in "Editions and Translations"; whenever possible, a translation in modern French or English will be provided. Translations provided within the essay are my own.

2. One contested point is whether the romance supports or undermines traditional gender roles. For a range of critical views and an extensive critical bibliography, see Regina Pskai, ed., "Special Issue on *Le Roman de Silence*," *Arthuriana* 7, 2 (1997).

3. See Aimé Petit, "Le traitement courtois du thème des Amazones d'après trois romans antiques: *Enéas, Troie,* et *Alexandre*," *Le Moyen Age* 89 (1983): 63–84.

4. Brigitte Cazelles, ed., *The Lady as Saint: A Collection of French Hagiographic Romances of the Thirteenth Century* (Philadelphia: University of Pennsylvania Press, 1991). Of particular interest is the female-authored *Life of St. Catherine* by Clemence of Barking presented in *Virgin Lives and Holy Deaths: Two Exemplary Biographies for Anglo-Norman Women: The Life of St. Catherine, The Life of St. Lawrence*, trans. Jocelyn Wogan-Browne and Glyn S. Burgess (London: J. M. Dent, 1996).

5. As discussed by Kathryn Gravdal, *Ravishing Maidens: Writing Rape in Medieval French Literature and Law* (Philadelphia: University of Pennsylvania Press, 1991), 104–21.

6. *Fabliaux érotiques*, ed. Luciano Rossi and Richard Straub (Paris: Librairie Générale Française, 1992), 93–105.

7. Alaisina Yselda and Na Carenza, "Na Carenza al bel cors avinenz," in *Songs of the Women Troubadours*, ed. Matilda Tomaryn Bruckner, Laurie Shepard, and Sarah White (New York: Garland, 1995), 96–97.

8. See the discussion by Helen Solterer, "Contrary to What Is Said: The *Response au Bestiaire d'amour* and the Case for a Woman's Response," in her *The Master and Minerva: Disputing Women in French Medieval Culture* (Berkeley: University of California Press, 1995), 97–130.

9. Jean de Meung, *Le Roman de la Rose*, ed. Félix Lecoy (Paris: Champion, 1973), ll. 12710–14516.

10. See, for example, the virtuous and wicked maidens portrayed by the Chevalier de la Tour Landry, who writes for his own young daughters in *Le Livre du Chevalier de la Tour Landry pour l'enseignement de ses filles*, ed. Anatole de Montaiglon (Paris: P. Jannet, 1854).

11. Marguerite Porete, *Le mirouer des simples ames*, ed. Romana Guarnieri (Turnholt: Brepols, 1986); trans. Ellen L. Babinsky, *The Mirror of Simple Souls* (New York: Paulist Press, 1993).

12. See *Joan of Arc in History, Literature, and Film: A Select Annotated Bibliography*, ed. Nadia Margolis (New York: Garland, 1990).

13. For a useful survey of the genre, see Douglas Kelly, *Medieval French Romance* (New York: Twayne, 1993). Fuller treatment of the literary context of twelfth- and thirteenth-century romance can be found in *Le roman jusqu'à la fin du XIIIe siècle*, ed. Jean Frappier and Reinhold R. Grimm, *Grundriss der Romanischen Literaturen des Mittelalters*, vol. 4 (Heidelberg: Carl Winter, 1978).

14. In the terms of this volume, most of these are life-cycle singlewomen rather than lifelong singlewomen. However, since many unmarried women who hail from the Other World seem free from the forces of biological age, and since we do not know the fate of so many anonymous damsels, the term "life-cycle singlewoman" must be applied with caution. See the discussion of life-cycle and lifelong singlewomen offered by Kowaleski and by the editors in the Introduction.

15. As Maureen Fries notes, "In Arthurian romance, only women who are not married are capable of consistent heroism" ("Female Heroes, Heroines, and Counter-Heroes: Images of Women in Arthurian Tradition," in *Arthurian Women: A Casebook*, ed. Thelma S. Fenster [New York: Garland, 1966], 66.

16. Studies of female characters in Old French romance abound, with greatest emphasis on individual heroines such as Iseut, Guinevere, and the named ladies of individual romances. For an early study, see Pierre Jonin, *Les personnages féminins dans les romans français de Tristan au XIIe siècle* (Aix-en-Provence: Ophrys, 1958), which includes analysis of Brangien, Iseut's unmarried servant. A recent anthology of criticism on Arthurian women, which includes a fine review essay and a current bibliography, is provided by Fenster in *Arthurian Women*; in the same series, see Lori J. Walters, ed., *Lancelot and Guenevere: A Casebook* (New York: Garland, 1996) and Joan Tasker Grimbert, ed., *Tristan and Isolde: A Casebook* (New York: Garland, 1995). For a detailed analysis of women's roles in Arthurian verse romances that stresses the importance of unmarried *damoiseles* and *puceles*, see Marie-Luce Chênerie, *Le chevalier errant dans les romans arthuriens en vers des XIIe et XIIIe siècles* (Geneva: Droz, 1986), 410–501. The many appearances of autonomous fairy-lovers, as epitomized by Morgan, are analyzed extensively by Laurence Harf-Lancner, *Les fées au moyen âge: Morgane et Mélusine, la naissance des fées* (Paris: Champion, 1984). Other recent works on heroines, secondary characters, or anonymous maidens in specific texts will be cited further on.

17. The significance of some Old French romances for their female audiences is the subject of my *Women Readers and the Ideology of Gender in Old French Verse Romance* (Cambridge: Cambridge University Press, 1993). On female patronage, see June Hall McCash, ed., *The Cultural Patronage of Medieval Women* (Athens: University of Georgia Press, 1996). Useful information about female audiences and patrons of Anglo-Norman literature is provided by Carol Meale, ed., *Women and Literature in Britain, 1150–1500* (Cambridge: Cambridge University Press, 1993). On the representation of women in romances written for female patrons, see Joan Ferrante, *To the Glory of Her Sex: Women's Roles in the Composition of Medieval Texts* (Bloomington: Indiana University Press, 1997), 107–35.

18. See, for example, Micheline de Combarieu, "Le *Lancelot* comme roman d'apprentissage: Enfance, démesure et chevalerie," in *Approches du Lancelot en prose*, ed. Jean Dufournet (Paris: Champion, 1984) and Elspeth Kennedy, "The Knight as Reader of Arthurian Romance," *Culture and the King: The Social Implications of the Arthurian Legend*, ed. Martin B. Shichtman and James P. Carley (Albany: State University of New York Press, 1994), 70–90.

19. Frédéric Godefroy, *Dictionnaire de l'ancienne langue française et de tous ses dialectes du IXe au XVe siècle*, 10 vols. (Paris: Vieweg, 1888–1920), 5:272–73. For detailed discussion of these terms, see the chapter "La jeune fille" in A. Grisay, G. Lavis, and M. Dubois-Stasse, *Les dénominations de la femme dans les anciens textes littéraires français* (Gembloux: Duculot, 1969), 156–87.

20. *Les dénominations de la femme*, 178.

21. Godefroy, *Dictionnaire*, 5: 273.

22. The spelling of *dameisele* (as found in Marie), has several Old French

variants. I will use *damoisele* as the generic OF form and will adopt the most prevalent spelling for individual texts and authors, as appropriate.

23. For example, the "damoiseles" of the *Prose Lancelot* are often alternately referred to as "puceles" and as "dames."

24. I take Marie de France, whatever her historical identity, to be the author and the compiler of the twelve *Lais* in the Harley manuscript, as the narrator suggests in the Prologue when she says that she has "collected" the lais and recounted them in rhyme—"m'entremis des lais assembler, / par rime faire e reconter" (47–48). On Marie's feminine narratorial persona, see Michelle A. Freeman, "Marie de France's Poetics of Silence: The Implications for a Feminine *Translatio*," *PMLA* 99 (1984): 860–83. Questions about the attribution of the *Lais* (as well as the *Fables* and the *Espurgatoire Seint Patriz*) to one Marie de France have been raised most forcefully in Richard Baum, *Recherches sur les oeuvres attribuées à Marie de France* (Heidelberg: Carl Winter, 1968).

25. Theories of Marie's historical identity are discussed in Philippe Ménard, *Les Lais de Marie de France* (Paris: Presses Universitaires de France, 1979), 13–28 and Michel Curley, ed., *Saint Patrick's Purgatory* (New York: Garland, 1993), 3–8.

26. On the originality of Marie's *assemblage* and on the ways she fulfills her Prologue program throughout the collection, see Matilda Tomaryn Bruckner, "Textual Identity and the Name of a Collection: Marie de France's *Lais*," in her *Shaping Romance: Interpretation, Truth, and Closure in Twelfth-Century French Fictions* (Philadelphia: University of Pennsylvania Press, 1993), 157–206.

27. See Freeman, "The Poetics of Silence" and her "Dual Natures and Subverted Glosses: Marie de France's 'Bisclavret,'" *Romance Notes* 25, 3 (1985): 288–301.

28. See, for example, Rupert T. Pickens, "Thematic Structure in Marie de France's *Guigemar*," *Romania* 95 (1974): 328–41, and, most recently, his "Marie de France and the Body Poetic," in *Gender and Text in the Later Middle Ages*, ed. Jane Chance (Gainesville: University of Florida Press, 1996), 135–71.

29. On Marie's *Fables* as a didactic work for young people, see Harriet Spiegel, "Instructing the Children: Advice from the Twelfth-Century Fables of Marie de France," *Children's Literature: Annual of the Modern Language Association Division on Children's Literature* 17 (1987): 25–46. Karen Jambeck argues that the *Fables* participate in the *speculum principis* tradition, "The Fables of Marie de France: A Mirror of Princes," in *In Quest of Marie de France*, ed. Chantal A. Maréchal, (Lewiston, Me.: Edwin Mellen Press, 1992), 59–106, but this need not exclude female audiences. See Harriet Spiegel, "The Woman's Voice in the *Fables* of Marie de France," in *In Quest of Marie de France*, 45–58. As they tell exemplary tales about male and female sexual and social development, the *Lais* can be shown to offer complex lessons to and about adolescents.

30. For her thoughtful comments on an earlier, unpublished paper on *Deux Amants*, and for introducing me to the *Lais*, I thank Kristine Baer.

31. See Kristine Brightenback, "The *Metamorphoses* and Narrative *Conjointure* in *Deux Amants*, *Yonec*, and *Le Laustic*," *Romantic Review* 72 (1981): 1–12.

32. On the role of female speech in instigating action throughout the collection, see Anne Paupert, "Les femmes et la parole dans les *Lais* de Marie de France," in

Amour et Merveille: Les "Lais" de Marie de France, ed. Jean Dufournet (Paris: Champion, 1995), 168–87.

33. As Peggy McCracken has argued, by locating the aunt in Salerno, site of a famous medical school, by calling her knowledge an art of "physik" [learned medicine], yet by refusing to call her a "miresse" [doctor], Marie allows the aunt to represent both "learned medical training" and "traditional healing practices"; see McCracken, "Women and Medicine in Medieval French Narrative," *Exemplaria* 5, 2 (1993): 260. McCracken notes that other romances characterize women healers as "enchantresses," as in Chrétien de Troyes's *Cligés*, where Thessala, the heroine's nurse and also a singlewoman, uses potions to remarkable effect.

34. The importance of women who write and tell stories in the *Lais*, and their affinity with the narrator, has been noted in Diana M. Faust, "Women Narrators in the *Lais* of Marie de France," *Stanford French and Italian Studies* 58 (1988): 17–28.

35. For edition and commentary of the 21 songs and song fragments constituting this thirteenth-century genre of "women's songs," see Michel Zink, *La Chanson de toile* (Paris: Champion, 1977). Many of the songs feature a young woman who sews; all feature either a young maiden or a *mal mariée* in love, as do Marie's *Lais*. Almost all the maiden's songs end either with the maiden's happy tryst with her lover, or with her eventual marriage to the man of her choice. The songs attributed to Audefroi le Bâtard are especially noteworthy for the ways their heroines overcome difficult obstacles (imprisonment by the father; pregnancy out of wedlock) to get what they want. Although some critics insist on the male authorship of these songs, Jane Burns has argued that, regardless of authorship, the songs combine female voice and women's work to construct alternative social scenarios (Burns, "Sewing like a Girl: Working Women in the *chanson de toile*," unpublished paper).

36. On the bonds between women in this lai, see Michelle Freeman, "The Power of Sisterhood: Marie de France's *Le Fresne*," *French Forum* 12 (1987): 5–26.

37. The fairy's interdiction may take various forms, from demanding that the affair be secret to forbidding that her body be seen under certain conditions. See Harf-Lancner, *Les fées au moyen âge*, 94–101 and 252–54. Such an interdiction heightens the reader's sense that the fairy's autonomous existence cannot be reconciled with the "real" social world.

38. Harf-Lancner, *Les fées au moyen âge*, 250. The motif of a fairy lady (or maiden knowing the arts of magic) who seeks out the lover will recur, for example, in *Partonpeu de Blois*, Aimon de Varennes's *Florimont*, and Renaut de Beaujeu's *Le Bel Inconnu*. These three romances are dedicated to fictional ladies whom the poet professes to love; in addition, *Partonpeu* and *Florimont* portray young women noted for their learning. On how poets writing for women valorize female autonomy, see Ferrante, *To the Glory of Her Sex*, 127–30.

39. On the significance of naming here and elsewhere in Marie, see Matilda Bruckner, *Shaping Romance*, 177–84.

40. Rupert Pickens notes the creative function of violence in this and other lais in "Marie de France and the Body Poetic."

41. On the economy of gifts and the poetics of largesse in *Eliduc* and Marie's other lais, see Milena Mikhaïlova, *Le présent de Marie* (Paris: Diderot, 1996).

42. For example, Philippe de Beaumanoir's *La Manekine*, in which the maiden

cuts off her hand so that her father will not marry her, and Jehan Maillart's *Le Roman du Comte d'Anjou*, in which the maiden enlists the support of other women after she escapes from her father's incestuous desire.

43. As in the romances discussed in "The Singlewoman Sets Forth," pp. 171–80.

44. On the power of women to subvert male appropriation of the female body in this text, see Jane Burns, "Beauty in the Blindspot: Philomena's Talking Hands" in *Bodytalk: When Women Speak in Old French Literature* (Philadelphia: University of Pennsylvania Press, 1993), 115–50.

45. Grace M. Armstrong, "Women of Power: Chrétien de Troyes's Female Clerks," *Stanford French and Italian Studies* 58 (1988): 29–46.

46. Marie-Noëlle Lefay-Toury, "Roman breton et mythes courtois: l'évolution du personnage féminin dans les romans de Chrétien de Troyes," *Cahiers de Civilisation Médiévale* 15 (1972): 193–204 and 283–93.

47. See Kathryn Gravdal's chapter, "The Poetics of Rape Law: Chrétien de Troyes's Arthurian Romance," in *Ravishing Maidens*, 42–71.

48. See Jane Burns, "Rewriting Men's Stories: Enide's Disruptive Mouths" in her *Bodytalk*, 150–202.

49. See "The Question of Women in *Yvain* and *Le Chevalier de la Charrette*" in my *Women Readers and the Ideology of Gender*, 33–67.

50. A complete enumeration of secondary "demoiselles" in *Erec*, *Yvain*, *Lancelot*, and *Perceval* is provided in Angelica Rieger, "Balade des demoiselles du temps jadis. Essai sur l'entrée en scène des personnages féminins dans les romans arthuriens de Chrétien de Troyes," in *Arthurian Romance and Gender. Masculin/féminin dans le roman arthurien médiéval. Geschlechterrollen im mittelalterlichen Artusroman*, ed. Friedrich Wolfzettel (Amsterdam: Rodopoi, 1995), 79–103.

51. Chênerie, *Le Chevalier errant*, 413.

52. Ibid., 434–51. Rieger's somewhat different schema posits 7 types in Chrétien: 1) the abandoned maiden 2) the escorting or escorted maiden 3) the wandering maiden 4) the "questing" maiden 5) Salomé, or the vengeful maiden 6) the nymphomaniac and 7) the chatelaine of a deserted castle ("Balade des demoiselles," 99).

53. As she later explains to her cousin, Erec, son of a king, took her "povre et nue" [poor and naked/ill-clothed] and so increased her "enor" that no "desconseilliee" [disconsolate/impoverished/endangered maiden] was ever so well provided for (6261–62).

54. She and her knight have made vows to each other, but they have come to the garden in secret, in contrast to Enide's public marriage. The cousin is referred to as a "pucele" (6002) and a "dameisele" (6023).

55. The way that Mabaograin's *amie* resists masculine appropriation and is subsequently "rejected" by the narrator has been discussed in Burns, *Bodytalk*, 184–96.

56. See my remarks on this manipulative character, who seeks to entrap Gauvain in her love-death machine in *Women Readers*, 90–100.

57. On Lunete's clever manipulations and their affinity with the narrator's moves, see Grace Armstrong, "Women of Power," 37–46.

58. Like Lunete, Thessala's creative powers link her to the narrator. She herself is a focus of the narrator's art, since she combines aspects of Ovidian nurses, Lavinia's mother in the *Roman d'Enéas*, and Brangien in the Tristan legend, as Michelle Freeman has demonstrated in *The Poetics of Translatio Studii and Conjointure: Chrétien de Troyes's "Cligés"* (Lexington, Ky.: French Forum, 1979), 92–97, 128–34.

59. With courage, determination, and ingenuity, Meleagant's sister seeks high and low until she discovers Lancelot in a tower, supplies him with a pick so that he can break free, and bathes and dresses him with great attention — all of which constitutes a fairly lengthy strand of narrative (ll. 6374–6706).

60. The appellation "dame" leaves open the possibility that the Lady of Norison may once have been married; the fact that she seeks Yvain as a permanent companion means that she no longer has a husband. On the motif of women under siege, see Elaine Newstead, "Besieged Ladies in Arthurian Romance," *PMLA* 63 (1948): 803–30.

61. On the motif of the *pucelle esforciée* and the function of rape in this and other episodes of Arthurian romance, see Gravdal, *Ravishing Maidens*, 42–71.

62. For more on the "costume de Logres" and the paradoxical status of women in *Yvain* and the *Charrete*, see my *Women Readers*, 39–41.

63. Gravdal, *Ravishing Maidens*, 66–67.

64. Female abjection subtends even a character as apparently malevolent as the Male Pucele, who has persisted in mocking and annoying Gauvain. As she finally explains to him, she engaged in her bizarre, haughty behavior in the hope that someone would punish her with death, which would comfort her for the loss of her love, killed by another knight (8879–8914).

65. "Roman breton et mythe courtois," 200.

66. The literary biography of Gauvain in later romances has been well told in Keith Busby, *Gauvain in Old French Literature* (Amsterdam: Rodopi, 1980).

67. Thessala also "succeeds" in manipulating events to her lady's advantage, thanks to her magic potions, but the matter of women's power in this romance is considerably complicated by *Cligés*'s frequent comic reversals and the narrator's antifeminist conclusion.

68. The magic ring Lunete gives to Yvain (*Yvain*, 1021–37) links her to the fairies.

69. His legacy also extends to numerous individual verse romances or continuations, where the representation of singlewomen owes much to Chrétien. On various aspects of Chrétien's legacy, see *The Legacy of Chrétien de Troyes*, ed. Norris J. Lacy, Douglas Kelly, and Keith Busby, 2 vols. (Amsterdam: Rodopi, 1988).

70. Harf-Lancner traces the evolution of the Lady and Morgan throughout the Arthurian corpus in *Les fées au moyen âge*, 264–315. Both women are variations of what Harf-Lancner calls the "Morganien" model in which a fairy carries a mortal off to her realm (leaving no issue in society), as opposed to a "Melusinian" model where the fairy visits a mortal on earth and bears progeny, before she disappears.

71. As has been remarked in Harf-Lancner, *Les fées au moyen âge*, 303–4. On the maternal qualities of the Lady of the Lake, whose sexuality has been repressed and whose selfless generosity has been heightened, see also Françoise Paradis, "La triple mise au monde d'un héros, ou trois images d'une féminité maîtrisée dans le début du

Lancelot en prose," in *Approches du Lancelot en prose*, ed. Jean Dufournet (Paris: Champion, 1984), 157–76.

72. See the discussion in Harf-Lancner, 264–88.

73. For further discussion of Morgan's evolution, chiefly in a negative direction, see Fanni Bogdanow, "Morgain's Role in the Thirteenth-Century French Prose Romances of the Arthurian Cycle," *Medium Aevum* 38 (1969): 123–33; Maureen Fries, "Female Heroes, Heroines and Counter-Heroes."

74. Fries, "Female Heroes, Heroines, and Counter-Heroes," 68–71.

75. See Sheila Fisher, "Leaving Morgan Aside: History, Revisionism, and Women in *Sir Gawain and the Green Knight*," in *The Passing of Arthur: New Essays in Arthurian Traditions*, ed. Christopher Baswell and William Sharpe (New York: Garland, 1988), 129–51.

76. Among these are Amite, daughter of King Pelles and mother of Galahad; her nurse, Brisane; the lady of Hungerford Castle who pursues Bors; the daughter of the King of Brandegorre whom Bors refuses to marry (and with whom he conceives a child, after being tricked); the young lady of Estroite March, who loves Hector and tries to make him promise to marry her; the false Guinevere, who attempts to usurp Guinevere's place as queen and as Arthur's wife; even a "damoisele de Grant Aage" [Maiden of Many Years] who pursues Lancelot.

77. Micha, *Lancelot*, 10:44–55. Micha's appendix also lists sixteen anonymous "dames" (43–44), not all of whom have husbands. There is considerable slippage between the terms "dame" and "damoisele" in the *Prose Lancelot*.

78. Burns, "La Voie de la Voix: The Aesthetics of Indirection in the Vulgate Cycle," in *The Legacy of Chrétien de Troyes*, 151–67.

79. Anne Berthelot, "From the Lake to the Fountain: Lancelot and the Fairy Lover," in *Arthurian Women*, 153–69.

80. Paradis, "La triple mise au monde."

81. Carol Chase, "Whatever Happened to Hector's *Amie*? Love, Marriage, and Land in the Prose *Lancelot*" (forthcoming).

82. Rieger suggests the proliferation of maidens in Chrétien's romances may, in part, be an appeal to the female audience; see "Balade des demoiselles du temps jadis," 103.

83. For elaboration, see Jeannine Horowitz, "La diabolisation de la sexualité dans la littérature du Graal, au XIIIe siècle, le cas de la *Queste del Graal*," in *Arthurian Romance and Gender*, 238–50; and Jacques Ribard, "Figures de la femme dans la *Quête du Saint Graal*," in *Figures féminines et roman*, ed. Jean Bessiere (Paris: Presses Universitaires de France, 1982), 33–48.

84. As discussed in greater detail in Susan Aronstein, "Rewriting Perceval's Sister: Eucharistic Vision and Typological Destiny in the *Queste del San Graal*," *Women's Studies: An Interdisciplinary Journal* 21, 2 (1992): 211–30.

85. See *La Mort le Roi Artu*, ed. Frappier, sects. 13–14, 25–29, 38–39, 70–71.

86. The recent publications and presentations of Nancy A. Jones have established the importance of these "femino-centric romances" to medieval women's history. Her work is part of an extensive project on medieval literature and women's production of textiles, especially embroidery. My debt to Nancy Jones's generosity in pointing me towards texts and criticism in this section is extensive. See Nancy A.

Jones, "The Uses of Embroidery in Jean Renart: Gender, History, Textuality," in *Jean Renart and the Art of Romance: Essays on "Guillaume de Dole,"* ed. Nancy Vine Durling (Gainesville: University Press of Florida, 1997), 14–44.

87. Although the category "roman réaliste" has been much discussed, the term need not preclude the sophisticated critique of courtliness that many of these romances perform. For a description of the genre, see Rita Lejeune, "Jean Renart et le roman réaliste," in *Grundriss der Romanischen Literaturen*, 400–453. Lejeune includes under this rubric Jean Renart's *L'Escoufle* and *Le Roman de la Rose et de Guillaume de Dole*, *Galeran de Bretagne*, Gerbert de Montreuil's *Le Roman de la Violette*, *Le Roman du Castelain de Coucy et de la Dame de Fayel*, *Joufroi de Poitiers*, Philippe de Beaumanoir's *La Manekine* and *Jehan et Blonde*, and *Le Roman du Comte d'Anjou*. Aside from the *Castelain de Coucy*, which treats an adulterous affair, and *Joufroi*, which centers on the hero's escapades (and the narrator's art), these romances all present maidens who overcome trauma (the threat of incest, as in *Manekine* and *Comte d'Anjou*), vindicate themselves from charges of slander (in *Roman de la Rose* and *Violette*), or surmount familial and social obstacles (*Escoufle*, *Galeran de Bretagne*, *Jehan et Blonde*).

88. Embroidery is a motif in *L'Escoufle*, *Guillaume de Dole*, *Galeran*, and *Le Comte d'Anjou*; the maidens work for pay in *Escoufle*, *Galeran*, and *Le Comte d'Anjou*. See Emmanuelle Baumgartner, "Les Brodeuses et la ville," *Una idea di città: l'imaginaire de la ville médiévale. 50 rue de Varenne* (Milan: A Mondadaori, 1992), 89–95; and Nancy A. Jones, "The Uses of Embroidery."

89. On interior feminine spaces or *gynécées* in French literature, see Danielle Regnier-Bohler, "Geste, parole et clôture: les représentations du gynécée dans la littérature médiévale du XIIIe au XVe siècle," *Mélanges . . . Alice Planche* (Paris: Belles Lettres, 1984), 392–404.

90. Jones notes (30–31) that Jean Renart was undoubtedly familiar with the female-dominated guilds described in Paris, Rouen, and Cologne by Judith Bennett and Maryanne Kowaleski, "Crafts, Guilds and Women in the Middle Ages: Fifty Years After Marian Dale," in *Sisters and Workers in the Middle Ages*, ed. Judith M. Bennett, Elizabeth A. Clark, Jean F. O'Barr, B. Anne Vilen, and Sarah Westphal-Wijl (Chicago: University of Chicago Press, 1989). But Jones observes that Jean Renart "downplays" the economic value of embroidery in the later scenes when Aélis and Isabelle take up embroidery (31). Our first encounter with women doing textile work is not of embroidery, but of wimple-making, and the narrator stresses the women's poverty and solitude.

91. As in many male-female "courtly" bedroom scenes, the erotic import of this exchange is inscrutable. But Jean Renart's positive portrayal of female love is noteworthy. It is generally admitted that the only explicit portrayal of lesbian sexual relations in medieval French literature is the scurrilous slander of Etienne de Fougères, *Li Livre des manières*, ed. R. Anthony Lodge (Geneva: L. Droz, 1979); see pp. 97–98. The nature of love between women in the poem by *trobairitz* Bieris de Romans has been the subject of great controversy; see Angelica Rieger, "Was Bieiris de Romans Lesbian? Women's Relations with Each Other in the World of the Troubadours," in *The Voice of the Trobairitz: Perspectives on the Women Troubadours*, ed. William D. Paden (Philadelphia: University of Pennsylvania Press, 1989), 73–94.

92. The seductive relationships between women in this romance have been noted in an astute article by George T. Diller, "*L'Escoufle*: une aventurière dans le roman courtois," *Le Moyen Age* 85 (1979): 33–43.

93. As set forth in the Introduction and Kowaleski, "The Demographic Perspective."

94. E. Hoepffner, "Les *Lais* de Marie de France dans *Galeran de Bretagne* et *Guillaume de Dole*," *Romania* 56 (1930): 227–30.

95. Helen Solterer, "At the Bottom of Mirage, a Woman's Body: *Le Roman de la Rose* of Jean Renart," in *Feminist Approaches to the Body in Medieval Literature*, ed. Linda Lomperis and Sarah Stanbury (Philadelphia: University of Pennsylvania Press, 1993), 227–28.

96. On the matrimonial politics at play in this romance and the historical realities that subtend them, see John W. Baldwin, " 'Once there was an emperor': A Political Reading of the Romances of Jean Renart," in *Jean Renart and the Art of Romance*, ed. Durling, 45–82.

97. A fine selection of recent articles on Jean Renart's literary techniques and an extensive critical bibliography are provided in *Jean Renart and the Art of Romance*, ed. Durling.

98. Baldwin, "A Political Reading," 70.

99. Nancy Jones, "The Uses of Embroidery in Jean Renart." From another perspective, I have argued that Jean Renart's narrator appropriates Lïenor for his metacritical enterprise (see *Women Readers*, 143–53).

100. Roger Dragonetti, *Le mirage des sources: l'art du faux dans le roman médiéval* (Paris: Seuil, 1987), p. 193.

101. Regina Psaki, "Jean Renart's Expanded Text: Lïenor and the Lyrics of Guillaume de Dole," in *Jean Renart and the Art of Romance*, ed. Durling, 122–41.

102. For resemblances between Renaut and Marie, see Hoepffner, "Les *Lais* de Marie de France dans *Galeran de Bretagne*," 212–24. See also Dragonetti, *Le mirage des sources*, pp. 229–60; Jean Dufournet, "Introduction," in Renaut, *Galeran de Bretagne*, trans. Jean Dufournet, 8–26; Paul Rockwell, "Twin Mysteries: *Ceci n'est pas un Fresne*," in his *Rewriting Resemblance in Medieval French Romance: ceci n'est pas un graal* (New York: Garland, 1995), pp. 25–42.

103. See, for example, Anne-Marie Plasson, "L'obsession du reflet dans *Galeran de Bretagne*," *Mélanges offerts à Pierre le Gentil* (Paris: SEDES, 1974), 673–94.

104. Christine de Pizan, *Le Ditié de Jehanne d'Arc*, ed. Angus J. Kennedy and Kenneth Varty (Oxford: Society for the Study of Mediaeval Languages and Literature, 1977). Christine's representation of Amazons, sibyls, maidens, and martyrs, her ways of telling of singlewomen's stories, and her advice to unmarried women in the *Livre de la Cité des dames* and the *Livre des Trois Vertus*, both of 1405, are subjects worthy of a chapter in their own right.

7

Having Her Own Smoke

Employment and Independence for Singlewomen in Germany, 1400–1750

Merry E. Wiesner

SCHOLARLY INTEREST IN SINGLEWOMEN in the medieval period has a very long history in Germany. In the late nineteenth century, when social commentators and academics throughout Europe (and the United States) were debating what to do with "surplus" and "redundant" women who were not able to marry, the German archivist and historian Karl Bücher looked backward to see if this had been a problem before. Using several population counts from the fifteenth century, he determined that there had been a significant "surplus of women" (*Frauenüberschuß*) in German cities during that time, perhaps as much as 125 women for every 100 men.[1] How did these women survive? By their own work, answered Bücher, who paid special attention to female occupations in his later exhaustive study of occupations in Frankfurt, and who, along with other nineteenth-century historians, saw the craft guilds in the late Middle Ages as a primary employer of women, including those not the wives or widows of guild masters.[2]

Bücher's statistics about the sex ratio in medieval cities have now been thoroughly questioned, as he used numbers drawn from wartime (when young men often fled cities to avoid being drafted into military service) or from only parts of cities.[3] Subsequent studies have also demonstrated, however, that even in cities with a balanced sex ratio, many households were headed by women. In Frankfurt, in 1354, for example, 17 percent of the households paying taxes were headed by women, and 24 percent in 1495; similar statistics — 25 percent in Trier in 1363, 22 percent in Schwäbisch-Hall in 1406, 25 percent in Basel in 1429 — come from the tax records of other cities.[4]

These tax records do not invariably divide female heads of household into widows and singlewomen, but occasionally they allow for rough estimates. Among the nearly 300 households headed by women in Trier that paid the least amount of taxes (and female-headed households were always overrepresented among the poorest in any city), 26 percent were headed by women labeled widows, 9 percent by beguines, 21 percent by women with an occupational designation, and 44 percent by women simply identified by name.[5] Some in the last group may well have been widows, and a few women with an occupational designation may have been widows as well — perhaps those whose husbands were long dead and who were known in the neighborhood for their work — but we can probably assume that most of the women with an occupational designation and some in the last group were singlewomen. Thus whether women actually outnumbered men in total, women did work and live independently in medieval cities; included among them were a significant share of singlewomen who lived independently, or in the words of the period, who "had their own smoke."

Statistical studies have also revealed that, in contrast to what Bücher wished had been the case, the sixteenth century brought little change in this situation.[6] Tax records from the sixteenth through the eighteenth centuries indicate that female-headed households continued to make up between one-fifth and one-quarter of the tax-paying households in most cities, and a few enumerations distinguish between singlewomen and widows. In Stuttgart in 1545, for example, a special tax levied to support military moves against the Turks (*Türkensteuer*) listed 3.5 percent of the households in the city as headed by women who were probably single (and another 11 percent by women labeled widow).[7] Tax lists from Frankfurt in 1593 and 1607 give similar numbers, as do those of Augsburg around 1600.[8] Tax records in villages do not begin as early as those in cities, but when they do they again reveal singlewomen as heads of household; during the eighteenth century in Egg, for example, a village of several hundred households in the south German area of the Vorarlberg, between 2 and 6 percent of the households were headed by singlewomen, with another 8 to 21 percent of the households made up of unmarried brothers and sisters who lived together.[9] These numbers may seem low by contemporary standards, but, as we shall see, legal and ideological sanctions on singlewomen living alone or heading households were so strong that even percentages in the single digits are surprising.

New and more extensive types of sources that began in the sixteenth century allow us to get a better idea about numbers of singlewomen. Marriage registers indicate that women's age of marriage was late, with the average age for women at first marriage in many villages of between 25 and 28, and in cities of between 21 and 25; in both rural and urban areas until the late eighteenth century, daughters from wealthier families married earlier than those from poorer families, who might not marry until they were in their forties.[10] Marriage registers thus suggest that some female-headed households were those of women who were not yet married but who would eventually marry. By the early eighteenth century church records of all types are complete enough to allow some calculation of the percentage of those who never married among the population; most estimates put this at about 10 percent.[11]

In addition to singlewomen who lived independently and thus show up in tax records as heads of household, many also lived as dependent domestic servants, of which there are increasingly specific enumerations in the early modern period. These records show that female domestic servants often made up between 5 and 15 percent of the population of urban areas, and that the majority of these were singlewomen.[12]

All these records indicate that Bücher's question may well be asked about early modern as well as medieval Germany, and it forms the key focus for this essay. What employment options were open to and pursued by singlewomen, and how did these change during the centuries in which so much about German society and culture changed dramatically?

Historiographical Issues

Though I have been using the terms "Germany" and "singlewomen" rather freely, it is important to recognize before going any further that both of these are somewhat problematic. There was, of course, no Germany in this period, only a loose conglomeration of hundreds of states making up the Holy Roman Empire, each with its own laws and traditions, and many including territory no longer within the boundaries of Germany. Though many of these states had roughly similar legal codes — and the smaller states often intentionally copied their larger and more powerful neighbors — there was often enough difference to mean that the laws regarding singlewomen could differ dramatically from place to place. We know that legal differences shaped employment and migration for single men, as the laws of certain cities favored journeymen at the expense of masters. These legal differences have been studied less systematically for women, but we do know that cities differed dramatically in the proportion of female to male servants, so that women may also have been influenced by legal differences as they migrated in search of work, choosing to go to those cities which offered more freedom as well as more employment opportunities. Thus, along with the types of personal and economic factors that made the experiences of singlewomen so varied in other parts of Europe — age, social class, ethnicity, regional economic development — the lack of legal uniformity in Germany makes generalizations difficult; even the geographic boundaries of "Germany" are hard to define.

"Singlewomen" also has rather loose boundaries. As noted above, the sources are not always clear about a woman's marital status, a problem exacerbated by the fact that most female-headed households are among the poorest in the city, often too poor to pay any taxes, so that officials do not record information about them carefully.[13] Poor widows and singlewomen often clustered in certain areas of town where rents were lowest, so that place of residence does not help us distinguish between the two groups.

There was also not a perfectly sharp line between being married and being single. Though the Catholic Church had taken a strong stand against clerical concubinage, in many cities and rural parishes priests still had concubines into the sixteenth century; these women were technically not wives, of course, but may have lived with the priest for many years.[14] Women who were vagrants or migrants often had longstanding relationships with men — again not technically "marriage" — and the children that resulted from these unions shaped the women's chances of employment and thus made their situation different from that of migrants without children.[15] At the other end of the social scale, noble and wealthy women sometimes spent much of their lives in conventlike institutions, termed *Stifte*, where they took no vows and so were not technically religious, but never married or did not marry until much later in life than most women of their social class.[16] In some parts of Germany this included Protestant women, who were forced to defend their single state to religious authorities who denied the value of celibacy; their words are some of the few we have from Protestant women about the value of virginity.[17]

Both Protestant and Catholic religious authorities and secular governments attempted to make the line separating the married from the single much sharper in the sixteenth century, however. Along with criticizing celibacy, Protestants attacked the Catholic understanding that consent of the two parties was the only necessary element in a marriage, pointing to irregular "marriages" (literally "dark-corner marriages," *Winckelehen*) in taverns and inns that were followed by pregnancy and then disputed by the "husband." Though they denied the sacramentality of marriage, Protestants put great emphasis on parental consent, a public ceremony, and the presence of a pastor for a valid marriage.[18] Reforming Catholics answered with the decree *Tametsi* at the Council of Trent, which required the presence of witnesses, including a parish priest, for an exchange of vows to be considered a valid marriage.[19] By the later sixteenth century both sides in the religious struggle saw setting clear boundaries between married and single, and other aspects of marital reform, as key parts of their drives toward confessionalization and social discipline; both Protestants and Catholics strengthened clerical, paternal, and state control of marriage.[20]

Attitudes Toward Single People

Along with a sharper distinction between married and single, the sixteenth century also brought with it a greater emphasis on marriage as the proper life for all (or most) individuals. This emphasis has traditionally been attributed to the Protestant Reformation, though recent scholarship has noted that decades before the Reformation Christian humanists also praised marriage, and city authorities viewed the marital household as the key political and economic unit. After the Reformation as well, manuals advising men how to be firm-yet-kindly household heads and women obedient-yet-capable wives flowed from both Protestant and Catholic pens.[21] Though their message was thus not completely new or different, Protestant reformers were particularly strong in both promoting marriage and attacking single people, arguing that those who did not marry went against God's command in the Garden of Eden and their divinely created and irresistible sexual desire; women who did not marry, they argued, also lacked the care and discipline the marital state provided.[22] With both religious and political ideology so firmly in favor of marriage, people who never married were regarded with increasing suspicion, except for those in Catholic areas clearly attached to religious institutions that themselves were becoming more like households during this period.[23]

Single men were often the targets of preachers and moralists for their flamboyant clothing and rowdy behavior, but the craft guilds depended on their labor as journeymen and apprentices and so were loath to support any meaningful restrictions, which would have simply led young men to migrate elsewhere.[24] Singlewomen were a different matter, for their work was rarely recognized as essential. Hostility toward never-married persons and a suspicion about women who were not under the control of men were not simply a matter of pastoral concern or religious ideology, but led to explicit legal restrictions on women's choice of work, place of residence, free-time activities, and even relations with their own family.

Some of these laws were directed primarily against women who migrated in search of employment, and are part of more general fear of migrants and transients.[25] Singlewomen were forbidden to move into cities unless they went into service, and those who left employers were banished. Innkeepers were prohibited from housing unattached women unless they received special permission, employment agents allowed to house domestic servants between jobs for only very short periods of time, and private citizens ordered never to take in singlewomen.[26] Such restrictions were gradually expanded to include the daughters of citizens, however, as they, along with foreigners, were forbidden to "have their own smoke" ("ihr eigene Rauch haben") or "earn their own bread" ("ihr eigene Brot verdienen").[27] Even girls whose mothers were still alive were suspect, as this ordinance from Strasbourg in 1665 makes clear:

> Numerous complaints have been made that some widows living here have two, three, or more daughters living with them at their expense. These girls go into service during the winter but during the summer return to their mothers, partly because they want to wear more expensive clothes than servants are normally allowed to and partly because they want to have more freedom to walk around, to saunter back and forth whenever they want to. It is our experience that this causes nothing but shame, immodesty, wantonness and immorality, so that a watchful eye should be kept on this, and if it is discovered, the parents as well as the daughters should be punished with a fine, a jail sentence, or even banishment from the city in order to serve as an example to others.[28]

Worries about women working and living on their own became particularly acute, as one would expect, in areas in which some type of wage labor made this possible. Textile production was the most common form of wage labor for women in Germany, and though spinners, weavers, and lace-makers were usually badly paid, local market conditions sometimes allowed them to make a living wage. It is thus in centers of textile production, such as Augsburg in the sixteenth century, Württemberg in the seventeenth, or Berlin in the eighteenth, that we find the most heated debates about women living on their own.

In 1577 in Augsburg the weavers' guild complained to the city council that they could not find enough young women willing to work as spin-maids in their households, as all the women coming into the city were working independently and living with other families or renting a small room somewhere. The weavers thus had to buy their thread from them at what they regarded as inflated costs. The city council responded by forbidding all noncitizen women to live and work independently, but the prohibition proved impossible to enforce as the need for thread was too great. In 1597 the weavers were even more incensed, as women were saying openly that they were not so dumb as to work as spin-maids for the weavers when they could earn three times as much spinning on their own; even those who agreed to live in weavers' households demanded the right to work for themselves two days a week. This situation was intolerable, according to the weavers, who included all sorts of moral issues in their complaint: the women had complete freedom as to when they worked and when not and so walked around with journeymen at all hours; they were a bad example for girls coming in from the countryside and even for local girls who would thus be inclined to live on their own rather than in a weaver's household. The council enacted a series of harsh ordinances banishing all women who made demands of their employers or worked on their own and all employers who made contracts with them, but these were also largely ineffectual, for unmarried citizen women continue to appear in the records as the employers of migrant women, all providing thread for the disgruntled but dependent weavers.[29]

In seventeenth-century Württemberg, a special pejorative, *Eigenbrötlerinnen* (women who earn their own bread), was used for women who lived on their own, and citizens were enjoined to report to authorities those who housed them. Tight control was exercised to make sure they did absolutely nothing else but spin (in other words, no other part of the cloth production process), with ducal authorities fining both village and city residents who employed singlewomen at other tasks and imposing a maximum piece rate for spinners, thus keeping their wages low.[30]

Similar anger at women who lived on their own and those who facilitated this arrangement also comes out in an eighteenth-century treatise by Johann Georg Krünitz, the author of a 242-volume political and economic encyclopedia:

The shortage of native domestic servants partly results when servants, especially maids, live by their own hands with other people in little rooms and support themselves by spinning, sewing, washing, or similar things. They usually do this at times when things are cheap. Through this they show nothing except a flight from hard work and an inclination towards comfort; they would rather have small earnings if they can only be their own masters and sit behind the stove. Yes, through this they seek to have better opportunities to indulge in their slovenly and immoral debaucheries more comfortably. The police cannot allow servants to live by their own hands in this way, but should send them away if they are not from this city, or bring them into the workhouse or jail; they should also punish with prison or something equally forceful those who shelter such servants and do not report them to the servant's office or the police-officials who have authority over servants.[31]

Krünitz's comments bring together all of the fears about singlewomen on their own: they affected the economy adversely by creating a shortage of servants so that employers had to pay servants more; they were "masterless" and thus a threat to a society that viewed male-headed households as the norm; they might be sexually active and have children out of wedlock, who would need public support. Pastor Brändle from the Vorarlberg was equally appalled at the activities of female cotton-spinners and lace-makers, who were wearing fancy clothes "because of the good wages in lace-making," ordering drinks from taverns for their lace-making sessions, and playing cards; he was especially upset at finding "a whole crowd of singlewomen" in a tavern on a Sunday.[32]

Singlewomen in early modern Germany thus faced continual criticism about their marital state and often about their type of employment and their living independently. Given the economic security, legal advantages, and higher social status that marriage promised, it is not surprising that marriage was the goal of most women and men. (Studies of early modern marriage courts reveal, for example, that many more women took cases to court in order to establish a marriage than to prevent or dissolve one.)[33] Nevertheless, despite the fulminations of preachers and officials, a large number of women, as we have seen, remained unmarried for most or all of their adult lives. In this milieu in which the behavior of singlewomen was under such intense scrutiny, what possibilities were open to them? Could any of them offer the "freedom" so feared by authorities, or was this simply a chimera of official imagination?

Domestic Servants

By far the largest number of singlewomen in Germany were employed in domestic service; indeed, as in English, one of the words for singlewoman and female domestic servant was the same: *Magd* (maid). As we have seen, domestic service was the most or only acceptable form of employment for singlewomen in the eyes of many commentators, for this generally put them into a male-headed household; population tallies indicate that most female-headed households were too poor to hire domestic servants. Conditions of service varied tremendously: many households, particularly in urban areas, had only one servant, almost always a woman who assisted in all domestic tasks and also at artisanal tasks if the household was one of a guild master; wealthier households might have many servants, and a woman could work her way up from goosegirl to children's maid to serving maid to cook; in some households, such as those of weavers in Augsburg noted above, women might spend most of their time in production, so that though officially counted as "maids" they were actually, in Olwen Hufton's terms, "residential industrial employees."[34] No matter what their tasks, however, they were always more poorly paid than male servants; both the regulations stipulating the amount of pay for servants and records of amounts actually paid indicate that women's wages were usually about half that of men's.[35] This proportion varied little from the fourteenth century to the eighteenth, and applied whether the place of employment was a patrician household in a large city, a noble estate in the countryside, or an artisanal household in a small town.

Some analysts of domestic service have pointed to the fact that *most* servants were between the ages of 15 and 29, and have thus seen service as a "life-cycle" phenomenon involving young people of all social classes, a period during which they learned the domestic and craft skills necessary to run a household.[36] Several more detailed analyses have demonstrated, however, that urban middle-class young women did not generally go through a period of service unless their parents, or at least their father, had died; most urban maids were thus lower class, from rural areas, or orphans.[37] They found their positions through friends or relatives or, beginning in the fifteenth century, through employment agents who were licensed by the city and were most often women.[38] On noble estates, maids might actually be "forced servants" (*Zwangsgesinde*), performing at least a year of service as part of their family's feudal dues; one study of a Westphalian estate has found that this continued into the late eighteenth century and involved only the daughters of dependent families, never the sons.[39]

Though service was praised because it put women into male-headed households, it was also problematic for that very reason. Increasing numbers of moralists and pamphleteers in the sixteenth and seventeenth centuries warned about the dangers of mixing classes within a household, and described maids as whores (*Huren*) who were out to seduce the head of household or one of his sons, though in actuality the reverse was more often the case. (This stereotype would have dangerous consequences for maids who actually did become pregnant, a situation that was often disastrous and occasionally led to imprisonment or infanticide.)[40] They increasingly compared maids with animals such as apes, donkeys, or pigs, or described them as a subhuman group distinct from the rest of the population. An entire subgenre of the "devil's books" (*Teufelsbücher*), popular works that described the evils associated with various occupations or activities, focused on maids.[41] The author of one of these, Philemon Menagius, for example, described maids as the "worst enemy," and viciously noted:

> Maids must also consider what they are in and of themselves. They are in themselves nothing but ashes and dirt, and, however they want to deck themselves out, they are shadows and nothings. In stink (*Stanck*) they were conceived, and in stink they lay hidden in their mothers' bodies. In stink they were born. They have nothing but filth and stink around them, and don't know to cover their stink, so that they don't often clear away the stink as the devil does, or their seams burst so that they cause a great stink and leave it after themselves.[42]

Such sentiments, though extreme, were not limited to moral treatises, but also began to shape laws in the later sixteenth century. Maids were accused of causing the general inflation of the sixteenth century, and their wages were strictly limited. They were criticized for extravagance in clothing and forbidden to wear silk or satin, even if they had gotten this from a generous employer as a hand-me-down.[43] Those found to be acting in a "disobedient, contrary, untrue, or otherwise inappropriate manner" were to be harshly punished, as were those who were found guilty of idleness.[44] Even their speech was restricted; a 1580 Munich ordinance ordered "headstrong and defiant" maids punished if they spoke against their masters, and the Memmingen city council ordered maids and other women not to discuss religion when drawing water at the neighborhood wells.[45]

Many of the regulations involving servants or the employment agents who found them positions were specifically concerned with limiting young women's mobility and independence. The 1580 Munich ordinance, for example, forbade anyone to coax servants away from their masters, not only with promises of gifts or money, but also with promises of "more freedom."[46] Many cities set draconian punishments for maids who left employers after serving less than six months or who demanded higher wages or gifts as conditions of employment; the frequency with which such laws were repeated suggests they were not as effective as authorities hoped, however. Frequently changing employment was one of the sins charged to maids in the "devil's books," with numerous authors repeating the same saying: "One thinks highly of journeymen who have wandered, but absolutely nothing of maids who have done so."[47] It is difficult to know whether this was a real issue or simply part of the stereotype about maids, however, for death records often describe women who had been in service with the same family for thirty, forty, or fifty years, and women appealing to gain entry into city and church hospitals in their old age noted similar periods of service.[48]

Despite the hostility towards maids and the restrictions on their independence, there were certain aspects of domestic service which made it attractive to young women. Though actual cash wages were low, room and board was included, allowing young women to save their wages for a dowry, spend them on clothing and jewelry, or even use them to make small investments or play city lotteries.[49] In some cities, maids who had worked a certain period with one employer were granted citizenship at a reduced rate, making them attractive marriage partners for husbands who were not citizens. In a few cities, public funds went to provide dowries for maids who had served long and honorably; though one would think the decades of service often required to gain such funds would have put a woman above marriageable age, the very late marriages recorded for many former maids demonstrates this was not always the case.

Domestic service also offered young women another means to gather a dowry: theft. Though servants who stole were harshly punished, the opportunities were great, and young women stole food, wine, bed-linens, spices, and money. They used these to trade for or buy drinks for their friends, or put them directly in their chests as a trousseau.[50] They bought gifts for young men they hoped to marry, or ribbons and lace collars for themselves. If caught, they sometimes justified their actions as simply taking back wages owed to them; a recent study of theft by maids has described this as both "retaliation and planning for the future."[51]

The pressure eventually to marry was not simply an ideological one for maids, but also reflected their understanding of what old age held for them if they did not. Though employers occasionally provided for servants who could no longer work, or servants used their own savings to buy places in hospitals or other care facilities, many were forced to move in with relatives and support themselves however they could.[52] The eighteenth-century judge Karl von Eckhartshausen described one woman who had simply been given a letter of good conduct that attested "that she had worked for our family as a children's maid for fifty years, and always conducted herself honorably, truly, and uprightly; she has been let go for no other reason other than that her eyes have gone bad so that she can no longer carry out her duties."[53] Aged ex-maids thus joined other singlewomen in the fluid pool of those who supported themselves by piecework, odd jobs, day laboring, and other forms of wage labor.

Wage Labor

Though wage labor has traditionally been seen as one of the hallmarks of capitalism, and thus a phenomenon of the "modern" economy, closer investigation of the medieval economy has indicated that many individuals, including many women, actually received wages at least as early as the fourteenth century, if not earlier. Estimates of urban populations in the eighteenth century note that one-quarter of the population may have supported themselves as day-laborers or by doing odd jobs, and, though accurate statistics are impossible, a good share of these were probably singlewomen. We know very little about how wage laborers were hired; certainly word of mouth and connections through relatives played a large part, and some cities appear to have had a corner of the public market where those seeking work gathered.

What types of work did women do? In the countryside they harvested grain, particularly in areas where grain was still cut with a sickle, or gathered and bound grain that men had cut with a scythe. Along with children, they gleaned, and they picked hops and grapes, sheared sheep, hauled manure, and harvested root crops. Beginning in the late seventeenth century, certain parts of Germany intensified stock-raising, with animals fed all year in stables instead of being allowed to range freely.[54] Feeding and caring for them was regarded as a female task, with women hired on a longer-term basis to care for pigs, cows, sheep, and poultry. In southern Germany and Switzerland, flax and linen production also provided employment for women in rural areas. We tend to think of the countryside as the domain of marital couples (and, indeed, the gender-specific nature of agricultural tasks meant that the proper functioning of a rural household necessitated at least one adult male and one adult female), but by the seventeenth century many rural areas actually offered more wage labor for women than men, and hiring records from large estates indicate that many of these may have been singlewomen.[55]

The cities also offered a range of possibilities for wage labor. As we have seen, in areas with significant cloth production there was always spinning, although wages for this varied considerably; they may have been adequate at times in Augsburg, but in Frankfurt in 1613 a woman appealing to the city council for support noted "What little I make at spinning will not provide enough for even my bread."[56] By the late seventeenth century some cities in Germany had manufactories for spinning or other stages of cloth production, in which large numbers of young women were paid by the piece for their labor; these were often linked to public workhouses that people could enter of their own free will or be forced to enter after being arrested for begging.[57] Laundering was another possibility, for especially the heavy laundry like bedding and linens was generally done by professional laundresses rather than the women resident in a household. Most laundry was done outside the house along river banks in both winter and summer, or in special laundering huts that city governments occasionally suspected of being locations for prostitution as well.[58] Laundresses in some cities were regulated, and had to swear an oath they would not overcharge customers or dump refuse in the city's rivers.

Laundresses were not the only women whose employment necessitated swearing an oath. As urban hospitals, pesthouses, and orphanages secularized in the sixteenth century, large numbers of women found employment in these caring for the ill, aged, handicapped, and children. Though most cities attempted to find widows or married women for the higher administrative positions, they also hired dozens of maids, cooks, seamstresses, shepherdesses, and women simply labeled "assistants" who were, judging by the names in some hospital records, often singlewomen.[59] Like domestic servants, these women received low cash wages, with the majority of their pay coming as room and board. They swore oaths to follow regulations that were often spelled out in great detail, including stipulations that they attend church services, pray daily, and not stand in dark corners talking to young men.[60] During times of the plague cities often opened special plague-hospitals or pesthouses, hiring women, as in Augsburg in 1563, "for lifting, turning, and whatever they were needed for, including sewing the dead into their burial cloths. We also used them if the parents of children died — one was either sent to the children or the children were sent into their homes until they each had three children."[61] Women were also hired by cities or privately to care for the needy outside of institutions; they took care of children, watched mentally ill adults, and fed war refugees. Though in times of great emergencies cities hired anyone available, in more peaceful times they were more restrictive; in 1532, for example, the Strasbourg city council paid people to care for the sick in their own homes and specifically wanted "elderly married men with good reputations and childless widows" for the job.[62] Singlewomen need not apply.

Some of the jobs available for women involved the care of healthy bodies as well as ill ones. Public baths employed women to help people undress or hold their clothes, wash customers' hair and bodies, shave them, or beat them with switches to increase circulation. Such women were called "bath maids," and many of them were probably unmarried, although this term is not a clear description of their marital status. The man or woman who ran the bathhouse was generally ordered to avoid taking anyone on who was known to have been a prostitute — and the bathhouses themselves were often suspected of prostitution — but otherwise there were few restrictions on who could be hired in this rather low-status occupation.[63]

Along with public baths, cities also ran municipal houses of prostitution from the fourteenth century until they were closed some time in the sixteenth century.[64] The man who ran a municipal brothel (*Frauenwirt*) was ordered not to take in young women from the city itself, but otherwise could take in anyone who looked to be healthy and clean. Most prostitutes came from poor families, and some appear to have been forced into prostitution by their parents or deceived into it through pimps or procurers.[65] Many more simply turned to prostitution when their attempts to support themselves in other ways failed, or combined prostitution with other types of wage labor such as laundering or spinning. (Indeed, in Ulm residents of the city's brothel were required to spin yarn every day for the *Frauenwirt* when they were not busy with customers, with the proceeds to go into a fund for women who were too old or sick to work.)[66] Women paid the *Frauenwirt* one-third of their earnings, and, though a few women may have earned fairly good pay at a young age, wills and inventories of prostitutes indicate that most earned very little.[67]

During the fourteenth and early fifteenth centuries, prostitutes — or at least those who lived in municipal brothels — were integrated fairly well into urban society, appearing as a group at city festivals and publicly welcoming visiting dignitaries. During the late fifteenth century this situation began to change, for complex ideological and political reasons, with prostitutes increasingly marginalized and attempts made to distinguish prostitutes from other women through special clothing and restrictions on their movement and places of residence.[68] This process resulted in the closing of municipal brothels (a process that took decades, from 1520 to 1590), and it also contributed to the hostility toward singlewomen. Singlewomen simply suspected of being "dishonorable" were ordered to move to special areas of cities reserved for prostitutes, "and not protect themselves that they do not carry out such sinful work in their houses."[69] In 1572 both Lucerne and Wismar ordered all young women not in service to leave, with the city council of Wismar noting that these women pretended to sew "in order to have a free life" but really "carried out great lewdness."[70] The borders between prostitution and other types of employment were often not rigid, as singlewomen (and also married women and widows) supported themselves occasionally by selling sex rather than, in the words of a woman from Stralsund in 1560, "suffer from poverty, hunger, and need."[71] Early modern authorities, however, both Protestant and Catholic, attempted to make them rigid, and increasingly viewed all singlewomen as potential whores.[72]

Craft Production and Sales

Though traditionally the Protestant and Catholic Reformations have been seen as the force behind the increased moralism of the sixteenth century, recent studies have pointed out that craft guilds also played a role in creating new types of familial and sexual ideology.[73] Certainly guild ordinances are one place where we can trace explicit restrictions on singlewomen, for, in contrast to what Bücher wished had been the case, access to craft guilds was only rarely the same for women as for men; the number of women working independently in guilds was always small, and most of these were master's widows.[74] The unmarried daughters of guild masters seem originally to have had the right to work in their father's shops as long as they remained unmarried, but this was not formally guaranteed through an apprenticeship contract, and by the seventeenth century was often disputed by journeymen. Daughters had to prove there were special circumstances that necessitated their working, and journeymen argued explicitly that masters' daughters should get married rather than take work away from men. Journeymen were even more adamant when it came to unrelated domestic servants, arguing that masters should utilize only apprentices and journeymen for production, and enforcing their aims by refusing to work next to men who had been trained in places where they still allowed "all sorts of servants, maids, women, and embroideresses."[75] Thus, though some singlewomen were employed in guild shops — occasionally even with the pretext of being "adopted" by the master so to avoid the restriction on their work in production—this was not a path toward an independent mastership, but akin to domestic service.

In any city, and in the countryside, a huge range of items existed that no guild bothered to oversee which could be made or gathered, and then sold rather freely. Singlewomen, along with widows and poorer married women, often combined these with wage work as opportunities fluctuated throughout the year, making brooms, brushes, soap, sauerkraut, or candles during the winter months, gathering firewood or herbs in the spring and nuts, berries, fruit, or mushrooms in the summer, and harvesting grain or picking grapes in the fall. They sold hot food items they had made or used clothing and other items—for which there was a flourishing market—sometimes combining this with petty pawnbroking or moneylending.[76] For such sales they had a small stand at the market or carried their wares around house-to-house; the opportunities to deal in stolen merchandise were great, so cities often required used-goods dealers to register and swear an oath. From lists of those registered we can tell that at least some of these women were not married—that is, they are not identified as "so-and-so's wife" but as "so-and-so's daughter" or with their own name.[77]

None of the women who sold at the market or peddled house-to-house became very wealthy, but the skills needed to earn at least a living through selling were those generally regarded as negative in women: verbal dexterity, independence, initiative, and a forceful personality. Market women appeared frequently in court defending their rights to sell certain items and their honesty and honor; they chased customers all over town to recover bad debts and took competitors to court to force them to stop selling.[78] Such skills and activities were bad enough, in the eyes of city authorities, in married women or widows, but even worse in singlewomen; a 1690 ordinance regulating fruit and vegetable vendors in Frankfurt, for example, blames "young female persons who could easily do some other kind of work, like being a maid" for "causing great disorder by selling fruit."[79] City officials often saw the license to sell or to have a stand as a substitute for poor relief, and wanted it limited to widows or married women whose husbands were away or injured. The Frankfurt ordinance noted above limits stands to those who are "aged and unsuitable for hard work, especially widows," and during the Thirty Years' War the city council of Strasbourg ordered all new brandy stands to go to widows or women whose husbands were away fighting "to support themselves better and live through this."[80]

Other Occupations

The types of employment I have discussed so far — domestic service, wage labor, craft production, and sales — certainly absorbed the vast majority of singlewomen during the late medieval and early modern period. A few other options were available, but these tended to be limited to much smaller groups. By the late seventeenth century, noble and wealthy urban households often hired singlewomen as governesses to train their daughters, at first favoring women from France or French-speaking Switzerland for the all-important French lessons, but gradually taking on women from Germany as well.[81]

At the other end of the scale of respectability were women who attached themselves to soldiers or supported themselves through crime; the two were equivalent, in the eyes of authorities, who banned women known to associate with the armies so often encamped in Germany during this period.[82] This suspicion of "soldiers' whores" at times extended to all singlewomen; in 1684 the Strasbourg city council ordered all singlewomen staying in the city who were not domestic servants to be registered "because so many immoral and indecent female persons have crept into the city and upset honorable citizens with their scandalous and animal-like lifestyles and have created noticeable problems among the king's garrison stationed here."[83] As in the case of maids and their employers, soldiers actually created more problems for women who associated with them than the reverse; by the eighteenth century in Prussia, soldiers were generally not liable to appear before local courts in fornication or paternity suits, and a significant share of the women who appeared before such courts alone described their impregnator as a soldier. Soldiers were forbidden to marry without the approval of their commanding officer, and sometimes made up the majority of unmarried men living in any area. This situation has led Ulrike Gleixner to note that in eighteenth-century Prussia "to a great degree the military system structured the sexual relationships between unmarried women and men."[84]

Conclusions

Whether servant, spinner, or "soldier's whore," singlewomen in Germany were often regarded as both animals and seductresses, living in filth and tempting men. They joined widows as an intellectual and moral problem for church and state authorities, inescapable given demographic and economic realities, but clearly outside the ideal that saw male-headed households as the only acceptable building blocks of society. Restrictions on their dress and employment, on the words they could speak, places they could go, and people they could talk to increased throughout the period, and a mistake in any of these could lead to suspicion of immorality, which further restricted their opportunities, or even to pregnancy, which could be catastrophic.

We might choose, as some historians have, to end the story here, with an assertion of the "bleak" conditions of life for singlewomen, the fact that "outside the family and the allotted roles of daughter, wife, and mother, women existed against considerable odds."[85] We might, however, read the sources slightly differently, not forgetting the restrictions, but also noticing how often they were ignored, laughed at, or directly confronted. Maids stole beer to drink with their friends, gathered at wells to discuss religion, or used their small earnings to buy jewelry and lace or play city lotteries; lacemakers ordered wine from taverns to drink while they worked and visited taverns or played cards openly when they were through for the day; used-goods dealers defended their livelihood and their honor when accused of trafficking in stolen goods or shortchanging their customers; spinners chose to keep "having their own smoke," living on their own or with other spinners despite all efforts to force them into male-headed households. These are, perhaps, small freedoms, but they indicate that, despite all the efforts of moralists and authorities, singlewomen did not always internalize the standard view of their condition or their character, nor did they necessarily require the support of their family to survive.[86]

Women's actions are only rarely accompanied by the type of self-conscious reflection we, as feminist historians, always hope to find. One of the few of these comes from the pen of Anna Bijns — actually a Dutch woman, not a German — who supported herself by teaching school and writing anti-Lutheran poetry. Though the hopes of most singlewomen rested with eventual marriage, her words indicate that at least a few women had a different opinion:

How good to be a woman, how much better to be a man!
Maidens and wenches, remember the lesson you're about to hear
Don't hurtle yourself into marriage far too soon . . .
Though wedlock I do not decry;
Unyoked is best! happy the woman without a man.[87]

This essay was written while I held the Association of Marquette University Women (AMUW) Chair in Humanistic Studies; my thanks to AMUW for providing me with the time to work on this and other writing projects. My thanks also to Susan Karant-Nunn for her suggestions about sources and references.

Notes

1. Karl Bücher, *Die Frauenfrage im Mittelalter* (Tübingen: H. Laupp, 1882).

2. Karl Bücher, *Die Berufe der Stadt Frankfurt im Mittelalter* (Leipzig: Teubner, 1914); Karl Weinhold, *Die deutschen Frauen in dem Mittelalter*, 2 vols. (Vienna: Gerold, 1851).

3. Kurt Wesoly, "Der weiblichen Bevölkerungsanteil im spätmittelalterlichen und frühneuzeitlichen Städten und die Betätigung von Frauen in zünftigen Handwerk (insbesondere am Mittel- und Oberrhein)," *Zeitschrift für die Geschichte des Oberrheins* 89 (1980): 69–117.

4. Merry E. Wiesner, *Working Women in Renaissance Germany* (New Brunswick, N.J.: Rutgers University Press, 1986), 4. (Specific archival references may be found in the notes of this book and for brevity's sake have not been reproduced here unless they concern a direct quotation.) Peter Ketsch, *Frauen im Mittelalter*, vol. 1, *Frauen im Mittelalter, Quellen und Materialen* (Düsseldorf: Schwann, 1983), 34–36.

5. Annette Winter, "Studien zur sozialien Situation der Frauen in der Stadt Trier nach der Steuerliste von 1364," *Kurtrierisches Jahrbuch* 15 (1975): 20–45.

6. Though he does not extend his own study into the period after 1500, when Bücher found increasing restrictions on women's work in the guilds in the late fifteenth century he asserted that there must have been "a gradual leveling of the significant sexual imbalance evident in the Middle Ages," for otherwise such "narrow-minded exclusion" would certainly have created "strong opposition in society and disturbance of the public order." As his own findings indicate a steady *increase* in the percentage of female taxpayers throughout the fifteenth century, his only solution was to propose a dramatic change, leading him to the odd claim that the sixteenth century was "peaceful times" (Bücher, *Frauenfrage*, 16).

7. Gerd Wunder, *Die Stuttgarter Steuerliste von 1545*, Veröffentlichung des Archivs der Stadt Stuttgart 26 (Stuttgart: Ernst Klett, 1974).

8. Friedrich Bothe, *Die Entwicklung der direkten Besteuerung in der Reichsstadt Frankfurt* (Leipzig: Duncker und Humboldt, 1906); Claus-Peter Clasen, *Die Augsburger Steuerbücher um 1600* (Augsburg: Hieronymous Mühlberger, 1976). Clasen attempts to sort out individual female taxpayers' marital status exactly, and notes that some women are explicitly labeled "single" (*ledig*), but because others are listed simply by name with no marital status, he is not able to do this in every case and his numbers are approximations.

9. Arno Fitz, *Familie und Frühindustrialisierung in Vorarlberg* (Dornbirn: Gütersloh, 1985), 110.

10. Heide Wunder, *"Er ist die Sonn', sie ist der Mond": Frauen in der Frühen*

Neuzeit (Munich: C. H. Beck, 1992), 48–49; Lotte C. van de Pol, "The Lure of the Big City: Female Migration to Amsterdam," in *Women of the Golden Age: An International Debate on Women in Seventeenth-Century Holland, England, and Italy*, ed. Els Kloek, Nicole Teeuwen, and Marijke Huisman (Hilversum: Verloren, 1994), 79. Though much of the discussion about the role of social class in determining age at first marriage is rather impressionistic and anecdotal, Renate Dürr has used unusually comprehensive death registers (*Totenbücher*) from Schwäbisch-Hall during the period 1635–90 to determine that over half the women who had previously worked as domestic servants did not marry until they were 30 or older (and 10 percent when they were 40 or older!), in contrast to only 12 percent of the women who had not worked as servants (Renate Dürr, *Mägde in der Stadt: Das Beispiel Schwäbisch Hall in der Frühen Neuzeit* [Frankfurt: Campus, 1995], 175). Jürgen Schlumbohm also has very complete records from a small rural area for the period 1650–1750 that indicate that not only familial wealth, but also whether one was an heir had significant effects on age at first marriage for both women and men (Jürgen Schlumbohm, *Lebensläufe, Familien, Höfe: Die Bauern und Heuerleute des Osnabrückischen Kirchspiels Belm in proto-industrieller Zeit, 1650–1850* [Göttingen: Vandenhoeck and Ruprecht, 1994], 100).

11. Ketsch, *Frauen*, 51, 97; Dürr, *Mägde*, 19; Erich Maschke, *Gesellschaftliche Unterschichten in den südwestdeutschen Städten* (Stuttgart: Kohlhammer, 1967), 29.

12. Arthur E. Imhof, *Lebenserwartungen in Deutschland vom 17. bis 19. Jahrhundert* (Weinheim: VCH, 1990).

13. In Frankfurt, Stuttgart, Memmingen, and Schwäbisch-Hall, 30 to 60 percent of the female-headed households in the sixteenth century were valued in the lowest category, and often identified as "have-nothings" (*Habenichtsen*) (Wiesner, *Working Women*, 5; Ketsch, *Frauen*, 40–45). In Wismar in 1475, 26 percent of the households listed as living in cellars or rooms (rather than houses) were women, most just listed by first name or termed "daughter" (Maschke, *Unterschichten*, 27).

14. James Brundage, *Law, Sex, and Christian Society in Medieval Europe* (Chicago: University of Chicago Press, 1987), 474–76, 568; Marc Forster, "The Counter-Reformation and the Traditional Church in the Villages of Speyer," *Fides et Historia* 2 (1989): 30–37; Wilhelm Kohl, "Die Durchsetzung der tridentischen Reformen im Domkapital zu Münster," in *Reformatio Ecclesiae: Beiträge zu kirchlichen Reformbemühungen von dem Alten Kirche bis zur Neuzeit*, ed. Remigius Bäumer (Paderborn: Schöningh, 1980), 729–47; Ulrike Strasser, "Farewell My Concubine: The Criminalization of Clerical Marriage in Counter-Reformation Munich," unpublished paper.

15. Robert Jütte, "Dutzbetterinnen und Sündfegerinnen: Kriminelle Bettelpraktiken von Frauen in der Frühen Neuzeit," in *Von Huren und Rabenmüttern: Weibliche Kriminalität in der Frühen Neuzeit*, ed. Otto Ulbricht (Cologne: Bohlau, 1995), 117–38; Helfried Valentinisch, "Frauen unterwegs. Eine Fallstudie zur Mobilität von Frauen in der Steiermark um 1700," in *Weiber, Menscher, Frauenzimmer: Frauen in der ländlichen Gesellschaft 1500–1800*, ed. Heide Wunder and Christina Vanja (Göttingen: Vandenhoeck and Ruprecht, 1996), 223–36.

16. Ute Braun, "Frauentestamente: Stiftsdamen, Fürstinnen-Äbtissinnen und ihre Schwestern in Selbstzeugnissen des 17. und 18. Jahrhunderts," *Beiträge zur Geschichte von Stadt und Stift Essen* 104 (1991/92): 13–99.

17. For translations of some of these writings, see Merry E. Wiesner and Joan Skocir, *Convents Confront the Reformation: Catholic and Protestant Nuns in Germany* (Milwaukee, Wis.: Marquette University Press), esp. 67–77.

18. Lyndal Roper, "Going to Church and Street: Weddings in Reformation Augsburg," *Past and Present* 106 (1985): 62–101.

19. Brundage, *Law, Sex*, 564.

20. Joel Harrington, *Reordering Marriage and Society in Reformation Germany* (Cambridge: Cambridge University Press, 1995); Thomas Robisheaux, *Rural Society and the Search for Order in Early Modern Germany* (Cambridge: Cambridge University Press, 1989), 95–120.

21. Wunder, *Er ist die Sonn'*, 89–118; Margo Todd, "Humanists, Puritans, and the Spiritualized Household," *Church History* 49 (1980): 18–34.

22. For discussion of convent life during this period, see many of the essays in Sherrin Marshall, ed., *Women in Reformation and Counter-Reformation Europe: Public and Private Worlds* (Bloomington: Indiana University Press, 1989).

23. On this point, see Harrington, *Reordering*, 59–83; Lyndal Roper, *The Holy Household: Women and Morals in Reformation Augsburg* (Oxford: Clarendon Press, 1989); Susan C. Karant-Nunn, "*Kinder, Küche, Kirche*: Social Ideology in the Sermons of Johannes Mathesius," in *Germania Illustrata: Essays on Early Modern Germany Presented to Gerald Strauss*, ed. Andrew C. Fix and Susan C. Karant-Nunn (Kirksville, Mo.: Sixteenth Century Journal Publishers, 1992), 121–40.

24. Merry E. Wiesner, "Wandervögel and Women: Journeymen's Concepts of Masculinity in Early Modern Germany," *Journal of Social History* 24 (1991): 767–82; Lyndal Roper, "Was There a Crisis in Gender Relations in Sixteenth-Century Germany?" and "Blood and Codpieces: Masculinity in the Early Modern German Town," both in her *Oedipus and the Devil: Witchcraft, Sexuality, and Religion in Early Modern Europe* (London: Routledge, 1994), 37–52, 107–24.

25. Robert Jütte, *Poverty and Deviance in Early Modern Europe* (Cambridge: Cambridge University Press, 1994), esp. 146–50; Robert W. Scribner, "Mobility, Voluntary or Enforced: Vagrants in Württemberg in the Sixteenth Century," in *Migration in der Feudalgesellschaft*, ed. Gerhard Jaritz and Albert Müller (Frankfurt: Ludwig-Boltzmann Institut, 1988), 65–88; Franz Irsigler and Arnold Lasotta, *Bettler und Gaukler, Dirnen und Henker: Außenseiter in einer mittelalterlichen Stadt* (Cologne: Greven Verlag, 1984); Bernd Roeck, *Außenseiter, Randgruppen, Minderheiten: Fremde im Deutschland der Frühen Neuzeit* (Göttingen: Vandenhoeck and Ruprecht, 1993). Beata Schuster has noted that this hostility toward migrants was part of what she terms a "morality of settledness" (*Moral der Seßhaftigkeit*) that also shaped treatment of prostitutes, who were usually migrants (Beata Schuster, *Die freien Frauen: Dirnen und Frauenhäuser im 15. und 16. Jahrhundert* [Frankfurt: Campus, 1995], 419).

26. Wiesner, *Working Women*, 6.

27. The quotations are from the Memmingen Stadtarchiv, Ratsprotokollbücher, June 12, 1612 and the Munich Stadtarchiv, Ratsitzungsprotokoll, 1607, fol. 238. A similar ordinance against "self-supporting maidens" was passed in Malmø, Denmark in 1549 and was part of the English Statute of Artificers in 1563 (Grethe

Jacobsen, "Nordic Women and the Reformation," in Marshall, *Women*, 56; Mary Prior, "Freedom and Autonomy in England and the Netherlands," in *Women*, ed. Kloek et al., 138).

28. Strasbourg, Archives Municipales, Statuten, vol. 33, no. 61 (1665), my translation. Poor parents in Essex were also ordered to send all children over the age of fifteen into service if they wanted to receive poor relief, with parishes often sending pauper girls to London (Pamela Sharpe, *Adapting to Capitalism: Working Women in the English Economy 1700–1850* [New York: St. Martin's Press, 1996]).

29. Claus-Peter Clasen, *Die Augsburger Weber: Leistungen und Krisen des Textilgewerbes um 1600* (Augsburg: Mühlberger, 1981), 133–34.

30. Sheilagh Ogilvie, "Women and Proto-industrialisation in a Corporate Society: Württemberg Woollen Weaving, 1590–1760," in *Women's Work and the Family Economy in Historical Perspective*, ed. Pat Hudson and W. R. Lee (Manchester: Manchester University Press, 1990), 86–92.

31. Johann Georg Krünitz, *Das Gesindewesen nach Grundsätzen der Oekonomie und Polizeywissenschaft abgehandelt* (Berlin, 1779), reprinted in Andrea van Dülmen, ed., *Frauenleben im 18. Jahrhundert* (Munich: C. H. Beck, 1992), 327, my translation.

32. Quoted in Arno Fitz, "Heimarbeit und Selbstbewußtsein von Vorarlberger Frauen im 18. Jahrhundert," in *Weiber, Menscher, Frauenzimmer*, ed. Wunder and Vanja, 67, my translation.

33. Thomas Max Safley, *Let No Man Put Asunder: The Control of Marriage in the German Southwest: A Comparative Study, 1550–1600* (Kirksville, Mo.: Sixteenth Century Journal Publishers, 1984). This was also true in eighteenth-century Pennsylvania; see Merril D. Smith, *Breaking the Bonds: Marital Discord in Pennsylvania, 1730–1830* (New York and London: New York University Press, 1991).

34. Olwen Hufton, "Women, Work, and Marriage in Eighteenth-Century France," *Studies in the Social History of Marriage*, ed. R. B. Outhwaite (New York: St. Martin's Press, 1981), 189.

35. Ketsch, *Frauen*, 58–67; Dürr, *Mägde*, 151.

36. Michael Mitterauer, "Gesindedienst und Jugendphase im europäischen Vergleich," *Geschichte und Gesellschaft* 11 (1985): 177–204.

37. Dürr, *Mägde*, 30; see also several of the essays in Gotthardt Frühsorge, Rainer Gruenter, and Beatrix Freifrau Wolff, eds., *Gesinde im 18. Jahrhundert* (Hamburg: Felix Meiner, 1995).

38. For a fuller discussion of employment agents, see Wiesner, *Working Women*, 83–85.

39. Wingolf Lehnemann, "Knechte und Mägde auf einem westfälischen Adelshof im 18. Jahrhundert," in *Wandel der Volkskultur in Europa*, ed. Nils-Arvid Bringius et al. (Münster: F. Coppenrath, 1988), 2: 709–24.

40. Dürr, *Mägde*, 220–65; Ulinka Rublack, "Women and Crime in Southwest Germany, 1500–1700" (Ph.D. diss., Cambridge University, 1994), 153–78; Richard von Dulmen, *Frauen vor Gericht: Kindsmord in der frühen Neuzeit* (Frankfurt: Campus, 1991); Susan Karant-Nunn, "The Rape of Servingmaids, Shameful Talk, and the Electress's Purity: Moral and Class Boundaries in an Age of Confessionalization and Social Disciplining" (unpublished paper).

41. Dürr, *Mägde*, 76–99. See also Paul Münch, "Tiere, Teufel oder Menschen? Zur gesellschaftlichen Einschätzung der 'dienenden Klassen' während der Frühen Neuzeit," in *Gesinde*, ed. Früsorge et al. 83–108.

42. Philemon Menagius, *Die Sieben Teuffel / welche fast in der gantzen Welt die heutige Dienst-Mägde beherrschen und verführen* . . . (Frankfurt, 1693), 66–67, my translation. Frances E. Dolan has discussed early modern literary portrayals of servants as "enemies within" in *Dangerous Familiars: Representations of Domestic Crime in England 1550–1700* (Ithaca, N.Y.: Cornell University Press, 1994).

43. Wiesner, *Working Women*, 87–88.

44. Strasbourg, Archives Municipales, Statuten, vol. 18, fol. 30. There is a good discussion of visual representations of idle maids in Wayne E. Franits, *Paragons of Virtue: Women and Domesticity in Seventeenth-Century Dutch Art* (Cambridge: Cambridge University Press, 1993), 108–10.

45. Munich, Stadtarchiv, Gewerbeamt, no. 1569 (1580); Barbara Kroemer, "Die Einführung der Reformation in Memmingen," *Memmingen Geshichtsblätter*, 1980: 11–23.

46. Munich, Stadtarchiv, Gewerbeamt, no. 1569 (1580).

47. This phrase was in one of the very popular "devil's books" about servants: Johann Balthasar Schupp, *Sieben böse Geister Welche heutiges Tages Knechte und Mägde regieren und verführen* (Hamburg, 1659), quoted in Dürr, *Mägde*, 210, and in an earlier, more general, anonymous devil's book, *Theatrum Diabolarum, Das ist: Warhaffte, eigentliche und kurtze Beschriebung allerley grewlicher, schreckliche und abschewlicher Laster* . . . (Frankfurt, 1575), quoted in Wesoly, "Weibliche," 77.

48. Dürr, *Mägde*, 178, 210–12; Wiesner, *Working Women*, 83.

49. Wiesner, *Working Women*, 91; Marybeth Carlson, "A Trojan Horse of Worldliness: Maidservants in the Burgher Household in Rotterdam at the End of the Seventeenth Century," in Kloek, *Women*, 95.

50. Rublack, "Women," 89–97.

51. Otto Ulbricht, "Zwischen Vergeltung und Zukunftsplanung: Hausdiebstahl von Mägde in Schleswig-Holstein vom 16. bis zum 19. Jahrhundert," in *Von Huren und Rabenmüttern: Weibliche Kriminalität in der Frühen Neuzeit*, ed. Ulbricht (Cologne: Böhlau, 1995), 139–71.

52. Dürr, *Mägde*, 176–80.

53. Karl von Eckhardtshausen, *Tagebuch eines Richters oder Beiträge zur Geschichte des menschlichen Elendes* (Munich, 1789), 104, quoted in Dülmen, *Frauenleben*, 331, my translation.

54. Wunder, *Er ist die Sonn'*, 90–95; David Warren Sabean, *Property, Production and Family in Neckarhausen, 1700–1870* (Cambridge: Cambridge University Press, 1990), 148–49; Christina Vanja, "Frauen im Dorf: Ihre Stellung unter besonderer Berücksichtigung langräflicher Quellen im Mittelalter," *Zeitschrift für Agrargeschichte und Agrarsoziologie* 34 (1986): 147–59.

55. Dorothea Rippman, "Frauenarbeit im Wandel: Arbeitsteilung, Arbeitsorganisation und Entlöhnung im Weinbau am Oberrhein (15./16. Jahrhundert)," in *Weiber*, ed. Wunder and Vanja, 26–59; Wunder, *Er ist die Sonn'*, 93–94.

56. Frankfurt, Stadtarchiv, Zünfte, Ugb. C-50, Ss, no. 4 (1615).

57. Rita Bake, *Vorindustrielle Frauenerwerbsarbeit: Arbeits- und Lebensweise von*

Manufakturarbeiterinnen im Deutschland des 18. Jhds. unter besondere Berücksichtigung Hamburgs (Cologne: Pahl-Rugenstein, 1984). This was also true in England, where poor law authorities organized spinstries and expected poor singlewomen to work there (Pamela Sharpe, "Literally Spinsters: A New Interpretation of Local Economy and Demography in Colyton in the Seventeenth and Eighteenth Centuries," *Economic History Review* 34 (1991): 46–65).

58. Wiesner, *Working Women*, 94.

59. Munich, Stadtarchiv, Heilig-Geist-Spital, no. 275, Pfrundner und Personalverzeichnis 1573–1598. In a few institutions, remaining unmarried was a condition of employment (Rublack, "Women," 98).

60. Wiesner, *Working Women*, 38–41.

61. Augsburg Stadtarchiv, Collegium Medicum, fasc. 5.

62. Wiesner, *Working Women*, 49.

63. Wiesner, *Working Women*, 74, 95–97.

64. Peter Schuster, *Das Frauenhaus: Städtische Bordelle in Deutschland 1350 bis 1600* (Paderborn: Schöningh, 1992).

65. P. Schuster, *Frauenhaus*, 77–85; B. Schuster, *Freien Frauen*, 194–204.

66. Georg Kriegk, *Deutsches Bürgerthum im Mittelalter* (Frankfurt: Rutten und Loning, 1871), 2: 316.

67. B. Schuster, *Freien Frauen*, 200–205; P. Schuster, *Frauenhaus*, 96–98.

68. This process has been traced in Wiesner, *Working Women*, 97–106; Lyndal Roper, "Discipline and Respectability: Prostitution and Reformation in Augsburg," *History Workshop Journal* 19 (1985): 3–28; P. Schuster, *Frauenhaus*. The most extensive discussion is B. Schuster, *Freien Frauen*, which also has a 55-page bibliography.

69. Strasbourg, Archives municipales, Statuten, vol. 2 fol. 137 (1497).

70. Quoted in B. Schuster, *Freien Frauen*, 399.

71. Ibid., 200.

72. Some authors have pointed out that not simply singlewomen, but *all* women came to be considered potential whores as marriage was also sexualized during this period, in a complex process that involved the Protestant and Catholic Reformations but did not start with them. See B. Schuster, *Freien Frauen*, esp. 224–55, 403–19; and Roper, *Holy Household*.

73. See Wunder, *Er ist die Sonn'*, 58–65; B. Schuster, *Freien Frauen*, 332–41; Merry Wiesner, "Guilds, Male Bonding and Women's Work in Early Modern Germany," *Gender and History* 1 (1989): 125–37.

74. I have traced the debate about women working in the guilds in "Gender and the Worlds of Work," in *Germany: A New Social and Economic History*, vol. 1, ed. Sheilagh Ogilvie and Robert Scribner (London: Edward Arnold, 1995), 221.

75. Frankfurt, Stadtarchiv, Züfte, Ugb C-36, Cc (1649, Huter).

76. Wiesner, *Working Women*, 123–37.

77. Munich, Stadtarchiv, Gewerbeamt, no. 5170; Strasbourg, Archives Municipales, Statuten, vol. 30, fol. 136 (1400). Nuremberg, Stadtarchiv, Aemterbüchlein, 1–81 (1400–1562). The Strasbourg list is interesting for the variety of ways in which women's names appear at this point in which surnames have not solidified. Some are listed as "(male name)'s daughter," or as "(male name)'s wife," while others have a first name and surname, a first name and place of origin or residence,

or a first name and identifying characteristic. From this we can probably assume that some of the women were not married, although we cannot be sure of exactly how many. The same is true of the earliest Nuremberg lists that show a variety of name forms; by 1480, however, the women are all listed simply with their own given name and surname, with no indication of marital status. Andrzej Karpinski has also found that more than half the female traders in the marketplace of Cracow were unmarried, though he cautions that the exact proportion of widows and singlewomen among this group is impossible to determine ("The Woman on the Market Place: The Scale of Feminization of Retail Trade in Polish Towns in the Second Half of the 16th and in the 17th Centuries," in *La Donna nell'Economia Secc. XIII–XVIII*, ed. Simonetta Cavaciocchi, Serie II, Atti delle "Settimane di Studi" e altri Convegni, 21 [Prato, Italy: Istituto International de Storia Economica "F. Datini," 1990], 283–92).

78. For a fuller discussion of market women, see Wiesner, *Working Women*, 134–42.

79. Frankfurt, Stadtarchiv, Verordnungen, vol. 1, no. 107, 1616 and 1690 Obsthocken Ordnung.

80. Strasbourg, Archives Municipales, Akten der XV, 1636, fol. 167.

81. Irene Hardach-Pinke, *Die Gouvernante: Geschichte eines Frauenberufs* (Frankfurt: Campus, 1993).

82. Ulinka Rublack, "Metze und Magd: Frauen, Krieg und die Bildfunktion des Weiblichen in deutschen Städten der frühen Neuzeit," in *Historische Anthropologie*, ed. Rolf Lindner and Norbert Schindler (Cologne: Böhlau, 1995), 412–32.

83. Strasbourg, Archives Municipales, Statuten, vol. 33, fol. 26b (1684).

84. Ulrike Gleixner, *"Das Mensch" und "der Kerl": Die Konstruktion von Geschlecht in Unzuchtsverfahren der Frühen Neuzeit* (Frankfurt: Campus, 1994), 106.

85. Olwen Hufton, "Women, Work, and Family," in *A History of Women in the West*, ed. Natalie Zemon Davis and Arlette Farge, Vol. 3, *Renaissance and Enlightenment Paradoxes* (Cambridge, Mass.: Harvard University Press, 1993), 45.

86. This point has also been made by Sharpe, "Literally Spinsters," 62; Rublack, "Women and Crime," 213–17; and Fitz, "Heimarbeit," 73.

87. Anna Bijns, "Unyoked is best!" trans. Kristiaan P. G. Aercke, reprinted in *Women Writers of the Renaissance and Reformation*, ed. Katharina M. Wilson (Athens: University of Georgia Press, 1987), 382.

8

Singlewomen in Early Modern Venice

Communities and Opportunities

Monica Chojnacka

WHEN ASKED WHETHER THERE WERE any known witches in her neighborhood, a witness in a 1625 Venetian witchcraft trial replied, "No, they are all married women [*sono tutte donne maritate*]."[1] Her statement expressed a social truth about early modern Venice: when they had no man to control them, women were perceived as particularly dangerous. The single state, then, was an undesirable condition for Venetian women. Women recognized this. Upper-class women left money to the dowries of their female servants and the poorer women in their neighborhoods. Hoping to increase the chances that such women might marry, testators sometimes even specified that the money or goods could only be delivered in the event of a successful union. Poor women had their own ways of increasing the odds of marriage; countless cases that came before the Venetian Inquisition related the stories of women who bought love-potions or charms to win the affection of a prospective husband.[2] Marriage guaranteed a measure of security, while spinsterhood seemed to promise poverty, marginalization, and loneliness. Yet, despite the desire on the part of most women to marry, early modern Venice was full of singlewomen who negotiated a hostile environment and managed to survive in a variety of ways.

This essay proposes that the worsening circumstances singlewomen confronted in the sixteenth century paradoxically produced responses that gave those women occupational, cultural, and social opportunities, some of which were new. One such opportunity was the continuation and creation of female communities in which singlewomen could find social and sometimes economic security. I first establish that singlewomen made up a sizable part of Venice's population, perhaps especially so in the sixteenth century, and briefly describe what we know about their living arrangements. I then examine singlewomen, a group primarily made up of poor women, in the context of their economic activity. This second section suggests that the economic opportunities traditionally open to singlewomen constricted in the sixteenth century, making them increasingly vulnerable. The third section examines in depth one formal community that was founded in the late sixteenth century partly in response to singlewomen's increasing vulnerability, the Casa delle Zitelle (The Home of Unmarried Girls). This Casa drew on traditional forms of female community — the family, the neighborhood, and the convent — and reconfigured them to offer some singlewomen a new sort of community all their own.

Singlewomen in Venetian Society

Singlewomen formed a marginal and sometimes ambiguous social group in early modern Venice. Thus, they are among the most difficult people for historians to identify and count today. For example, singlewomen made only sporadic appearances in the tax rolls of the city, since most of them held little property. When we turn to church records, however, the sources are more promising. The post-Tridentine church was interested in the souls of men and women, old and young, regardless of their marital or financial status. After the Council of Trent (1547–1563), local parishes throughout Italy were instructed to carry out soul counts (*status animarum*) to determine how many parishioners had been baptized and confirmed.[3] Venetian parish priests conducted such surveys in the 1590s.[4] In each parish, a census-taker (sometimes the priest himself) proceeded house by house, street by street, noting the name and position of each member of every household. People were listed in the order of their household status, with the head of the household always listed first. Thus, a typical house with a married couple, two children, and a servant was listed in the following way:

Jacopo, son of Giuseppe, butcher, baptized and confirmed
Susanna, his wife, baptized and confirmed
Elena, his daughter, baptized
Filippo, his son, baptized
Lucia, his servant, baptized and confirmed

A typical household headed by a singlewoman looked like this:

Margarita, daughter of Tommaso
Elisabetta, a Greek woman, who boards with her

The extant parish censuses cover two-thirds of Venice's parishes and represent every district of the city. The total number of persons covered by them is 94,862 (almost two-thirds of a city population of about 150,000).[5] Thus these status animarum offer representative information about Venice's population and household structure. By using these censuses, we can examine the population of singlewomen in Venice at the end of the sixteenth century by looking for women who were identified by their father's name (as in the example above) rather than that of their husband, and who were not identified as widows.

The parish censuses suggest that singlewomen were a sizable part of the Venetian population in the second half of the sixteenth century, perhaps more so than in previous periods. Table 1 shows that a considerable number of the city's adult population was single or widowed — at least 25,301, or over one-quarter.[6] Of these unmarried (single or widowed) people, 53.3 percent were women.[7] Almost one-third of the unmarried women who appear in these censuses (32 percent) headed their own households.

The censuses make clear that unmarried women and men were plentiful in sixteenth-century Venice: 13,534 women and 11,767 men. If the numbers of unmarried men and women were similar, however, their living patterns were not. While unmarried women and men found shelter with their relatives in nearly equal numbers, women far outstripped men as unmarried heads of households. In fact, unmarried women were about twice as likely as unmarried men to head their own households.[8] This suggests that the unmarried state gave some women an independence that unmarried men did not have, or need.

How many of these women were single as opposed to widowed? Among women who were heads of their own households, a singlewoman can be identified by the absence of both a husband and the title of widow (*vedova*). There, we find that of 4,285 women with no apparent husband, a full 30 percent are single (1,311).[9] The single women in the categories of servant and others (mostly boarders) can be tracked the same way. More than half of the unmarried women in the other category (691 out of 1,206) appear to have been single, and, as is discussed below, most female servants were singlewomen. Single offspring and siblings are the most difficult to identify, since they may be children. The numbers of unmarried females that I have found in these categories include few singlewomen, since the

TABLE 1   Unmarried, Adult Venetians by Position in the Household, 1589–94

HOUSEHOLD POSITION	WOMEN (%)	MEN (%)	TOTAL (%)
Head of household	4,285 (32)	2,533 (21.5)	6,818 (27)
Widowed parent	1,063 (8)	65 (0.5)	1,128 (5)
Offspring	151 (1)	88 (1)	239 (1)
Sibling	952 (7)	915 (8)	1,867 (7)
Servant	5,877 (43)	6,188 (52)	12,064 (47)
Others	1,206 (9)	1,978 (17)	3,184 (13)
Total	13,534 (100)	11,767 (100)	25,301 (100)

Source: Archivio Storico della Curia Patriarcale di Venezia (ASCP), Archivio Segreto, Sezione Antica, Status Animarum, B. I–III.

only way to establish a woman's adulthood is to find her identified by a profession (which is listed only sporadically) or marital status. For example, if the head of household has a sister, Caterina, we have no way of knowing if she is ten years old or thirty years old, unless she is listed as Caterina, Widow, or Caterina, Seamstress.

Because the age of the women listed in the categories of offspring and sibling is impossible to ascertain, in most cases I can only count the exceptional singlewomen who are explicitly described as adults. Thus, my estimate of singlewomen in early modern Venice is almost surely an underestimate. Even so, that estimate reveals a substantial number of singlewomen.[10]

Most of these women were poor; some were immigrants.[11] The sixteenth century witnessed several waves of immigration by people fleeing the Italian peninsula, northern Europe, and the Balkans to escape religious intolerance, economic hardship, and political turmoil. The particular vulnerability of female immigrants meant that they were likely to cluster at the bottom of the economic scale, with limited prospects for marriage.[12] As Maryanne Kowaleski discusses in her contribution to this collection, a woman's decision to migrate to a city increased her chances of remaining single.[13]

As immigration crowded the city's neighborhoods, singlewomen relied on a variety of living situations. The parish censuses reveal households with women who appear to be unrelated and often from different countries or regions of Italy, suggesting that immigrant women sometimes banded together. Other singlewomen turned to their families. Table 1 shows that a singlewoman might remain with aging parents or live with a married brother; Merry Wiesner has noted the same phenomenon for early modern

TABLE 2   Venetian Singlewomen by Position in the Household, 1589–94

HOUSEHOLD POSITION	NUMBER OF WOMEN (%)
Head of household	1,311 (15)
Offspring	47 (1)
Sibling	818 (9)
Servant	5,745 (67)
Others	691 (8)
Total	8,612 (100)

Source: ASCP, Status Animarum, B. I–III.

Germany.[14] Singlewomen found support from other family members as well. Some, according to the censuses, moved in with their married sisters. Others shared lodgings with another unmarried sister. Together, single sisters could pool their resources to survive, or even thrive. The records for the Venetian head tax of 1582 reveal at least forty-seven cases in which two or more sisters declared property in common, either independent of male family members or as equals alongside them.[15]

Singlewomen and the Venetian Economy

Singlewomen rarely found employment as artisans, but they did find work in the shops of artisans, especially in the silk industry. Although a 1682 description of the Venetian silk industry claimed that "wives and daughters of *maestri* [masters] are an unimportant consideration because they just do household work, cleaning up and occasionally preparing bobbins or warping the looms, but the bulk of the routine work is done by the journeymen and apprentices,"[16] this claim was deceptive. In fact, women regularly filled the ranks of low-level jobs in the profitable textile industries of silk and wool, as elsewhere in Italy.[17] Singlewomen worked on the textiles at their preliminary stages, such as reeling, winding, and throwing. By the seventeenth century, this opportunity may have diminished in Venice, since Richard Rapp has pointed out that by the seventeenth century Venetian merchants had turned to the mainland for much preparatory textile work, in order to lower their costs.[18]

Although a few women worked as sailmakers and journeywomen,[19] singlewomen participated in the city's industrial growth by providing the services that grew along with artisanal production. They sold food and other goods on the streets, and offered domestic services as laundresses (*lavandera*). The parish censuses also list singlewomen and widows who worked as second-hand clothes dealers (*strazzaruola*), linen-makers (*linaruola*), bakers (*fornera*), fruit vendors (*fruttaruola*), and spice vendors (*spiciera*). A few practiced traditionally male occupations, like boatwomen (*barcaruola*), cobblers (*zavatera, cassellera*), and one sail-maker (*vellera*) who appear in the censuses. Three principal occupations of singlewomen — domestic service, prostitution, and the magical arts — became increasingly difficult to practice in the late sixteenth century. These occupations are discussed below.

DOMESTIC SERVICE

One of the most common occupations for singlewomen throughout medieval and early modern Europe was domestic service. The parish censuses confirm that Venice was no exception. Of 11,901 servants listed in the status animarum, 5,877, or 49.4 percent, were women.[20] Only 93 of these seem to have been married. By contrast, we find 5,772 unmarried women and 6,189 unmarried men who found employment in service. While these numbers may be slightly inflated (a few wives may have hired themselves out as domestic labor while their husbands were in prison or away at sea), the percentage of single and widowed people serving as domestic laborers remains impressive: 98.2 percent of all women and 97.4 percent of all men in domestic service appear to have been unmarried. Research by Klapisch-Zuber on female domestics in sixteenth-century Florence found that the majority of female domestics there were unmarried, but the percentage of singlewomen in service was only slightly higher than that of widows.[21] In Venice, by contrast, the censuses show the ranks of servants overwhelmingly filled by singlewomen, who made up over 97 percent of the female servant population, with only a tiny number (0.5 percent) of female servants identified as widows.

Dennis Romano believes that in this period female domestics may have faced growing competition from men, although the balance was still even at the close of the century.[22] Romano has suggested that in the sixteenth century, wealthy Venetian households increasingly hired male servants rather than female ones as a result of changing notions of honor.[23] In addition, the presence of immigrant women may have meant added compe-

TABLE 3   Domestic Servants by Sex, Marital Status, and Age, 1589–94

MARITAL STATUS	WOMEN (%)	MEN (%)
Single	5,745 (97.7)	6,180 (97.3)
Widowed	27[1] (0.5)	8 (0.1)
Married	93 (1.6)	93 (1.5)
Children[2]	12 (0.2)	66 (1.1)
Total	5,877 (100)	6,347 (100)[3]

Source: ASCP, Status Animarum, B. I–III.

[1] Eleven female servants are identified as widows in the censuses. An additional 16 women are listed with children but no husband; I have also counted these as widows.

[2] Few ages are listed in the parish censuses, making it impossible to assess how many children actually worked as servants (the larger number of boys in Table 2 reflects the number of apprentices whose ages were given). The children identified above ranged in age from 7 to 16 years; undoubtedly there were many more. See Romano, *Housecraft and Statecraft*, 152–55.

[3] A slightly larger number of men than women worked as domestic servants: 52% contrasted with 48%. This is partly because of a few wealthy households that boasted 20 or more male servants. The actual number of households that employed female servants is almost exactly equal to that of households with male domestics: 3,403 contrasted with 3,409.

tition among female domestics themselves. With or without increased competition, life as a domestic servant was not easy, particularly for women.[24] Young women often found themselves at the mercy of employers who paid none or only part of the agreed-upon wage, who forced them to live in squalid conditions, and who occasionally raped them or physically abused them. Poor, alone, and totally dependent on her employer's good will, a female servant had little support if she protested bad treatment, especially if she came from the countryside. Romano's study of sixteenth-century legislation on servants shows that female servants were systematically disadvantaged. For example, they were expected to receive the lowest wages by law, and were tied to the longest contracts.[25]

But singlewomen who remained in the service of one family could sometimes build affective bonds as well as economic ones. Apart from the wealthiest patricians and citizens, most Venetians lived in tight quarters. This produced tense relationships in some cases, and intimate ties in others. Employers and servants might work together at the same task, or at least alongside one another; this was especially true of artisanal households.[26] According to Romano, female servants were more likely than males to form affective ties to their employers. More often than male servants, female servants asked their employers to execute their wills, and requested burial alongside the families they had served.[27]

In addition, Venetian law sought to protect female servants in several ways. Contracts had a maximum duration of ten years, to be renegotiated at the end of that period if both the employer and the servant were amenable. For young girls sent into service,[28] this sometimes meant a guarantee of freedom and the option to move to another household, to marry, or to leave the city.[29] Moreover, women who were sexually violated by their employers were guaranteed, at least in theory, full payment of their wages for their entire tenure, release from the terms of their contract, and money for a suitable dowry. By the early sixteenth century, however, the execution of this legislation became more difficult.[30] For the poorest women and men, finding another employment that promised decent wages and a fair work-load was not always an easy endeavor, and thus many were probably forced to remain in difficult situations and endure unjust treatment. Women had fewer options than their male counterparts; those who dared to leave do-mestic service in search of better working conditions risked being forced into prostitution.

PROSTITUTION

A second common method of survival for poor singlewomen was prostitu-tion. It is impossible to count accurately the number of *meretrici*, or pros-titutes, who lived in Venice in the early modern period. In the early six-teenth century, the patrician Marin Sanudo recorded that they made up more than 10 percent of the population, which shows how pervasive pros-titution seemed to the chronicler.[31] The parish censuses identify only 204 prostitutes by their profession, suggesting that Venetian priests and their assistants were reluctant to record, and thus reveal, the number of pros-titutes living in their parishes.[32] Of this small number, almost two-thirds, or 128, were listed as head of household. Another 30 percent, or sixty-three, lived as boarders or companions in the home of another prostitute.

In the early modern period, Venetians increasingly associated prosti-tutes with the problems of overcrowding, poverty, and crime in their city. City crises, such as the food shortages and plague of 1576–77, were inter-preted by some as divine retribution for the city's sinful ways. By the mid-sixteenth century, the legislation against prostitution was growing, due in

part to Counter-Reformation pressures. Immigrant women formed a particular target; in 1539 and 1572 legislators attempted to expel "fallen women"
who were recent immigrants.[33] What had always been a supremely regulated
urban institution[34] came under attack from the government, as prostitutes
were identified with the social and economic crises of the period.[35]

MAGIC

Another risky but popular source of income for singlewomen was magic.
Although we have long known that married and widowed women as well as
singlewomen filled the ranks of those who practiced magic and were accused of witchcraft in Venice,[36] Sally Scully recently suggested that for some
women magic and sorcery offered a viable alternative to the economic
security of marriage.[37] The practice of charms and incantations, often in
tandem with other occupations such as laundering or huckstering, could
provide a singlewoman with relative economic security. It also offered her a
means for controlling her environment, decreasing her social vulnerability,
and acquiring a sort of power. In her capacity as a wise woman, a poor
woman—single, married, or widowed—was sought after, and her skills
were recognized, valued, and sometimes feared.[38]

With the establishment of the Holy Inquisition, or *Sant'Uffizio*, in
Venice in 1547, women who practiced healing and magic found themselves
particularly vulnerable. Initially, the Inquisition's work was directed primarily at heretics, such as the Lutheran artisans who dominated the print-
ing industry.[39] As the century progressed, however, the Inquisition began
to focus its attention increasingly on practitioners of magic and demonol-
ogy. In this area, their main targets were the *popolane*, or humble women, of
Venice, many of them singlewomen, who offered charms to heal the sick or
promised a glimpse into the future. By the late sixteenth century, then,
"wise women" found it increasingly difficult to practice their craft.[40]

The Casa delle Zitelle

By the mid-sixteenth century, increased demographic pressure combined
with economic changes and religious fervor made the single life increasingly difficult for women. Religious factionalism in the period of reform

and counterreform meant that neighbors and even relatives sometimes turned on one another in new and more aggressive ways, with the aid of the Inquisition.[41] The entry of more immigrants into neighborhoods may have made for greater tensions as well, since their arrival swelled the poorer sectors of the city and increased competition for local resources like housing and employment. The immigrants themselves often lacked the common foundations of local communities — a network of family members and long-standing neighborhood ties — which heightened their vulnerability.

As the character of neighborhood life changed, wider Venetian society began to address problems that had previously been left to local authorities and private charity. One result was a subtle shift toward a centralized system of charity to deal with the city's poor.[42] Out of that system came new ways of conceptualizing female communities, which would offer some women a new set of options for survival outside of marriage. Thus, in the second half of the sixteenth century, a number of institutions were founded by wealthy laypeople to help poor women. One of these, the Casa delle Zitelle, was a female community that embraced a new philosophy of education and re-form (always within the parameters of Venetian society) and incorporated singlewomen from all levels of the Venetian class hierarchy.[43]

Founded in 1568, the Zitelle's mission was to take in young girls who were clearly at risk of becoming prostitutes, and shelter and educate them in a way that would make them marketable wives or nuns when they reached adulthood. Upon admittance, girls ranged in age from nine to thirteen years old.[44] They typically remained at the Casa until their early twenties, although one list of inhabitants from the late sixteenth century shows that a few charges stayed on into their forties, presumably having become mem-bers of the Casa's staff. Admission to the Casa was competitive: girls were interviewed by members of the governing board, who also visited their homes, to ensure that candidates fulfilled the requirements of being poor, physically attractive, and at clear risk of falling into prostitution. As the constitution of the Zitelle noted, girls who were merely "poor, or those without beauty, can find shelter elsewhere."[45]

Behind the foundation of this house was a group of deeply religious noblewomen, both single and widowed, who saw the problem of prostitu-tion not in the innate sinfulness of the women involved, but in the poverty and lack of choices that increasingly confronted them in the late sixteenth century. In response, they created the Zitelle, establishing a community that, while most important for some of the city's poor singlewomen, came to offer a new career alternative to a few wealthier women as well.

Staffed and administered almost entirely by women, the Zitelle consciously modeled itself as an alternative family, or an alternative community, for the girls in its care. But this family was almost exclusively female, and almost exclusively single. The head positions of *Madre* (Mother or Headmistress) and *Coadjutrice* (Assistant) were filled by noblewomen who had decided to dedicate their lives to helping their less fortunate sisters. The Madre was often a widow, but the rest of the staff were singlewomen. The *Maestre* (Mistresses), or female staff, were former *zitelle* who had elected to stay on in the house rather than marry or enter a convent. As former "daughters" themselves, the Maestre were supposed to serve as older sisters to the younger women, and act as liaisons between them and the administrators. The administrators had regular contact with the zitelle as well, and that contact was expected to continue throughout the girls' lives.

The young zitelle lived in seclusion, and except for the necessary visits by the women's confessor and the casa's doctor, contact with men was forbidden outright. The doctor himself examined patients only under the supervision of the Madre or one of her assistants. Both the girls' spiritual upbringing and their daily activities were determined by the governing board, made up of noblemen and -women. The Zitelle charter describes how the zitelle should dress, eat, and interact with one another. One concern on the part of the governors was the risk of homosexual activity among these young women. The charter hints at the type of behavior that governors feared, and outlines the procedure that should be followed if two girls were suspected of such activity: "When it is noted that one of the *zitelle* is too affectionate with another girl, the two must be separated from each other and accompanied by others."[46]

The Casa delle Zitelle was founded to help poor women, but it played an important role in the lives of some upper-class women as well. Noble and wealthy singlewomen confronted some of the same problems as their humbler counterparts. Though they rarely found themselves in the dire economic straits that forced poorer women into prostitution, they also lacked an accepted social identity, and may have lacked even an informal community of singlewomen. Singlewomen from the popular classes had multiple opportunities for encounters with one another as they ran errands for their employers or worked as hucksters, prostitutes, or healers. Upper-class singlewomen were absent from the streets, and are largely absent from our sources, except for the work of early modern Venetians like Lucrezia Marinella, Moderata Fonte, and Arcangela Tarabotti. These writers railed against the injustice of their limited options as women, and asserted the need for alternatives beyond marriage or the monastic life. A recent article on Marinella and Fonte has suggested that their works were at least in part a reaction to the constriction of the marriage market for upper-class women in late sixteenth-century Venice.[47] If in fact increasing numbers of elite women found themselves unable to marry, how did they cope?

We know almost nothing about the individual women who worked at the Casa, but we do know that their responsibilities were greater than those traditionally assumed by singlewomen. These elite women directed a female community based on loving support, mixed with discipline. As the administrators, they enjoyed a considerable amount of authority. They oversaw the education of the young women in their care, managed the financial concerns of the house, raised funds, and arranged the marriage or entry into a convent for the young women who left them. The Zitelle charter mandates that the Madre and Coadjutrici be excellent managers as well as appropriately pious, and it appears that for the most part they were, since the Casa delle Zitelle continued to shelter and educate young women into the twentieth century.[48]

In addition to operating the Zitelle, Venetian singlewomen and widows from the upper classes ran other charitable institutions designed to help the poor. These included the Convertite, a home for experienced prostitutes to retire into permanent seclusion; the Soccorso, also a refuge for prostitutes and for women fleeing troubled marriages; and the Derelitti, an orphanage for girls and boys. The dedication of elite, unmarried women was crucial to the survival of these houses. Not only did their presence ensure a certain legitimacy of purpose and prestige, but their connections also helped solicit funds for these institutions, and thus to create networks of charity that ensured institutional survival.

THE CASA AS FAMILY

The charges of the Zitelle were isolated from the traditional communities of family and neighborhood. The Zitelle building was deliberately constructed to limit even visual access to the outside world.[49] The aim behind this rule was clear: to keep the girls and women away from the dangers and influences of the outside world. In this way, the Casa emulated a convent by creating a secluded environment of prayer, discipline, and contemplation. This emulation was to some degree intentional; the women who founded the Zitelle had themselves been members of the evangelical *barnabiti* movement around Milan, a movement that similarly encouraged a life of seclusion.[50] Yet wards of this Casa were not cloistered in the religious sense, because during their seclusion the staff prepared them to reenter wider society. The zitelle were expected to marry, and were taught skills to make them good helpmates for potential husbands. In this way, the house fulfilled a familial duty by sheltering its wards from the outside world while at the same time preparing them to return to it.

Language illustrates how the founders of the Zitelle consciously modeled their institution on that of the family. For example, just as widows in notarial documents described themselves as *Procuratrici* (executors) for their orphaned children, so too do the dowries of the zitelle describe their wealthy benefactresses as Procuratrici of the recently married girls.[51] In this way, these noblewomen identified themselves as motherly figures through legal terminology. As we shall see, they did so through affective language as well.

Even after a girl was settled in either a marriage or a convent, the responsibilities of the Zitelle's administrators did not end. The charter states that:

When these daughters are in need, they must notify the Congregation of *Governatrici* [female members of the Casa's Board of Governors] who will have [already] visited them, to ask advice regarding what they should do to resolve the issue [*provedere*]. . . . The *Governatrici* must remember that these daughters do not have mothers other than themselves [the *Governatrici*], in order not to miss a visit to them, . . . because visiting them frequently will keep the fear of God in them, . . . which they had at the Casa and they will love [the *Governatrici*] always when they see the motherly concern that the *Governatrici* show for them. It is also good that with these visits the husband will not treat [the daughters] badly, since they will see that [their wives] are under the protection of many matrons.[52]

The noblewoman's duty, then, was not simply to guide the zitella from a distance, as an expression of noblesse oblige. Rather, she was to be the girl's mother, to protect and advise her, to give her love and discipline even after she left the family fold of the Casa's walls. Like a girl's relationship with her natural mother, the female bonds forged within the institution should remain strong even after a zitella had departed for a new home.

These examples suggest an atmosphere of familial or at least enduring connection on the part of the administrators. If this was not always the reality (and we have no way of knowing if it was), at least it was the intention of those who founded the casa and others like it, and established their rules. By using this terminology, the founders of the zitelle asserted their aim to create familial communities for girls and women who found themselves, either permanently or temporarily, without the resources of the traditional one.[53] The importance of the family structure — its cornerstone being loving discipline — was recognized, and reconfigured as an almost entirely female community where the children and parents were single-women and where singlewomen set the standards of behavior, education, shelter, and support — all with the sanction of the city's leaders.

Conclusion

On the one hand, we are faced with a grim picture when we consider the plight of singlewomen in early modern Venice. Singlewomen were pro-liferating, and most lived difficult lives. Their economic options were few, their social status low. Forced to scramble for a living, often through do-mestic labor or the risky occupations of prostitution and witchcraft, single-women faced countless obstacles (many of them faced by widows as well) with few opportunities to surmount them. By the mid-sixteenth century, the traditional obstacles faced by singlewomen may have increased. As the population rose, domestic service became more difficult and competitive, and two other occupations, prostitution and witchcraft, came under in-creasing attack.

Yet a few opportunities existed that singlewomen could seize. For-mally and informally, singlewomen negotiated the barriers around them to fashion a life for themselves through family (especially sisters), friends, and the new institutions emerging in Counter-Reformation Venice. They found ways of building communal bonds that could offer them a part of the social net usually generated through marriage. Their sheer numbers made single-women a presence to be reckoned with, both within the social confines of the parish and as a subject of discussion among the city's elite. Through formal institutions and traditional society, community and opportunity combined to offer singlewomen agency in early modern Venice.

Finally, while the single state generally imposed on women a poorer, more difficult life than they would have as wives, some women actively rejected marriage and embraced the single state. The famous trio of Moder-ata Fonte, Lucrezia Marinella, and Arcangela Tarabotti consciously ex-pressed such attitudes. Moreover, some married women actively rejected marriage by choosing to leave it. In the sixteenth and seventeenth centuries, Venetian women filed more petitions for separation than did men, even though, practically speaking, women had much more to lose by leaving a marriage.[54] In doing so, these women in effect created an alternative for themselves by declaring that no marriage was better than a bad one. The married women who petitioned for separation may have recognized what the women of the Zitelle already knew: within a marginalized space, there is still room to maneuver. Some singlewomen made the most of that space in early modern Venice.

Notes

1. Archivio di Stato di Venezia (ASV), Sant'Uffizio, Processi, B. 80, no. 3, doc. 12.

2. For examples, see Guido Ruggiero, *Binding Passions: Tales of Magic, Marriage and Power at the End of the Renaissance* (New York and Oxford: Oxford University Press, 1993).

3. On these *status animarum* as a source, see Athos Bellettini, "La démographie italienne au XVIe siècle: sources et possibilitiés de recherche," *Annales de Demographie Historique* (1980): 19–38.

4. For a description of these *status animarum*, see Paolo Ulvioni, *Il gran castigo di Dio: carestia ed epidemie a Venezia e nella Terraferma, 1628–1632* (Milan: F. Angeli, 1989), 8.

5. On the population of Venice in the sixteenth century, see Daniele Beltrami, *Storia della Popolazione di Venezia dalla Fine del Secolo XVI alla Caduta della Repubblica* (Padua: CEDAM, 1954); and Domenico Sella, "L'Economia," in *Storia di Venezia, vol. VI: Dal rinascimento al barocco*, ed. Gaetano Cozzi and Paolo Prodi (Rome: Istituto della Enciclopedia Italiana, 1994), 651–712.

6. For the total number of unmarried adults, I have counted the number of unmarried heads of household, single sisters, brothers, widowed parents, and "other" men and women in the household. "Other men" and "other women" are the categories in which I placed adults found in the censuses who are not described either as relatives or servants. Often these people are described as living "in affitto" or "a mese"; i.e., they rented rooms from the head of the household. I list them as unmarried if, in the case of women, they are not identified by their husband's name or, in the case of men, no wife was listed in the same household. I have also included both female and male servants for whom no spouse is noted. Since it is fairly clear that these servants lived with their employers, their spouses should be listed in the same household; it was common practice for servants to lodge with their employers. See Dennis Romano, *Housecraft and Statecraft: Domestic Service in Renaissance Venice, 1400–1600* (Baltimore: Johns Hopkins University Press, 1996), esp. chap. 4. The category of "children" is particularly tricky when trying to calculate the number of single adults. Many single adults continued to live with their parents, and some — mostly women — returned to their parental home after being widowed. But of course most of the offspring living with their parents were still young, and cannot be considered part of an unmarried adult population. Therefore, I have included in

these figures only those offspring who are unambiguously adults, usually because either an age or a profession is given. Since almost certainly more adults were living in the homes of their parents in the censuses than those who are explicitly identified as such, my figures both for the number of adult offspring and for the total number of single adults are somewhat conservative.

7. Karl Julius Beloch shows that by the 1580s, women outnumbered men in Venice. See his "La popolazione di Venezia nei secoli xvi e xvii," *Nuovo Archivio Veneto* 3 (1902): 5–49, esp. 29–32.

8. 2,533 unmarried men were identified in the censuses as household heads, contrasted with 4,285 women.

9. The figure is 1,311 out of 4,285.

10. It is not possible to count the number of single men for comparison purposes, because men were not identified by marital status, especially when widowed. A man living alone could be widowed, single, or married but separated from his wife—we have no way of knowing which.

11. The best summary of the evidence for high immigration in sixteenth-century Venice is Domenico Sella's "L'Economia," 652.

12. On the plight of female immigrants in early modern Europe, see Olwen Hufton, "Women and the Family Economy in Eighteenth-Century France," *French Historical Studies* 9 (1975): 1–22; Joan W. Scott and Louise A. Tilly, *Women, Work and Family* (New York: Holt, Rinehart and Winston, 1978); and Natalie Zemon Davis, "City Women and Religious Change," in *Society and Culture in Early Modern France* (Stanford, Calif.: Stanford University Press, 1975), 69.

13. Kowaleski, this volume.

14. Wiesner, this volume.

15. Many of these, of course, were wealthy women who had received the property in question from their parents. Many appear to have been single, since no husband is mentioned in the declaration. See, for example, ASV, Dieci Savii Sopra le Decime, B. 157, n. 357; B. 157 bis, n. 451; B. 161, n. 801; B. 162, nos. 260, 289, 394; and B. 170, nos. 450, 525, 563, 582, 643, and 684.

16. Cited in Richard Rapp, *Industry and Economic Decline in Seventeenth-Century Venice* (Cambridge, Mass.: Harvard University Press, 1976), 28.

17. See Judith C. Brown, "A Woman's Place Was in the Home: Women's Work in Renaissance Tuscany," in *Rewriting the Renaissance: The Discourses of Sexual Difference in Early Modern Europe*, Margaret W. Ferguson, Maureen Quilligan, and Nancy J. Vickers, ed. (Chicago: University of Chicago Press, 1986), 206–24.

18. Rapp, *Industry and Economic Decline*.

19. Amintore Fanfani, *Storia del lavoro in Italia dall fine del secolo XV agli inizi del XVIII* (Milan: 1943), 1123–24, cited in Rapp, *Industry and Economic Decline*.

20. Judith Brown has found that two-thirds of servants identified in a seventeenth-century Florentine census were female (Brown, "A Woman's Place").

21. Klapisch-Zuber's figures for female domestics for the years 1500–1529 are as follows: 33.3% single or presumed single; 29.2% widowed or presumed widowed; for a total of 62.5% unmarried women in domestic service, and 37.5% married or presumed so (Christiane Klapisch-Zuber, "Women Servants in Florence During the Fourteenth and Fifteenth Centuries," in *Women and Work in Prein-*

dustrial Europe, ed. Barbara Hanawalt [Bloomington: Indiana University Press, 1986], 63). For more on female domestics and unmarried women in fifteenth-century Florence, see Klapisch-Zuber, "Female Celibacy and Service in Florence in the Fifteenth Century," in *Women, Family and Ritual in Renaissance Italy* (Chicago: University of Chicago Press, 1987), 165–77.

22. See Romano's discussion of servant populations in *Housecraft and State-craft*, 109–16. Karl Julius Beloch's research for the Venetian population in the six-teenth century offers contrasting information regarding the number and ratio of male and female servants. He has found, for 1593, almost twice as many female ser-vants as male ones: 5,753 as contrasted with 3,632. This ratio remains roughly the same from the mid-sixteenth century to the mid-seventeenth. (Beloch's chart also implies that there were more nobles than servants in Venice in this period.) Beloch seems to have relied on only two terms to describe the servants under study: *famiglio* for a male servant, and *massera* for a female one. But *massere* and *servo* were also com-mon terms for male servants, and *serva* was often used to identify women in domes-tic service; see Beloch, "La Popolazione di Venezia nei Secoli XVI e XVII," 27–28. The population of servants is difficult to pin down in part because of rather fluid definitions of what constituted a servant in early modern Venice, which influenced the way their numbers were recorded. On this issue, see Romano, *Housecraft and Statecraft*, 105, 108. Klapisch-Zuber has noted for Florence that by the late fifteenth century men were entering the domestic labor force in increasingly large numbers due to a shortage of better-paying work (Klapisch-Zuber, "Female Celibacy," 177).

23. Romano bases his findings on the examination of legislation regarding servants from the late thirteenth through the sixteenth century. He concludes that by the later period the owning and displaying of servants became more closely associated with the employer's prestige; since male servants were usually employed for more public activities, such as rowing a boat, it became more important for wealthy Venetians to hire them than to hire female domestics, who were usually hidden away in the house and thus carried little prestige (Dennis Romano, "The Regulation of Domestic Service in Renaissance Venice," *Sixteenth Century Journal* 22, 4 (1991): 661–77).

24. For research on domestic servants, see Susan Mosher Stuard, "To Town to Serve: Urban Domestic Slavery in Medieval Ragusa" and Christiane Klapisch-Zuber, "Women Servants in Florence During the Fourteenth and Fifteenth Cen-turies," both in *Women and Work in Preindustrial Europe*, ed. Hanawalt 39–55 and 59–80 respectively; Mary Prior, "Women and the Urban Economy," in *Women in English Society 1500–1800*, ed. Mary Prior (Cambridge: Cambridge University Press, 1985), esp. 95; Olwen H. Hufton, "Women, Work and Marriage in Eighteenth-Century France," in *Marriage and Society: Studies in the Social History of Marriage*, ed. R. B. Outhwaite (New York: St. Martin's Press, 1981), 186–203; and Louise A. Tilly and Joan W. Scott, *Women, Work, and Family*, pt. 1.

25. For example, "Men who received clothes from their masters (as part of their upkeep or salary) could keep the clothes after only six months' service; women could do so only after a year" (Romano, "Domestic Service," 674).

26. Romano, *Housecraft and Statecraft*.

27. Ibid., 206.

28. The parish censuses record servants as young as 10.

29. Dennis Romano, "Domestic Service in Venice," 663, 664. On the working conditions of women servants more generally, see Hufton, "Women, Work, and Marriage."

30. Romano, "Domestic Service in Venice," 667–71.

31. Marin Sanuto, *I diarii*, Rinaldo Fulin, ed. (Venice: F. Visentini, 1879–1902), 8: 414, cited in Margaret F. Rosenthal, *The Honest Courtesan: Veronica Franco, Citizen and Writer in Sixteenth-Century Venice* (Chicago: University of Chicago Press, 1992), 11.

32. On the flourishing of prostitution in Venice throughout the early modern period, see Roman Canosa and Isabella Colonnello, *Storia della prostituzione in Italia, dal Quattrocento all fine del Settecento* (Rome: Sapere 2000, 1989), 149–64.

33. Brian Pullan, *Rich and Poor in Renaissance Venice: The Social Institutions of a Catholic State, 1580 to 1620* (Cambridge: Cambridge University Press, 1971), 380.

34. Frederic Lane, *Venice: A Maritime Republic* (Baltimore: Johns Hopkins University Press, 1973), 347.

35. "If the sixteenth century was the glorious age of the courtesan, this was also the century in which we note a significant change in the public attitude toward the common prostitute. Where she was once seen as a necessity and sometimes as a public good, by the end of the sixteenth century we see her viewed as a type of disease which is weakening the entire social structure" (Ruggiero, "Vizi e virtù nel rinascimento," *La storia della prostituzione*, ed. Guido Ruggiero, *Storia Dossier: Storia*, 4, 25 (January 1989): 35; my translation).

36. On the presence of married, widowed, and singlewomen in the Inquisition trials for witchcraft, see Ruth Martin, *Witchcraft and the Inquisition in Venice, 1550–1650* (Oxford: Oxford University Press, 1989).

37. Sally Scully, "Marriage or a Career?: Witchcraft as an Alternative in Seventeenth-Century Venice," *Journal of Social History* 28, 4 (1995): 857–76.

38. See Keith Thomas, *Religion and the Decline of Magic* (New York: Wiedenfeld and Nicholson, 1971).

39. On heretics and the Venetian Inquisition, see John Martin, *Venice's Hidden Enemies: Italian Heretics in a Renaissance City* (Chicago: University of Chicago Press, 1993).

40. See Ruth Martin, *Witchcraft and the Inquisition*.

41. See John Martin, *Venice's Hidden Enemies*.

42. On this shift, see Pullan, *Rich and Poor in Renaissance Venice*.

43. The Casa delle Zitelle is discussed at greater length in Chojnacka, "Women, Charity and Community in Early Modern Venice: The Casa delle Zitelle," *Renaissance Quarterly* 51 (1998): 68–91.

44. Ibid.

45. Istituzione di Ricovero e di Educazioni (IRE), ZIT A 1, sect. 4, ch. 4. See also Pullan, *Rich and Poor*, 389. This policy of accepting only those girls who were beautiful and in direct danger of becoming prostitutes was not unique to Venice. For Bologna, see Luisa Ciammitti, "Quanto costa essere normali: la dote nel Conservatorio femminile di Santa Maria del Baraccano (1630–1680)," *Quaderni Storici* 53 (1983): 469–97.

46. IRE, Zit A 1, ch. 15. The rest of the Zitelle charter is silent on the issue of overly intimate relations between the women living there. On the nature of female sexuality and female communities in early modern Italy, see Judith C. Brown, *Immodest Acts: The Life of a Lesbian Nun in Renaissance Italy* (Oxford: Oxford University Press, 1986); especially the helpful introduction on homosexuality in medieval and early modern Europe. On the changing perceptions of homosexuality in Counter-Reformation Italy, see Nicholas Davidson, "Theology, Nature and the Law: Sexual Sin and Sexual Crime in Italy from the Fourteenth to the Seventeenth Century," in *Crime, Society and the Law in Renaissance Italy*, ed. Trevor Dean and K. J. P. Lowe (Cambridge: Cambridge University Press, 1994), esp. 94–96.

47. Virginia Cox, "The Single Self: Feminist Thought and the Marriage Market in Early Modern Venice," *Renaissance Quarterly* 48, 3 (Autumn 1995): 513–81.

48. In the 1920s the Casa shifted identity to become, more broadly, a home for female orphans. In the 1930s, it was absorbed into a broader network of charitable institutions administered by the civic government (Silvia Lunardon, "Le Zitelle alla Giudecca: una storia lunga quattrocento anni," in *Le Zitelle: architettura, arte e storia di un'istituzione veneziana*, ed. Lionello Puppi [Venice: Albrizzi, 1994]).

49. Ibid., 28.

50. See Giuseppe Ellero, "Vergini christiane e donne di valor," in *Le Zitelle*, esp. 54–59, and Lunardon, "Le Zitelle alla Giudecca," 33.

51. ZIT, G 4, no. 61. Similar language is found in sixteenth-century statutes concerning a new women's hostel in Bologna. There, too, the women staff were specifically called upon to behave as "loving mothers of the family of the poor" (Nicholas Terpstra, "Apprenticeship in Social Welfare: From Confraternal Charity to Municipal Poor Relief in Early Modern Italy," *Sixteenth Century Journal* 25, 1 [1994]: 119).

52. IRE, Zit A 1, parte II, cap. 12.

53. Silvia Lunardon writes of wealthy Venetian society, "there was little faith in the salvation by the family of a girl either of the popular classes or of the middle classes in economic difficulty, unless she was aided by one of the institutions" (Lunardon, "Le Zitelle," 16).

54. Archivio Storico della Curia Patriarcale, Sezione Antica, Repertoria Causarum Civilium et Criminalium Curiae Patris Venetiarum, Causarum Matrimonialis. For more on these petitions, see Joanne Ferraro, "The Power to Decide: Battered Wives in Early Modern Venice," *Renaissance Quarterly* 48, 3 (Autumn 1995): 492–512.

9

Marital Status as a Category of Difference

Singlewomen and Widows in Early Modern England

Amy M. Froide

WHEN FANNY BURNEY'S NOVEL *Camilla* appeared in 1796, it featured a singlewoman, Mrs. Mittin, who provided a telling comment on the importance of marital status to women in her time. She confided to a close friend: "Do you know, for all I call myself Mrs., I'm single. . . . The reason I'm called Mrs. is . . . because I'd a mind to be taken for a young widow, on account everybody likes a young widow; and if one is called Miss, people being so soon to think one an old maid, that it's disagreeable."[1] Mrs. Mittin knew what modern historians of women have often ignored: although a singlewoman and a widow were both unmarried women, people in early modern England did not at all think of these two groups of women in the same way. This crucial distinction is one that most historians of women have overlooked in our preoccupation with comparing married to unmarried women. We have privileged the distinction between married and unmarried women for primarily two reasons. First, widows and singlewomen both lived without husbands, as opposed to (most) married women. And second, all unmarried women, or *femes soles*, enjoyed an independent legal status that wives, or *femes coverts*, surrendered upon marriage.[2] Merging singlewomen and widows into one category, and taking the experiences of widows as representative of both groups of women, we have too often left the unique experiences of singlewomen unexamined.[3]

Our tendency to see widows as representative of all unmarried women is especially problematic since at any given time singlewomen outnumbered widows in the English population. A sample of 100 rural and urban communities throughout early modern England has revealed that while widows made up 14.9 percent of the adult female population, singlewomen were twice as numerous, comprising 30.2 percent of adult women. Likewise, in the urban environment of Southampton, widows made up at least 16.3 percent of adult females but singlewomen comprised at least 25.7 percent.[4] Since singlewomen formed a larger proportion of the female population than did widows, we have been generalizing from the experiences of a smaller group to the experiences of a larger one. Moreover, in so doing we misrepresent how contemporaries in early modern England viewed women of different marital states. Today we differentiate women with men (usually wives) from women without men (widows and singlewomen); then, people distinguished between women who were, or had been, wives and mothers of legitimate children, from women who were, and had been, neither. Marital status was an important differentiating factor between women, but the significant difference in the past was not between married and unmarried women; rather it was between what I will call *ever-married* (women who had ever been married in their lifetimes — thus, both wives and widows) and *never-married* women.[5] This distinction was a result of the very disparate roles of widows and wives on the one hand, and singlewomen on the other, in a society where the conjugal household was the basis of social, economic, and political thought and structure.

The differing experiences of ever-married and never-married women make sense in light of the prominence of the conjugal household and family in early modern English society. Early modern England was a patriarchal society in which contemporaries thought of women in terms of their familial roles: as daughter, wife, mother, and widow. The position of women who had married was clear: wives assisted their husbands in the running of households, and widows, by virtue of being the deputies of their deceased husbands, headed households. But contemporaries did not conceive of singlewomen as heading or even assisting in running households of their own. Rather, singlewomen were expected to remain in a dependent position in which they lived as daughters, or if their parents were deceased, as sisters, kin, or servants in another male's household. The only acceptable role for the singlewoman was as a household dependent, not as an independent female head of household, outside the control of a father or master. This expectation was a problem for the many singlewomen who could not or did not live as dependents. Widows had a public and independent place within the patriarchal society; singlewomen did not.

Marginalized singlewomen faced more scrutiny and operated under more disadvantages than did widows, who at least occupied a sanctioned social role.[6] This essay will illuminate the differing experiences of single-women and widows throughout various communities in early modern England by focusing on three areas: residential options, employment, and poor relief, which best illustrate the differences between ever-married and never-married women. We will find that while singlewomen and widows may have shared a theoretical legal status, in practice singlewomen labored under practical disadvantages that ensured never-married women seldom enjoyed the residential, employment, and welfare options that ever-married women did. Nevertheless, while such distinctions between ever-married and never-married women were the rule, we will see how age and social status allowed a small number of singlewomen to achieve a "widow-like" status, so that they experienced contingently the opportunities reserved legitimately for matrons who had married.

Residence

Singlewomen and widows had very different residential options available to them. For one thing, widows had more alternatives from which to choose. The dominance of the nuclear family and household in early modern England meant that, once a husband died, his widow did not return to her natal family or go to live with her husband's family. Instead, she became the head of her deceased husband's household.[7] In assuming the role of head of household a widow gained authority over the house, the family, the ser-vants and apprentices, and the family business. She had earned this role by marrying and helping to create a household, which it was her responsibility to continue after her husband was gone. This pattern of nuclear households is evidenced by the 70 percent of households in early modern England that were headed by married couples, as well as the 12.9 percent (the next most common arrangement) headed by widows.[8] Of the residential options a widow entertained on her spouse's death, heading her own household was the most likely. For example, between 72 and 79 percent of widows headed their own households in eighteenth-century Lichfield, Stoke-on-Trent, and Corfe Castle.[9] In the port town of Southampton it was customary for a widow whose husband left her with property to take over his lease and remain in the family home. For instance, in 1705 the widow Elizabeth Rowte took out a new lease on a tenement on French Street (that her husband John Rowte had originally leased in 1679), and she continued to head a household made up of herself and several adult children.[10] Of course, poverty prevented some widows from establishing their own households, but even poor widows had options. They might move in with kin (such as adult children, siblings, or even parents if they were young), with friends, or board in another family's home. By opening their homes to lodgers or boarders, some poor widows retained their headship of households. And some widows coheaded households with other women who lived without husbands. For example, in 1696 widow Flood and widow Weeks lived together with Weeks's two children in St. Lawrence's parish, Southampton. These two widows shared household expenses and housework, and perhaps provided emotional as well as material support to one another.[11] Even if they could not always exercise it, widows enjoyed the privilege of living on their own, or at least heading a household with another woman, and in many communities a majority chose to do so. Widows made use of the independence their marital status gave them. If poor, they still had the option to retain their household and bring in lodgers, or to lodge them-selves with other women — for widows, no matter what their social status, were allowed to live outside a male-controlled household. And if more prosperous, widows could opt to establish their own households, where they could gather around them whichever children, servants, relatives, and friends they could accommodate.

The residential situation of a singlewoman was quite different from and far more limited than that of a widow. Because a lifelong singlewoman did not marry there was never a definitive public moment when she became a householder in her own right. And precisely because she did not marry, a singlewoman never earned the privilege to set up her own nuclear house-hold.[12] While widows headed 12.9 percent of households in early modern England, singlewomen headed only 1.1 percent.[13] There were twice as many singlewomen as widows in England, but they headed only a tiny fraction of households. Since it was rare for a singlewoman to head her own household, she typically lived as a dependent daughter in her parents' household until they died or she left. A singlewoman then usually went to live as a servant, lodger, or relative in someone else's home.[14]

Contemporaries expected singlewomen to live as dependents in the households of their fathers, male relatives, or masters, and those who did not do so caused local authorities a good amount of worry. The household, the family, and service were all institutions of authority and control — two things contemporaries thought singlewomen should be under.[15] From at least the fifteenth century and continuing well into the seventeenth, munici-

pal authorities throughout England issued edicts against singlewomen who
lived independent of fathers or masters, or in other words outside a family
or male-headed household.[16] As early as 1492 the civic officers of Coventry
ordered that "no singlewoman . . . take or keep from henceforth houses or
rooms to themselves, nor that they take any room with any other person,
but that they go into service."[17] A century later, in 1582, the officers of
Southampton's Court Leet defined the single female objects of their concern as charmaids, or "maid servants that take chambers and so live by
themselves masterless and are called by the name of charwomen which we
think not meet or sufferable."[18] In other sixteenth- and seventeenth-century
towns such as Norwich, the town fathers issued orders against young people living "at their own hand." Almost all of those prosecuted under such
orders were singlewomen and female servants, who lived either on their
own or in female-headed households.[19]

Town fathers worried about independent singlewomen for various
reasons. Diane Willen suggests authorities in York were concerned about
singlewomen living on their own because they thought such women "represented a threat to the patriarchal social order" by living outside the authority of the household and a male master.[20] Some local officers raised
suspicions about the morality of singlewomen who lived alone and accused
them of serving as a bad example. In 1584 Manchester's Court Leet stated
"women being unmarried be at their own hands . . . also abusing themselves
with young men and others having not any man to control them to the
great dishonor of God and evil example of others."[21] Urban authorities,
such as those in Manchester, assumed that sexual immorality would be the
by-product of any singlewoman living on her own. Officials elided singlewomen who lived in their own lodgings with prostitutes who rented lodgings from which they plied their trade. The line between a singlewoman
who worked and lived on her own and a prostitute became a (perhaps
purposely) thin one. Thus, the morality of all singlewomen was called into
question and, perhaps more important, allowed town fathers to demand
that singlewomen be put under the authority of a male head of household.[22]

Town officials addressed in the strictest terms the supposed social and
moral threat posed by singlewomen living on their own. When Southampton's officials failed to impel independent singlewomen back into household dependency, they forced them to leave the town. In 1609 they told the
charmaid Elizabeth Green to put herself into service within two weeks or to
depart from Southampton. Green was only one of many singlewomen that
Southampton's authorities examined for living independently in the early

part of the seventeenth century.[23] While enforced departure was a common threat in Southampton, singlewomen in Norwich who took chambers or otherwise lived out of service were more commonly incarcerated in the local bridewell, or house of correction, where they would be whipped and set to work.[24]

Persecution of singlewomen whose only "crime" was to live and work on their own was no accident. Scholars have noted the intense fear of disorder evidenced by Tudor and early Stuart contemporaries. The targets of this fear were often poor, female, and young: those people who seemed to threaten a social order run by adult, married males of middling and elite status.[25] The singlewomen who found themselves the subject of much local legislation were not only from the lower classes, but also young, female, and of an anomalous marital status in a society that privileged the marital state. Singlewomen might well have been the early modern patriarch's worst nightmare — encompassing multiple characteristics of disorder all at once. Nevertheless, views of singlewomen do seem to have modified over the early modern era. By the 1640s urban authorities became less overtly concerned about independent singlewomen and punishments of such women waned, although they did not disappear completely. Despite less antipathy toward them, no consequent increase in the numbers of singlewomen living on their own came about. Even at the end of the seventeenth century only 8 percent of never-married women (22 out of a total of 292 possible singlewomen) headed their own households in Southampton.[26] Most singlewomen still remained within the household of a relative or master.

Nevertheless, as the above figure indicates, a minority of singlewomen did manage to form their own households. These women shared three characteristics: advanced age, the loss of a surviving parent, and elevated social status. When urban authorities legislated against singlewomen living on their own, they were assuming that all women married and that any woman who was single was also young. But not all women did marry in early modern England, and for older singlewomen residence with a parent was not always an option (since they might very well be deceased), nor were positions in service always available or consonant with a woman's social status.[27] These lifelong singlewomen predominated among the few never-married women who established their own households.

Two events seem to have enabled a singlewoman to establish her own household. The first was passing the age of menopause, which would have signified the end of the myth that a singlewoman would inevitably marry, produce a family, and assist in running her husband's household. Menopause and older age may have also signaled a rise in autonomy for the singlewoman, thus allowing her to live more independently.[28] For instance, in a sample of three eighteenth-century communities in Staffordshire and Dorset, only between 4.5 and 5.9 percent of singlewomen under 45 years of age headed their own households. But between 36.4 and 40 percent of singlewomen age 45 and older headed their own households. Age, in other words, resulted in an eight- or nine-fold increase in the number of single female householders.[29] Forty-five is an arbitrary age picked by demographers to differentiate between life-cycle and lifelong singlewomen, but it seems close to the age at which contemporaries decided a singlewoman might acceptably live on her own. For instance, according to officials in Coventry, "no singlewoman . . . under the age of fifty years, [should] take or keep from henceforth houses or rooms to themselves."[30]

The second event that allowed a singlewoman to set up her own household was the death of a surviving parent. This circumstance heralded the end of a singlewoman's tenure as daughter, as well as the loss of a parental household in which to reside.[31] The small but significant number of single female householders who began to appear in seventeenth-century Southampton all shared the circumstance of their surviving parent's recent death. Barbara Richards was 38 years old when she leased her own town house in 1705. Her mother had died in 1698 and the messuage that Richards leased had been her mother's before she died. A few years after their widowed mother died, Elizabeth and Joanna Shergold, who were 47 and 39 years old respectively, leased a large house together in 1721.[32] And in 1733 forty-nine-year-old Ann Goodridge was living in her own house one year after she had served as her father's executrix.[33] An older singlewoman, who had neither a parent's nor a husband's household to live in, may have now resembled a widow, and like a widow now had the privilege of living on her own.[34] However, there was no distinct age at which a singlewoman might strike out on her own. Instead, it seems she had to judge what her own community would condone. This may have left many singlewomen in their thirties and forties unsure of their options, and at a loss if they had no family or master with whom to reside.

While advanced age and parental demise were sufficient reasons for a singlewoman to become a householder, middling to elite social status was a necessary factor. It is telling that all the singlewomen who headed their own households in seventeenth-century Southampton were not only mature women, but also women of independent and ample means. For example, Barbara Richards was the daughter of a Southampton gentleman who supported herself by lending money when she began to lease a house of her own.[35] The never-married sisters Elizabeth and Joanna Shergold (also the daughters of a Southampton gentleman) employed themselves as both managers of (an unspecified) trade and keepers of a boarding house for young ladies. The latter occupation required them to have their own residence, so together they rented one of the largest buildings in Southampton.[36] Women like Richards and the Shergolds had the means to support themselves, a matter of considerable importance to civic officers. Early modern towns did not want to play host to singlewomen who might become economic charges as they aged and who had no family on which to rely for assistance. Through various measures town fathers discouraged any but the self-sufficient from establishing households in their towns.[37]

Nevertheless, some of the singlewomen who had the economic means to set up their own households chose not to do so. Sometimes they opted to live in the households of relatives or friends. For example, the Southampton singlewoman Jane Bracebridge lived in the household of her kinsman Robert Richbell, despite the fact that she was mature, well-off, and enjoyed the partial ownership of two houses in which she could have lived on her own.[38] Why did Bracebridge choose to live as a dependent? Perhaps she had heard too many stories about the harassment of independent singlewomen; perhaps she too felt the concern contemporaries voiced over the virtue of never-married women living on their own. Bracebridge knew that while an ever-married woman might legitimately maintain her own household, the never-married woman who lived on her own did so contingently, and never legitimately.[39] Only if she were older and had the financial means could a singlewoman head a household, and even then her neighbors might not approve of such an arrangement. Younger and poorer singlewomen were in an even more constrained situation; they seem to have never enjoyed the full freedom or choice to live on their own.

Employment

If the residential options available to singlewomen were more limited than those enjoyed by widows, singlewomen fared even worse in employment opportunities. Widows enjoyed the most extensive economic rights and privileges of any working women in the early modern period. Most women living in English towns in this period had a difficult time breaking into formal trades, which were often organized into male-run guilds and companies. In Southampton, for example, women had apprenticeship and entry into the freedom (a status that conveyed the right to trade in the town) denied to them. Other towns were slightly more open to female apprentices and mistresses, but women never operated on an equal par with men. Nevertheless, wives often worked as partners in their husbands' businesses and both guild and civic officials permitted widows to continue the trades of their deceased husbands. By virtue of their status as "deputy husbands," widows in towns like York and Southampton formed the majority of women independently engaged in formal trades.[40] For example, the widow Judith Delamotte carried on her husband's cloth trade and even expanded the family business, becoming one of seventeenth-century Southampton's most successful businesswomen.[41] Not only did widows inherit their husbands' trades, but urban authorities also on occasion allowed widows to succeed to their husbands' public offices, which provided them with a source of both income and prestige.[42] In 1586 the Southampton assembly allowed the widow Alice Harvey to assume the office of a porter for her lifetime.[43] Widow Harvey had to hire a male laborer to do the actual carrying, but she did appropriate a portion of the fees collected for the service, and thus was able to maintain herself.

The widows of wealthy craftsmen, merchants, and officials were not the only ever-married women to benefit from economic privileges. Most working women, even most widows, did not engage in formal trades. Rather, they found employment in informal and casual work. Widows and wives engaged in various stages of textile production; they worked as petty retailers of food, alcohol, and other small goods; they ran lodging houses and alehouses; and they assisted the sick and the poor. Urban authorities often regulated, but also condoned and assisted the widows and wives who worked in these informal employments. For instance, in 1650 Southampton's assembly questioned the widow Anne Janverine about her huckstering and decided to allow her to retail "fish, salt, candles, butter and other victuals provided that she [did] not sell any other thing and [did] not forestall, regrate or do any other thing contrary to the law or order of the town."[44] Sometimes town fathers not only condoned, but actively recruited working widows and wives. In York and Southampton civic officers regularly paid widows and wives for distributing relief to the poor, instructing poor children and "idle" singlewomen in a trade, assisting in the births of illegitimate and poor children, nursing the sick, and laying out and burying the dead.[45] In London and Salisbury, widows and wives comprised the majority of women who let out lodgings, retailed food, brewed and sold beer, and managed alehouses.[46] Officials in Southampton, Salisbury, and many other communities regularly granted licenses to work as victualers, tipplers (sellers of ale), and alehousekeepers to poor widows in particular. The predominance of widows among such licensees can be explained by the fact that local officials used such casual work as a form of poor relief for needy widows.[47] Urban officials could give licenses to anyone they wished, but they singled out widows; in so doing they deemed widowed female householders especially worthy of economic assistance.

Town officials not only allowed widows to engage in both formal and informal trades, they also doled out more active assistance to these women. When widows did not possess the money or goods necessary to continue the family business, they were sometimes able to borrow money from local authorities in order to establish a livelihood. In Southampton and other towns, testators sometimes endowed loans or grants of money to individuals (usually young men) starting up in a business or trade. In 1670 Southampton's assembly reiterated that only those persons holding the freedom to trade in the town (that is, men) were to receive such assistance, but in practice widows also received loans.[48] Between 1641 and 1721, 560 people received money from the Lynch endowment, 22 of whom were women — all widows.[49] The widows obtained loans of £10 apiece, the same amount that men received.[50] While widows made up only 4 percent of those persons receiving money from Mr. Lynch's gift, they did relatively well since they comprised only 9 to 14 percent of the adult population in Southampton.[51] Widows were the only women acknowledged as legitimate recipients of business loans in Southampton.

This is not to say that widows always found themselves welcome in the urban economy. A widow who remarried and attempted to continue in her prior husband's occupation could encounter opposition. In 1674 Southampton's assembly heard various complaints from the hatters against Mrs. Lyne and told Lyne that she had to forbear selling any hats within the town because she had "no right to the trade"; she had forfeited it by remarrying. Nor could a widow practice a trade different from that of her deceased husband. Protests against such women even came from fellow widows, as was the case in 1718 when Southampton's assembly ordered widow Fry not to sell any more grocery or other wares upon the complaint of widow Dummer and other grocers' widows.[52] These examples show that Southampton's authorities did not hesitate to restrict the trading activities of widows on occasion. But local authorities dealt with widowed women on a case-by-case basis. This was very different from how local officials treated working single-women, whom they refused to help and, in fact, punished as a group.

Working singlewomen faced many disadvantages, for they enjoyed neither the toleration nor the assistance extended to working widows. Life-long singlewomen obviously could not inherit a trade or office from a husband, and it was not customary for fathers to leave their businesses to their daughters. Some singlewomen did learn skills and work in their par-ents' shops or trades, while a few others even apprenticed themselves into a formal trade. But most of these women did not enjoy the possibility of independently exercising these trades, because in early modern England to be a master or mistress in a trade also meant being a householder. Just as local authorities believed that the proper residence for a singlewoman was as a dependent in someone else's household and not as an independent householder, so they also believed that the only appropriate economic role for a never-married woman was a subordinate one. A singlewoman was encouraged, even expected, to work for her family, other relatives, or as a servant in a master's household, but she was not supposed to establish a business of her own or work independently as widows did. Even when a singlewoman worked with her siblings, if they were male or widowed, urban authorities viewed the singlewoman as a dependent worker. For example, in 1697 singlewoman Ann Faulkner and her widowed sister Mary Stotes jointly inherited their mother's trade. The following year "widow Stotes and her sister" paid the annual "Stall and Art" licensing fee to trade in Southampton. But the tax assessors in Holy Rood parish didn't even bother to mention Faulkner when they assessed the widow "Mrs. Stotes' stock in trade" at a value of £12 10s.[53] In the eyes of Southampton's officials, widow Stotes was an independent tradeswoman, but the singlewoman Ann Faulk-ner was a dependent worker, sometimes noted as Stotes's sister and some-times not mentioned at all.

As the sisters Mary Stotes and Ann Faulkner illustrate, even though singlewomen shared the legal status of *feme sole* with widows and thus had the legal ability to trade, in practice widows were allowed to engage in formal trades but singlewomen usually were not.[54] When singlewomen tried to exercise their *feme sole* status they met with opposition from urban officials. In towns such as Oxford and Southampton legal theory and local economic practice often diverged sharply.[55] While Oxford's officials toler-ated the business activities of both married women and widows, "the inde-pendent singlewoman had no place in the Oxford commercial community."[56] In the first two decades of the eighteenth century singlewomen who made the popular loose overgarments called mantuas faced prosecution for intruding upon the work of the Oxford tailor's gild. In Southampton, while widows formed a consistent minority of those individuals who paid the Stall and Art fees each year to trade in the town, only one singlewoman paid such a charge before the 1680s. Mary Sherwood, who inherited her widowed mother's shop and trade in 1639, was for a short period of time the only officially acknowledged single tradeswoman in Southampton. But she died in the following year.[57] If Sherwood had lived she would have most likely shared the treatment that singlewoman Mary Shrimpton Junior received from the town assembly. In 1649 the justices of the peace examined the widow Shrimpton and her daughter Mary Jr. about the theft of two cheeses from a shop. They decided that Mary Jr. "appeared to be an idle and suspicious housewife and therefore sent [her] to the workhouse."[58] Eight years later Mary Jr. again aroused the disapproval of the town officials, but this time for very different behavior. The assembly gave her "one month's space to put off and dispose of her sackcloth and whalebone which she has now in her house and custody and from that time forward to forbear to use the trade of bodice making unless she be employed by the freemen of the town."[59] While Shrimpton had at first appeared too idle to Southampton's authorities, now she seemed too industrious and independent, and the officers punished her for both behaviors. Mary Shrimpton Jr. illustrates the difficult position in which singlewomen found themselves: they were punished for not supporting themselves, but they were also penalized for working independently in formal trades.

One option for a singlewoman like Shrimpton was to find work in the informal and casual trades such as victualling and huckstering that employed so many wives and widows. But even in these occupations never-married women were treated differently than ever-married women. Widows made up the majority of women working as tipplers and alehouse-keepers, but singlewomen were less active in these trades. In early modern London, out of a sample of 53 women engaged in catering or victualling, 32 were wives, 18 were widows, and only 3 were singlewomen.[60] In South-ampton, it was not until 1739 that Mary Smith became the first single-woman to keep a licensed alehouse in the early modern era.[61] Ever-married women could gain licenses to victual, but never-married women usually could not. If it was the case that urban officials reserved licenses for ale-housekeeping and tippling for those persons they deemed worthy of help, it is not surprising to find so few singlewomen in these occupations.[62] As we shall see, contemporaries did not usually number singlewomen among the "worthy" poor.

Singlewomen found a few more employment opportunities in huckstering, or selling small goods and victuals, than they did in tippling or alehousekeeping, but the handful of never-married women who made a living by petty retailing in towns like London and Southampton never compared to the consistent number of ever-married women who did so.[63] Perhaps the clearest example of the relative privilege of widows can be seen in the starkly different manner Southampton's officials treated petitions to trade made by widows and singlewomen. In 1607, Mrs. Ecton and her stepdaughter appeared before Southampton's assembly, where Mrs. Ecton asked if "her daughter [might] be admitted to open a shop above the Bar and sell small wares by retail." The assembly's response was an unequivocal no; they were unwilling to permit the singlewoman to establish herself independently in trade.[64] Things were very different when, in the summer of 1629, widow Tirrell came before the same assembly asking if she might be allowed to sell goods in the town. The local authorities had a different response for Tirrell, whom they allowed to "have free liberty, license, and toleration from henceforth to retail all sorts of saltfish and herring within this town."[65] Even though Ecton's daughter and widow Tirrell were both *femes soles*, and despite the fact that Ecton's daughter had family-backing for her venture (which made her a good economic risk), Southampton's officials favored the widow and frowned on the singlewoman.

If a singlewoman found herself unwelcome in formally organized and more casual trades and did not have a family member for whom she could work, then she was most likely to enter into service. This was exactly the type of subordinate economic position that English contemporaries condoned for singlewomen.[66] By not allowing singlewomen to enter into trade, local authorities could ensure such women would have to enter service and thus be under the roof and control of a master or mistress. What this meant was that most singlewomen did work in service — an occupation that covered a variety of duties ranging from housework and child care to assisting in the master's trade or minding the master's shop or alehouse. Unfortunately for singlewomen, good service positions were not always to be found.[67] In addition, lifelong singlewomen might not want, or be able, to remain in service for their entire working lives. Singlewomen who would or could not maintain themselves through service struck out into various types of day labor or other independent occupations, and in doing so ran into trouble with local authorities. In Southampton such women were called "charmaids" and in Norwich these women were referred to as "out of service," or in other communities as "out of place."[68] The assumption was that singlewomen should be employed as the servants of adult males, which was their proper "place."

Just as early modern towns punished singlewomen for attempting to set up their own households, town fathers also prosecuted singlewomen for working independently or in occupations other than service. The opposition that these day-laborers, or charmaids, faced offers some of the clearest evidence of the official antipathy toward independent, working single-women. Singlewomen in Norwich who were found "out of service" were given the options of incarceration in the local bridewell or of finding a position in service within a set period of time.[69] In the late sixteenth and early seventeenth centuries Southampton's officials issued repeated proclamations against charmaids who kept "themselves out of service and [worked] for themselves in diverse men's houses."[70] Southampton's authorities did not stop at general pronouncements against independent working women, for they also singled out and punished individual single-women for working outside of service. These women would "disappear" from their employers' homes after a reprimand or punishment, but then inevitably reentered casual employment until the next time they came to the attention of the authorities. For instance, between 1608 and 1616 Southampton's beadles arrested Elizabeth Quinten for working as a charmaid at four separate times. In 1609 Quinten briefly responded to town pressure by getting a job as a servant; in 1615 she was thrown in the cage (a prison for petty criminals); and by 1627 she was resorting to petty thievery to sustain herself.[71] Like many other singlewomen, Elizabeth Quinten lived a precarious life on the economic margins — moving from job to job, eking out a living, while simultaneously trying to avoid the notice of the authorities.

Economic legislation was specifically crafted with social considerations in mind so that singlewomen would not compete with householders, and so that never-married women would have no option but to work for someone else (and preferably in that person's household). For instance, Manchester's Court Leet railed at the "inconvenience" caused by "single-women . . . at their own hands [who] do bake and brew and use other trades to the great hurt of the poor inhabitants having wife and children."[72] Singlewomen, in other words, were discouraged from trading independently because they might compete with married male householders, who plied their trades to support their families. By living and working on their own singlewomen were assuming the privileges of householders, which their contemporaries did not think they deserved. Since contemporaries believed singlewomen were not proper householders and had no children to support, they were seen as unnecessary competition and so were not allowed to trade. This situation is similar to what Merry Wiesner has noted for Germany, where spinner's wages were purposely kept low so that singlewomen could not support themselves on their own, and thus would move into the household of some male master or artisan and work for him.[73] The work of singlewomen was never restricted for purely economic reasons; such restrictions had as much to do with social expectations about who was a legitimate, independent worker, and in these cases, singlewomen were not viewed as such.

Despite the considerable opposition they faced from local officials, a few intrepid singlewomen did manage to work independently in early modern towns. In Southampton, small numbers of singlewomen began to establish their own businesses beginning in the 1680s, so that by 1750 at least 36 singlewomen had independently plied a trade or established a shop in the town.[74] On their own, or with the assistance of female family members, singlewomen in Southampton succeeded in establishing themselves as milliners, linendrapers, clothiers, glovers, ironmongers, shopkeepers, schoolteachers, and bathhousekeepers. Many of these women were quite successful. Jane Martin, a singlewoman and a milliner, had amassed such a considerable stock of merchandise that she figured among the major traders in Southampton who were fined for using metal-wheeled carts to transport their wares. Elizabeth and Joanna Shergold ran two businesses in Southampton for close to 30 years and could afford to live in one of the largest properties in the town.[75]

Just as age and social status were mitigating factors that allowed a few singlewomen to set up their own households, these same characteristics enabled a minority of singlewomen to work independently. Almost all of the single tradeswomen in Southampton were over 30, and a good number were in their forties and fifties. For example, Anne Goodridge started to work as an independent glover beginning in her fifties.[76] Similarly, when Mary Rowte's widowed mother died she inherited her mother's ironmongery business and began to ply the trade herself at the age of 45.[77] Single tradeswomen like Goodridge and Rowte were not only mature but also well-off. The never-married women who established their own businesses in Southampton were usually also householders in their own right, as well as property-holders and investors. For instance, Ann Fleming kept a coach house and paid tax on one of the more expensive properties in All Saints

Infra parish.[78] When the linendraper Alice Zains died in 1701 she left behind an estate worth over £240 in cash, as well as jewels, household and shop goods, and loans she had yet to collect.[79] In other towns it was also singlewomen of at least middling social status — most definitely not the average singlewoman — who established themselves as independent traders. In Oxford it was the daughters of former mayors who broke into the male-dominated millinery trade.[80] In London and Edinburgh it was singlewomen from middling families — the daughters of merchants, ministers, and significant tradesmen — who independently plied the trades of milliner, mantua-maker, and shopkeeper.[81]

These few singlewomen who established their own businesses also did so without any public or charitable assistance. When widows established their own businesses they had somewhere to turn. As noted above, between 1641 and 1721–22 Southampton widows received loans from Lynch's endowment, and 11 more widows received economic aid from John Steptoe's endowment.[82] While this may seem a small figure, it is considerable when compared to the fact that not one singlewoman received a business loan. Moreover, singlewomen often had to pay exceptionally high fees to trade. In Southampton, most male and widowed female traders paid 2d. each year for the privilege to trade in the town. But Jane Zains, one of the first singlewomen to pay a Stall and Art fee so that she could open a linendrapery business, paid a fee of 2s. 6d. (15 to 30 times higher than what most men and widows paid).[83] In other words, those singlewomen who managed to ply an independent trade never did so on equal terms with other businesswomen. If a singlewoman was old enough that she resembled a widow, if she had her own household, and if she was wealthy enough to establish her own business and pay the discouragingly high trading fees, then urban officials might turn a blind eye to her trading. But civic officials were not going to assist or encourage a singlewoman in taking on the role of a householder and an independent tradesperson. Once again a few singlewomen managed to carve out an independent space for themselves, but they only did so contingently, not because they were viewed as legitimate tradespeople, worthy of the same rights and privileges as others.

When urban authorities allowed widows to continue in their husbands' trades, licensed widows and wives to engage in casual employment, and assisted widows in establishing their own businesses, they acted not out of any conviction that ever-married women had the right to engage in trade, but because they believed in supporting the household and the family economy. If a wife worked in a by-employment or assisted her husband, then authorities viewed her as helping to maintain her household rather than functioning as an individual worker. A widow was the deputy of her deceased husband, and if she could support herself and her children through her trade, then her family and her household would not become an economic burden on the town. By tolerating and even assisting the business activities of ever-married women town fathers aided in the maintenance of a family and a household.[84] These same civic officials regularly chose not to assist, and even to oppose outright, never-married women who worked for themselves. If they allowed singlewomen to trade, the town fathers seem to have believed that they would be supporting never-married women in independent and aberrant roles, since they expected these women to confine themselves to subordinate residential and economic positions within a household. Put simply, early modern people did not think of singlewomen as heads of household, even if in reality some were, and thus they saw no reason to support such women as independent workers.

Poor Relief

Widows not only had more economic opportunities open to them than did singlewomen, but if they were unemployed, widows also had an easier time than singlewomen in securing poor relief. As with employment assistance, parochial officials dispensed poor relief in accordance with patriarchal beliefs about who was or was not a worthy recipient of aid. Widows typically found themselves included among the "deserving poor," along with orphans, the aged, sick, or lame, as well as householders overburdened with children. Because widows were usually either elderly, or young and "overburdened" with children for whom they were the sole support, widowed women were some of the most common recipients of poor relief from the local parish. For instance, in the villages and towns of early modern Norfolk, widows comprised an average of 50 percent of those receiving poor relief.[85] Likewise, in the Oxfordshire town of Abingdon widows were the largest group of poor relief recipients.[86] And in Southampton, widows comprised two-thirds of the persons receiving money from the poor rates at the end of the sixteenth century.[87]

Widows also figured among the most common beneficiaries of assistance from private charities and almshouses. Each year seven poor people in Southampton received new clothing (usually gowns) from the endowment of John Cornishe. In the years between 1617 and 1636 ever-married women such as widows and goodwives received at least three to four of these gowns (the remainder went to aged men), and sometimes, as in 1625, all the gowns went to ever-married women.[88] The women who lived in Southampton's numerous almshouses were also usually widows.[89] For example, in 1675 the widow Mary Jenkins was living in the lower almshouse in St. Mary's parish when she petitioned Southampton's justices for some assistance because she was suffering from "the [skin] disease called the King's Evil."[90] Widows also made up a considerable proportion of the inhabitants of almshouses in York and the Hertfordshire community of Aldenham. In fact, throughout Europe institutions for poor women generally seem to have favored widows over singlewomen.[91]

While needy widows were thus able to obtain various types of assistance, local officials expected singlewomen to shift for themselves. In an age that did not comprehend systemic unemployment, young, single individuals found themselves characterized as the "able-bodied" or "undeserving" poor. Paradoxically, civic officials required singlewomen to work and support themselves, but at the same time they limited these women's employment options and channeled them into less remunerative and less autonomous occupations, thus giving singlewomen little control over their work or the length of their employment. Employment conditions such as these meant that singlewomen sometimes found themselves in need of relief, but they did not often get it.

The relatively small number of singlewomen who figure in various lists of poor relief recipients illustrate the lack of assistance meted out to never-married women. In 1552, the officers of St. Michael's and St. John's parish in Southampton provided assistance to four widows, seven men, four wives, and 16 children, but not to any known singlewomen.[92] The position of singlewomen in Southampton was not unique, for such women also were rarely recipients of poor relief in other communities. The census of the poor conducted by Norwich in 1570 identified 40 singlewomen as paupers, but only 6 of the 40 obtained relief. By comparison, out of the 177 poor widows living in Norwich in the same year, 64 received relief.[93] The likelihood of widows obtaining more economic assistance than singlewomen was even more striking in the seventeenth-century community of Aldenham, Hertfordshire. Here widows formed 48 percent of those receiving assistance, but singlewomen comprised an average of only 4.5 percent of the recipients of poor relief.[94] Historians of early modern England have largely characterized the "deserving" poor as women, but the above examples caution against such a generalization. Ever-married women, especially widows, made up the majority of women counted as the "deserving" poor; however, never-married women most definitely did not.[95]

While parish officials assisted poor parents and their young children, they did not extend that assistance to teenagers and young adults who were yet living at home and not yet married. The contemporary correlation between singleness and "undeserving" poverty is illustrated by the predicament of the Veere family of Southampton.[96] In 1697 the parish officers of St. Mary's gave widow Veere 2s. 6d. because she was otherwise unable to support herself and her young children. But the officers granted this money to widow Veere upon the condition that she would make her eldest son and daughter "go abroad into service."[97] The churchwardens of St. Mary's felt it was necessary to provide for poor widows and their young children, but not for their equally poor but able-bodied daughters and sons, whom the officers believed were capable of supporting themselves. In Norwich, children deemed old enough to be in service (14-year-old boys and 15-year-old girls) were ordered out of their mothers' households.[98] Likewise in Aldenham, the parish officers refused to aid young people who could go into service, dispensing relatively little to individuals between the ages of 15 and 30—those who were old enough to leave home but not yet old enough to marry.[99] It is important to note that for lifelong singlewomen who never married (and so could not hope to earn the economic assistance officials extended to the heads of households), the years they spent without relief extended far beyond the age of 30.

As part of the "undeserving" or "able-bodied" poor, singlewomen were not ignored, but, in contrast to the economic assistance obtained by widows, singlewomen received more punitive attention.[100] Urban governors preferred to force poor singlewomen into compulsory labor rather than giving them monetary aid. Communities throughout England enrolled young girls and singlewomen in their teens into pauper apprenticeships where they learned skills such as sewing, spinning, and housewifery.[101] After the passage of the Poor Law Act of 1598 (reenacted in 1601), unemployed singlewomen in towns like Norwich were set to work on stocks of raw materials such as flax, hemp, and wool.[102] Towns such as Salisbury and Southampton set up workhouses for the poor in the early seventeenth century. In 1632 Southampton's corporation established a workhouse wherein 20 resident children and up to 40 other compulsory day-workers (including adult singlewomen) would be forced to make bonelace, or to knit, card, and spin.[103]

Most historians agree, however, that schemes to set able-bodied paupers to work never successfully employed many people, singlewomen included.[104] Instead, local authorities did a much better job incarcerating and punishing those who did not find employment. Indeed, alongside workhouses—and often in the same building—towns established houses of correction for those persons deemed particularly idle, unwilling to work, or more generally "lewd." Southampton's officers installed a house of correction, or bridewell, in their workhouse. Here the governor and his officers incarcerated and "corrected" (or punished, usually by whipping) idle, vagrant, and incorrigible persons. Then they set these "idle" paupers to work.[105] Women consistently made up a majority of the prisoners in Hampshire's house of correction (situated in the county town of Winchester) between 1680 and 1750 and, indeed, women vastly outnumbered men in most of the urban bridewells of seventeenth- and eighteenth-century England.[106] In fact these houses of correction were designed for exactly the sorts of petty crimes associated with singlewomen: prostitution, living out of service, petty larceny, idle or disorderly behavior, and bastard-bearing. For example, in the summer of 1706 Joanne Fisher was residing in Hampshire's house of correction "for living an idle and disorderly life and [for being] out of service."[107] Although Fisher may not have been able to find work due to the limited employment options for singlewomen like herself, the authorities only recognized her idleness and disorderliness, not her possible poverty. They punished this singlewomen instead of offering her any assistance.

This is not to say that the poverty of singlewomen always went ignored and unassisted. Certain characteristics guaranteed particular singlewomen a place among the "deserving" poor. Sickness, infirmity, old age, or motherhood enabled a poor singlewoman to appear worthy of at least temporary aid. For instance, in 1696 widow Beele and her never-married daughter Alice received assistance from the churchwardens of St. Mary's parish, Southampton, who judged both women to be "very poor and sickly and not able to earn their maintenance." Significantly, just a year earlier the parish officers had been willing to support widow Beele, but not her daughter. What had elevated Alice Beele to the status of "deserving" poor was her illness, not simply her poverty; the churchwardens now granted Alice half the sum of 4s. that they provided to her mother each month.[108] Following the same logic, the parish officers extended relief to the singlewoman Ann Call in her mid-teens because she was "unable to get her livelihood" due to a crippled left leg. But in 1725 the parish officers apprenticed the 19-year-old Call against her will to a silk thrower, who twice absconded and left her without provision.[109] In this case, Call's infirmity had been worthy of temporary assistance, but the parochial officers eventually decided Call's singleness overshadowed her disability, so they forced her to work instead of providing her with regular relief over her lifetime.

While sickness or disability might merit a singlewoman some aid, old age was the characteristic that entitled never-married women to the most relief. The singlewoman Elizabeth Downer of Southampton received a significant amount of assistance in the form of money, food, and lodging throughout the 1730s, when she was in her seventies and eighties.[110] Of the 40 pauper singlewomen listed in Norwich's census of the poor, only 6 received relief. All 6 women were over 40 years of age, and half of them were sick or "lame" as well.[111] Advanced age allowed some singlewomen to establish their own households and businesses just as widows did. Similarly, old age allowed never-married women to resemble ever-married women by entitling them to the same poor relief that widows enjoyed. Nevertheless, we should not assume that all of the elderly singlewomen in need received assistance. Even though singlewomen outnumbered widows in the population, the number of widows who obtained poor relief was always much higher than the number of never-married women.

In addition to sickness and old age, certain life events allowed singlewomen to earn temporary economic assistance. Local governors rewarded singlewomen who opted to enter one of the dependent or traditional roles contemporaries urged on all women: singlewomen on the verge of becoming servants, wives, and even mothers were sometimes able to obtain a measure of parochial relief. In Southampton, parish officers paid 15s. for a pair of stays for Robert Butcher's daughter when she went into service. Likewise, the community of Aldenham offered monetary help to children who left home to become servants.[112] Southampton's churchwardens were also willing to disburse large sums of money when poor singlewomen decided to alter their marital status and become wives. For example, Holy Rood parish paid £3 5s. 6d. for the marriage of Wellow's daughter, and Mary Chandler received £3 1s. to clothe herself on her marriage day.[113] Chandler was the illegitimate daughter of singlewoman Elizabeth Chandler—a continual thorn in the side of Southampton's governors. It seems that Southampton's churchwardens were willing to pay dearly to ensure that the second generation did not repeat the mistakes of the first. They believed they would accomplish this by ensuring that the younger female Chandler was under the authority of a husband.

Ironically, one of the most common times for singlewomen to receive relief from the parish was when they were pregnant or were the mothers of young children.[114] Parochial and town officers paid out large amounts of money to assist single mothers in giving birth, find clothes for new babies, and nourish mother and child, at least through the first few months. For example, the officers in Holy Rood parish, Southampton paid £2 15s. 2d. for Mary Andrew's lying in and for clothing her child. This amount was comparable to the amount (£2 8s.) a widow like Eleanor Metcalf received in parish relief for the entire year.[115] Although singlewomen did not regularly reside in Southampton's almshouses, singlewomen with children found lodging in houses for the poor. In 1746 Mary Benson alias Edminston and her illegitimate daughter were staying in a house in St. Mary's that was "made use of for lodging poor persons of the said parish."[116] Likewise, single mothers in eighteenth-century London found that parish assistance and institutions such as hospitals and workhouses, which were normally intended for the more "deserving" and moral poor, provided them with a temporary "safety-net" in their time of need.[117]

On the surface it seems odd that singlewomen would receive aid after giving birth to illegitimate children. It was, after all, by this act that these women accomplished what authorities most feared and tried to avoid: the creation of disorder. The single mother had taken it upon herself to create a family outside the bonds of marriage and the male-controlled household, thereby disrupting the social order. She also had disrupted the economic order by producing a child, and thus a family, who might very well become an economic burden on the community. Much like today, people in early modern England saw single mothers as undeserving and immoral, and as such they were punished, usually by a year-long stint in the house of correction.[118] But at the same time paternalistic town fathers could not desert a child in need, even if that child was illegitimate. Bastards and single mothers benefited from this contradiction. Such a paradox is understandable, especially if seen as yet another example of the favoring of the family and household over the individual in early modern England. While single mothers were not wives, they could, by giving birth, become mothers; if so, they then resembled widows with children to support. With the birth of a child a single mother became the de facto head of a family and household, and as such she was entitled to more assistance than a singlewoman on her own. While local officials were willing to ignore a solitary woman, they were less likely to neglect a child, who, while illegitimate, was still one of the deserving poor. Single mothers throughout England benefited from their association with deserving children, although for how long is unclear.[119] For

example, in 1743, All Saints parish, Southampton was offering relief to
Argentine Long's two-year-old bastard, but not to the singlewoman herself
(who bore two more illegitimate children in 1748 and 1751).[120] In the
same way that singlewomen managed to establish their own households
and work independently, such women earned economic assistance contingently, and not legitimately. A singlewoman might receive assistance while
pregnant and nursing, but this was based on the contingency of her pregnancy and not on the fact that singlewomen were legitimate recipients of
poor relief.

Only one sort of benefactor looked especially benevolently on all poor
singlewomen. Poor singlewomen did not have to be sick, disabled, or old,
nor did they have to seek service, marriage, or motherhood to obtain relief
from other singlewomen. They merely had to be single. In 1741, singlewoman Susanna Shreckenfox bequeathed £20 to the "poor widows, maids,
and decayed housekeepers" of Holy Rood parish, Southampton. Shreckenfox distinctly mentioned the three marital states of women, noting that
widows, singlewomen, and wives might all be in need. In her 1697 will Jane
Bracebridge focused purely on women of her marital status, stipulating that
four to six servant maids from Southampton should carry her "corpse to the
grave and that they each [should] have a hood and gloves and 2s. 6d in
money."[121] Shreckenfox and Bracebridge were both relatively wealthy singlewomen, suggesting that singlewomen of all classes may have been particularly aware of how difficult it was for a never-married woman to maintain herself. Only singlewomen, it seems, recognized that singleness could
be enough of a detriment itself to merit economic assistance.

As this examination of residence, employment, and poor relief has shown, a
woman's marital status was a key determinant of how she would live her life
in early modern England. When a woman married she lost legal, economic,
and social independence, but she also gained protection and earned certain
privileges from both her family and the local community. By virtue of being
a wife, a mother, and her husband's deputy, a widow earned the right to
head a household. An ever-married woman could live where she wished,
support herself through various trades, or receive financial assistance if she
could not. But never-married women merited no such assistance or privileges. Town governors limited where singlewomen could live, in what
trades they could work, and the circumstances under which they might
claim poor relief. These constraints made never-married women much
more vulnerable than ever-married women. By fulfilling neither the role of

wife nor that of mother, a singlewoman earned neglect or even outright repression in early modern England.

But there is also another side to this story. While local governors may have put singlewomen at a disadvantage, many of these women refused to respond passively to their hated circumstances. Instead, they constantly pushed against the limitations placed on them. There would have been no need for repeated proclamations against singlewomen living on their own in towns like Norwich, Manchester, and Southampton if singlewomen had in fact acquiesced to living in male-controlled households. There would have been no need for Southampton's authorities to prosecute over and over again singlewomen such as Elizabeth Quinten for working as a charmaid, or living "out of service," if Quinten and women like her had docilely chosen the path of a servant or just gone away. And what of those singlewomen who, at the slightest hint of opportunity, took advantage of their age or social status and established their own households and set up their own businesses? Such women illustrate how far off the mark contemporaries were when they assumed that an independent woman could only create disorder. Given the chance, singlewomen performed the duties of upright householders — paying taxes and poor rates, holding property, running successful businesses, and even performing the service of loaning money to local individuals and municipalities.[122] Singlewomen were paragons of citizenship, rather than the evil examples and originators of disorder presupposed by patriarchal theory. Many widows were good citizens as well, but they achieved their success with assistance and acknowledgment, while singlewomen achieved theirs with neither.

The experiences of women in early modern England suggest that there is another category of difference to attend to in our examinations of women in premodern Europe. Women's historians have long acknowledged the differences of gender, have become comfortable examining the differences of class, and more recently have become attuned to differences in race, but we have not fully explored one of the critical differences between women: that of marital status. While most of us have acknowledged that married women's lives were unlike those of unmarried women in many ways, this essay has shown that such a binary distinction is incomplete. Not only did married women differ from unmarried women, but the lives of ever-married women also contrasted with those of never-married women. Widows, wives, and singlewomen all experienced life differently in early modern England, but it was perhaps the singlewoman's experiences that were the most distinct from those of the other two groups. Certainly we do not

want to confine our understanding of women in early modern England (or
any other region or time for that matter) to the experiences of only those
women who conformed closely to the roles sanctioned by their patriarchal
societies. We must, therefore, pay clearer attention to how marital status
differentiated the experiences of women in the past, and how women who
never conformed to the roles of wife and mother managed to live and
sometimes even to thrive.

I would like to thank the following organizations who supported the dissertation research upon which this essay is based: the North American Conference on British Studies, the Center for International Studies, the History
Department and the Women's Studies Program at Duke University, the
Local Population Studies Society, the British Academy, and the Hunting-
ton Library. I am also thankful for the help and suggestions I have received
from Judith Bennett, Cynthia Herrup, Terry Bouton, Colleen Seguin, Philippe Rosenberg, and Ann Claycombe in the writing of this essay.

Notes

1. Fanny Burney, *Camilla* (London: 1796), 468–69.
2. In other words, both adult women and widows had the ability — lost to
wives — to make contracts, to own and dispose of property, and to sue or be sued in
a court of law. Some English towns did extend the status of *feme sole* to married
women engaged in trade, and some courts did treat married women as *femes soles* if
they wanted to hold such women liable for their criminal behavior (for as *femes
coverts* wives were not legal adults and thus were not legally culpable for their
actions). But these were exceptions to the general rule. See Amy Louise Erickson,
Women and Property in Early Modern England (New York: Routledge, 1993), 24, 30,
100, 146; Carole Z. Wiener, "Is a Spinster an Unmarried Woman?" *American Journal
of Legal History* 20 (1976): 27–31.
3. The French historian Olwen Hufton has written one of the few articles
examining singlewomen, but the title of the piece, "Women Without Men: Widows
and Spinsters in Britain and France in the Eighteenth Century," *Journal of Family
History* 9, 4 (1985): 355–76, is indicative of how scholars have grouped singlewomen with, and subsumed them under, widows. Even Amy Erickson, whose
attention to marital status led her to divide her book on women and property in
early modern England into separate sections on maids, wives, and widows, has
conflated these discrete categories. Two of her chapters in the section on widows,
"How Lone Women Lived" and "Lone Women's Wills," discuss the experiences of
both widows and singlewomen (Erickson, *Women and Property*). See also B. A.
Holderness's articles on credit: "Credit in a Rural Community, 1660–1800," *Mid-
land History* 3, 2 (1975): 94–115; and "Credit in English Rural Society Before the

Nineteenth Century, With Special Reference to the Period 1650–1720," *Agricultural History Review* 24, 2 (1976): 97–109, both of which focus on widows but assume that singlewomen shared the same moneylending patterns. In Southampton and throughout Hampshire singlewomen and widows did not, in fact, lend money in similar ways (Amy Froide, "Single Women, Work, and Community in Southampton, 1550–1750" [Ph.D. diss., Duke University, 1996], chap. 7).

    4. Peter Laslett looked at 100 English communities for which population listings are extant for the years 1574–1821. By taking into account Laslett's assumption that female children under the age of 16 comprised 41.5 percent of all single females, I have produced my own calculations for percentages of adult women (Peter Laslett, "Mean Household Size in England Since the Sixteenth Century," in *Household and Family in Past Time*, ed. Peter Laslett and Richard Wall [Cambridge: Cambridge University Press, 1972], 145). The figures for Southampton are derived from that town's 1696 Marriage Duty assessments — a tax that came close to recording almost all inhabitants in England. A further 8.7 percent of adult women in Southampton were either single or widowed (it is impossible to assess which), so the estimates for singlewomen and widows in the adult female population are both conservative (Southampton Record Office [hereafter SRO], SC 14/2/66a–68b, 70a–74c).

    5. I am grateful to Judith Bennett for the term "ever-married."

    6. In exploring the differences between widows and singlewomen I will focus on the disadvantages experienced by the latter because historians have not paid much attention to never-married women. This does not mean that I believe that widows failed to encounter difficulties in a patriarchal society such as early modern England. However, both the positive and negative experiences of widows have been studied much more. See Charles Carlton, "The Widow's Tale: Male Myths and Female Reality in 16th and 17th Century England," *Albion* 10, 2 (1978): 118–29; Barbara J. Todd, "Widowhood in a Market Town: Abingdon, 1540–1720" (D.Phil. thesis, University of Oxford, 1983); Vivien Brodsky, "Widows in Late Elizabethan London: Remarriage, Economic Opportunity and Family Orientations," in *The World We Have Gained: Histories of Population and Social Structure*, ed. Lloyd Bonfield, Richard M. Smith, and Keith Wrightson (New York: Blackwell, 1986), 122–54; and Jeremy Boulton, "London Widowhood Revisited: The Decline of Female Remarriage in the Seventeenth and Early Eighteenth Centuries," *Continuity and Change* 5, 3 (1990): 323–55. While Todd in particular points out the loss in standard of living that many women experienced after their husbands died, the evidence I have seen suggests that widows still enjoyed both more autonomy and more public assistance than either wives or singlewomen of the same socioeconomic status.

    7. If an elderly widow had living with her an adult son or an adult daughter and son-in-law, then a male in the next generation might take over the headship of the household. But Todd found that only 4 percent of married male testators left their dwelling houses to their children and that fully three-fourths of these testators expected their wives to become the head of household (Todd, "Widowhood," 8, 256; Laslett, "Mean Household Size," 125–26).

    8. Laslett, "Mean Household Size," 147.

9. Richard Wall, "Woman Alone in English Society," *Annales de Démographie Historique* 17 (1981): 313. Wall examined the living arrangements of widowed and never-married women using population listings from the Staffordshire towns of Lichfield (1695) and Stoke-on-Trent (1701), as well as the rural community of Corfe Castle, Dorset (1790). Calculations are my own.

10. SRO, SC 4/3/359.

11. SRO, SC 14/2/66a, b.

12. When couples in premodern England married it was most common for them to set up their own household, separate from those of their parents or other family members. An individual achieved entry into full social adulthood upon marriage, full participation in trade, and the establishment of a household. See John Gillis, *For Better, For Worse: British Marriages, 1600 to the Present* (New York: Oxford University Press, 1985), 57; Paul Griffiths, *Youth and Authority: Formative Experiences in England, 1560–1640* (Oxford: Clarendon Press, 1996), 32. It is difficult to judge when the adulthood of singlewomen who never married began.

13. Laslett, "Mean Household Size," 147.

14. Wall found that between 43.9 and 53.8 percent of never-married women below the age of 45 lived with at least one parent, while between 3 and 7.6 percent lived with some other relative, between 30.2 and 39.4 percent lived as a servant, and between 5.4 and 11 percent lived as a lodger. Only between 4.5 and 5.9 percent of singlewomen below the age of 45 headed their own households (Wall, "Woman Alone," 311).

15. Griffiths says that "the household and service were the most widely discussed forms of disciplining youth" in early modern England (Griffiths, *Youth and Authority*, 13). These institutions served the same purpose for singlewomen, whether young or old.

16. Concern over independent singlewomen was by no means limited to England. See Bronislaw Geremek, *The Margins of Society in Late Medieval Paris* (New York: Cambridge University Press, 1987), 221; Merry E. Wiesner, *Working Women in Renaissance Germany* (New Brunswick, N.J.: Rutgers University Press, 1986), 6, 88; and Wiesner's essay in this volume.

17. Cited in P. J. P. Goldberg, ed., *Women in England, c. 1275–1525* (New York: Manchester University Press, 1995), 212.

18. F. J. C. Hearnshaw and D. M. Hearnshaw, eds., *Southampton Court Leet Records A.D. 1578–1602*, Southampton Record Society, vol. 2 (Southampton, 1905–6), 236.

19. Griffiths, *Youth and Authority*, 358, 381–82.

20. Diane Willen, "Women in the Public Sphere in Early Modern England: The Case of the Urban Working Poor," *Sixteenth Century Journal* 19, 4 (1988): 561.

21. J. P. Earwaker, ed., The *Court Leet Records of the Manor of Manchester*, vol. 1: 1552–1686 (Manchester, 1884), 241; Griffiths, *Youth and Authority*, 380.

22. Goldberg believes that Coventry's ordinance forbidding singlewomen to live on their own was aimed at prostitutes (P. J. P. Goldberg, *Women, Work, and Life Cycle in a Medieval Economy: Women in York and Yorkshire, c. 1300–1520* [Oxford: Clarendon Press, 1992], 155–56). Also see the essays in this volume by Ruth Mazo

Karras and Sharon Farmer, who discuss the identification of adult singlewomen with prostitutes. This conflation was due to the fact that contemporaries in medieval England and France had no acknowledged social category for adult lay women who had never married, except for that of the prostitute.

23. J. W. Horrocks, ed., *Assembly Books of Southampton 1609–10*, Southampton Record Society, vol. 21 (Southampton, 1920), 59. Southampton's assembly prosecuted 14 charmaids between 1607–8, 10 more between 1609–10, none between 1611–14, and 9 again between 1615–16 (J. W. Horrocks, ed., *Assembly Books of Southampton 1602–8, 1609–10, 1611–14, 1615–16*, Southampton Record Series, vols. 19, 21, 24, 25 [Southampton, 1917, 1920, 1924, 1925]; W. J. Connor, ed., *The Southampton Mayor's Book of 1606–1608*, Southampton Records Series, vol. 21 [Southampton, 1978]).

24. These punishments may have differed because the Norwich singlewomen who were accused of being "out of service" were commonly residents of the town, while the residential status of Southampton's charmaids is not always possible to discern. Those who can be identified as residents were less likely to be told to depart (Griffiths, *Youth and Authority*, 380; Froide, "Single Women," 269–70). Bridewells were used to incarcerate petty offenders, including those who were "idle" or anyone who had run away from service or refused to serve (Joanna Innes, "Prisons for the Poor: English Bridewells, 1555–1800," in *Labour, Law, and Crime: An Historical Perspective*, ed. Francis Snyder and Douglas Hay [New York: Tavistock Publications, 1987], 70, 74, 85).

25. The period c. 1560–1640 is now recognized as one of socioeconomic upheaval in England (characterized by high population growth, inflation, unemployment, increasing poverty, and vagrancy) that resulted in much contemporary worry about disorderly elements in society. On a crisis in gender relations, see Susan D. Amussen, *An Ordered Society: Gender and Class in Early Modern England* (New York: Oxford University Press, 1988); Michael Roberts, "Women and Work in Sixteenth-Century Towns," in *Work in Towns 850–1850*, ed. Penelope J. Corfield and Derek Keene (New York: Leicester University Press, 1990), 86–102; and David Underdown, "The Taming of the Scold: The Enforcement of Patriarchal Authority in Early Modern England," in *Order and Disorder in Early Modern England*, ed. Anthony Fletcher and John Stevenson (New York: Cambridge University Press, 1985). On youth and disorder, see Griffiths, *Youth and Authority*, 6–7, 13, and chap. 7.

26. The 1696 Marriage Duty Assessments for Southampton reveal there were also 21 possible singlewomen living with unrelated persons in 1696. If these women are considered cohousehold heads, and are added to the 22 singlewomen above, then 15 percent of singlewomen would have headed their own households. This small percentage does not even compare to the 86 percent of widows who headed or coheaded their own households in Southampton (SRO, SC 14/2/66a–68b, 70a–74c).

27. Wrigley and Schofield found that between 10 to 27 percent of the English population remained single for their entire lives, with the number of lifelong single people rising to a particularly high level in the late seventeenth century (E. A.

Wrigley and Roger Schofield, *The Population History of England, 1541–1871: A Recon-*
struction [London: Edward Arnold, 1981], 260). Wrigley and Schofield's high-end
estimate has been criticized by demographers, but most, including Schofield himself, still believe 10 to 20 percent of the English population remained permanently
single between 1500 and 1750 (Roger Schofield, "English Marriage Patterns Revisited," *Journal of Family History* 10 [Spring 1985]: 14).

28. Contemporary literature placed menopause between the ages of 40 and 50
(Patricia Crawford, "Menstruation in Seventeenth-Century England," *Past and*
Present [1981]: 65–79). Keith Thomas theorizes that advancing age may have resulted in rising female authority (Keith Thomas, "Age and Authority in Early Modern England," *Proceedings of the British Academy* 62 [1976]: 205–48).

29. Wall, "Woman Alone," 311.

30. Goldberg, *Women in England*, 212.

31. Lee Chambers-Schiller believes a singlewoman's adulthood began when
she passed what contemporaries viewed as marriageable age, which she loosely
defines as a woman's thirties or forties (Lee Chambers-Schiller, *Liberty, a Better*
Husband. Single Women in America: The Generations of 1780–1840 [New Haven,
Conn.: Yale University Press, 1984], 84–86).

32. SRO, transcript of the parish registers of Holy Rood (29 July 1667,
1 August 1674, 3 April 1682).

33. SRO, D/ABC 1/1, f 56v, 59.

34. More rarely, age could also affect the householder status of widows. For
example, in 1613 Margaret Griffin was widowed and living in her brother's house in
Southampton. Griffin was young and had no children, so Southampton's authorities treated her more like a singlewoman than a widow. They did not allow Griffin
the option of living wherever she chose, but instead told her brother that she must
either leave Southampton or put herself into service by Michaelmas (*Assembly Books*
of Southampton 1611–14, 66).

35. SRO, SC 7/1/21 (1703); SC 4/3/360a & b, 453.

36. SRO, D/MC 10/11, 8 a & b.

37. For instance, the 1662 Settlement Act stipulated that if newcomers to a
town were questioned within 40 days of their arrival they could only remain if they
had rented property worth at least £10 a year (Paul Slack, *The English Poor Law 1531–*
1782 [Basingstoke: Macmillan Education, 1990], 36).

38. Hampshire Record Office (hereafter HRO), 1697 B6; SRO, SC 14/2/37a.

39. Carlton, "The Widow's Tale," 126.

40. Diane Willen, "York Guildswomen, 1560–1700," *Historian* 46 (February
1984): 204–18, esp. 209.

41. *Assembly Books of Southampton 1615–16*, 1–2. Delamotte leased one of the
largest houses in the town, employed many townspeople in her business, and her
son Joseph (also a clothier) became mayor.

42. The antiquarian John Speed noted that anyone interested in the place of a
porter in Southampton negotiated with his predecessor or his widow, for this office
was inherited by a porter's wife (John Speed, *The History and Antiquity of South-*
ampton, Southampton Record Society, vol. 8 [1770; reprint, Southampton, 1909],
61–62).

43. Porters carried goods from ships anchored in the harbor to storehouses and cellars in Southampton (A. L. Merson, ed., *Third Book of Remembrance of Southampton 1514–1602*, Southampton Records Series, vol. 2 [Southampton, 1952], 3: 41).

44. SRO, SC 2/1/8, f 69v. To forestall was to buy up goods before they reached the market in order to sell them again for profit, and to regrate was to buy up goods to sell them again at a higher price. Both practices were frowned on because they supposedly increased the cost of food and goods.

45. SRO, PR 9/15/5; Willen, "Women in the Public Sphere."

46. Earle found that widows and wives comprised virtually all of the hawkers, caterers, and victualers in early modern London (Peter Earle, "The Female Labour Market in London in the Late Seventeenth and Early Eighteenth Centuries," *Economic History Review*, 2d ser., 42, 3 [1989]: 339). Wright believes that petty retailing was particularly suited to poor wives and widows, and that widows frequently engaged in victualling (Sue Wright, "'Churmaids, Huswyfes and Hucksters': The Employment of Women in Tudor and Stuart Salisbury," in *Women and Work in Pre-Industrial England*, ed. Lindsay Charles and Lorna Duffin [London: Croom Helm, 1985], 108, 110).

47. Paul Slack, "Poverty and Politics in Salisbury 1597–1666," *Crisis and Order in English Towns, 1500–1700: Essays in Urban History*, ed. Peter Clark and Paul Slack (London: Routledge, 1972), 182, 190; Judith Bennett, *Ale, Beer, and Brewsters in England: Women's Work in a Changing World, 1300–1600* (New York: Oxford University Press, 1996), 56 and n. 75. Willen also found that authorities in York assisted poor, unmarried women by paying them to in turn nurse, assist, and look after other poor people (Willen, "Women in the Public Sphere," 560, 564–65).

48. SRO, SC 2/1/8, f 261v.

49. SRO, D/MC 7/1, 6/1, 8/1.

50. SRO, D/MC 7/1.

51. I have derived these figures from the 1696 Marriage Duty assessments.

52. SRO, SC 2/1/8, f 307 and SC 2/1/9, f 521.

53. HRO, 1697 A48; SRO, SC 6/1/73, SC 14/2/97. Southampton's assembly allowed people who did not hold the freedom to trade in the town (and so all female traders) to trade in practice if they paid an annual fee called a Stall and Art fee.

54. Although she does not explain why singlewomen failed to enjoy economic freedom, Katherine Kittredge also notes that it was beneficial for a singlewoman in early modern England to "remain attached to a widow, since in this way she could share in economic opportunities available to her as a single woman" (Katharine Ottaway Kittredge, "'Tabby Cats Lead Apes in Hell': Spinsters in Eighteenth Century Life and Fiction" [Ph.D. diss., State University of New York at Binghamton, 1991], 71).

55. In her study of working women in Oxford, Mary Prior noted that "whilst common law might not hinder singlewomen and widows from trading, borough custom might do so" (Mary Prior, "Women and the Urban Economy: Oxford 1500–1800," in her *Women in English Society, 1500–1800* [London: Methuen, 1985], 103).

56. Ibid., 110–12.

57. SRO, SC 6/1/50; HRO, 1641 A100/1.

58. SRO, SC 9/3/12, f 25. Housewife was an occupational term as well as an indicator of marital status, which explains why town officials used it to describe a singlewoman.

59. SRO, SC 2/1/8, f 132.

60. Earle's sample consisted of 201 singlewomen, 156 widows, and 256 wives, for a total of 613 women (Earle, "The Female Labour Market," 339, table 10).

61. SRO, SC 6/1/98.

62. See n. 47 above for the argument that local officials doled out petty trading licenses as a form of poor relief.

63. Earle, "The Female Labour Market," 339, table 10.

64. *The Southampton Mayor's Book of 1606–1608*, 102.

65. SRO, SC 2/1/6, f 237.

66. According to the Statute of Artificers (1563) people without independent trades could be compelled into service. But the majority of those punished for being out of service were young women. For instance, 80 percent of such cases in Norwich dealt with women (Griffiths, *Youth and Authority*, 358).

67. A rising population, unemployment, poverty, and a youthful age-structure made it difficult to find a position in service at the turn of the seventeenth century (Griffiths, *Youth and Authority*, 360). Even if one had a position in service it was precarious; servants were often dismissed, and both sickness and pregnancy were causes for losing one's position (Bridget Hill, *Servants: English Domestics in the Eighteenth Century* [Oxford: Clarendon Press, 1996], 95–99).

68. Griffiths, *Youth and Authority*, 71, 353. A charwoman was someone who did "char" work — cleaning, laundering, or performing other household chores for a daily wage. However, in Southampton at least, town officials seemed to have used the word "charmaid" to refer to women who performed any kind of day labor. It was the conditions of such work, and not the type of work being done, that were important to civic officers. They targeted singlewomen (char*maids* more specifically than char*women*) who neither lived with a master nor worked for that master for a contractual period of time.

69. Ibid., 354.

70. *Southampton Court Leet Records A.D. 1578–1602*, 186.

71. *Assembly Books of Southampton 1602–8*, 98; *Assembly Books of Southampton 1609–10*, 3; *Assembly Books of Southampton 1615–16*, 11; and R. C. Anderson, ed., *Books of Examinations and Depositions 1622–44*, Southampton Record Society, vol. 31 (Southampton, 1931), 15. For similar examples of repeat offenders in Norwich see Griffiths, *Youth and Authority*, chap. 7, esp. p. 351.

72. *Court Leet Records of Manchester*, 241. This 1584 ordinance was reissued in 1589 and once more (Griffiths, *Youth and Authority*, 357).

73. Merry E. Wiesner, *Women and Gender in Early Modern Europe* (New York: Cambridge University Press, 1993), 99.

74. SRO, SC 6/1/50, 67, 70–108.

75. For more on these independent tradeswomen see Froide, "Single Women," chap. 6.

76. SRO, D/ABC 1/1, f 59; SC 4/4/479/2; SC 6/1/98.

77. HRO, 1708 A108; SRO, SC 6/1/76.

78. SRO, PR 7/5/1; SC 14/2/337; SC 6/1/93–94.

79. HRO, 1701 A107.

80. Prior, "Women and the Urban Economy," 112.

81. Margaret R. Hunt, *The Middling Sort: Commerce, Gender, and the Family in England, 1680–1780* (Berkeley: University of California Press, 1996), chap. 5; and Elizabeth C. Sanderson, *Women and Work in Eighteenth-Century Edinburgh* (New York: St. Martin's Press, 1996), chap. 3.

82. This charity was endowed by John Steptoe in 1675. Two-thirds of the money was distributed annually as £10 loans to "young beginners" in trade, while one-third was to go to the poor. A few singlewomen received some of the money allotted to the poor but no known singlewomen obtained any of the business loans. Four named widows received loans, as well as 7 other women who can be identified as widows from other sources. There were 7 additional female recipients for whom no marital status was indicated. Some of these women may have been singlewomen, but even so they would not have equaled the number of widowed recipients.

83. Froide, "Single Women," 282; SRO, SC 6/1/70–73.

84. Roberts also believes that "widows' rights to engage in trade and production seem . . . to have rested on the assumed priority of family survival" (Roberts, "Women and Work," 91).

85. Tim Wales, "Poverty, Poor Relief and the Life-Cycle: Some Evidence from Seventeenth-Century Norfolk," in *Land, Kinship and Life-Cycle*, ed. Richard M. Smith (New York: Cambridge University Press, 1984), 361, 377.

86. Todd, "Widowhood in a Market Town," 5.

87. SRO, SC 10/1/5, 10.

88. SRO, SC 2/1/6.

89. SRO, D/MC 1, 2.

90. SRO, SC 9/1/19.

91. Willen, "Women in the Public Sphere," 563; W. Newman Brown, "The Receipt of Poor Relief and Family Situation: Aldenham, Hertfordshire 1630–90," in *Land, Kinship and Life-Cycle*, ed. Richard M. Smith (New York: Cambridge University Press, 1984), 414; Hans Christian Johansen, "Never-Married Women in Town and Country in Eighteenth-Century Denmark," in *Poor Women and Children in the European Past*, ed. John Henderson and Richard Wall (New York: Routledge, 1994), 202.

92. SRO, SC 10/1/1. Three women whose marital status cannot be identified also received relief, some of whom may have been singlewomen.

93. J. F. Pound, ed., *The Norwich Census of the Poor*, Norfolk Record Society, vol. 40 (Norwich, 1971). Calculations are my own. The census also includes 43 daughters over the age of 14. Nineteen of these single daughters lived in households that received relief payments, but such relief was assisting the household and not these singlewomen in particular. Of an additional 63 women in the census whose marital status cannot be identified, 30 obtained economic assistance.

94. Brown, 412.

95. A. L. Beier, "Vagrants and the Social Order in Elizabethan England," *Past and Present* 64 (1974): 6–9; Paul Slack, *Poverty and Policy in Tudor and Stuart England* (London: Longman, 1988), 166; Wales, "Poverty, Poor Relief," 361. For

instance, while Wales shows that women comprised an average of 63 percent of all poor relief recipients in his sample of Norfolk villages and towns, 50 percent of this total percentage were widows, while only the remaining 13 percent was made up of wives and singlewomen. Calculations are my own.

96. The Norwich census of the poor also provides an illustration of this correlation. The census listed all paupers in the town, whether they received relief or not. But it also included some singlewomen whom officials did not characterize as paupers, but whom they nevertheless chose to "note" in the census. These included ten singlewomen identified as harlots, three maids living with unrelated individuals who officers either noted or ordered to depart, and four grass maids, a term for singlewomen who had given birth to bastards or who lived in common-law unions. Three other grass women did make it into the category of pauper. While officials found they could not fit these singlewomen into conventional categories for never-married females, such as servant or daughter, they also did not view most of these women as potential recipients of poor relief.

97. SRO, PR 9/15/2.

98. Griffiths, *Youth and Authority*, 381, 383.

99. Brown, "The Receipt of Poor Relief," 418–19.

100. Historians of vagrancy and the poor have not paid much attention to the fact that singlewomen were part of the undeserving poor. Studies of vagrancy have most often characterized the able-bodied poor as young, single males. Paul Slack found that, of a sample of 3,000 vagrants in the seventeenth century, one-fourth were singlewomen, but he did not discuss female vagrants to any degree (Paul Slack, *Poverty and Policy*, 98). A. L. Beier noted that in his sample of vagrant arrests just over half were of single males, but did not discuss the arrests of women (A. L. Beier, "Vagrants and the Social Order in Elizabethan England," *Past and Present* 64 (1974): 6–9). The title of Beier's synthetic work on vagrancy in early modern England — *Masterless Men* (London: Methuen, 1985) — indicates his focus on male vagrants.

101. A. J. Willis, comp., and A. L. Merson, ed., *A Calendar of Southampton Apprenticeship Registers 1609–1740*, Southampton Records Series, vol. 12 (Southampton, 1968); Pamela Sharpe, "Poor Children as Apprentices in Colyton, 1598–1830," *Continuity and Change* 6, 2 (1991): 253–70.

102. *Norwich Census of the Poor*, 19.

103. Slack, *Poverty and Policy*, 180–81; SRO, SC 2/1/6, f 254v.

104. Slack, *Poverty and Policy*, 180; Wales, "Poverty, Poor Relief," 379, 386.

105. Slack, *Poverty and Policy*, 181; SRO, SC 2/1/6, f 254v.

106. Innes, "Prisons for the Poor," 100.

107. HRO, Q 9/1/1-256.

108. SRO, PR 9/15/2.

109. SRO, SC/AG 6/1, #238.

110. SRO, SC/AG 8/6/1.

111. *Norwich Census of the Poor*.

112. SRO, SC/AG 8/6/1; Brown, "The Receipt of Poor Relief," 418.

113. SRO, SC/AG 8/6/1.

114. Referring to singlewomen in the late eighteenth and early nineteenth centuries, John Gillis says that "a pregnancy, previously something to be kept quiet,

now became an instrument for securing either marriage or parish maintenance" (Gillis, *For Better, For Worse*, 115). The evidence from Southampton indicates that Gillis's observation can be applied to an earlier period as well.

115. SRO, SC/AG 8/6/1.

116. SRO, SC 9/4/347.

117. Tim Hitchcock, "Unlawfully begotten on her body': Illegitimacy and the Parish Poor in St. Luke's Chelsea," in *Chronicling Poverty: The Voices and Strategies of the English Poor, 1640–1840*, ed. Tim Hitchcock, Peter King, and Pamela Sharpe (New York: St. Martin's Press, 1997), 70–86.

118. Mark Jackson, *New-Born Child Murder: Women, Illegitimacy and the Courts in Eighteenth-Century England* (New York: Manchester University Press, 1996), 31.

119. On the (sometimes generous) support given to single mothers see Hitchcock, "Unlawfully Begotten," 73–75; and Pamela Sharpe, "The bowels of compa-tion': A Labouring Family and the Law, c.1790–1834," in *Chronicling Poverty*, ed. Hitchcock et al., 92–93, and n. 27.

120. SRO, SC/AG 8/3/1; transcript of the All Saints parish registers (16 Aug. 1741, Nov./Dec. 1748, 7 July 1751).

121. HRO, 1741 A119; 1697 B6.

122. For examples, see Froide, "Single Women," chaps. 6 and 7.

10

The Sapphic Strain

English Lesbians in the Long Eighteenth Century

Margaret R. Hunt

SOMETIMES A PICTURE SAYS IT ALL — or almost all. "Dear, the whole family wants to know why you're not married!" says a harried 1950s cartoon mother to her handsome, mannishly dressed daughter in a pinup postcard much loved by lesbians of my generation. Her daughter, on her way out the door (we assume) to some gay assignation, hunts for a response and comes up with: "Tell them . . . tell them I forgot." This picture wittily parodies traditional injunctions to women to find a man, highlighting, for the lesbian viewer at any rate, their irrelevance to women who have discovered the erotic and social attractions of their own sex. In these postmodern, post-euphoric days we know it's more complicated than this; still, what makes this cartoon so wonderful is the lighthearted way it challenges the long and weighty association in the public mind of never-married women with loneliness and sexual frustration. But does the imputation of lack make more sense for a period when (we assume) never-married women had a good deal less freedom to form close relations either with other women or with men than is the case today? This essay challenges the received image of the isolated and sexually and emotionally thwarted "spinster" of the early modern period. It does so in order to lay the base for an exploration of same-sex sexual and emotional relations among singlewomen in England in the eighteenth century.

Let us start by reflecting a little on what we hope to find when we search for lesbians[1] in the past. Unquestionably many lesbian and gay historians feel a powerful urge to locate and celebrate historical lesbians who can, as it were, function politically in the present. The story they look for can be detailed quite precisely. A young woman who has early manifested discom-fort with prevailing gender roles braves ridicule or worse in order to win the love of a good woman. In the end she and her true love settle down perma-nently in a remote cottage in something very like connubial bliss. This narrative combines romantic pastoralism with monogamous yearnings and latent strains of lesbian feminist separatism. Its precedents include produc-tions like Isabel Miller's *Patience and Sarah* (1970), a well-loved early les-bian historical novel set in nineteenth-century America, as well as the real-life case of the Ladies of Llangollen, two Anglo-Irish gentlewomen who fell in love, eloped in 1778 to a secluded cottage in Wales, and lived there together for more than forty years.[2]

In this essay I want to try to de-romanticize eighteenth- and early nineteenth-century lesbians, not because I am an unromantic person, but because this particular scenario is only one of many that could obtain in the eighteenth century.[3] Not only is the "Ladies of Llangollen" archetype a largely aristocratic ideal, but it implies that eighteenth-century lesbians had to withdraw from the world and go into romantic rural seclusion in order to love women. In fact, most lesbians in the eighteenth century were poor or hailed from the middling sort rather than the gentry and aristocracy, who together constituted somewhat less than 5 percent of the population. And, whereas lesbians lived in both town and country, they seldom lived in seclu-sion — if only because true seclusion demands an income that few women, and even fewer singlewomen, possessed. Even those who lived in their own room, rooms, or cottages — and there were probably more of these than we tend to think — were out and about, working for a living, provisioning themselves, forming part of a community, for better or for worse. Women who engaged in lesbian acts were in fact a relatively unproblematic, unob-trusive feature of mainstream society, not an alienated minority.[4]

Some, no doubt, will object that we don't have enough information to say even this much. But, as I hope to show, one can only sustain this position if one thinks that lesbian impulses are extremely rare. If they are a fairly common, naturally occurring aspect of many girls' and women's lives, as a good deal of modern opinion thinks they are, then it is probable that lesbian activity was actually quite common in the eighteenth century. One may compare the problem of lesbianism with that of premarital heterosex-ual sex in the eighteenth century. Most social historians assume that a great many heterosexual acts (petting, bundling, coitus interruptus, and so on) went on *other* than what Henry Abelove calls "vagina around penis followed by ejaculation."[5] Yet in fact we have rather little evidence for this, because

most contemporaries didn't write about it.[6] We presume it to be true based
on a tiny number of first-person accounts, on exaggerated notions about
the universality of heterosexuality, and on extrapolation from our own adolescent heterosexual fumblings. We need to remind ourselves that the most
explicit account of non-penetrative sex in the premodern period comes, in
fact, from a lesbian (Anne Lister of Halifax, 1791–1840) — and this particular lesbian seldom lacked for sexual partners. Homo- and bisexual impulses
may not be as common in women as heterosexual ones, but they are certainly very widespread even in a time (ours) when far more active efforts
are made to repress them than ever took place in the eighteenth century. It is
not surprising that some of the best recent work on lesbianism has implicitly assumed that there was probably quite a bit of it going on.[7] What I
propose to do here is to examine in detail what we know about the opportunities for same-sex sexuality among ordinary (that is, for the most part,
unaristocratic) women in the eighteenth century, focusing especially on the
experience of singlewomen — those allegedly isolated and sexually thwarted
women who have so dogged the study of women in history.

Patriarchy and the Question of What Women Knew

Let us look in a general way at the status of eighteenth-century women, or
rather at the way that status has tended to be understood by many historians of the period. Women's historians, feminists, and others have worked
hard to develop a nuanced picture of the way patriarchal structures and
male supremacy worked in the past — and works in the present. A great deal
of attention has been given to continuities, but also to women's resistance
and to the way patriarchal systems change over time.[8] However, the way
patriarchy is understood by nonspecialists, including some people quite
indifferent to the project of women's history, often works against such
subtlety. Thus it is fairly common for people to assume that eighteenth-
century patriarchy was so extreme and so pervasive that it made women's
lives into nothing but a litany of suffering. Women, so this argument goes,
were faced with overwhelming cultural taboos against disobeying male
authority, possessed no real alternatives to marriage, were psychologically
incapable of mounting a sustained critique of male privilege (and lacked the
educational sophistication even to start), and almost universally lived lives
of sexual constraint followed by years of debilitating pregnancies. Early
modern women, with the possible exception of a few aristocrats, appear

colonized in mind and body, the gendered equivalent of natural slaves. They cease to be human enough to populate real history. Needless to say, this picture leaves few spaces for any resistance whatsoever, much less for lesbian sexuality. And it is a great boon to people who believe that studying women is pointless or worse.

Let me be clear. I am not disputing the fact that early modern England was dominated by men; clearly it was. Rather, I want to examine some of our assumptions about what this meant in real life. Male supremacy, both as a set of institutions and as personified by individual men, was a real force in women's lives, but it was frequently inefficient and often contested. Men (especially male moralists) were so endlessly insistent about male prerogatives in part because their power was never complete. It is reasonable to see "patriarchy" as hegemonic in the Gramscian sense; it is a mistake to view it as a totalitarian system. Thus, it is only by examining its weaknesses and its less-than-total reach that we can begin to see how lesbians could have survived and even prospered in eighteenth-century society.

To search for lesbians is to be on the lookout for agency, whether of an economic, political, spiritual, or sexual sort. It is therefore important at the outset to combat the claim that women seldom disobeyed male authority, and its corollary, the belief that those few who did were, without exception, brutally punished. It is certainly possible to find examples of women who were punished or persecuted in some way for "getting out of hand." By the eighteenth century witchcraft persecution and the more life-threatening public punishments of out-of-control women had largely disappeared from the English scene. But it was not a level playing field. So for instance, a study of late seventeenth- and early eighteenth-century London and Middlesex finds that women were considerably more likely to be apprehended for "sexual" crimes—such as "nightwalking," prostitution, or adultery— than men, and that they accounted for two-thirds of those sent to houses of correction for offenses against the peace. Moreover, it is likely that most of these women were unmarried and poor.[9] Double standards based on gender, socioeconomic status, and marital status are clearly evident. Similarly, those women (there were more of them than we used to think) who disguised themselves as men in order to pursue better job opportunities, to travel more easily, and—sometimes—to marry other women were sometimes unmasked and punished for it, as Henry Fielding's notorious *The Female Husband* (1746), based on a true story, clearly shows.[10] But it is by no means the case that women were merely victims of law and patriarchal custom.

It is also a misrepresentation to claim that all women were so ignorant that they were unable to stand up for themselves. Two forces are at work here. One is an exaggerated perception of the extent of female illiteracy, which was in sharp decline, especially in the cities, from the mid- to late seventeenth century. The other is the notion that one had to be literate to possess a public voice. Civic identity is not an easy thing to define, much less to quantify. But it is surely significant that from the late seventeenth century on quite large numbers of women (urban women especially) resorted to justices of the peace, the courts, or parish officials to defend themselves against a wide array of wrongs and abuses and to argue for benefits they believed they were owed. Women constituted one-third of the plaintiffs in informal settlements before one Wiltshire justice of the peace in the 1740s — and many of these cases involved domestic abuse. In urban Middlesex in the first half of the eighteenth century female plaintiffs accounted for about half of all prosecutors of recognizances (a species of peace bond).[11] The equity and borough courts contain thousands of cases of women suing parents, stepmothers or fathers, employers, guardians, former sweethearts, the government (notably the Navy), and even husbands for debts, inheritances, land, nonpayment of wages, and the like.[12] Significant numbers of eighteenth-century women resorted to the ecclesiastical courts to obtain legal separations, often on grounds of marital cruelty.[13] Additionally, there exist hundreds of extant petitions to poor law commissioners and other bodies, penned or dictated by women who were very poor indeed, asking for financial assistance and other benefits.[14] Now clearly a woman who had been able to get an education was in a more advantageous position in such a milieu than a woman who had not. It is not unreasonable to suppose that illiterate people had a harder time standing up for themselves in court. And marital status *did* matter. Though singlewomen (and widows) did resort to justice, they do not seem to have done so in the same proportions that married women did.[15] But the really interesting thing about these cases is how very many illiterate people, both male and female, initiated actions. It is simply not true that people who lacked an education or were poor (states that were, of course, highly correlated with one another) were condemned to civic passivity.

Nor is it realistic to think that early modern women were completely taken in by patriarchal conditioning, or that recognizably feminist ideas were confined only to a few middle- or upper-class intellectuals. Witness a comment one Roger Lowe, a shopkeeper's apprentice in Lancashire, made to his diary in 1664: "I was in some grief by reason of Cooke's wife, a very wrathful, malicious woman, had reported that I said such things concerning women's natural infirmities, which I never did and troubled me extremely."[16] It is anyone's guess what Lowe said that was so objectionable. What is interesting about this, first, is that one of the standard preoccupations of feminist writers through the ages, the defense of women against gratuitous attacks on their mental or physical capacities by men, tripped as easily from the lips of a (presumably) illiterate villager as it might from the quill of an educated gentlewoman. What is still more revealing is that Cooke's wife had the power, with accusations like these, to affect Lowe's reputation in his own village, and both of them knew it. In a more urban context, the Reverend William Gouge's *Of Domesticall Duties* (1622), the most famous family advice manual of the seventeenth century, contains hints that the women among his London parishioners did not take kindly to his lecturing them about their duty to obey their husbands.[17] Plenty of men cast aspersions on women's characters and abilities verbally and in print in the early modern period. But we should not assume that women never stood up to them when they tried it. What this, in turn, suggests is a climate that may have been more hospitable to lesbianism than we have previously thought. It is not, of course, the case that all lesbians are somehow natural feminists. Still, an atmosphere in which women debated among themselves about the legitimacy of male power (and more occasionally, even confronted men about it) is one where we can imagine some women being hospitable to attempts to usurp male prerogatives, whether sexual or otherwise.

Lesbianism: Natural or Learned?

Contrary to what has been thought, it was no secret to people in the eighteenth century that some women were erotically drawn to other women. Ros Ballaster and Emma Donoghue, in two recent studies, have uncovered numerous references to lesbian activity in seventeenth- and eighteenth-century English pornography, novels, private letters, newspapers, and popular slang. The claim that no such category existed before Krafft-Ebbing, Havelock Ellis, and others "invented" it in the nineteenth century has been quite thoroughly discredited.[18] It would not have been especially difficult for someone who really wanted to know and who could read (or had a friend who could read) to turn up information from printed books about erotic alternatives to married heterosexuality. In a tract by Nicolas de Venette entitled *The Art of Conjugal Love*, which was translated into English in

1712, discussion of lesbianism comes a mere twenty pages in, conveniently located right after a paean to the clitoris ("which I may justly term the Fury and Rage of Love" and the "seat of Pleasure and Lust").[19] The famous early eighteenth-century tract against masturbation, *The Onania, or the Heinous Sin of Self-Pollution*, which I discuss in more detail below, contains much to interest the inquiring mind, as do a number of more overtly pornographic texts, most famously John Cleland's *Fanny Hill: The Memoirs of a Woman of Pleasure* (1748–50) with its much imitated scene of lesbianic initiation in the brothel.[20] Most of these productions rely on recurring sexual scenarios that may not be "lesbian" in the modern sense, but which are, nonetheless, specific to female-female sex — that is, they don't turn up in the same form when representing other kinds of sexuality. These include the notion of women teaching other, usually younger women sexual secrets so as to prepare them for heterosexual intercourse, servants teaching their charges to masturbate, without any apparent desire to prepare them for anything, references to sexual practices supposedly originally invented by the poet Sappho, and erotic behaviors allegedly linked to oversized clitorises.[21] By at least the 1740s, Emma Donoghue tells us, lesbian sex had come to be known by the slang term the "game of flats," and as early as 1732 the word "lesbian" was being used in literary contexts to refer to sexual relationships between women.[22] Those with an interest in the Classics, including such texts as Juvenal's *Sixth Satire* with its notorious account of Roman lesbian orgies, could find a number of English translations.[23] Anne Lister of Halifax, the early nineteenth-century lesbian diarist, was well aware of the classical accounts, and records a conversation in which she apparently used a reference to Juvenal to search out whether another acquaintance of hers was also having sex with women.[24] No known explicitly lesbian diaries from the eighteenth century have been found, but there is also no good reason to think that earlier lesbians of a literary bent could not have drawn similar connections to their own behavior.

They could have, but did they? More to the point, did they need to? It is well known in the contemporary lesbian community that very large numbers of women first began having homosexual sex in their early to mid-teens, without — and this is the key point — linking it initially to "lesbianism" as a sexual category. Either they have never heard the word (this tends to be more common among older lesbians, obviously; in the era of lesbian chic the term is hard to escape) or they don't acknowledge, until somewhat after the fact, that it applies to them. For these women acts that the more knowing identify as "lesbian" (e.g., genital to genital contact, vaginal penetration, feelings of deep emotional and physical connection to another girl or woman) are a natural part of powerful girlhood attachments, or grow out of the sexual "play" of early to mid-adolescence. They do not constitute a thought-through, much less a "political" lesbianism that seems to speak to the very core of their identities — at least not at this early stage. In fact, this is not even necessarily a distinctively "lesbian" route. Many women who "end up" straight have similarly erotic experiences with other girls in late childhood or adolescence, though they are a good deal less likely to acknowledge them in retrospect than self-identified lesbians are. My point is that girl-to-girl or woman-to-woman sexual activity, which may or may not stop short of genital contact, is not something that relies — any more than heterosexuality does — on the adopting of some prior "identity" or specialized knowledge. And neither heterosexual nor homosexual acts require that one have read up on technique beforehand. As far as we can tell, "Lesbian" eroticism is made up of naturally occurring sexual acts that an indeterminate, but probably large number of girls and women hit upon at some time in their lives and understand and rationalize in ways that are very diverse indeed.[25]

Why is this important for studying the eighteenth century? Because it is most unlikely that this particular aspect of human sexuality has changed. Eighteenth-century lesbians learned by doing, by seizing the opportunities that were available to them and following the same experimental routes by which most people discover sex and sexuality. As we will see, young girls and women probably had more rather than fewer opportunities to engage in same-sex acts than is the case today, and at least as much motivation. That having been said, the evidence on real flesh-and-blood eighteenth-century lesbians is tantalizingly meager. What we have instead are "suspected" lesbians: generally literate, relatively privileged individuals, couples, or coteries, such as the Ladies of Llangollen or the circle around Mary Astell, Sarah Fielding, or Anne Conway Damer, some of whom were suspected of lesbianism by their contemporaries.[26] In the rest of this essay I will try to identify a different class of lesbians and to clothe these women's lives in as much complexity as I can.

Singlewomen in Eighteenth-Century England

Late seventeenth-century English parish registers suggest that as much as 27 percent of the population never married. But the frequency of clandestine (and usually untraceable) marriages in this period, along with other complicating factors, means that these figures are certainly inflated. A "conservative" estimate from Wrigley and Schofield, authors of a well-known book on the historical demography of early modern England, is that the proportion of women and men never marrying in the second half of the seventeenth century hovered around 15 percent for England as a whole.[27] Two things do seem clear. First, the number of people who never married was not constant. It peaked in the late seventeenth century, dropped toward the middle of the eighteenth, then crept up again from the 1780s into the first half of the nineteenth century, where it oscillated between 6 and 10 percent (by this later date the figures are somewhat more reliable).[28] Second, factors such as socioeconomic status, whether one had previously been married, and where one lived all had a powerful impact on nuptiality rates. Thus, there is evidence that poorer women were more likely never to marry than better-off women, that widows rather seldom remarried, and that, in at least some places where employment for women was fairly abundant, they tended to marry late or not at all.[29] The point is that in most locales people were perfectly accustomed to the notion that appreciable numbers of women (at least one in ten, and in some places two in ten or more) would never marry.

There was a good deal of pressure to marry in the eighteenth century, but it was less successful than comparable pressure is today. What explains the disparity? Historical demographers tend implicitly to assume that all early modern women wanted to marry, but that some were deterred from doing so due to poverty (especially unemployment or underemployment on the part of the woman herself or her prospective groom(s), and inability or unwillingness on her or family's part to raise a dowry), personal unattractiveness, women's heavy concentration in domestic service (a job deemed by employers to be inconsistent with matrimony), and unfavorable sex ratios, at least from a heterosexual female vantage point. There can be no doubt that the above factors were correlated, in a number of times and places, with a higher incidence of never-married women. However, statistical correlations are not the same as historical causation. Useful evidence at times, they are often read in such a way as to gloss over individual experience and choice, substitute rote supply and demand for much more complicated causal sequences, and support untenable assumptions about what all women want.

Feminist historians, unlike some historical demographers, have no difficulty seeing that some eighteenth-century women had no wish to be married. Marriage in the early modern period carried with it terrible risks: "cruel servitude . . . for life" (as one eighteenth-century woman put it) to a physically or emotionally abusive man,[30] the dangers of pregnancy and childbirth, and the insecurity of living with another's financial ineptitude. The fabled benefits of marriage — economic security, sexual fulfillment, greater prestige in one's community, loving children who would support you in your old age — often failed to materialize. Lesbians today often joke about what a bad deal heterosexual marriage is for women, but it is indisputable that, with readily available birth control, modern medical care, the right to divorce, and the right to one's own property, it is a much better bargain than it used to be. We know that when eighteenth-century women contemplated marriage, they often went to great pains to increase the odds of achieving happiness. Women routinely turned down suitors who did not offer them a generous enough financial settlement (one of the sticking points was often whether women would be allowed control over their own money or would get a generous jointure), husbands who they thought would prove authoritarian or miserly, and situations that would require unusual amounts of work (like caring for stepchildren or keeping shop). Sir John Fryer, a pewterer and sometime Lord Mayor of London, was rebuffed by Abigail Brand, "a single gentlewoman," because "she . . . objected against my children [from a previous marriage] as she had always done saying she could not be a Mother in law [i.e., stepmother]."[31] We know of numerous instances of women who refused to marry particular suitors (or indeed any suitors) because the man or men left them cold emotionally or physically, seemed too far beneath them socially, or seemed to lack connections or ambition. Other women didn't marry because they were deemed to be in delicate health and therefore unfit for childbearing.[32] These are people we know about because they turned up in someone's diary or correspondence; they are undoubtedly the tip of a large iceberg. We have no way of knowing how many other women simply discouraged male suitors from the outset. It is often rightly pointed out that for many women domestic service functioned as a way of accumulating money that would permit one to marry in time. But for those who managed to find tolerable employers, it could also become a convenient semi-permanent refuge for women who were ambivalent about matrimony or wanted no part of it.

It is often assumed that most women before the twentieth century were so economically dependent on men (fathers, brothers, or husbands) that they were not in any position to pursue their own interests, whether political, cultural, or erotic. This picture is a poor representation of the diversity that characterized the lives of singlewomen in the eighteenth-century. We can see this especially clearly in terms of access to wage work, often (though not always) a marker of women's independence. The evidence we have suggests that the work force participation of widowed or never-married women was extremely high in the early modern period. The best study of women's work in London in the period 1695 to 1725 suggests that 77.8 percent of singlewomen and 71 percent of widows were wholly maintained by their own paid employment, while another 4 percent of singlewomen and 8 percent of widows were partially self-supporting. These data are especially significant because they derive from women's own self-descriptions.[33] We do not know exactly what these figures meant: some of the people who considered themselves wholly self-supporting may have lived with parents, husbands, or brothers and simply handed over their earnings. Moreover, we do not have comparable figures for other towns or for rural areas. Still, these data belie the claim that all or even most single-women were dependent on male relatives.

Women workers in the eighteenth century were heavily concentrated in a small number of difficult, often dangerous, and very poorly remunerated jobs. A full quarter of London women were domestic servants, most of them live-in, which imposed its own restraints on their sex lives as well as, it bears saying, offering certain opportunities (a topic to be examined in more depth below).[34] Other women worked for a pittance and often under terrible conditions as hod-carriers, laundresses, agricultural laborers, or street vendors. On the other hand, we know of thousands of women in the eighteenth century — whether married, widowed, or never-married — who had relatively well-paying, if not necessarily secure jobs as milliners, pawnbrokers, grocers, schoolteachers, midwives, publishers, and the like.[35] For that minority of women who commanded enough capital to permit it, a career was a viable possibility, and not too surprisingly, we often find women seizing on such activities in preference to marriage. Taken all together this evidence suggests that female economic independence, partial or entire, was not only not unusual but, in the case of widows and single-women, the norm in the vast majority of cases, though we must again remind ourselves that this was often a hardscrabble and precarious independence that grew still more insecure with old age.

Looking for Lesbians

When looking for lesbians in the past it is useful to keep in mind the diversity and complexity of the erotic and residential arrangement that people make in the present day. This does not mean that they are the same — we live in a very different world from eighteenth-century women — but they may give us clues to the way women loved women in past times.

Let us trace the stages of life of a singlewoman in eighteenth-century England, beginning with late childhood and early adolescence, and try to insert within her story, at appropriate moments, the lesbian possibilities that are generally excluded from any investigation of women's lives in the past. Girls from poor and middling families generally began working very young. They minded their mothers' or other people's children, helped with rural tasks, such as gathering greens or firewood or carrying water, sold things on the street, ran errands, did other sorts of casual labor, and, where necessary, begged. At some point between about age ten and fifteen many of them were put out to service or (less often) apprenticeships. From this point on they were self-supporting and to a large extent independent of their natal families, though they remained dependent on their employers, whom they had a legal as well as customary responsibility to obey. The standard assumption was that they would save their money (perhaps, if they still had a family, sending some of it home) so as to be able to marry some time in their mid- to late twenties. During this lengthy period, often fifteen or more years, they habitually slept in the same bed with a succession of other girls or women, other female servants if there were any, the daughters of other women of the household, or not uncommonly, the mistress of the house herself. Court records and other accounts make it very clear that few people, and certainly not servants, slept alone; they also make it clear that the turnover of servants was very high. Many female servants would have experienced the sleeping arrangements of half a dozen households before they turned thirty, and that during a period when they were lonely, often deprived of affection, and, at least part of the time, at a high libidinal pitch.[36] The potential this system offered for risk-free, same-sex erotic activity was very great.

It is probable that we don't hear much about erotic relations between servant girls because for the most part they struck contemporaries as harmless and beneath their notice, especially if the women were fairly young. Most people assumed that girls of all classes would have close and affectionate friendships with others of the same status, which included physical endearments and sleeping in the same bed. There was more concern attached to cross-class homoerotic activity, and over time, this may have served to cast doubt on lesbian acts more generally, though we have little evidence either way. A classic statement of cross-class sexual anxiety comes from the already mentioned *Onania, or the Heinous Sin of Self-Pollution*, or more precisely, from the *Supplement to the Onania*, which probably appeared first in 1725. It is worth quoting in the original, because it is one of the very few purportedly first-person accounts of lesbian activity from the eighteenth century. In fact, it is clear that the author of the *Supplement* has doctored the account to make it fit with his own preoccupations — the main one being that masturbation causes all sorts of health problems. Still, if one leaves aside the scare tactics, the scenario described here is very plausible. Here is the writer, E.N., describing how she was initiated into mutual masturbation (today we would call it lesbianism) by an older girl, one of the family maids:

I began, Sir, the folly at 11 Years of Age, was taught it by my Mother's Chamber Maid, who lay with me from that Time all along till now which is full seven Years, and so intimate were we in the Sin, that we took all Opportunities of committing it, and inventing all the ways we were capable of to heighten the Titillation, and gratifie our sinful Lusts the more. We, in short, pleasured one another, as well as each our selves.

In this tale, the opportunity provided for sexual activity by sleeping together — which the two were still doing seven years later — and cross-class solidarity between women, is very clear. The purpose of inserting this story into the *Supplement* was to draw attention to the way servants allegedly debauched their young charges by teaching them how to masturbate, the end result being illness, uncontrollable sexual urges, or worse. Thus it was claimed that E.N., "of a tender make, and naturally inclin'd to be weakly," had developed an enlarged clitoris, heightened libido, cessation of the menses, back pains, a swollen belly, weakness, a pallid complexion, and loss of appetite. Conversely, the servant who had been the cause of the problem "ails nothing, [and] is a strong wench of twenty seven." Obviously those of rougher grain could stand treatment that their betters could not, thus making it even more essential that intimacy between the classes be strictly controlled. Ironically, though, this story could also be read as saying that mutual masturbation is largely unproblematic if confined to the servant class alone. Indeed, there is no evidence that most people cared what servant girls did on their own or together in bed after dark, so long as they didn't get pregnant. Harder to read are the cases where servants were of essentially the same "class" (if not the same status) as their master's family, something that was extremely common in a world where people often took in relatives' and friends' children as servants. These girls would have been especially likely to sleep with members of the family, and it is anyone's guess what sorts of activities went on.

Within a master-servant relationship questions about sexual agency and consensuality (or lack of it) inevitably present themselves. In fact, the field of possibilities was very wide, rendered doubly complex by hierarchies of age and status. Servant girls, as is well known, were very vulnerable to advances by the men of the household. All other things being equal, forging a close alliance with the mistress must have at times seemed safer, and, under some circumstances, more appealing. It is very striking how often such alliances turn up in troubled marriages, though this may be a function of the fact that we know far more about them than we do of more harmonious ones. Married women commonly talk of sleeping with their maids in order to garner some measure of protection from their husbands,[37] and there is also some evidence that husbands were jealous of their wives' relationships with their servants. In a case related by Tim Meldrum one husband raped his wife's servant, a woman named Susannah Yeareley, "saying he had done it because Yeareley was too kind to her mistress, his wife."[38] It is not surprising that literary renditions of close alliances between mistresses and servants (for example, the relationship between Roxana and Amy in Daniel Defoe's *Roxana*) often seem homoerotic in tone.[39]

But then, by our standards, the mistress-servant relationship in the eighteenth century seems possessed of a degree of bodily intimacy much more akin to a love relationship than a job. Thus maids were often expected to bathe their mistresses, wash their feet, dress and undress them, arrange their hair, massage them, sit up with them when they were sick, and sleep in their bed or in the same room with them. It would be naive to think that when these acts shaded into the lesbian they always involved free consent of both parties, especially given the very great age and status differences that often obtained. Conversely we should not assume that master-servant erotics were always nonconsensual. What is certainly the case is that, if both parties were willing, intimacy between mistress and maid took little in the way of skills of seduction to turn into something else.

Sex with one's mistress offered several advantages: love and affection under one roof, potential for "promotion" from servant to companion, and greater economic security were the obvious ones. A possible case of something like this (at least contemporaries thought so) was the love affair between Queen Anne (reigned 1702–1714) and Abigail Masham, her bed-chamber woman, who became her most influential female companion and the wife of a peer.[40] But there is no reason to think this sort of thing didn't happen further down the social scale. We suspect something of the sort in the case of Eleanor Coade (1733–1821) who set up a very successful artificial stoneworks in Lambeth, never married, lived for many years in her own home with a female housekeeper and companion, Hannah Wootten, and left that companion a good part of her substantial fortune (though only in trust) when she died at the age of almost ninety.[41]

What about girls who did not go into service? The eighteenth century, especially the second half of the eighteenth century, was a very important period for the rise of girls' schools, many of which were boarding schools.[42] Though a minority of girls went to such schools, it was a significant minority, and there immediately developed many of the features we still associate with girls' boarding schools: schoolgirl crushes that sometimes developed into much more enduring alliances, experiments with sex and power, petty pecking orders, and so on.[43] Anne Lister apparently had her first sexual experiences in such a school in the early 1800s, and several other women with whom Lister later had affairs were people she had met there. Somewhat later, Charlotte Brontë, who fell deeply in love with one of her own boarding school friends, Ellen Nussey, memorialized a similar if more shortlived relationship (complete with sharing a bed) in *Jane Eyre* (1847).[44]

The mid- to late twenties was the age when women were expected to marry. As we have seen, significant percentages of them, throughout the period, failed to do so — some purposely and some not. It is tempting to imagine a young woman who had already discovered homoeroticism in her teenage years using this time to organize stable living arrangements with another woman, and this does seem to have motivated at least some of the many women who sought to pass as men. Thus in the late seventeenth century, Anne Poulter, going by the name of James Howard, courted a singlewoman, Arabella Hunt, "and seemed to be very much in love with her." The two got married in Marylebone parish church in London and set up house together in Hunt's mother's home. Unfortunately the idyll lasted only a few months before Poulter was unmasked as female and already married to a man.[45] Less dramatically, some middle-class women with small incomes from writing or investments also set up as "companions." Others found positions as teachers, milliners, or in a few cases, ladies-in-waiting,[46] that would permit them to live together.

A good many other women probably hedged their bets, and were willing to consider the possibility of heterosexual marriage if a good offer came their way. While they weighed their options, it would have been quite easy to sustain homosexual liaisons, largely because, unlike marriage, most homosexual connections did not have to involve lengthy negotiations, moving house, or changing one's job. In fact, female homoeroticism was so seamless a part of everyday life that it may have been difficult to conceive of it as a vocation, something to be planned and worked for in the way that marriage was. Either way it is abundantly clear that, whereas marriage put logistical obstacles in the way of lesbian activity, it did not put a stop to it. In most of the (probable) lesbian couplings we know about from the late seventeenth through the early nineteenth century, at least one and some-times both partners were married (here Poulter and Hunt are typical).[47] This arrangement is certainly a function of the fact that so many women did get married at some point in their lives; though it also reflects the higher prevalence of married, separated, and widowed women as well as women in their thirties or older among those for whom private papers, written ac-counts by others, and legal records have survived. Lesbianism (or lesbian-like activity) within marriage left reverberations in the sources because husbands and others often knew or suspected that something was going on, and made waves about it. A recently discovered case from the London Court of Exchequer shows clearly how powerful emotional ties between women, combined with strong suggestions of homoeroticism, could both thrive on a troubled marriage and contribute to its breakdown.

Elizabeth Tobin, a widow, had been employed for several years as a nurse at the Charterhouse in London, and had managed to accumulate a considerable amount of money and some household goods. At some point in the 1690s, while living in the parish of Cripplegate in Greater London, she became friendly with her neighbor Anne Ellis, the wife of William Ellis, a coachman. Ill and short of money, Elizabeth prevailed upon Anne to let her use the Ellises' fire for cooking, since she had none of her own. Over time a close relationship grew up between the two women, which was expressed, among other things, in terms of fictive kinship: "[Elizabeth] would be frequently calling . . . Anne by the name of her Daughter" and telling her that when she [Elizabeth] died she would bequeath all her money to her. By 1708 the Ellises' marriage was in a wretched state, at least in part due to Elizabeth: two witnesses would later depose that Elizabeth Tobin "was very instrumental in parting the said William Ellis and his wife." The couple separated and William Ellis went into service in a distant parish. Elizabeth immediately set about helping Anne to break definitively with her husband. She got Anne to sell a hackney coach and horses her husband had left with her, and gave her additional money to set up in business as a chandler so that she could "continue to live apart from her husband." A married woman's liquid assets were, in theory, the property of her husband, so Elizabeth enjoined Anne "not to give her husband any part of the money or acquaint him with [its existence]." Elizabeth gave Anne £20 in all, in two £10 increments. With the first she said before witnesses that "she gave [the money] freely to [Anne] as she had a Soul to be saved and would never call it her own unless . . . Anne's husband came to take it away from her by force." On the occasion of the second gift she said "I give it [the money] to her freely and . . . I do not expect it back again for I will live with her."[48] Accordingly the two women moved together into their own house; the one time that William Ellis came to visit he was obliged to sit up all night while Elizabeth and his wife "lay together" on the only bed.

For reasons that will never be known the arrangement did not work. Perhaps one or the other woman proved hard to live with. The money may have run out, or the neighbors may have disapproved. Certainly William Ellis put pressure on his wife to come back to him. In any case, Elizabeth ended up homeless and £20 poorer than she had been before, and, in the manner of many a jilted lover before and since she sued her former friend and her friend's husband for the money. She claimed in her statement to the court that she had *lent*, not given the money to Anne, that the latter had merely been acting at the behest of her husband William, and that the whole sorry affair had been a plot by the Ellises to defraud her. Meanwhile the Ellises brought in witnesses to prove that the money had been a gift and concentrated on Elizabeth Tobin's efforts to break up her friend's marriage.[49]

We cannot prove that these two women were lesbians. It is quite possible that Anne Ellis *did* see Elizabeth as a mother figure more than a lover. After all, mothers and daughters "lay together" (slept in the same bed) too. Moreover, there were numerous cases in this period of real mothers encouraging their daughters to leave bad marriages and helping them out financially when they did. This story makes as good sense as a (fictive) mother/daughter tale as it does a lesbian one. For our purposes what is most interesting about it is that it shows that marriage (and the process of exiting from a bad marriage) did not constitute a sharp break with the homoeroticism and female bonding that probably characterized the lives of most young unmarried women.

Those women who did remain unmarried into their thirties, forties, and beyond were generally fully self-supporting. The traditional picture of the long-suffering "spinster" forced by convention to throw herself totally on the reluctant hospitality of brothers and sisters-in-law is quite misleading, though it did sometimes obtain among upper middle-class or upper-class families (again, a tiny percentage of the population). A surprising number of singlewomen lived in female-headed households, their own or others'. Such households, which could be headed by widows, singlewomen, deserted or runaway wives, or some combination of these, varied in frequency from place to place but were certainly far more common than most historians have tended to acknowledge. Around 15 percent of households in London for much of the seventeenth century were headed by women, and the proportion was somewhat higher in rural areas (20 percent or more in the same period, with variations) and as high as 27.7 percent in later seventeenth-century Southampton.[50] Insurance records (which are, however, heavily biased toward better-off people) routinely record singlewomen and same-sex couples (some of them blood relations, such as sisters, some not) living in houses of their own and taking out fire insurance policies for their houses or their goods (including, often, their book collections);[51] wills show that it was common to bequeath dwelling places to unmarried daughters, whether single or widowed. Many more households (though they are hard to reconstruct from the records) consisted of women heads of household who kept lodgers, themselves often singlewomen or widows, or unmarried female servants.[52] The point is that no one was especially shocked by the spectacle of one woman living alone or with her children, or two women living together with or without children. Enough explanatory scenarios were available to cover a wide variety of residential arrangements. Singlewomen who stayed with relatives (as many certainly did) tended in the eighteenth century to do so not as humble dependents but as paying lodgers, who went out to work or provided service in exchange for bed and board. Many of them were fully capable of finding lodging elsewhere if the situation grew too tense or if they felt they were being taken advantage of. One imagines there was much moving about. Other women lived in female-headed households, with, say, a widowed sister or sister-in-law.[53] Women who had their own domiciles routinely kept lodgers who were themselves often singlewomen. And poorer women, those on the parish rates, were often encouraged (or forced) to move in with other women in order to keep down costs. Thousands of others, the less fortunate, spent time in houses of correction, where the majority of the adult population was female. Indeed, as Tim Hitchcock remarks, "by the end of the third quarter of the eighteenth century, upwards of forty-five thousand adult women were sharing beds and huddling to keep warm in these institutions. Amongst this variegated population it is difficult to accept that no 'grubbling' [lesbian activity] took place."[54]

This section has stressed once more the everyday character of close relations between women, as well as the fact that it was more normal for young singlewomen as well as older women, whatever their marital status, to sleep together than it was to sleep alone. The comparison with today, when girls and women sleep together only in unusual circumstances, and tend to arouse suspicion by doing so, is striking. All in all, this system provided a great deal of scope for homoerotic relationships, permitting them to coexist easily with the life cycle of most women while also offering some possibilities for stepping out of the prescribed route as women grew past marriageable age.

The Advantages of Lesbianism

One of the signal advantages of a relationship with a woman, as opposed to being married to a man, was that a woman could have control over her own money without going through complicated legal maneuvering. A good example of this is the case of Charlotte Charke, a mid-eighteenth-century actress and writer, well known to lesbian and gay historians for her penchant for dressing — and sometimes passing — as a man. Charke was not a singlewoman: she had married young and disastrously. But sometime in the 1740s she abandoned her unfaithful husband and, around the same time — just as Anne Ellis had done — she moved in with a woman.[55] Charke seems to have been a notably bad manager of money, but one thing she was later to boast about was the way she cheated her estranged husband out of her profits after she had left him (he was, of course, legally entitled to them, and had apparently been coming around trying to collect). According to Charke she "gave and took all Receipts . . . in the name of a Widow Gentlewoman, who boarded with me, and I sat quiet and snug with the pleasing Reflection of my Security."[56] This is a most suggestive episode that encourages us to think about the very real advantages a lesbian relationship might offer to a woman in eighteenth-century society. We do not know whether Clarke and the unnamed "Widow Gentlewoman who boarded with [her]" were having a lesbian affair, but the benefits would have been substantial if they had. Few people put all their money in someone else's name on a whim. Sex is very often tied up with security, defined frequently in financial terms. People expect, sometimes naively, to be able to repose greater trust in those they sleep with than in other people — even, often, than in their blood relations. We have a good deal of evidence that this expectation was a conventional part of eighteenth-century sexual bargaining, both in and out of marriage, but it is easy to see why a woman on the run from her husband might find it advantageous, both emotionally and financially, to establish a relationship with a woman, either a singlewoman or a widow. As researchers turn up more evidence about lesbianism in the eighteenth century it is very likely that they will discover that a good many women who established close emotional, physical, and financial ties to other women were precisely women at that crucial turning point in their lives.

Women in the eighteenth century moved in together because it was more economical to live that way, because they were seeking allies and confederates in their struggles with men over money and other resources, because they wanted companionship, and, at times, because they sought sexual fulfillment. And without idealizing lesbian relationships, which surely had their own problems in the eighteenth century, it seems clear that under some circumstances a lesbian relationship might have seemed a much better risk than marriage, remarriage, or cohabitation with a man. In a partnership between two women it was not the case that all one's earnings automatically went to one's husband, or that one was largely barred from bequeathing away one's own possessions. It was not the case that a woman's real property passed out of her control, or that she lost custody of her children if she broke off the relationship. Lesbian relationships also carried advantages over non-regularized heterosexual unions (e.g., cohabitation with a man). They did not carry the heavy weight of the cultural assumption that the man would rule the household. And, finally, homosexual relations did not raise the possibility of pregnancy.[57]

As we have seen, several of the traits we associate with lesbians today, such as not marrying, being economically self-supporting (albeit often at a rather low level), and living on one's own or with someone of the same sex (as opposed to a male relative) were not especially unusual for women in eighteenth-century England. Nor is it the case that women were always subservient to men, or that they were so sexually ignorant that they could not possibly have known about alternatives to heterosexuality. Eighteenth-century English women were certainly disadvantaged on account of their gender. They lived in a society which limited the range of jobs they could do and the pay they could get for them, which allowed a tremendous amount of discretionary authority to men who were above them in the status hierarchy, and which was overt in its support for male prerogatives. But they also had available to them a larger number of opportunities than we have sometimes realized for pursuing lives that were not tied to marriage to one man. Moreover, some of the motives that still propel women into close relationships with other women, whether or not those include lesbian relationships, have recognizable antecedents in the eighteenth century.

In the case of relationships between servants or other coresidents (other servants, lodgers, family members, and so on) and indeed with most relationships involving women, it is again worth stressing the ease of access of women to other women. In a society as homosocial as eighteenth-century England, lesbian acts fitted easily into the fabric of everyday life. They did not go entirely unnoticed, but there was little effort to wipe them out unless an individual case seemed to constitute a barrier to hetero-sexuality. This is why they thrived in such places as servant's quarters, girls' schools, and houses of correction. We do get hints of friction, but these tended to be in places where male prerogatives were at stake. We need to look more at the rivalry that often obtained between husbands and the household maid(s) for the wife's attention and affection, at con-temporary concerns about relationships between older servants and their younger charges, and — perhaps — at family displeasure at a woman's re-sources going to her companion in preference to her blood relations (there are hints of this with Eleanor Coade).[58]

Eighteenth-century English society was not a place of infinite oppor-tunity for women and what chances there were varied enormously by age, class, place of residence, and other factors. Nonetheless, there were enough cracks in the edifice that some women could do that cost-benefit calculus themselves and arrive, by direct or indirect route, at cohabitation with another woman in their own room or rooms instead of marriage to a man. It seems likely that this was a minority experience however. Probably more often the sheer abundance of lesbian opportunities within the household, the school, or the workhouse, while it did not lead easily to coupled lesbian domesticity along modern lines, nevertheless combined to render the life of many an eighteenth-century woman the very opposite of sexually and emo-tionally thwarted.

The question of the degree to which such activities challenged or failed to challenge the status quo is perhaps the most interesting one to come out of this inquiry, and it is one that is difficult to answer. On the one hand, the very lack of attention to lesbianism where it was most likely to have been happening (among adolescent girls) suggests that these mostly young women's erotic activities threatened no one. On the other hand, the faint but discernible evidence of tension around sexual prerogatives (visible in some husbands' jealousy of their wives' maids and in the outcry over female husbands), around control and bequeathing of money (evident in the case of Charlotte Clarke, Elizabeth Tobin, Anne Ellis, and perhaps Eleanor Coade) and around cross-class sexual encounters (as decried in the *Supplement to the Onania*) may provide clues to a more complex sexual and emotional family economy than we have yet imagined for eighteenth-century Britain.

Notes

1. I use the term "lesbian" in this essay to denote women who sometimes engaged in homosexual or homoerotic acts. I mean neither to assume nor to discount the possibility that some of these women thought of themselves as having a distinct "identity" related to their sexual practice, though I think it likely that many of them did not.

2. See Isabel Miller, *Patience and Sarah* (New York: McGraw-Hill, 1972). The Ladies of Llangollen have themselves inspired at least two novels: Doris Grumbach, *The Ladies* (New York: E. P. Dutton, 1984), and Morgan Graham, *These Lovers Fled Away* (Austin, Tex.: Banned Books, Edward William Publishers, 1988).

3. Tim Hitchcock, *English Sexualities, 1700–1800* (London and New York: Macmillan and St. Martin's, 1997), 87–88, 91–92, speculates that the romantic friendship model of lesbian activity may have become more popular over the course of the eighteenth century, at least among the middling sort and upper class.

4. Hitchcock, *English Sexualities*, suggests something similar; see especially, p. 87.

5. Henry Abelove, "Some Speculations on the History of 'Sexual Intercourse' During the 'Long Eighteenth Century' in England," in *Nationalisms and Sexualities*, ed. Andrew Parker, Mary Russo, Doris Sommer, and Patricia Yaeger (New York and London: Routledge, 1992), 335–42.

6. An important exception is the excise officer John Cannon (b. 1684), whose sexual career (including much non-penetrative sex) is outlined in Hitchcock, *English Sexualities*, 28–38.

7. See especially Emma Donoghue, *Passions Between Women: British Lesbian Culture 1668–1801* (London: Scarlet Press, 1993). Donoghue's encyclopedic reach and indefatigable research will form the basis for all future work on the subject, and has had a powerful influence on this essay. The excellent chapter entitled "Tribades, Cross-Dressers and Romantic Friendship" in Hitchcock, *English Sexualities*, 76–92, begins the work of trying to think about lesbianism in terms of what we know about the social history of ordinary women in the eighteenth century, a project the present essay also takes up.

8. See especially Judith M. Bennett, "Medieval Women, Modern Women: Across the Great Divide," in *Culture and History 1350–1600: Essays on English Communities, Identities, and Writing*, ed. David Aers (London: Harvester Wheatsheaf, 1992), 147–75.

9. Robert B. Shoemaker, *Prosecution and Punishment: Petty Crime and the Law*

in London and Rural Middlesex, c. 1660–1725 (Cambridge: Cambridge University Press, 1991), 185 (table 7.3), 187, 213–14.

10. Henry Fielding, *The Female Husband: or the Surprising History of Mrs. Mary, alias Mr. George Hamilton, Who was Convicted of Having Married a Young Woman of Wells and Lived with Her as her Husband. Taken from her own Mouth since her Confinement* (London: Printed for M. Cooper, 1746).

11. Shoemaker, *Prosecution and Punishment*, 207. However, as Shoemaker also shows, women were considerably less likely than men to pursue the more formal avenue of indictments or trying to get people committed to houses of correction. It is impossible to know whether this represents a real preference on women's part or is the result of JPs pressuring women in the direction of informal mediation (still a common practice in the courts today).

12. I base this assertion on my own work-in-progress on women litigants in borough courts, the courts of Chancery and Exchequer, the ecclesiastical courts, and the High Court of Admiralty.

13. Margaret Hunt, "Wife-Beating, Domesticity and Women's Independence in Eighteenth-Century London," *Gender and History* 4 (1992): 10–33.

14. Numerous examples are quoted in the important new collection edited by Tim Hitchcock, Peter King, and Pamela Sharpe, *Chronicling Poverty: The Voices and Strategies of the English Poor, 1640–1840* (London and New York: Macmillan and St. Martin's, 1997). For women approaching JPs to help them coerce parishes into coming up with poor relief payments, see Richard Connors, "Poor Women, the Parish and the Politics of Poverty," in *Gender in Eighteenth-Century England: Roles, Representations and Responsibilities*, ed. Hannah Barker and Elaine Chalus (London and New York: Longman, 1997), 141–47.

15. Shoemaker, *Prosecution and Punishment*, 209 (table 8.3).

16. Roger Lowe, *Diary of Roger Lowe of Ashton-in-Makerfield, Lancashire, 1663–74* (London: Longman, Green, 1938), 55 (entry for 18 March 1664).

17. See, for example, William Gouge, *Of Domesticall Duties; Eight Treatises*, The English Experience No. 83 (1622; Norwood, N.J. and Amsterdam: Walter J. Johnson and Theatrum Orbis, 1976), 343, where he wishes women "would not so lightly think of their husband's place, nor so reproachfully speak against God's Ministers who plainly declare their [women's] duty unto them, as many do."

18. See especially Randolph Trumbach, "London's Sapphists: From Three Sexes to Four Genders in the Making of Modern Culture," in *Body Guards: The Politics of Gender Ambiguity*, ed. Julia Epstein and Kristina Straub (New York and London: Routledge, 1991), 121–41; Donoghue, *Passions Between Women*; Ros Ballaster, "'The Vices of Old Rome Revisited': Representations of Female Same-Sex Desire in Seventeenth- and Eighteenth-Century England," in *Volcanoes and Pearl Divers: Essays in Lesbian Feminist Studies*, ed. Suzanne Raitt (London: Onlywomen Press, 1995), 13–36.

19. Nicolas de Venette, *The Mysteries of Conjugal Love Reveal'd* (London, 1712; abridged translation of de Venette's *Tableau de l'amour considéré dans l'estat du mariage*, originally published 1687), 20. De Venette goes on to say that "this part [the clitoris] lascivious women often abuse," and that "The Lesbian Sappho would

never have acquired such indifferent Reputation, if this part of hers had been less [i.e., smaller]" (20–21). This plays on the old notion that lesbians possessed over-sized clitorises and used them on other women the way men use penises on women. For a detailed discussion of this theme see Donoghue, *Passions Between Women*, 25–53.

20. See Donoghue, *Passions Between Women*, 183–219, for a well-informed discussion of lesbian tropes in contemporary pornography including Cleland's *Fanny Hill*.

21. See, e.g., Luisa Sigea Toletana and Nicolas Chorier, *Dialogues on the Arcana of Love and Venus* (1660; Lawrence, Kans.: Coronado Press, 1974); and Cleland, *Fanny Hill*. See also Donoghue, *Passions Between Women*, 40–45.

22. Donoghue, *Passions Between Women*, 3–5, 259–61.

23. Lesbian references in Juvenal and other classical authors, as well as the question of accessibility in the eighteenth century, are masterfully discussed in Do-noghue, *Passions Between Women*, 28–33, 212–14, 243–53.

24. Anne Lister, *I Know My Own Heart: The Diaries of Anne Lister, 1791–1840*, ed. Helena Whitbread (New York: New York University Press, 1992), 268 (entry for 26 July 1823).

25. I am not seeking here to distinguish the "natural" from that which is consciously named, nor am I trying to claim that early sexual experimentation is not affected by cultural surround. I am assuming that, in general, human beings are relatively polymorphous in their desires until pushed into narrower channels by forces outside themselves. I also think that childhood and adolescence tend — albeit briefly — to offer more scope for same-sex sexual experimentation than adulthood.

26. Donoghue, *Passions Between Women*, 125–26, 145–48.

27. Wrigley and Schofield, *Population History of England*, 265. For discussions of the methodological complexities of figuring nuptiality rates, especially in the late seventeenth century, see 28–29, 190–91, 257–65. See also Jeremy Boulton, "London Widowhood Revisited: The Decline of Remarriage in the Seventeenth and Eigh-teenth Centuries," *Continuity and Change* 5 (1990): 323–55.

28. Wrigley and Schofield, *Population History of England*, 260, table 7.28: Esti-mated proportions of people never marrying by cohort.

29. For a subtle discussion of singlewomen, sex-ratios, poverty, and women's work in the context of one East Devon town, see Pamela Sharpe, "Literally Spin-sters: A New Interpretation of Local Economy and Demography in Colyton in the Seventeenth and Eighteenth Centuries," *Economic History Review* 44 (1991): 46–65.

30. Elizabeth Ashbridge, *Some Account of the Early Part of the Life of Elizabeth Ashbridge, Who Departed this Life in Truth's Service, in Ireland, the 16th of the 5th Month, 1755* (with additional biographical material by her third husband) (Dublin: C. Bentham, 1820), 16. Ashbridge's second husband was both physically and men-tally abusive (17–50).

31. London Guildhall MS. 12017, "Some Account of the Life &c of John Fryer & of Several of his Relations Written by Himself 1715 &c," fol. 33. The issue of caring for children was also an issue in more plebeian courtships. See, for example, Edmund Harrold, "Edmund Harrold: His Book of Remks and Obs'ns. 1712," in

Collectanea Relating to Manchester and its Neighbourhood, at Various Periods, ed. John Harland, Chetham Society Publications 68 (Manchester: Chetham Society, 1866), 172–208.

32. Margaret R. Hunt, *The Middling Sort: Commerce, Gender, and the Family in England, 1680–1780* (Berkeley and Los Angeles: University of California Press, 1996), 150–51; William Stout, *Autobiography of William Stout of Lancaster, 1665–1752*, ed. J. D. Marshall (Manchester and New York: Manchester University Press and Barnes & Noble, 1967), 87. Stout writes: "My sister had the offers of marriage with several country yeomen, men of good repute and substance; but being always subject to the advice of her mother, was advised, considering her infirmities and ill state of health, to remain single, knowing the care and exercises that always attended a married life, and the hazard of happiness in it."

33. Peter Earle, *A City Full of People: Men and Women of London, 1650–1750* (London: Methuen, 1994), 114.

34. Younger women were especially likely to be servants. Thus for the cohort of women aged twenty-four or less, 63.9 of employed women were in domestic service. For women aged twenty-five to thirty-four the figure was 30.5 percent. From age thirty-five on the percentage fell off markedly as women moved into the needle trades, shopkeeping, and nursing, among other activities (Earle, *City Full of People*, 119).

35. For discussions of the scope and dimensions of women's work, see L. D. Schwarz, *London in the Age of Industrialization: Entrepreneurs, Labour Force and Living Conditions, 1700–1850*, Cambridge Studies in Population, Economy and Society in Past Time 19 (Cambridge: Cambridge University Press, 1992); Maxine Berg, "Women's Work, Mechanization and the Early Phases of Industrialization in England," in *On Work*, ed. R. E. Pahl (Oxford: Basil Blackwell, 1988), 61–94; and Hunt, *Middling Sort*, 125–46.

36. It was during the comparable period in young boys' lives that a number of indictments for sodomy come. In these cases pre-adolescent or early adolescent youths were preyed on either by other older servants while sharing a bed or by their masters. See Alan Bray, *Homosexuality in Renaissance England* (London: Gay Men's Press, 1982), 45–49. Girls were much more likely to be servants than were boys, and we periodically find traces of their having been raped or sexually abused by male masters: see Tim Meldrum, "London Domestic Servants from Depositional Evidence, 1660–1750," in *Chronicling Poverty*, ed Hitchcock, King, and Sharpe, 47–57. I know of no complaints of servants being sexually abused by their mistresses, though it is hard to think this never occurred.

37. I base this assertion on my own reading of Consistory Court divorce cases. See also Margaret Hunt, "Wife-Beating, Domesticity, and Women's Independence in Eighteenth-Century London," *Gender and History* 4 (1992): 10–33.

38. Meldrum, "London Domestic Servants," 56 (Meldrum's words).

39. Donoghue, *Passions Between Women*, 139–43, gives a good account of the homoerotic overtones in a number of literary servant-mistress love relationships.

40. The bedchamber woman, as Edward Gregg makes clear in his biography of queen Anne, was a much more menial position than that of the Ladies of the Bedchamber, in large part because it involved some of the intimate personal tasks

that were normally associated with personal servants. Before she caught the queen's eye Abigail Masham was a poor dependent of Anne's earlier love, Sarah, Duchess of Marlborough. See Edward Gregg, *Queen Anne* (London: Routledge, 1980), 110–11.

41. For Eleanor Coade's career see Alison Kelly, *Mrs. Coade's Stone* (Upton-upon-Severn, Worcs.: Self-Publishing Association and Georgian Group, 1990). For Coade's will and insurance policies see Hunt, *Middling Sort*, 144, 271n–272n. Hannah Wootten was left the money in trust for her lifetime only, which may mean that Coade considered her to be of a lower social status than herself.

42. Susan Skedd, "Women Teachers and the Expansion of Girls' Schooling in England, c. 1760–1820," in *Gender in Eighteenth-Century England: Roles, Representations and Responsibilities*, ed. Hannah Barker and Elaine Chalus (London and New York: Longman, 1997), 101–25.

43. The first girls' school novel also dates from this period, Sarah Fielding, *The Governess, or Little Female Academy* (1749; London: Pandora Press, 1987). Fielding herself never married and has been linked with female companions.

44. For an excellent account of Charlotte Brontë's longtime attachment to Ellen Nussey see Elaine Miller, "Through All Changes and Through All Chances: The Relationship of Ellen Nussey and Charlotte Brontë," in Lesbian History Group, *Not a Passing Phase: Reclaiming Lesbians in History 1840–1985* (London: Women's Press, 1989), 29–54.

45. For a full description of this interesting case see Patricia Crawford and Sara Mendelson, "Sexual Identities in Early Modern England: The Marriage of Two Women in 1680," *Gender and History* 7 (1995): 362–78. This was a rather complex form of impersonation (at least as Hunt later described it in court). Poulter allegedly pretended to be a man dressed as a woman, claiming that "he was forced so to disguise himself till he came of Age being (as he gave out) a Bachelor Heir to a great Estate, for fear his Mother's Brothers should kill him" (London Metropolitan Archives, DLC/240 fol. 141, Arabella Hunt v. Anne Poulter). Very likely Arabella Hunt knew that "John Howard" was a woman but concocted this slightly implausible tale of double impersonation so as to save her reputation.

46. The Bath Abbey contains memorial stones for two such women, Martha Caroline Goldsworthy (d. 1816), for thirty-three years a sub-governess to the daughters of George III, and her "beloved friend" Jane Gomm (d. 1822), also in the service of the royal family. The two were laid to rest in the same grave along with their favorite niece.

47. See, e.g., Charlotte Charke (discussed below); Elizabeth Steele and Sophia Baddeley, discussed in Donoghue, *Passions Between Women*, 167–73; and of course Anne Lister, whose lengthy affair with Marianne Lawton (née Belcome) provides much of the sexual energy of her remarkable memoirs.

48. Elizabeth Tobin's insistence on laying out the terms of the gift before witnesses (if true; after all this came from a hostile testimony) was fairly unremarkable in a world where few people could read or write a contract. Tobin herself was apparently illiterate or only partially literate.

49. The discussion of the case is taken from Public Record Office, London, E112/847 Suit 1418 (*Tobin v. Ellis*), 1710.

50. Jeremy Boulton, *Neighbourhood and Society: A London Suburb in the Seventeenth Century* (Cambridge: Cambridge University Press, 1987), 128–29.

51. The Sun Fire and Royal Exchange Insurance policies in the hundreds of thousands maintained at the London Guildhall Archives show numerous cases of women living together and separately.

52. The keeping of servants reached down into the laboring classes in the eighteenth century, so we should not assume that, just because a woman had a servant, she was rich. In practice, too, the category of "servant" overlapped with that of "lodger." Many heads of household, both male and female, had "lodgers" who discharged all their rent in "household service" and never received a money wage.

53. This seems to have been especially common among sailors' wives, though this may be an artifact of these women's heavy representation in the civil courts in the early part of the eighteenth century.

54. Hitchcock, *English Sexualities*, 86.

55. Charlotte Charke, *Narrative of the Life of Mrs. Charlotte Charke (Youngest Daughter of Colley Cibber, Esq.)* (London: Printed for W. Reeve, A. Dodd, and E. Cook, 1755). See also Hunt, *Middling Sort*, 96–99, 142–43.

56. Charke, *Narrative of the Life of Mrs. Charlotte Charke*, 76.

57. Custody of children went automatically and irrevocably to the father in the eighteenth century. In practice, of course, children often remained with the mother after a separation, but the threat (rather often carried out) of taking a woman's children away was a powerful weapon in the hands of a vengeful husband.

58. Hunt, *Middling Sort*, nn. 271–72.

I I

Singular Politics

The Rise of the British Nation and the
Production of the Old Maid

Susan S. Lanser

IN 1713 a fiercely misogynist twelve-page poem appeared anonymously on a London scene where venomous satires against women were commonplace. But instead of attacking women in general, as such works were wont to do,[1] this pamphlet singled out a constituency that formal satire had hitherto overlooked: never-married women, now known as old maids.[2] Indeed, one explicit objective of this *Satyr Upon Old Maids* was to fill a discursive vacuum: while "*Antiquated Maids*" have been "everlasting Theams for Railery," says the author, they have hitherto "gone free" from sustained attack because they are so "odious" and "impure" a "*Dunghil*" as to contaminate the satirist and even his muse. Evoking old associations of unmarried women with "Witchcraft," the *Satyr* designates singlewomen for "*Pestilence*" on earth and "the *Devil*'s Dish" thereafter and reviles them through a language of bestiality, wantonness, decay, and disease: single-women are "nasty, rank, rammy, filthy Sluts" so disgusting and dangerous that they are urged to throw themselves into the "vilest" marriages to "*Lepers* and *Leachers*," "*Zanies*," or "*Dolts*" just to avoid being "piss'd on with Contempt" for their singleness.[3]

What social conditions or anxieties could have prompted such rhetorical excess? How did singlewomen become by 1713 a target for venom, a new caste defined and maligned solely on the ground of their never-marriedness? Why did England lead Europe in producing the old maid as a despicable cultural identity?[4] And how does the foul "scourge of Providence" of the 1713 *Satyr*, seething with moral and physical contagion, become in just a century the merely foolish and irksome maiden aunt whom

Austen's Emma Woodhouse will be chastised for ridiculing? By tracing the contours of a dialogic discourse about singlewomen produced across the eighteenth century, I hope to expose England's construction of the old maid as inseparable from the emergence both of modern heteropatri-archy — by which I mean a system of male dominance that posits sexual complementarity as the basis not only of personal desire but of social order — and also of the (re)productive economy that will underwrite a specifically British national and imperial identity.[5]

As the *Satyr Upon Old Maids* itself tells us, in 1713 hostility toward singlewomen was not new but also not yet commonplace. Sixteenth- and early seventeenth-century mockery was comparatively infrequent and re-strained, often centering on the curious proverb that singlewomen "lead apes in hell," which appeared in such plays as Shakespeare's *The Taming of the Shrew* and *Much Ado About Nothing*, *The London Prodigal*, and Shirley's *The School of Compliment*, and persisted into the eighteenth century.[6] It is possible that Elizabeth I's singleness curtailed public criticisms of never-married women during her reign, but it is also likely that such criticisms, especially in view of relatively high marriage rates, would not at that time have served particular social needs. In the late sixteenth century, however, at a time when the population of never-married people of both sexes was increasing, English law did begin routinely to identify singlewomen in legal documents, usually with the designation "spinster," which had earlier re-ferred to persons engaged in the spinning trade.[7] This legal development heralded the recognition of singlewomen as "a new group in society."[8]

A movement from recognition to derision, however, is not an inevita-ble phenomenon. Indeed, the source text for the Oxford English Diction-ary's first substantial reference to "old maid," Richard Allestree's 1673 *Ladies Calling*, recognizes negativity toward singlewomen as both constructed and new: "An old Maid is *now thought* such a Curse as no Poetic fury can exceed, look'd on as the most calamitous Creature in Nature." Allestree urges singlewomen not to be "frighted" by society's "vulgar contemt" and "causeless Reproaches," yet he also places on singlewomen the burden of proving their innocence: "If the superannuated Virgins would behave themselves with Gravity and Reservedness, addict themselves to the strict-est Virtue and Piety," the world would esteem them as "espoused to the Spiritual Bridegroom."[9]

Allestree's early articulation of the terms around which the old maid is being constructed begins to address the dialogic interplay of ideologies that will produce the old maid during the eighteenth century. By examining pairs of texts published at successive moments between the Restoration and the Regency, I want to propose that through a dialectical process, opposing but disparate discourses — discourses that talk *past* as much as *to* each other — compete and ultimately converge to define singlewomen as a social category. This dialectic, polarized at the beginning of the eighteenth century, seems to move at century's end toward a synthesis that will reify the old maid into a negative but also socially recuperated (second-class) identity that will change very little from the late eighteenth century to the late twentieth. The fact that by 1800 the term "old maid" had lost much of its venom though not its ridicule helps to identify the historically specific needs served by both the nastier constructions of the earlier period and the more domesticated negative images that persisted into the next.

The emerging contest was already taking shape by the 1690s when Mary Astell published her *Serious Proposal to the Ladies* (1694–97) advocating a "Retreat from the World" where well-born singlewomen could pool their resources in the service of their intellectual and spiritual development. Astell presents singleness not simply as one option but as *the* option: marriage is "slavery" and celibacy the optimal path for fulfilling a woman's full God-given destiny. Yet even as Astell insists on singleness as the ideal for all "Ladies" she echoes Allestree's concern that women might opt to marry simply because they are "terrified with the dreadful Name of *Old Maid*, which yet none but Fools will reproach her with, nor any wise Woman be afraid of."[10] The forms of this reproach are made vivid in John Dunton's compendium, *The Challenge, . . . Or, The Female War* (1697), an epistolary debate on "all the *Disputable* Points relating to women." Its attack "Against Old Maids" anticipates the 1713 *Satyr* in representing singlewomen as envious, malicious, loquacious, ugly, deceitful, odoriferous, and vain "Lump[s] of *Diseases*" with "terrible Fangs" who resemble *"She-Cannibals," "Man-Catchers,"* and "Flesh-Crows." This calumny is countered in the next chapter by a "Defense of Old Maids" that derides "old Batchellor[s]," who enter their dotage in need of "the same Watching, the same Tucking up," as children, and with so little virility that a singlewoman might enter his bed "without any Scandal or Danger; alas!"[11] Clearly these paired constructions of "old maids" and "old bachelors" are far from parallel: the old bachelor may be infantile and impotent, but he lacks the moral and physical repulsiveness of *The Challenge*'s old maid.

The wide popularity of Astell's *Serious Proposal* and the defense of singlewomen built into Dunton's *Challenge*, however, suggest that singleness is still a viable ideological position for women at the onset of the eighteenth

century, although the negative charge of "old maid" is already so prevalent
that outspoken advocates like Astell are compelled to confront and defuse
the term. At the same time, Astell's and Dunton's texts also trace the diver-
gent semantic fields on which discourses for and against singlewomen will
be based until late in the eighteenth century. Texts advocating or affirm-
ing singleness for women, written primarily but not exclusively by singlewomen themselves, usually rest their case on a critique of marriage and/or
men, arguing that marriage as presently practiced actively harms women or
at least denies them the possibility for spiritual and intellectual fulfillment.
The mostly man-made and more frequent discourses against singlewomen,
by contrast, obsessively write the old maid's body as morally and physically
repugnant, incarnating her as woman reduced to materiality in its repellent
rather than its seductive form, as a danger to younger marriageable women
and especially to men. As I will discuss more fully later, this discourse
insistently reconstructs old maids as both heterosexually desperate and vehemently unwanted by men.[12] Neither of these discourses can respond
adequately to the other, for the positive presentations erase the female body
and its desires while the negative discourses avoid or recuperate any critique
of marriage and men.[13]

These divergences are nowhere more intense than in two texts published during the reign of Queen Anne:[14] the virulent 1713 *Satyr Upon Old
Maids* and a surprisingly positive predecessor, Bernard Mandeville's 1709
*The Virgin Unmask'd: or, Female Dialogues Between an Elderly Maiden Lady
and her Niece, on several Diverting Discourses on Love, Marriage, Memoirs and
Morals, &c. of the Times.* A complex book that has received far too little
scholarly attention, *The Virgin Unmask'd* attempts a compelling empirical
case against marriage for women while also analyzing the political systems
of several countries and advancing its own political and social philosophy. Lucinda, positioned as Mandeville's unchallenged mouthpiece and
authorized on the very grounds of her never-marriedness, claims that

we can conclude nothing [about marriage], unless first we examine the Old Maids,
how they have throve, and how they like their being Single at Long-run; and
afterwards look into the vast numbers of [wedded women] . . . and see likewise,
how Marriage has agreed with them. . . . [Moreover,] if you would come to a fair
Trial, you must take your Married Women of the same Age with the maids, and if
you do, you will not find One in Five Hundred, but what has repented a Thousand
Times, that ever she submitted to the Yoak: Whilst all the Old Maids, as soon as that
troublesome [sexual] Itch is over, rejoice at having kept their Liberty, and agree
unanimously in the Comforts of a Single Life.[15]

Lucinda then extends her critique of male dominance to larger political institutions from the absolute monarchy of Louis XIV to the English class system.

The ideological distance between *The Virgin Unmask'd* and the *Satyr Upon Old Maids* makes sharply evident the incommensurate polarities of discourse about singlewomen in the early eighteenth century. The *Satyr* creates a kind of hysteria around the bodies of old maids, on which, as I have already suggested, are heaped a compendium of repulsive conditions from ugliness and uncleanness to a malice that corrupts young virgins and "stud[ies] Mankind's Destruction" (8). *The Virgin Unmask'd* sees *men* as the destroyers and names the body of the *wife/mother* as distorted and destroyed: "is it not a Thousand pitys, to see a Young Brisk Woman, well made, and fine Limb'd? as soon as she is Poyson'd by Man, reach, Puke, and be Sick, ten or twelve times in a Day, for a Month or Six Weeks; and after that, Swell for Seven or Eight Months together; till, like a Frog, she is nothing else but Belly" (119–20). The *Satyr*'s old maid longs grotesquely for men she cannot have; Lucinda sees heterosexual desire as a temporary illness and holds an "ill Opinion of Men, which they deserve" (18).

Little is known about the reception of either *The Virgin Unmask'd* or the *Satyr*, but other writings suggest that the *Satyr* was the far more representative construction of singlewomen at the beginning of the eighteenth century; a spate of new evocations of the old "apes in hell" proverb, for example, surfaced around 1708 and 1709.[16] By the 1720s, the institutionalization of the old maid is setting in; the condition of singleness becomes a social problem that women need to address, and defenses of singleness take a more fatalistic tack. This shift is visible when we pair Jane Barker's 1723 *Patch-Work Screen for the Ladies*, a compendium of poems, stories, and fictional autobiography, with the writings about singlewomen attributed to Daniel Defoe that appeared in *Applebee's Journal* between 1723 and 1725. Barker's Galesia, like Astell and like Mandeville's Lucinda, extols the single life and offers illustrative anecdotes about the disasters of marriage and the destructive behaviors of men. But while Astell and Mandeville presented celibacy as the wisest universal choice, Galesia marks it simply as her own "Fate." After one tragic experience and several lesser skirmishes with men, she had come "to believe Providence had ordain'd for me a *Single Life*." Along with her compulsion to write poetry, her love of learning, and her gift for medicine — all clearly men's prerogatives — singleness is Galesia's *"fatal Necessity,"* for *"Nature,"* even when "thrust off . . . by Force," will "still return to her old Course." Galesia does see singleness as "bear[ing] the

Impress of all Good" and comprising "all Vertue" and "Modesty," and she
cannot fathom those who deride this *"happy State"* with "mad Conceptions" of singleness as "foul Deformity, in vilest Dress."[17] But what the
earlier texts offered as the superior option for all women is here reconfigured as an individual destiny for which Galesia bears no agency.

Defoe's first *Applebee's Journal* entry, a 1723 "Satire on Censorious Old
Maids," echoes the 1713 *Satyr Upon Old Maids* in more than name: singlewomen are "Amazonian Cannibals," "the Terror and Aversion of all Mankind," and "the foreboder of Diseases and Death," with "Sour, and acri-
monious Liquids" in their veins and spewing a poisonous animal venom, so
that "if an Old-Maid should bite any body, it would certainly be as Mortal,
as the Bite of a Mad-Dog." This reinscription is only weakly contested in a
subsequent protest (also apparently authored by Defoe), which claims that
not all singlewomen fit this bill. Most of the material in *Applebee's*, however,
lacks this virulence, taking the negativity of the singlewoman as a given,
often adopting the fiction of a female voice, and focusing on such "practical" issues as the age at which a woman shall be considered an old maid
(possibilities range wildly from twenty-four to forty-three); whether it is
better to remain single than to marry a pauper, a person beneath one's
station, or a rake; whether women might avoid singleness by adopting a
"Polish" custom of courting men; and other strategies for avoiding the
"most scandalous Circumstances of Women, call'd an *Old Maid*."[18] Similar
practicality surfaced in a 1719 proposal for an "office of marriage" to help
the "despicable" victims of a "censorious world" who would do anything
rather than "sink with that heavy luggage of virginity into their graves."[19]

In these 1720s writings that straddle older and newer positions, singleness is neither as idyllic nor as repulsive a state as the more polar images of
the late Stuart period constructed it. Preoccupied with both definitions and
practicalities, Defoe's journalism emphasizes ways of constructing — and of
avoiding — membership in the class of old maids. Marriage is presented as
effectively the only path to female respectability, so that even those who
recognize its drawbacks opt for it, focusing their attention on when, whom,
and how to wed. By mid-century, when novelists such as Henry Fielding
and Tobias Smollett are representing singlewomen as blameworthy comic
types,[20] even the more benevolent representations will take on an apolo-
getic tone. That one of the few mid-century attempts to authorize the singlewoman itself yields to the title *The Old Maid* is significant, since virtually
every previous effort to defend singlewomen has avoided or overtly rejected
that term.

The *Old Maid* I have in mind, only incidentally about singleness, is a set of essays on diverse subjects by the not-yet-married Frances Brooke, published serially in 1755–56 under the pseudonym Mary Singleton and reprinted later in book form. Singleton confesses that her never-married state has given her "scruples of conscience" because "an old maid is, in my opinion, except an old bachelor, the most useless and insignificant of all God's creatures." Recounting a history almost identical to that of Mandeville's Lucinda, she explains that after being abandoned by a suitor she was called on to care for her orphaned niece. But while Lucinda urges her own niece not to marry, Singleton acquiesces eagerly to the norm: "if any old maid is excusable, I hope I am; for tho, I have not had the honor of being a mother, I have had all the cares of one, and hope I have executed this trust in such a manner as to make some worthy man happy in a wife; for marry [my niece] certainly shall: one old maid is quite enough in a family; nay to be plain, I sometimes think too much."[21]

Mary Singleton's retrenchment is echoed even in Sarah Scott's *Millenium Hall* (1762), which offers probably the most positive mid-century representation of singlewomen, especially in contrast to Arthur Murphy's nasty farce, *The Old Maid*, produced just a year earlier. Scott creates a utopian all-female space devoted to the welfare of women and girls, but bent less on improving its (already improved) founding "ladies"—mostly widows or women circumstantially unable to marry—than on educating the lower-class objects of its benevolence. In ways dramatically different from discourses of Mandeville, Barker, and especially Astell, to which it is sometimes compared, *Millenium Hall* embraces a marital economy as the "ladies" assist girls of the lower classes to become virtuous and productive wives. *Millenium Hall* does allow singleness to be a blessing and a benefit, but it is careful to detail the history of each unmarried woman in elaborate justification of her state. Within this framework, *Millenium Hall*'s most apparently radical gesture is also potentially its most conservative: in clustering unmarried women in a separate, isolated space where they perform the work of reproducing patriarchy, the novel doubly defuses the threat that female affiliation could have posed.

Scott's popular novel thus stands in apparent but only partial contrast to perhaps the most negative representation of singlewomen of this period, Arthur Murphy's very popular play, *The Old Maid* (1761). Murphy's protagonist, Miss Harlow, is "sour," "vain," "peevish," and deeply envious of married women. On the verge of accepting the elderly Captain Cape, she becomes convinced, through a case of mistaken identity, that a more eli-

gible man is courting her; actually, that suitor has confused her with
her younger but already-married sister-in-law. Once Miss Harlow's self-
delusion has been exposed, Murphy could have married her off to Captain
Cape and integrated her into the reestablished social order that comic resolution conventionally entails. Instead, Miss Harlow is banished from the
stage and indeed from society, sent to "bewail [her] virginity in the moun-
tains." The old maid herself assents to this exile; unable to "bear to be thus
disgraced," she will "go and hide myself from the world for ever." Given her
eager participation in the marriage market, her parting lament that "men
are all savages, barbarians, monsters, and I hate the whole sex" discredits
and recuperates the serious charges against male dominance offered by an
Astell or a Mandeville or even, if more mildly and surreptitiously, the ladies
of Millenium Hall.[22] According to Katharine Kittredge, ridicule and exile
are also the fate of Miss Patty Ravensworth, Anne Skinn's eponymous *Old
Maid* (1771), whose nephew reviles her as a "sapscull" and "old fusta ket-
tle" and proclaims that "if I was such a stinking tawney as you, I should not
in conscience pack myself out of the world, that I might be no disease to
wholesome mortals."[23]

Across the span of almost a century, then, English discourse has staged
a contest in which the virtuous and respectable singlewoman is opposed
to the dangerous and disgraceful old maid who is not simply a personal
failure — so lacking in adult authority that even a youngster can mock her
openly, so widely reviled that popular theatre can ban her with impunity —
but a contaminant, a signifier whose very presence is dangerous. This unbalanced dialectic of textual encounters between the respectable and the disrep-
utable old maid seems to me to reach a kind of (still-unbalanced) synthesis
in the 1780s as the oppositions are subsumed into a more unified image of a
singlewoman with both vices and virtues — an object of polite pity, slight
admiration, and temperate ridicule. The text that dramatically illustrates
this coalescence is the popular poet William Hayley's three-volume *Philosophical, Historical, and Moral Essay Upon Old Maids* (1785), an extraordinary work to which I cannot begin to do justice here. Hayley's table of
contents itself recognizes its project of synthesis: the book begins with a set
of chapters on "the particular failings of old maids" — curiosity, credulity,
affectation, envy, and ill-nature — and then discusses singlewomen's "particular good qualities" — ingenuity, patience, and charity. Illustrating these
traits through a series of narrative episodes in which he creates a panoply of
singlewomen, Hayley turns even alleged virtues to vices, rendering the
problems singlewomen encounter as signs not of social disorder but of

moral defect in the women themselves. The most extraordinary aspect of this wide-ranging book, which treats singlewomen not only in present-day England but from ancient times, is Hayley's re-creation of the kind of all-female Protestant space envisioned by Astell and Scott (and by Defoe and Richardson), as a literal convent in which Hayley himself becomes not simply a ministering priest but a kind of a messiah who, after preaching his ultimate sermon, dies and is resurrected to live forever for all future old maids.[24]

Hayley insisted that his *Essay* was intended to "promote" never-married women; his first chapter offers his book as a "little fence" that he will raise around "this blasted tree" so that it "not suffer the wild asses . . . to kick and wound it."[25] Given such rhetoric, it is no surprise that single-women rejected and resented his book, and it is a sign of his own lack of consciousness that Hayley was allegedly bewildered and wounded when his efforts did not meet with gratitude from such singlewomen as Elizabeth Carter, to whom it is dedicated, or Anna Seward, who was apparently so outraged that she broke her ties with him.

It has been said of Hayley's poetry that it was wildly popular in its day — and forgotten thereafter — because it expressed so precisely the hegemonic values of its time. Hayley's acute encapsulation of the patronizing ideology surrounding singlewomen in the 1780s also became a forgotten text but not a forgotten ethos. In 1822, for example, the self-identified sapphist Anne Lister copied into her diary the following newspaper passage that addresses just the stereotypes Hayley perpetuates:

I am inclined to believe that many of the satirical aspersions cast upon old maids tell more to their credit than is generally imagined. Is a woman remarkably neat in her person? "She will certainly die an old maid." Is she particularly reserved toward the other sex? "She has the squeamishness of an old maid." Is she frugal in her expenses & exact in her domestic concerns? "She is cut out for an old maid." And, if she is kindly humane to the animals about her, nothing can save her from the appellation of an "old maid." In short, I have always found that neatness, modesty, economy, & humanity, are the never-failing characteristics of that terrible creature, an "old maid."[26]

This is not far from the portrait that Austen's Emma Woodhouse evokes, both in her mockery of Miss Bates and in her insistence that, even were she herself not to marry, she would still not be an old maid.[27] It is this portrait, too, that has come down to this century: not the virulent, physically and morally repulsive old maid of the 1713 *Satyr* but the irksome, prattling, and small-minded one, not the castrating "she-Cannibal" but the frugal and inconsequential bore, not a threat to family but a kind of "extra" tolerable insofar as she can be of use. So naturalized does the fiction of the old maid become that the OED can define the term tautologically, as "an elderly spinster: usually connoting habits characteristic of such a condition" as if it were self-evident what those habits must be.[28]

But both the unprecedented horror of singlewomen in the early eighteenth century and their ultimate recuperation into a domestic economy remain to be explained, as does the role of Britain as the avant-garde in creating the old maid as a fixed social identity. Surely the first contributing factor is simple demography—the significant increase in singlewomen, probably of all social classes, in the seventeenth century. E. A. Wrigley and R. S. Schofield's extrapolated data suggests that the proportion of adults not married by age forty rises dramatically in the seventeenth century, from only 84 per 1000 in 1596 to 135 in 1616, peaking at 270 in 1681–86.[29] David Weir's data, intended as a corrective to Wrigley's, still locate the peak of English celibacy in the late seventeenth century.[30] T. H. Hollingsworth's study of the peerage also shows "remarkable increases" in the proportions never marrying: in the cohort born between 1550 and 1574, only 4 percent of males and 9 percent of females never married, but for cohorts born in the seventeenth century the number was well over 20 percent for both sexes.[31] Pamela Sharpe's data indicate that celibacy rates were also exceptionally high among the poor, and Wrigley estimates the number of all singlewomen in 1680 at about 15 percent.[32]

As I suggested earlier, the increased number of singlewomen in late seventeenth-century England may account for increased *attention* to singlewomen, but I do not believe the numbers can in themselves explain the intense *negativity* of this attention or the specific forms of that negativity. First, the rise in celibacy seems to hold for men as well as women, yet negative references to never-married men seem to be uncommon and relatively mild; the bachelor does not become a despised social category in eighteenth-century England. Second, celibacy rates also rise at this time in some other countries, especially France and Italy, apparently without a negative discourse taking hold.[33] Conversely, singlewomen were apparently regarded quite negatively in Puritan New England even though rates of singleness in both sexes were very low.[34] Third, English old-maid discourses do not discuss singlewomen as a problem of numbers; it seems that the presence of *any* singlewoman is odious. Moreover, if Hollingsworth and Sharpe are right to locate the highest celibacy rates within the upper and lower classes, the fact that the discursive attention is focused on gentry women suggests that a deeper agenda is at work. Finally, hostility toward singlewomen increases in intensity during the first decades of the eighteenth century when their numbers are actually in decline; in Wrigley and Schofield's data, for example, from 267 per 1000 in 1696 to only 96 per 1000 in 1746 and 73 in 1761.[35] In sum, late seventeenth-century demographic changes probably directed attention to singlewomen, but I do not think that numbers alone can explain the extent of the intensity or its hostile shapes.

On the other hand, increased numbers surely intersected with patriarchal anxieties to stir old fears of women unattached to men. It is, after all, only in the early eighteenth century that European persecutions of women as witches died out. Both singlewomen and widows were singled out for particular persecution as witches, and it is plausible to speculate that distrust of the singlewoman simply continued in the castigation of the old maid. But the connection with witchcraft does not explain why England led Europe in producing discourses hostile to singlewomen, especially since witch trials were far more widespread on the continent and in Scotland than in England per se. Nor does it explain why widows, highly suspect as witches, would be spared the onus directed at never-married women.

Some scholars have theorized the seventeenth and eighteenth centuries as a period of changing constructions of gender — from a "single-sex" model of sameness that sees women as inferior versions of men, to a "two-sex" model of difference that refigures the sexes as complementary.[36] And it is during the later seventeenth century that one can first speak of any widespread feminist "movement" in Europe — by which I mean not an organized or systematic intervention but a range of more or less simultaneous writings and activities, from the Paris salons of the *précieuses* and Poulain de la Barre's treatises on female equality to the resistant writings and actions of Margaret Cavendish in England, of Sor Juana de la Cruz in Mexico, or of Sweden's cross-dressing and ultimately abdicating Queen Christina. As an effect of feminist interventions or of patriarchal accommodations to women as men's "separate but equal" counterparts, discourses critical of women in general did grow more restrained and superficially more respectful as the eighteenth century progressed, at least until the backlash against "unsex'd females" of the late French Revolutionary period. In this climate, it is feasible that the denigration and hostility once bestowed verbally on all women became localized within particular scapegoat groups. That one such group might be singlewomen would hardly be surprising, since female singleness not only threatens the patriarchal control of individual women, but undermines an entire system that depends on women's control by men. At the same time, the phenomena I am describing here occur throughout western Europe and not in England alone. Yet attacks on singlewomen are more occasional in other countries: hostile texts such as La Fontaine's fable "La Fille" or Lessing's play *Die alte Jungfer* (1749) do not seem to generate a widespread phenomenon.

Numbers of singlewomen in England must surely have intensified patriarchal anxieties about female economic and social agency. Singlewomen were both legally privileged over married women and disproportionately involved, not only in what Jürgen Habermas has called the "literary public sphere" but in many other economically productive activities, from shopkeeping to speculation, that were traditionally the province of men. Defoe's Roxana understands English law and practice well when she says "that while a woman was single, she was Masculine in her politick Capacity; that she had then the full Command of what she had, and the full Direction of what she did."[37] Although historians disagree about whether women's economic opportunities improved or declined during the eighteenth century, it seems that some occupational possibilities—from lacemaking to shopkeeping to education—were increasing, especially, as both Linda Colley and Elizabeth Child have argued, within the burgeoning provincial towns.[38] Once again, other European countries become an important point of comparison. Female agency in the French literary public sphere dates from the seventeenth century and features such never-married women as Madeleine de Scudéry, and in the seventeenth and eighteenth centuries French singlewomen also engaged in a wide range of economic activities.[39] And if French (and Catholic German) women might be safely ensconced in convents, any perceived problem of German Protestant singlewomen could not be so readily resolved, yet neither country produced at this time a significantly increased body of discourse about old maids. Nor do social attitudes toward marriage seem relevant: if there was a widespread negativity toward marriage in France, in Germany religious pietism reinforced conceptions of married domesticity.[40]

Taken together, then, the factors I have mentioned, while surely contributory, strike me as still insufficient to explain English leadership in the production of the old maid. I want to suggest, therefore, the possibility of a specifically national prism through which these various contributing elements might have been organized. In so doing, I turn to a trope that is already embedded in many of the texts I have been discussing: the sense that women who don't marry are a national detriment. The *Satyr Upon Old*

Maids of 1713 implies that singlewomen have failed in responsibility not only to God but to Country: they are called *"Rebels* both to *God* and *men"* at a time when such words surely echo recent national threats from the Civil Wars and the Popish Plot to the Jacobite rebellions. Woman's rebellion is explicitly identified as a failure to (re)produce: women are "design'd / To propagate the Species of Mankind," but old maids are "impious Traytors," useless while they, "like *wicked Vermin*, feed upon / The Fruits the Earth produce, yet bring us none" (5–6). Dunton's *Challenge* announces that "an *old Maid* in a *Commonwealth* is much such another Impliment as an *Eunuch* in a *Seraglio"* and holds that " 'tis not easie to know for what else she was design'd (since it looks harsh to grant that Nature made any thing in vain)" (141). Antonia, Lucinda's niece in *The Virgin Unmask'd*, also sees reproduction as a patriotic goal: "Aunt, you are enough to ruine, and unpeople a Common-Wealth: When yesterday I was Reading, how sollicitous the Emperor *Augustus* was, in Stocking of his Empire, what Care and Pains he took, to perswade all Young People to Matrimony, and how he Honoured, and Encouraged such as would Marry, I could not forbear thinking of you: If you had Lived in his Days, and Ventilated this Doctrine, you would have certainly come to some Untimely end or other" (116). Defoe compares the "Tea-Table Courts" of the "censorious old maids" to those of "the *Spanish* Inquisition" (125) — that paradigm of un-Englishness — while Brooke's Mary Singleton says that raising her niece "has been so great a pleasure to me that I should never have regretted my condition, had I not thought myself wanting in duty to my country" (5). *Sir Charles Grandison's* notion of a "Protestant Nunnery" is identified "a *national* good" especially because its unmarried inhabitants would provide a "seminary for good wives."[41] And Samuel Johnson's *Rambler* No. 39 implies a metaphoric link to national identity when he refers to singlewomen as "barren countries."[42]

Why in the early and mid-eighteenth century should singlewomen have been a particular affront to nationhood? I would like to speculate that the English construction of the old maid is connected to an urgent perceived interest in increasing the British population, and that promotion of fertility in an England with high numbers of unmarried people was abetted by the dramatic discrediting of the female body that did not reproduce. In other words, I suggest that the recognition of population growth as a key to Britain's political and commercial future fostered a pronatalist domesticism in which negative discourses against singlewomen could prove materially significant.

Numerous scholars have recognized Britain's strong interest in population growth during this period. Increased population meant both expansion of markets for consumer goods and plentiful labor power to hold down wages and production costs.[43] Early modern societies also tended to assume that "a nation's political strength was determined largely by the sheer number of men who could be called to bear arms," and since 1689, England had been "caught up in a succession of major wars," especially with France.[44] For these reasons, Neil Tranter argues, "all writers of the period . . . remained convinced that the total size of a population was a crucial, if not the only, determinant of political power."[45]

Seventeenth- and eighteenth-century thinkers were vocal in articulating such a national population need. An anonymous 1690 work titled *Marriage Promoted* claimed that "the neglect of marriage" would "occasion the destruction of these kingdoms" through depopulation.[46] John Cary in a 1695 *Essay on the State of England* stressed the importance of population growth both to economic development and to social organization generally.[47] Charles D'Avenant's 1698 *Discourses on the Public Revenues and on the Trade of England* considered "the bodies of men . . . the most valuable treasure of a country; their encrase or decrease must be carefully observed by any government that designs to thrive."[48] Defoe lamented in 1704 that England was poor because "there is more labour than hands to perform it. . . . From the dearnesse of wages, which in England outgoes all nations in the world," and in 1728 he surmised that "Trade has increas'd the People and People have increas'd Trade; for Multitudes of People, if they can be put in a condition to maintain themselves, must increase Trade." According to Felicity Nussbaum, Thomas Man's *The Benefits of Procreation* (1739) raised the issue to a "feverish millennial pitch" and recognized an increase in children as the means to make Britain "the Terror of all *Europe*, and the most formidable Power upon the Face of the Globe."[49] David Hume identified an abundance of people, along with "commodities and riches," as the signifiers of a nation steering a wise and just moral course.[50] In 1755 Josiah Tucker argued that England needed bigger markets and more customers,[51] and Ruth Perry cites the arguments of Jonas Hanway in 1756 that "England's expanding colonial power" necessitated "more citizens."[52]

As Defoe's participation in this discourse reminds us, the period of English anxiety about population coincides quite precisely with the decades in which England produced most intensively its negative old maid. The population of England during this period was indeed small and static, putting the island at a distinct disadvantage economically and militarily especially in relationship to its archrival France: at 4.9 million, England's population in 1680 constituted only 6.8 percent of western Europe's total, while France had the region's largest percentage (30 percent) with 21.9 million; Spain, 8.5 million; and Italy and the German states, 12 million each.[53] In the late decades of the seventeenth century, England saw no appreciable population growth, and increases before 1780 were modest — remaining, except for one five-year period, at 0.1 to 0.6 percent annually, with the slowest reproduction rate occurring between 1711 and 1740.[54] During this period, the populations of many other European nations, including Holland, Belgium, Norway, Ireland, Spain, and to a lesser extent France, were growing at a faster pace. Given the interests of eighteenth-century Britain to gain power and assert nationhood through an imperialist mercantile capitalism, the population problem would easily become critical in perception and perhaps in fact.

Extraordinary changes in the later eighteenth century testify eloquently to England's success in reversing its own demographic practices. From the 1740s through the 1770s, English population growth was more than twice that of the first decades of the century, and beginning in 1781 it "accelerated dramatically." Malthus's warnings of 1798 notwithstanding, by 1820 England's population had risen to 11.5 million through an annual growth rate that seems literally to have doubled within a decade: from 0.5 percent in the 1770s to 1 percent in 1781 and 1.8 by the 1810s. During the same period from 1680 to 1820, France's population grew only from 21.9 to 30.5 million and Spain's from 8.5 to 14 million. By 1900 England would number 30.5 million, while France's increased only to 38.5 — staggering differences when we note that in 1550 England had only 3 million people compared to 17 million in France.[55] It is not surprising that Britain achieved its greatest commercial and imperial success at the time of its highest population growth; Tranter asserts that "both the expansion of international trade and English dominance over it owed much to the fact that the rate of population increase was high." Population growth triggered vast increases in the demand for raw materials and foodstuffs from the colonies and also for manufactured goods, and a strengthened domestic economy "made it that much easier for English businessmen to take advantage of the new overseas opportunities offered to them."[56] But never did the population increase more dramatically within a brief period than around 1780, giving a major "jump start" to British national and imperial economy.

Historians seem to agree that England's "population revolution" resulted less from improvements in diet and health than from a drop in the age of first marriage from 26 to just over 23 years and a dramatic decrease in the number of singlewomen from about 15 percent in the late seventeenth century to about half that number in the late eighteenth. In other words, during the decades of the eighteenth century that I associate with the English construction of the old maid, "the percentage of women who lived through the child-bearing ages without ever marrying" seems to have dropped a startling 50 percent.[57] David Weir believes that "it was celibacy and not age at marriage that accounted for most of fertility variation before 1750,"[58] but in any case these two factors converge when discourses such as Defoe's encourage early marriage by setting up women of eighteen or twenty to fear ending up as old maids.

In light of this agenda, then, it would be "logical" for the singlewoman to be represented as a deterrent to national enterprise. Since she (presumably) did not procreate, the singlewoman directly retarded the economic and military might that depended — or was perceived to depend — on population growth. If historians such as Amy Froide and Pamela Sharpe are right to suggest that some work opportunities for women were expanding at this time and thus diminishing women's economic incentives to marry, ideological pressure might well have been even more imperative. It is plausible to speculate that the negative construction actually helped both to reduce the numbers of singlewomen and to increase Britain's population by the late eighteenth century — the time I have also identified with a weakening of the vituperation against old maids and arguably also a time of yet another decrease in Englishwomen's opportunities for independent work. The successful continuance of England's population growth during the Victorian age might also explain why, although the numbers of singlewomen rose again in the nineteenth century, the earlier, virulent hostility toward singlewomen did not recur. In this light, we can think of vituperative texts such as the 1713 *Satyr* as signifiers of a historically specific hysteria over the national dependence on women to procreate. We might also read the intense and vivid disgust reflected in the early discourses as an attack upon the nonproductive female body, which gets figured as a tomb of contagion, putrefaction, and disease.

This hysteria may also explain why old-maid discourse so frequently exposes its own seams of illogic, its artificiality — indeed its status *as* ideology. The very fact that the discourses can discuss the age at which a woman becomes an "old maid" suggests that there is no natural moment — or identity — that separates singlewomen from women generally. Most of the discourses admit that there is nothing intrinsically negative about being single; the problem lies in social hostility, which is thus implicitly (and often explicitly) identified as the major reason to avoid singlehood: even the *Satyr* urges women to marry because otherwise they "are the Scorn and Sport of *All*." Insofar as the texts themselves are writing the scenario that makes singlewomen such "Scorn and Sport," it is *discourse* that creates the desire for marriage and the fear of singleness. Several texts openly recognize the effectiveness of this strategem. Afraid of "new Contempt" each day, says Barker's Galesia, women "fling themselves" into the marital *"Lyon's Den"* (91). And Samuel Johnson writes that singlewomen, tiring of the "disposition always shewn to treat old maids as the refuse of the world," are often "persuaded, by powerful rhetoricians, to try the [married] life which they had so long contemned" — thereby suffering in marriage still worse "miseries."[59] All these texts also suggest that marrying is solely a woman's choice — a patent contradiction in a social system that makes women the passive parties in courtship rituals. Thus women are blamed for failing to achieve what they have little agency to bring about.

The harnessing of singlewomen into a domestic social economy might also be explained partly by population needs. Linda Colley notes the extent to which women were "encouraged by British legislators, pundits, and charitable bodies . . . for practical as well as humanitarian reasons" to rescue orphans and foundlings, and she cites as "frank and typical" the motto of the Lying-in Charity for Married Women: "Increase of Children a Nation's Strength."[60] In this way, when Richardson's "Protestant nunnery" or Scott's *Millenium Hall* co-opts single women into a system of national service that entails preparing other people's daughters to be good mothers and wives, a potentially feminist solution turns into a nationalist one. Not only do such gestures remove women from an economy of goods and hence from independent entrepreneurial productivity, but they position the old maid as a kind of national maiden aunt, devoted to the work of reproduction both within and beyond her extended family. Hayley's very project in the recuperative *Essay on Old Maids*, indeed, is to turn singlewomen into "pillars of the state."

Yet this explanation by which I have linked nationalist pronatalism to the construction of the old maid does not account for one other significant aspect of the negative English construction of the old maid: its almost complete repression of homoerotic or even homoaffectional bonds. In eighteenth-century England, such an absence of the homoerotic cannot be attributed either to a more general discursive silence about female homosexuality or to a lack of investment in heterosexuality as a national goal. Discourses about female homoeroticism, under such labels as tribadism, sapphism, and hermaphroditism, appear with some frequency in England in the seventeenth and eighteenth centuries. In contrast to an apparent silence about female homosexuality in eighteenth-century German writings, and a French discourse often fascinated with female homoeroticism despite some disapproving gestures, England produces, especially after 1740, writing that is notably vocal in its negativity.[61] This position is illustrated perhaps most dramatically in Fielding's *The Female Husband* (1746), which sensationalizes the case history of a woman prosecuted for masquerading as a man, but female homosexuality is also explicitly rejected in writings as pornographic as Cleland's *Memoirs of a Woman of Pleasure* (1749), in which Fanny Hill's homosexual initiation in the brothel is "naturally" exchanged for "finer" heterosexual "food"; as self-satisfied as the anonymous and sensational *Satan's Harvest Home: or the Present State of Whorecraft, Adultery, Fornication, Procuring, Pimping, Sodomy, And the Game at Flatts, And other Satanic Works, daily propagated in this good Protestant Kingdom* (1749), whose title makes clear its agenda and which attempts to relocate tribadism ("the game at flatts") to an orientalized East; and as chaste as Richardson's *Sir Charles Grandison* (1753–54), in which the masculine Miss Barnevelt is rejected for both her demeanor and her amorous attentions to women.

Several scholars have already persuasively argued that heterosexuality became a British national project in the late seventeenth and eighteenth centuries for purposes sometimes linked to but not circumscribed by population needs. Henry Abelove, in a provocative and speculative essay of 1989, links population growth to the institutionalization of coitus over other sexual practices.[62] Ruth Perry claims that eighteenth-century motherhood "effected the colonization of women for heterosexual productive relations."[63] Valerie Traub, perceptively reading the borders and frontispieces of early modern maps, argues for the emergence in this period "of heterosexual desire as a national project" with colonialist and racialist purposes.[64]

If the institutionalization of heterosexuality is in England's national interest, and if a negative discourse about sapphism is readily available, why does the old maid *not* get discredited as a tribade or sapphist? The absence of explicit homoeroticism from discourses that support singlehood is more understandable. Critics have identified suggestions of homoeroticism and signs of homoaffectionality in Astell's *Serious Proposal*, Barker's *Patch-Work Screen*, and especially Scott's *Millenium Hall*; *The Virgin Unmask'd* likewise suggests that Lucinda's deep connection to her niece is a motivating factor in her efforts to discourage Antonia from marrying. But for fairly obvious strategic reasons, these texts advocating singlehood and/or communities for women are careful not openly to advocate homoeroticism as well. This strategic caution may explain the presence in some of these texts of homo-eroticism that is treated as untenable: in *The Virgin Unmask'd*, Lucinda chastises Antonia for provocatively kissing another girl (as "practice" for heterosexuality); in *Patch-Work Screen*, Galesia inserts the curious tale of the "Unaccountable Wife" who abandons her own household for her hus-band's servant and former mistress;[65] in *Sir Charles Grandison*, the negative case of Miss Barnevelt coexists with advocacy for a "Protestant nunnery."

But the silence about sapphism in those discourses that seek to dis-credit the singlewoman is, I think, even more revealing. For to acknowl-edge the possibility of homosexual desires in the "old maid" would dis-mantle and expose the entire system of old-maid ideology, in which the singlewoman's physical and moral deficiencies rest on the presumption of her heterosexual desire — on the presumption that she wants a man and cannot get one and as a result has become the miserable person she is. This scenario explains both the repeated insistence that old maids should marry anyone at any cost, however late in life — clearly not just a reproductive question — and the approval bestowed even by some of the most vitupera-tive discourses on women who purportedly choose for spiritual reasons to be celibate. The *Satyr* itself, having spent its venom for twelve pages, adds a brief postscript that posits as an "Exception" some women "who continue *Maids* to *Old Age* through Choice, on *prudent* or *pious Considerations.*" Hav-ing vilified singlewomen as "Rebels," it now belatedly accords to these dutiful women "all the *Encomiums* can be merited by the *Best* of their *Sex*" (12). One of Defoe's pieces, "Old Maids. The Other Side of the Picture," similarly excepts from "Buffoonery" those who "either by Religious Vows or by other private Engagement, by Choice, not Necessity, remain Single and Unwed" (129). Women can choose, in other words, to be heterosex-ually nonsexual. In this way singlewomen remain attached to the heterosex-ual order just as much in these discourses as they do in Hayley's phallo-centric "sisterhood" with its male savior-priest. And in this way, too, these negative discourses join with the more positive representations in their avoidance of a homosexual alternative.[66] This discourse, I suggest, is espe-cially effective in serving a nation such as Britain in which the combined project of national and imperial power depends on acts of conquest, and the attendant acquisition of capital, that reorders class relations and could in theory reorder gender relations as well. That, for example, some (often cross-dressing) women seem to have participated in British entrepreneurship underscores the need for English discourses to reaffirm the dependence on men even — or especially — of women who are sexually unattached to them.

I want to end with the speculation that heterosexualizing single-women as old maids may also constitute a backlash response to possibilities, inherent in projects such as Astell's and Scott's, that singlewomen could join not only themselves but their incomes and property and thus control both land and capital. In a century before the Married Woman's Property Act gave English wives some financial rights, ideology might have been especially important in encouraging singlewomen to yield possession and control of their earthly goods, such as they were, to men. In this light, the discourses in which old maids remain avid to marry even as they are spurned by men might constitute a kind of inversion that masks men's fear that women might in fact spurn them. How, after all, could the men of Britain "rule the waves" if they could not rule British women first? In order to produce a British empire, I would suggest in closing, England had to produce Europe's first — and worst — old maids: one more of the equivocal achievements of the Empire on which the sun has still not set.

I am grateful to Sharon Groves, Ann Kelly, Joan Radner, Michael Ragussis, Kathryn Temple, Valerie Traub, and the coeditors of this volume for their invaluable responses to various versions of this essay and to Sharon Groves for crucial research assistance.

Notes

1. The popularity of Juvenal's *Sixth Satire*, which its most famous seventeenth-century translator, John Dryden, acknowledged to be "a bitter invective against the fair sex," is one sign of the pervasiveness of misogynist satire after the Restoration. On this question of misogynist satire, see Felicity Nussbaum, *The Brink of All We Hate: English Satires on Women 1660–1750* (Lexington: University Press of Kentucky, 1984). As some early modern women themselves recognized, even purportedly selective satires were occasions for attacking all women; Esther Sowerman, writing in 1617, charged an author of "pretend[ing] to write against lewd, idle, and unconstant women" but actually "most impudently rag[ing] and rayl[ing] generally against all the whole sexe" (in *Ester Hath Hang'd Haman*, excerpted in *First Feminists: British Women Writers 1578–1799*, ed. Moira Ferguson [Bloomington: Indiana University Press, 1985], 75).

2. Throughout this essay, I use the term "old maid" without quotation marks in order to signify its solidity as a *social category*. I do not use the term to designate — or denigrate — actual women, but to denote a real effect of ideology.

3. *A Satyr Upon Old Maids* (London: W. Denham, 1713), 12 pp. The microfilm entry in the English Short Title Catalogue manuscript collection suggests that the *Satyr* is "sometimes attributed to Marshall Smith."

4. My research suggests that in comparison to England, the old maid engenders relatively little attention in France and Germany during the eighteenth century and becomes highly prominent only in the next. Cécile Dauphin, for example, identifies only occasional references to the singlewoman before the nineteenth century, whereas Balzac's *Comédie humaine* numbers "several dozen" singlewomen among 5,000-odd characters and includes a novel titled *La Vieille fille*; see Dauphin, "Histoire d'un stéréotype: la vieille fille," in *Madame ou mademoiselle? itinéraires de la solitude féminine XVIIIe–XXe siècle*, ed. Arlette Farge and Christiane Klapisch-Zuber (Paris: Montalba, 1984).

Although German literature counts at least one eighteenth-century work titled after the old maid (Lessing's 1749 *Die Alte Jungfer*, a little-known comedy that Lessing considered inferior and suppressed from editions of his collected works), the evidence suggests that old-maid ideology intensified in the German states in the nineteenth century. For a new study of German representations of both old maids and bachelors, see Katrin Baumgarten, *Hagestolz und Alte Jungfer: Entwicklung, Instrumentalisierung und Fortleben von Klischees und Stereotypen über Unverheiratetgebliebene* (Munich: Waxmann, 1997).

5. The use of the terms "England" and "Britain," or "English" and "British," is unstable in the eighteenth century. "Great Britain" is itself, of course, an eighteenth-century invention following on the Act of Union that joined Scotland to England and Wales in 1707. But Britain remained, as Roy Porter notes, "a euphemism for greater England" (see Porter, *English Society in the Eighteenth Century* [London: Penguin, 1982], 34), and his own title, appearing in a series titled "the Penguin Social History of Britain," testifies to the insistent and persistent *Englishness* of concepts of eighteenth-century "Britain." Although, as Linda Colley notes, the press made efforts at "grimly substituting the words 'Great Britain' in place of the more parochial references to 'England,'" it is not entirely meaningful to speak of a British *culture* in the eighteenth century; see Colley, *Britons: Forging the Nation 1707–1837* (New Haven, Conn.: Yale University Press, 1992), 41 and passim. At the same time, as the island becomes a national and imperial power, it is certainly the *British* and not the *English* Empire on which the sun will never set, and such popular signifiers as the song "Rule Brittania" suggest that England's military and political identity was becoming a British one. I have therefore tended to use the words "England" and "English" when I speak of culture, and "Britain" and "British" to refer to political systems. Most of my source texts both past and present, however, tend to retain the emphasis on England or to use the terms interchangeably. To further complicate the matter, most demographic studies concentrate exclusively on England.

6. See *Much Ado About Nothing* II, i; *Taming of the Shrew* II, i; *London Prodigal* I, ii. The "logic" of this formulaic phrase is expounded in some later writings, including the 1708 issue of *The British Apollo*, reasoning not only that apes alone are fit companions for singlewomen, but that "even apes imagine old maids worse than They, for They must all be led you see, or would not follow them" (*The British Apollo*, 2 February 1708, cited in Katharine Ottaway Kittredge, "'Tabby Cats Lead

Apes in Hell': Spinsters in Eighteenth Century Life and Fiction," Ph.D. diss., SUNY-Binghampton, 1992). William Hayley also speculates on the possible origins of the "apes in hell" trope in his three-volume *Philosophical, Historical, and Moral Essay on Old Maids* (London: T. Cadell, 1785). Hayley finds himself "unable to ascertain the origin of this remarkable saying," but speculates that it might have been a ruse "invented by the Monks, to allure opulent females into the cloister," or a "superstition of Aegypt" stemming from "a passage in Hermes Trismegistus, which says, that those who die childless are, immediately after their death, tormented by demons"; however, he dismisses this because of "the very high respect which the Aegyptians entertained for the ape," and settles on the possibility that "the saying in question might have arisen in some country where it bore a very different meaning from what we annex to it at present; where this destiny of the ancient virgin was intended, not as the punishment, but the reward of her continence" (3: 157–58). On this proverb, see also B. J. Whiting, "Old Maids Lead Apes in Hell," *Englische Studien* 70 (1935–36): 337–51.

7. Although "spinster" eventually became the standard legal appellation, other terms including "virgin" were also used until the late seventeenth century. E. Cobham Brewster's *Dictionary of Phrase and Fable* (London, 1894) explains the interconnection between singlewoman and spinner in this way: "Wife is from the verb to weave. (Saxon *wefan*, Danish *vaevc*, German *weben*, whence *weib*, a woman, one who works at the distaff.) Woman is called the distaff. Hence Dryden calls Anne 'a distaff on the throne.' While a girl was spinning her wedding clothes she was simply a spinster; but when this task was done, and she was married, she became a wife, or one who had already woven her allotted task. Alfred, in his will, speaks of his male and female descendants as those of the spear-side and those of the spindle-side, a distinction still observed by the Germans; and hence the effigies on graves of spears and spindles" (1299–1300).

8. Amy Froide, "Single Women, Work, and Community in Southampton, 1550–1750," Ph.D. diss., Duke University, 1996, 375.

9. [Richard Allestree], *The Ladies Calling in two parts. by the author of the Whole Duty of Man, &c.* (London: At the Theater in Oxford, 1673), 158–60.

Lee Virginia Chambers-Schiller, *Liberty, a Better Husband: Single Women in America: The Generations of 1780–1840* (New Haven and London: Yale University Press, 1984), cites as evidence of a particular hostility toward singlewomen in Puritan New England the following pronouncement by John Dunton: "an old (or Superannuated) Maid, in Boston, is thought such a curse as nothing can exceed it, and look'd on as a dismal Spectacle" (in *Letters Written from New England, A.D. 1686*, ed. Wm. Whitmore, Publications of the Prince Society 4 [1867]: 99). That Dunton's language almost copies Allestree's suggests, however, that what Dunton claims for Boston is simply a replication of attitudes already present in the mother country. Dunton's penchant for masking plagiarism as originality supports such a reading.

10. Mary Astell, *A Serious Proposal to the Ladies, for the Advancement of their True and Greatest Interest, By a Lover of her Sex* (London: R. Wilkin, 1694, 1697), 159–61.

11. [John Dunton], *The Challenge, Sent by a Young Lady to Sir Thomas — &c. Or, The Female War* (London: E. Whitlock, 1697), 139–47.

12. I would agree with Katherine Kittredge that some of this negativity stems

from "society's preoccupation with the aging female body" ("'Tabby Cats Lead Apes in Hell,'" 120). I will also suggest additional social contexts below.

13. While avoidance is far more common than recuperation, one of Defoe's journalistic pieces, purportedly written by a woman, acknowledges men to be "Brutes to us on many Occasions" but uses even this to argue that therefore "we had better trust them, under the bounds of Law, than trust them without Law." See the 20 March 1725 entry, "On Matrimony, and the most Suitable Age for the Ladies," in William Lee, *Daniel Defoe: His Life, and Recently Discovered Writings Extending from 1716 to 1729* (London: John Camden Hotten, 1869), 3: 369.

14. It is not impossible that Anne's presence as queen stimulated both supportive discourses about powerful women unattached to or independent from men and backlash attacks. Astell explicitly claimed Anne's rulership as a sign of women's right to intellectual and moral authority and as a boon to her project for a female monastery. I am not, however, suggesting a causal link between Anne herself and the discourses about singlewomen produced during her reign. It should be noted parenthetically that, although Anne was married, her intimacies with other women, particularly Sarah Churchill and Abigail Masham, were the butt of sapphic innuendo.

15. Bernard Mandeville, *The Virgin Unmask'd: or, Female Dialogues Betwixt an Elderly Maiden Lady and her Niece, On several Diverting discourses on Love, Marriage, Memoirs, and Morals, &c of the Times* (London: J. Morphew, 1709), 31–32. Further references will appear in the body of the text.

16. In addition to the 1708 passage in *The British Apollo* cited above, this period produces a 1708 *Modern World Disrob'd* in which a "haughty Madam" with "an Aversion to the leading Apes in Hell, resolves to lay fast Hold of the next Offer" of marriage even if it comes from "an unbenefic'd Curate" or "some tottering Apothecary" (quoted in Kittredge, "'Tabby Cats'") and a *Female Tatler* entry of 1709 claiming that people "do so jeer" "old maids" that "they had rather marry the most impudent young rake than bear the continual reflection of leading apes" (*The Female Tatler written by Mrs Crackenthorpe*, No. 22 [24–26 August 1709], ed. Fidelis Morgan [London: Dent, 1992], 53).

17. Jane Barker, *A Patch-Work Screen for the Ladies* (London: E. Curll, 1723), 90–91 and passim. Further references will appear in the body of the text.

18. Daniel Defoe, writings from *Appleby's Journal* (1723–25), in Lee, *Daniel Defoe: His Life, and Recently Discovered Writings*, 3: 125–28, 323–25, 330–32, 359–61, 367–69.

19. Cited in Bridget Hill, *Eighteenth-Century Women: An Anthology* (London: Allen and Unwin, 1984), 124.

20. For an extended discussion of such characters as Fielding's Bridget Allworthy and Sister Western and Smollett's later Tabitha Bramble, see Kittredge, "'Tabby Cats.'" Kittredge's dissertation is to my knowledge the first book-length treatment of singlewomen in English literature.

21. Mary Singleton, *The Old Maid* (London: A. Miller, 1755), Letter 1, pp. 2, 5. Singleton's jibe at old bachelors is not wholly without precedent, but, as I will note later, I have found no evidence that eighteenth-century English discourse mounts a critique of single men.

22. Arthur Murphy, *The Old Maid. A Comedy in Two Acts* (London: P. Vaillant, 1761), 52–54. Murphy's play was performed more than twenty-five times at Drury Lane Theatre, published in print form later that year, revised for publication in 1786, and maintained as a staple of the English stage until at least the mid-nineteenth century. The first edition, from which I have cited here, is reprinted in *The Plays of Arthur Murphy*, vol. 2, ed. Richard B. Schwartz (New York: Garland, 1979), 155–214; the revised edition in *The Way to Keep Him and Five Other Plays by Arthur Murphy*, ed. John Pike Emery (New York: New York University Press, 1956), 245–48.

I am grateful to Traci Abbott for showing, in an excellent seminar paper at the University of Maryland (1997), the ways in which *Millenium Hall* represents men as beyond reform even by virtuous women.

23. See Kittredge, "'Tabby Cats,'" 36–37.

24. Hayley, *A Philosophical, Historical, and Moral Essay on Old Maids*, 3: 231.

25. Ibid., 1: 16.

26. Anne Lister, diary entry of 15 Dec 1822, reprinted in *I Know My Own Heart: The Diaries of Anne Lister*, ed. Helena Whitbread (London: Virago, 1988), 231. Lister's diary specifies that this passage came to her "without date or reference."

27. See Jane Austen, *Emma*, chap. 10. Emma's associations of the "old maid" with poverty expose a class bias in the late eighteenth-century construction of the old maid: "a single woman with a very narrow income must be a ridiculous, disagreeable old maid — the proper sport of boys and girls; but a single woman of good fortune is always respectable." Emma sees the poor singlewoman's temperament as the effect of her situation: "a very narrow income has a tendency to contract the mind and sour the temper."

The distinction Emma makes is still present in the French *Petit Robert*, which, after providing a pejorative definition of the "vieille fille," offers as an exemplary sentence: "Elle ne s'est jamais mariée, mais elle n'est pas du tout vieille fille" [She has never married, but she's not at all an old maid] (*Le Petit Robert I* [Paris: Dictionnaires Le Robert, 1986], 784).

28. An unusually large number of OED entries characterizing various qualities of the "old maid" follows the standard definitions. These date almost entirely from the late eighteenth through the nineteenth century, and the fact that they are not in any chronological order testifies to the stasis of representation in that period.

29. E. A. Wrigley and R. S. Schofield, *The Population History of England 1541–1871* (Cambridge, Mass.: Harvard University Press, 1981), 260.

30. David R. Weir, "Rather Never Than Late: Celibacy and Age at Marriage in English Cohort Fertility, 1541–1871," *Journal of Family History* (Winter 1984): 340–54.

31. See T. H. Hollingsworth, *The Demography of the British Peerage*, supplement to *Population Studies* 18, 2 (1965).

32. Pamela Sharpe, "Literally Spinsters: A New Interpretation of Local Economy and Demography in Colyton in the Seventeenth and Eighteenth Centuries," *Economic History Review* 44, 1 (1991): 56. Sharpe states that 12.9 percent of poor women but only 5.2 percent of gentry women never married in this period.

33. See, for example, Maura Palazzi, "Female Solitude and Patrilineage: Unmarried Women and Widows During the Eighteenth and Nineteenth Centuries," *Journal of Family History* 15, 4 (1990): 446.

34. See Chambers-Schiller, *Liberty, a Better Husband:* 3, 11.

35. Wrigley and Schofield, *Population History of England*, 260.

36. On the "two-sex" model and its implications for modern patriarchy, see Tom Laqueur, *Making Sex: Body and Culture from the Greeks to Freud* (Cambridge, Mass.: Harvard University Press, 1990); Michael McKeon, "Historicizing Patriarchy: The Emergence of Gender Difference in England 1660–1760," *Eighteenth-Century Studies* 28, 3 (Spring 1995): 295–322; and Anthony Fletcher, *Gender, Sex and Subordination in England 1500–1800* (New Haven, Conn.: Yale University Press, 1995). On "heteropatriarchy," see my essay, "Sapphic Picaresque: Heteropatriarchy and Homoadventuring," in *Queering the Eighteenth Century*, ed. Jonathan Kramnick, forthcoming.

37. Daniel Defoe, *Roxana* (Oxford: Oxford University Press, 1964), 148. The late eighteenth century does show some negative associations between "old maid" and "woman writer," such as the labeling of the long married and at that moment recently widowed Anna Barbauld as a "fatidical spinster," but this seems to occur well after old-maid ideology has reached its peak of hostility.

38. See Colley, *Britons*, 241, and Elizabeth Child, "'To Sing the Town': Women, Place, and Print Culture in Eighteenth-Century Bath," forthcoming in *Studies in Eighteenth-Century Culture* (1998), and Child's dissertation in progress, "Local Attachments: Eighteenth-Century Women Writers and English Provincial Towns."

39. See, for example, Wendy Gibson, *Women in Seventeenth-Century France* (New York: St. Martin's Press, 1988). I recognize that these are both Catholic countries where convents often "took care of" the problem of singlewomen.

40. According to Gibson, both religious and secular ideology in seventeenth-century France posited marriage as a negative. On domestic pietism in eighteenth-century Germany, see, for example, the excellent introduction to *Bitter Healing: German Women Writers, 1700–1830*, ed. Janine Blackwell and Susanne Zantop (Lincoln: University of Nebraska Press, 1990), 9–50.

41. Samuel Richardson, *Sir Charles Grandison*, vol. 4, letter 18 (Oxford: Oxford University Press, 1986), 2: 355–56.

42. Samuel Johnson, *The Works of Samuel Johnson, in Sixteen Volumes* (Troy, N.Y.: Pafraets Book Company, 1903), 1: 252.

43. N. L. Tranter, *Population Since the Industrial Revolution: The Case of England and Wales* (New York: Barnes and Noble, 1973).

44. Colley, *Britons*, 322. In this light, the mandate to marry advanced in France late in the Revolution might well stem from a similar military need — all the more as the legal pressure was exerted primarily on men. See Michèle Bordeaux, "Droit et femmes seules: Les pièges de la discrimination," in *Madame ou mademoiselle*, ed. Farge and Klapisch-Zuber, 29–30.

45. Tranter, *Population*, 180.

46. Cited in Froide, "Single Women, Work, and Community," 388.

47. Cited in Tranter, *Population*, 189.

48. Cited in Tranter, *Population*, 139.

49. Thomas Man, *The Benefit of Procreation Together with Some Few Hints toward the better support of Whores and Bastards* (London, 1739), 26, cited in Felicity Nussbaum, *Torrid Zones: Maternity, Sexuality, and Empire in Eighteenth-Century English Narratives* (Baltimore: Johns Hopkins University Press, 1995), 27.

50. David Hume, "Of the Populousness of Ancient Nations," in *Essays Moral, Political, and Literary* (Edinburgh, 1825), 1: 376, cited in Catherine Gallagher, "The Body Versus the Social Body in the Works of Thomas Malthus and Henry Mayhew," in *The Making of the Modern Body: Sexuality and Society in the Nineteenth Century*, ed. Catherine Gallagher and Thomas Laqueur (Berkeley: University of California Press, 1987), 83.

51. Cited in Tranter, *Population*, 138–39.

52. Ruth Perry, "Colonizing the Breast: Sexuality and Maternity in Eighteenth-Century England," *Journal of the History of Sexuality* 2 (1991): 207.

53. See E. A. Wrigley, *People, Cities and Wealth* (London: Blackwell, 1987), 216.

54. See Tranter, *Population*, 41ff.

55. Wrigley, *People, Cities and Wealth*, 216.

56. Tranter, *Population*, 150.

57. Ibid, 53.

58. Weir, "Rather Never than Late," 340.

59. Johnson, *Works*, 1: 252.

60. Colley, *Britons*, 240.

61. On German silence, see Alice A. Kuzniar, ed., *Outing Goethe and His Age* (Stanford, Calif.: Stanford University Press, 1996), 20–22 and passim. On the French production of sapphic "mystery," see Marie-Jo Bonnet, *Les relations amoureuses entre les femmes* (Paris: Editions Odile Jacob, 1995), pt. 2.

62. Henry Abelove, "Some Speculations on the History of 'Sexual Intercourse' During the 'Long Eighteenth Century' in England," *Genders* 6 (1989): 125–30.

63. Perry, "Colonizing the Breast," 209.

64. Valerie Traub, "Mapping the Global Body," in *The Visual Culture of Early Modern England*, ed. Peter Erickson and Clark Hulse (Chicago: University of Chicago Press, forthcoming).

65. On this fascinating tale, see Kathryn R. King, "The Unaccountable Wife and Other Tales of Female Desire in Jane Barker's *A Patch-work Screen for the Ladies*," *The Eighteenth Century: Theory and Interpretation* 35 (Spring 1994): 155–72.

66. The repression of female homosexuality may also underlie later constructions of the old maid, from Hayley through present-day dictionaries, as prudish, squeamish, or listless — that is, of a body which, not desiring men, is simply denied erotic energy. The German *Duden* gives as its second definition of the "alte Jungfer" [old maid] an "*ältere, prüde, zimperliche, unverheiratet gebliebene Frau*" [older, prudish, squeamish, never-married woman] (*Deutsches Universalwörterbuch* [Mannheim: Dudenverlag, 1996], 794). More cerebral but no more complimentary, the French *Petit Robert* provides as its "pejorative" definition a woman with "des idées étroites, une vie monotone" [narrow ideas and a dreary life] (*Petit Robert* 1: 784). That these

definitions became intensified in other parts of Europe in the nineteenth century and follow so obviously on the model England had already set, allows at least a playful speculation that the English construction of the old maid was pervasive enough to constitute a kind of British export in itself. Hayley's *Essay on Old Maids* was translated into French, and the popularity of English fiction would surely also have helped to give England's version of the old maid an international prominence.

Appendix

Demographic Tables

Maryanne Kowaleski

Tables for Chapter 2, "Singlewomen in Medieval and Early Modern Europe: The Demographic Perspective"

The following five tables provide data on the proportions of life-cycle and lifelong singlewomen in medieval and early modern Europe. Culled from a wide variety of demographic studies, the data focus in particular on two measures: the timing of marriage (as reflected in the mean age at first marriage) and the incidence of marriage (as reflected in the proportions of women over about age 45–50 who never married).

TABLE A1   Proportions of Singlewomen in Some European Populations Before 1550

PLACE AND TYPE OF COMMUNITY	DATE	% SINGLE WOMEN	(AGE OF ADULTHOOD)	% UNMARRIED (WIDOWS & SINGLEWOMEN)	MEAN AGE AT 1ST MARRIAGE	(No. OF CASES)
England						
Towns						
Bristol elite[1]	1341–1428				16.8	(18)
London merchant elite[2]	1352–1509				17.0	(41)
London elite[3]	14th–15thC				19.1	(17)
Oxford (2 parishes)[4]	1377		(14)	41.2		
Carlisle	1377		(14)	44.5		
Colchester	1377		(14)	39.7		
Hull	1377		(14)	45.0		
Coventry[5]	1523	43.0	(15)			
Villages						
19 vills in Rutland	1377		(14)	32.6		
125 vills in Essex[6]	1381		(15)	39.8		
1377 *Tax Overall*[7]	1377	29.9	(14)	33.6		
Low Countries						
Zierikzee urban elite[8](B)	1500–49				25.3	(65)
Germany						
Frankfurt urban elite[9]	14th–15thC				18.8	(28)
Freiburg[10]	1447	31.0				
Württemberg urban elite[11]	16thC				21.4	(34)

	Date				
France					
Reims[12]	1422	41.2	(14)	21.9	
Dijon[13]	1500–50				(32)
Switzerland					
Zurich[14]	1467	49.0	(15)		
Italy					
Towns[15]					
Prato (Tuscany)	1372			16.3	
	1427			17.6	
	1470			21.1	
Florence (Tuscany)	1427	21.4	(12)	17.6	
	1458			19.5	
	1480			20.8	
6 large towns (Tuscany)	1427	18.2	(12)	17.9	
15 small towns (Tuscany)	1427	17.7	(12)	17.9	
Verona & Vicenza elite[16]	1425–c.1510			20.1	(26)
Villages					
around Prato (Tuscany)	1372			15.3	
	1427			17.3	
	1470			19.5	
around Florence (Tuscany)	1427	18.0	(12)	18.4	
	1470			21.0	
around Lucca (NW Tuscany)[17]	1411–13	2.4	(15)		

Notes: Note that the data presented here were collected in different ways from widely varying sources, as detailed in the notes below. Dates for mean age of marriage generally refer to marriage cohorts, except for those marked (B), which refer to birth cohorts. 1. Based on marriages of Bristol orphans of the urban elite; I thank Elaine Clark for allowing me to cite these figures, which are from Bristol Record Office, Register of Recognizances for Orphans. Sylvia Thrupp, *The Merchant Class of Medieval London* (Ann Arbor: University of Michigan Press, 1948), 196, n. 10, found 20 cases of Bristol girls orphaned in 1385–1485 and calculated that the median age of marriage was 17.0.

TABLE A1 *Continued*

2. The figure represents the median age at marriage and is based on marriages of London orphans of the merchant elite that were recorded in Letter Books G–L and the London Journals; see Thrupp, *Merchant Class of Medieval London*, 196.

3. Barbara Hanawalt, *Growing Up in Medieval London: The Experience of Childhood in History* (New York: 1993), 205, 263; the data refer to the marriages of London orphans, which would have included the wealthier strata of the urban population. Note also that orphans tended to marry earlier than non-orphans.

4. This and the following figures are from the 1377 poll tax; see P. J. P. Goldberg, *Women, Work, and Life Cycle in a Medieval Economy: Women in York and Yorkshire c. 1300–1520* (Oxford: Clarendon Press, 1992), 215. The column for "single and widowed women" is a minimum figure since singlewomen were often underenumerated in the tax.

5. Charles Phythian-Adams, *Desolation of a City: Coventry and the Urban Crisis of the Late Middle Ages* (Cambridge: Cambridge University Press, 1979), 84, 306–7; figure is derived from a detailed town census and is probably slightly inflated by the inclusion of some widows and girls.

6. L. R. Poos, *A Rural Society After the Black Death: Essex 1350–1525* (Cambridge: Cambridge University Press, 1979), 152–57; figure is based on 1381 poll tax and has been adjusted by using model life tables so as to include excluded taxpayers (the largest group of which is singlewomen) and by assuming that one-half of the male exclusions were married.

7. Caroline Fenwick, "The English Poll Taxes of 1377, 1379 and 1381: A Critical Examination of the Returns," Ph.D. thesis, University of London, 1983), 179.

8. H. van Dijk and D. J. Roonda, "Het Patriciaat in Zierikzee Tijdens de Republiek," *Archief: Mededlingen van het koninklijk zeeuwsch genootschap der wetenschappen* (Rotterdam: 1979), 37.

9. Richard Koebner, "Die Eheauffassung des ausgehenden deutschen mittelalters," *Archiv für Kulturgeschichte* 9 (1911): 139.

10. Roger Mols, *Introduction à la démographie historiques des villes d'Europe du XIVe au XVIIIe siècle* (Louvain: Duculot, 1954–56), 3: 129.

11. J. Hajnal, "European Marriage Patterns in Perspective," in *Population in History: Essays in Historical Demography*, ed. D. V. Glass and D. E. C. Eversley (London: Edward Arnold, 1965), 115; the figures are drawn from genealogical records.

12. Pierre Desportes, "La population de Reims au XVe siècle d'après un dénombrement de 1422," *Le Moyen Age* 72 (1966): 472, 486, 495; figure is drawn from a census extant for two of the city's richest parishes that together contain 3,195 people, about one-third of the town's population.

13. Jacques Rossiaud, *Medieval Prostitution*, trans. Lydia G. Cochrane (Oxford: Blackwell, 1988), 15; the figures are from declared age at marriage made in depositions of witnesses to crimes.

14. Hajnal, "European Marriage Patterns," 116–17; the figures are drawn from head taxes and might include some widows.

15. All Tuscan data are from David Herlihy and Christine Klapisch-Zuber, *Tuscans and Their Families: A Study of the Florentine Catasto of 1427* (New Haven, Conn.: Yale University Press, 1985); for age at marriage, see pp. 87, 207, 210, and note that those for 1458 and 1480 are based on samples of one-tenth of the taxed households. For percentage of singlewomen, see p. 216; the data are from the catasto of 1427 and include women of indeterminate marital status, who represent 2.8% of the Florentine population, 4.9% in the cities, 2.9% in the towns, and 1.4% in the countryside. The figures also exclude nuns, who represented about 2.4% of adult singlewomen (25, 214, n.16).

16. James S. Grubb, *Provincial Families of the Renaissance: Private and Public Life in the Veneto* (Baltimore and London: Johns Hopkins University Press, 1996), 221.

17. Franca Leverotti, "La famiglia contadina Lucchese all'inizio del '400," in *Structure familiari, epidemie, migrazioni nell'Italia medievale*, ed. Rinaldo Comba, Gabriella Piccinni, and Giuliano Pinto (Naples: Edizione Scientifiche Italiane, 1984), 261; data are from an *estimo* recording 1,148 women aged 15 or over; 17 were single (1.5%), 10 of indeterminate marital status (.9%), 954 married, and 167 widowed.

TABLE A2   Proportions of Singlewomen in Some European Populations after 1550 (as measured by mean age of women at first marriage)

PLACE AND TYPE OF COMMUNITY	DATE AND MEAN AGE AT FIRST MARRIAGE		
	16TH CENT.	17TH CENT.	18TH CENT.
Denmark and Sweden[1]			
Kolbäck (Sweden)		1581–1700 26.7	1740–90 25.5
Västerfärnebo (Sweden)		1585–1700 25.2	
		1581–1700 27.4	
Glostrup (Denmark)		1677–1740 28.2	1741–90 26.8
Scotland			
Lowlands[2]		1660–1770 26.8*	
Kilmarnock[3] town part			1732–53 23.5
rural part			1745–63 26.5
Ireland			
County Dublin[4]		1652–53 23.8	
County Munster[5]		1652–53 22.6	
Quaker women[5]		1650–99 23.5	1700–40 24.1
County Antrim[6]			1755–1802 22.9
Killyman (Ulster)[7]			1771–1810 21.8
England			
Country 26 parishes[8]		1610–24 25.5	1700–24 26.1
		1625–49 25.5	1725–49 25.3
		1650–74 25.8	1750–74 24.6
(B) 404 parishes[9]	1566 26.8	1616 25.7	1716 25.5
	1591 25.8	1641 26.8	1741 25.1
		1666 26.7	1766 24.3

TABLE A2 *Continued*

PLACE AND TYPE OF COMMUNITY	DATE AND MEAN AGE AT FIRST MARRIAGE					
	16TH CENT.		17TH CENT.		18TH CENT.	
Cities						
London[10]			1598–1619	22.3		
London Quakers[11]			1650–99	27.1	1700–49	25.6
Villages and small towns (B)[12]						
Alcester (Warwicks)	1550–99	22.4	1600–49	25.0	1700–49	28.2
Banbury (Oxford)	1550–99	24.9	1600–49	25.4	1700–49	26.7
Colyton (Devon)	1550–99	26.9	1600–49	27.3	1700–49	28.6
Terling (Essex)	1550–99	24.5	1600–49	24.6	1700–49	24.4
Regions[13]						
Southern counties			1615–21	24.6		
Southern England Quakers			1650–99	24.9	1700–49	26.3
Yorkshire, 6 parishes			1691–1710	23.1		
Nottinghamshire, 3 parishes					1701–10	24.2
Low Countries						
Cities						
Amsterdam[14]			1626–27	24.5	1726–27	27.2
			1676–77	26.5	1776–77	27.8
Villages						
Elversele (Flanders) (B)[15]			1608–49	24.8	1700–49	28.0
Someren (Brabant)[16]			1664–69, 1693–95	26.7		
N. Belgium[17]			1620–99	26.4	1700–49	26.7

Germany

Cities

	Period	Age	Period	Age	Period	Age
Nördlingen[18]	1611–50	25.1	1651–90	26.0	1691–1730	30.2

Villages

	Period	Age	Period	Age
Schwalm region[19]	1600–1799	24.7		
Hesel (E. Friesland)	1600–1799	25.2		
Vasbeck (Walbeck)[20]	1700–49	26.6		
Werdum (E. Friesland)	1700–49	24.3		
Rust (Baden)	1700–49	25.5		
Giessen[21]	1631–1730	24.5		

Switzerland

	Period	Age	Period	Age
Geneva[22]	1625–44	24.8	1650–74	26.0

France

Country[23]

	Period	Age	Period	Age	Period	Age
Country[23]	1675–99	24.7	1700–24	25.0	1775–99	26.3

Cities

	Period	Age	Period	Age	Period	Age	Period	Age
Rouen (Normandy)[24]	1640–69	25.8	1700–29	26.2				
Meulan (Paris Basin)[25]	1560–79	20.5	1580–99	21.5	1660–1739	24.9	1740–64	26.0
Bourg en Bresse (Ain)[26]	1600–19	21.6	1760–89	27.0				

Villages

	Period	Age	Period	Age
Crulai (Normandy)[27]	1674–1742	24.6		
Athis (Ile de France)[28]	1578–99	19.1	1635–79	23.4
Lambesc (Provence)[29]	1630–69	19.1	1700–40	23.0
Saint-Savin (Pyrenees)[30]	1670–1709	22.3	1710–49	25.4

TABLE A2 *Continued*

PLACE AND TYPE OF COMMUNITY	DATE AND MEAN AGE AT FIRST MARRIAGE		
	16TH CENT.	17TH CENT.	18TH CENT.
Regions			
Paris Basin[31]		1671–1720 24.5	
Lorraine[32]	1575–1625 22.1		
Vexin[33]		1685–89 23.6	
		1695–99 25.1	
Portugal			
Villages[34]			
Moncarapacho (Algarve)	1545 21.1*		
Rebordaos (Bragança) (B)		1610–29 25.3	1721–1800 26.4
Spain			
Towns and Cities			
Cuenca (New Castile)[35]	1560–1600 21.6	1601–50 20.7	1701–5 22.4
Cartagena (Murcia)[36]		1646–50 19.6	
		1674–79 21.3	
Villages			
Cirauqui (Navarre)[37]		1640–99 22.0	1700–9 23.0
			1770–89 21.1
Villabáñez (Old Castile)[38]		1590–1605 20.2	1701–50 22.4
		1651–1700 21.8	1751–1800 22.6
S. Pablo de Zaragoza (Aragon)[39]		1600–50 22.8	
Los Molinos (New Castile)		1638–89 21.7	
Felanitx (Mallorca)	1580–1601 19.6	1602–50 20.9	1690–1729 22.3

Regions[40]

	(A) Date	Age	(B) Date	Age	(C) Date	Age	(D) Date	Age
Galicia							1787	25.0*
Aragon								23.2*
New Castile								23.0*
Estremadura								22.0*
Murcia								22.2*
Andalusia								22.2*

Italy

Cities[41]

	(A) Date	Age	(B) Date	Age	(C) Date	Age	(D) Date	Age
Venice (Venetia)					1701–5	28.8*		
					1740–44	29.3*		
Pavia (Lombardy)					1700	22.0*		
Chieti (Abruzzi)					1732	25.0*		

Villages

	(A) Date	Age	(B) Date	Age	(C) Date	Age	(D) Date	Age
Valdarno (Tuscany)[42]			1684–1707	24.2				
S. Ippolito & Galciana[43] (Tuscany)			1646	19.9*	1735	25.1*		
			1678	22.2*	1786	26.2*		
Altopascio (Tuscany)[44]			1625–49	18.6	1700–49	21.9		
			1650–99	20.4	1750–84	25.5		
Prato contado (Tuscany)[45]			1678	23.6*	1786	25.2*		
Chieti contado (Abruzzi)					1732	24.0*		
Eboli (Campania)			1629	18.5*	1750	19.0*		
Solofra (Campania)			1631	23.5*	1730	25.3*		
Bitetto (Puglia)	1585	17.3*						
	1522	19.8*						
	1561	15.3*						
	1586	15.8*						
Taurisano (Puglia)			1643	19.0*	1747	21.5*		

Unless noted otherwise, all data are drawn from family reconstitution studies, except for ages marked with a *, which represent the singulate mean age of marriage calculated according to the method developed by J. Hajnal. All dates refer to marriage cohorts, except for those marked (B) which are based on birth cohorts.

1. Michael W. Flinn, *The European Demographic System* (Baltimore: Johns Hopkins University Press, 1981), 127. The 1581–1700 figure is a weighted mean of reconstitutions (only 3 of which cover this whole period) from 6 villages. The 1740–90 figure includes data from 3 reconstitutions.

TABLE A2 *Continued*

2. R. A. Houston, "Age at Marriage of Scottish Women, c. 1660–1770," *Local Population Studies* 43 (1990): 63–66. The figures are based on 849 female deponents between the ages of 15 and 49 who appeared before the High Court of Justiciary; the sample is probably biased toward town-dwellers and underrepresents the poorest classes.

3. Michael W. Flinn, ed., *Scottish Population History from the Seventeenth Century to the 1930s* (Cambridge: Cambridge University Press, 1977), 276.

4. David Dickson, "No Scythians Here: Women and Marriage in Seventeenth-Century Ireland," in *Women in Early Modern Ireland*, ed. Margaret MacCurtain and Mary O'Dowd (Edinburgh: Edinburgh University Press, 1991), 230. The County Dublin data refer to 103 women in a listing of Catholic and Protestant inhabitants of the baronies of Upper Cross and Newcastle; the age at marriage was calculated by subtracting the reported age of the eldest child plus 1 year from the reported age of the mother. The Munster data are calculated in a similar way but refer to 34 women appearing in transplantation certificates.

5. Richard T. Vann and David Eversley, *Friends in Life and Death: The British and Irish Quakers in the Demographic Transition, 1650–1900* (Cambridge: Cambridge University Press, 1992), 105.

6. V. Morgan and W. S. Macafee, "Irish Population in the Pre-Famine Period: Evidence from County Antrim," *Economic History Review* 2nd ser. 37 (1984): 186.

7. W. S. Macafee, "Pre-Famine Population in Ulster: Evidence from the Parish Register of Killyman," in *Rural Ireland, 1600–1900: Modernisation and Change*, ed. Patrick O'Flanagan, Paul Ferguson, and Kevin Whelan (Cork: Cork University Press, 1987), 154; Killyman was a linen-weaving parish.

8. E. A. Wrigley, R. S. Davies, J. E. Oeppen, and R. S. Schofield, *English Population History from Family Reconstitution, 1580–1837* (Cambridge: Cambridge University Press, 1997), 149. The data have been corrected for compositional change and "splicing" and refer to marriages between bachelors and singlewomen; singlewomen who married widowers were generally 3 to 4 years older than the ages noted here. Note also that data are not available for all 26 parishes for every period.

9. These data represent corrected versions of figures derived by back projection for 404 parishes; see David R. Weir, "Rather Never Than Late: Celibacy and Age at Marriage in English Cohort Fertility," *Journal of Family History* 9 (1984): 342.

10. Vivien B. Elliot, "Single Women in the London Marriage Market: Age, Status and Mobility, 1589–1619," in *Marriage and Society: Studies in the Social History of Marriage*, ed. R. B. Outhwaite (London: Blackwell, 1981), 84, 87. Data are drawn from applications for a licence to marry in the diocese of London and thus are probably biased in favor of higher status groups, although servants and other low-status groups often applied as well.

11. John Landers, "Fertility Decline and Birth Spacing Among London Quakers," in *Fertility and Resources*, ed. Landers and Vernon Reynolds (Cambridge: Cambridge University Press, 1990), 93.

12. Richard M. Smith, "Population and Its Geography in England 1500–1730," in *An Historical Geography of England and Wales*, ed. R. A. Dodgshon and R. A. Butlin (New York: 1979), 217.

13. All regional data are from Flinn, *European Demographic System*, 124–25, except for Quaker data, which are from Landers, "Fertility Decline," 93.

14. A. M. Van der Woude, "Population Developments in the Northern Netherlands (1500–1800) and the Validity of the 'Urban Graveyard' Effect," *Annales de Démographie Historique* (1982): 63.

15. P. Deprez, "The Demographic Development of Flanders in the Eighteenth Century," in *Population in History*, ed. Glass and Eversley, 615.

16. Mols, *Introduction à la démographie historique des villes d'Europe*, 3: 137.

17. Jacques Houdaille, "Nuptialité et fécondité en Flandre et au Brabant du XVIIe au XIXe siècles," *Population* 32 (1977): 1005.

18. Christopher R. Friedrichs, *Urban Society in an Age of War: Nördlingen, 1580–1720* (Princeton, N.J.: Princeton University Press, 1979), 69; data based on a sample of 263 women whose fathers or husbands had surnames that began with a G.

19. Schwalm and Hesel data are from A. E. Imhof, "Remarriage in Rural Populations and in the Urban Middle and Upper Strata in Germany from the Sixteenth to the Twentieth Century," in *Marriage and Remarriage in Populations in the Past*, ed. Jacques Dupâquier, Etienne Hélin, Peter Laslett, Massimo Livi-Bacci, and Solvi Sogner (London: Academic Press, 1981), 338.

20. Data for Vasbeck, Werdum, and Rust from John Knodel, *Demographic Behavior in the Past: A Study of Fourteen German Village Populations in the Eighteenth and Nineteenth Centuries* (Cambridge: Cambridge University Press, 1988), 122–23.

21. Data for Giessen and Massenhausen are from Flinn, *European Demographic System*, 126–27.

22. A. Perrenoud and D. Zumkeller, "Caractères originaux de la démographie genevoise du XVIe siècle. Structure ou conjoncture," *Annales de Démographie Historique* (1980): 130.

23. David R. Weir, "Life Under Pressure: France and England, 1670–1870," *Journal of Economic History* 44 (1994): 33; the dates are the years in which the cohort reached age 25.

24. Jean-Pierre Bardet, *Rouen aux XVIIe et XVIIIe siècles: les mutations d'un espace social* (Paris: Société d'Edition d'Enseignement Supérieur, 1983), 1:55.

25. For the period 1660–1739, exact ages are known only for 16% of the women marrying; for 1740–64, this rises to 36.9%; see Marcel Lachiver, *La population de Meulan du XVIIe au XIXe siècle (vers 1600–1870)* (Paris: SEVPEN, 1969), 138–39.

26. Denise Turrel, *Bourg en Bresse au 16e siècle: les hommes et la ville* (Paris: Société Démographique Historique, 1986), 198–202. The average age rises by 6 to 7 months if women whose status at marriage was unclear (single or widowed) are included in the calculations.

27. Etienne Gautier and Louis Henry, *La population de Crulai, paroisse normande: étude historique* (Paris, 1958), 84.

28. François Lebrun and Antoinette Fauve-Chamoux, "Le mariage et la famille," in *Histoire de la population française*, ed. Jacques Dupâquier et al. (Paris: Presses Universitaires de France, 1988), 2: 305, citing Jean-Marc Moriceau, *La population du sud de Paris aux XVIe et XVIIe siècles* (Paris, 1978): 81.

29. M. Terrisse, "Note à propos des aspects démographiques de la vie provençale au XVIIe siècle," *Provence Historique* 39 (1989): 163.

30. Yves Guy, *Saint-Savin: démographie d'un village bijourné* (Paris: Centre National de la Recherche Scientifique, 1988), 163.

31. François Lebrun, "Amour et mariage," in *Histoire de la population française*, 2: 305.

32. Jean-Pierre Kintz, "Démographie en pays lorrains au XVIe siècle," *Annales de Démographie Historique* (1975): 411.

33. Jacques Dupâquier, "L'autorégulation de la population française (XVIe–XVIIIe siècle)," in *Histoire de la population française*, 2: 429.

34. Robert Rowland, "Sistemas matrimoniales en la Península Ibérica (siglos xvi–ix): una perspectiva regional," in *Demografía histórica en España*, ed. Vicente, Pérez Moreda and David S. Reher (Madrid: El Arquero, 1988), 90.

35. David S. Reher, *Town and Country in Pre-Industrial Spain: Cuenca, 1550–1870* (Cambridge: Cambridge University Press, 1990), 75.

36. Francisco Chacón Jiménez, "Notas para el estudio de la familia en la región de Murcia durante el Antiguo Régimen," in *La familia en la España mediterránea (siglos XV–XIX)*, ed. James Casey et al. (Barcelona: Centre d'Estudis d'Història Moderna Pierre Vilar, 1987), 155.

37. Fernando Mikelarena Peña, *Demografía y familia en la Navarra tradicional* (Pamplona, 1995), 160.

38. Bartolomé Bennassar, *Valladolid au siècle d'or: une ville de Castille et sa campagne au XVIᵉ siècle* (Paris: Mouton, 1967), 197.

39. Rowland, "Sistemas," 91, for Los Molinos, S. Pablo de Zaragoza, and Felanitx.

40. Rowland, "Sistemas," 95.

41. City data from Marzio Barbagli, *Sotto lo stesso tetto: Mutamenti della famiglia in Italia dal XV al XX secolo* (Bologna: Il Molino, 1984), 534, 536.

42. Andrea Menzione, "Composizione delle famiglie e matrimonio in diversi gruppi contadini nella Toscana del secolo XVII," in *Popolazione, società e ambiente: Temi di demografia storica italiana (sec. XVII–XIX)*, ed. Eugenio Sonnino et al. (Bologna: Società Italiana di Demografia Storica, 1990), 200.

43. Marco Della Pina, "Famiglia mezzadrile e celibato: le campagne di Prato nei secoli XVII e XVIII," in *Popolazione, società e ambiente*, 136.

44. Frank McArdle, *Altopascio: A Study in Tuscan Rural Society 1587–1784* (Cambridge: Cambridge University Press, 1978), 61.

45. Following data are from Barbagli, *Sotto lo stesso*, 535–36, 538; most are also listed in Gérard Delille, *Famille et propriété dans le royaume de Naples (XVe–XIXe siècle)* (Rome: Ecole Française de Rome, 1985), 192–93.

TABLE A3   Proportions of Lifelong Singlewomen in Some European Populations

PLACE AND TYPE OF COMMUNITY	DATE AND % OF ADULT WOMEN NEVER MARRIED					
	15TH–16TH CENT.		17TH CENT.		18TH CENT.	
Ruling Families[1] (B)	1480–1579	24.1	1580–1679	24.9	1680–1770	13.2
Norway[2]					1750	14.1
Sweden[3] (B)					1700	10.4
					1750	11.7
Scotland[4]						
Villages						
Kilmarnock (W. Lowlands)					1740s	26.0
Torthorwald (Borders)					1763–80	33.0
Tranent (E. Lowlands)					1750s	9.7
					1770s	14.5
Fordoun (E. Lowlands)					1790s	13.5
Ireland						
Quaker women[5]					1700–49	1.9
					1750–99	15.1
England						
Country[6] (B)	1536	4.7	1616	22.1	1716	12.1
(men & women)	1591	14.6	1641	19.4	1741	10.0
			1666	9.2		
			1691	8.4		

Location	Period	%	Period	%	Period	%
British peerage[7] (B)	1550–74	9.0	1600–24	12.8	1700–24	26.3
	1575–99	4.2	1650–74	15.1	1750–74	23.9
Quakers[8]						
Urban			1700–49	3.5	1750–99	14.7
Southern England				3.0		14.9
Northern Britain				0		7.2
Low Countries						
E. Flanders[9]			1699–1703	15.2	1742–57	18.8
France						
Country[10] (B)			1660–64	7.1	1710–14	6.6
			1675–79	5.6	1730–34	9.6
			1690–94	6.6	1760–64	11.7
All départements[11] (BC)					1756	12.9
Cities and Towns						
Paris (St. Sulpice parish)[12]			1640–69	16.0	1715–44	15.0
Rouen (Normandy)[13]			1670–99	22.0	1700–29	19.0
					1730–59	21.0
					1760–89	17.0
Meulan[14]			1660–1739	7.9+	1740–89	10.2
Villages and Regions						
Saint-Savin (Pyrenees)[15]			1618–99	8.6+	1700–99	14.9+
Normandy[16]					1740–89	5.3
Northern France						8.1
Eastern France						6.6
Manche[17] (B)					1756	16.4
Seine-et-Marne (B)						7.3
Jura (B)						14.2
Dordogne (B)						12.4
Hautes Pyrénées (B)						20.7

TABLE A3   *Continued*

PLACE AND TYPE OF COMMUNITY	DATE AND % OF ADULT WOMEN NEVER MARRIED		
	15TH–16TH CENT.	17TH CENT.	18TH CENT.
Switzerland			
Cities			
Geneva elite[18] (B)	1550–99 2.0	1600–49 7.0 1650–99 25.0	1700–49 29.0 1750–99 31.0
Geneva[19]	1580–89 12.0	1650s 15.0	
Spain			
Country[20] (C) villages			1787 10.0
cities			17.1
Cities			
Cuenca[21] (C)			1752 13.3
Regions (C)			1787
Galicia			16.5
León			7.8
Catalonia			12.4
Old Castile			7.8
New Castile			7.5
Valencia			8.6
Andalusia			17.9
Italy			
Cities			
Florence (Tuscany)[22] (C)	1427 5.8 1457 2.9 1480 1.9		

Location	Date	%	Date	%	Date	%
6 Cities (Tuscany) (C)	1427	5.4				
15 Towns (Tuscany) (C)	1427	2.5				
Pavia[23] (Lombardy)					1700	11.0
Villages						
around Florence (C)	1427	2.0				
around Prato[24]						
sharecroppers (mezzadri)					1786	18.1
renters (pigionali)						9.3
around Pisa[25] (C)			1684–1707	11.6		
Lucera (Apulia)[26] (C)			1621	.6	1750	8.2
Eboli (Apulia) (C)			1629	7.6	1730	22.7
Solofra (Campania) (C)			1631	1.0	1730	21.0
S. Cipriano (Campania) (C)			1610	10.1		

All figures are based on never-married women, but at ages that varied from 45 to 55 and by using different methods, as noted below. Dates refer to death cohorts, except for those marked (B) which are birth cohorts and those marked (C) which refer to the year of the census recording marital status and age.

1. Sigismund Peller, "Births and Deaths Among Europe's Ruling Families Since 1500," in *Population in History*, 89; data drawn from family genealogies (age 50).

2. Louis Henry, "La population de la Norvège depuis deux siècles," *Population* (1979): 547 (age 50 or older).

3. Erland Hofsten and Hans Lundstrom, *Swedish Population History: Main Trends from 1750 to 1970* (Stockholm, 1975), 35 (aged 45–49).

4. Flinn, ed., *Scottish Population History*, 280 (dying aged 50 or older).

5. Vann and Eversley, *Friends in Life and Death*, 108 (dying aged 50 or older); figures are calculated using the method of Henry and Houdaille (n. 9 below).

6. Roger S. Schofield, "English Marriage Patterns Revisited," *Journal of Family History* 10 (1985): 14 (aged 40 or older). The figures are derived from back projection with further modifications, refer to birth cohorts, and are for both men and women (which means they probably underestimate lifelong singlewomen).

7. T. H. Hollingsworth, "The Demography of the British Peerage," *Population Studies* Supp. 18 (1964): 20 (age 50 or older).

8. Vann and Eversley, *Friends in Life and Death*, 108 (dying aged 50 or older).

9. Jacques Houdaille, "Nuptialité et fécondité en Flandre et au Brabant du XVIIe au XIXe siècles," *Population* 32 (1977): 1006 (ages 40–49 or older); figures are derived from *états des âmes*.

10. Louis Henry and Jacques Houdaille, "Célibat et âge au mariage aux XVIIIe et XIXe siècles en France. I. Célibat définitif," *Population* 33 (1978): 50 (aged 50 or older). Their method draws on data in burial registers and is designed to take into account the relatively large number of women whose exact marital status at death could not be determined.

TABLE A3 *Continued*

11. Etienne Van de Walle, "La nuptialité des Françaises avant 1851, d'après l'état civil des décédées," *Population* 32, special no. (1977): 458–59. His method takes data on age and marital status in 1806 and makes adjustments for differential mortality by marital status; the data refer to the proportion of women dying aged 50–74 years old who never married.

12. Henry and Houdaille, "Célibat," 53 (aged 60 or older).

13. Bardet, *Rouen aux XVIIe et XVIIIe siècles*, 1:322 (dying aged 50 or older).

14. Lachiver, *La population de Meulan*, 136 (dying aged 50 or older). It is likely that up to half of the 20 women of "indeterminate" status of the 380 total in 1660–1739 were spinsters. For the period 1740–89, the marital status of only 8 of the 433 went unrecorded, and for 1790–1839, only 7 of the 573 total.

15. Guy, *Saint-Savin*, 154 (dying aged 50 or older). The figures exclude those whose marital status was not recorded in the burial register, which includes 70.2% of the women in the first period and 40.5% of those in the second period.

16. Henry and Houdaille, "Célibat," 52 (dying aged 50 or older). The figures represent the average of the proportions derived by two different methods; the three regions were chosen because the number of women of undetermined marital status was less than 10%.

17. See n. 11 above for the data from 1756.

18. Louis Henry, *Anciennes familles genevoises: étude démographique: XVIe–XXe siècle* (Paris: Presses Universitaires de France, 1956), 52 (dying aged over 50 in the families of the ruling elite).

19. E. William Monter, "Historical Demography and Religious History in Sixteenth-Century Geneva," *Journal of Interdisciplinary History* 9 (1979): 417; the 1580s figures are based on the marital status of 404 women dying in this period aged 50 or older, 47 of whom died single. The 1650s figures are those of A. Perrenoud, cited by Monter in n. 33, of women dying single aged 50 or older.

20. Reher, *Town and Country*, 80, n. 20 for the overall figures and Rowland, "Sistemas matrimoniales," 95, for the individual regions. Figures based on never-married women aged 40–50.

21. Reher, *Town and Country*, 75 (ages 40–50).

22. All 1427 data from David Herlihy, "Deaths, Marriages, Births, and the Tuscan Economy (ca. 1300–1500)," in *Population Patterns in the Past*, ed. Ronald Demos Lee (New York: Academic Press, 1977), 143. Figures refer to women, aged 48–52, who were listed in the Florentine catasto with no indication of ever having married, and excludes nuns. The 1480 figure for Florence is from Molho, *Marriage Alliance*, 217–18 (aged 46–55); it excludes 0.9 per cent of women whose marital status is unclear.

23. Hajnal, "European Marriage Patterns," 137, citing G. Aleati, *La popolazione di Pavia durante il dominio spagnolo* (Milan: A. Giuffre, 1957); figures based on women dying single aged 40–59 in three parishes.

24. Della Pina, "Famiglia mezzadrile e celibato," 131; figures based on women aged 50–54.

25. Menzione, "Composizione delle famiglie e matrimonio in diversi gruppi contadini nella Toscana," 207; data are based on women aged 50–54.

26. This and the following from Delille, *Famille et propriété dans le royaume de Naples*, 190 (aged 50); data are from a series of censuses that give age and marital status. The Apulia villagers were largely sharecroppers in a grain-exporting region, while the villagers of Campania were essentially subsistence hill farmers.

TABLE A4 The Effect of Migration on the Proportions of Singlewomen
(as measured by mean age of women at first marriage)

PLACE	TYPE OF COMMUNITY	DATE	MEAN AGE AT 1ST MARRIAGE
England			
London-born[1]	city	1598–1619	20.5
Migrants to London			24.2
Netherlands[2]			
Amsterdam-born	city	1796	
Spouse Amsterdam-born			24.6
Spouse migrant			25.6
Migrant			
Spouse Amsterdam-born			26.6
Spouse migrant			28.4
Spain			
Cuenca-born[3]	city	1680–1750	22.4
Migrants	city	1701–50	24.0
Italy			
Altopascio (Tuscany)[4]	village	1625–49	
Marry and remain			18.6
Marry and leave			21.0
Marry and remain		1650–99	20.4
Marry and leave			22.5

Data are drawn from family reconstitution studies unless noted otherwise. Dates refer to marriage cohorts.

1. Vivien Brodsky Elliott, "Single Women in the London Marriage Market," 84, 87. The data are drawn from applications for a licence to marry in the diocese of London, are probably biased in favor of higher status groups because of the expense of the licence, although servants and other low-status groups were included and the author thinks the ages are generally representative of all single women in London.
2. Jan de Vries, *European Urbanization 1500–1800* (Cambridge, Mass.: Harvard University Press, 1984), 191, citing Herman A. Diederiks, *Een stad in verval. Amsterdam omstreeks 1800* (Amsterdam: Historisch Seminarium van de Universteit van Amsterdam, 1982), 92.
3. Reher, *Town and Country*, 82.
4. McArdle, *Altopascio*, 63.

TABLE A5   The Effect of Wealth and Status on the Proportions of Singlewomen (as measured by mean age of women at first marriage)

PLACE AND TYPE OF COMMUNITY	STATUS	DATE AND MEAN AGE AT FIRST MARRIAGE					
		15TH–16TH CENT.		17TH CENT.		18TH CENT.	
Ruling Families[1] (B)		1500–99	20.2	1600–99	22.7	1700–99	21.7
England							
Nobility[2] (B)	British peers	1550–74	20.3	1600–24	20.7	1700–24	23.5
		1575–99	19.7	1675–99	22.7	1775–99	25.5
London[3]	2 rich parishes			1580–1650	22.3		
	2 poor parishes				24.0		
Colyton (Devon)[4]	Gentry	1550–99	24.6	1600–49	24.1	1750–99	26.2
(village)	Crafts		25.4		25.7		26.8
	Laborers		25.6		24.2		26.8
	Poor		25.2		26.5		28.0
Low Countries							
Zierikzee[5] (B)	Urban patriciate	1500–49	25.3	1600–49	26.0	1700–49	25.5
		1550–99	24.2	1650–99	25.0	1750–99	24.1
Germany							
14 villages[6]	Farmers					1700–99	24.1
	Artisans and skilled						25.3
	Proletarians						26.4
	All (incl. unknown)						25.6
9 villages[7]	Land-rich					1761–70	24.8
(in Belm)	Smallholders						25.7
	Landless						27.3

France

Nobility[8]	Dukes and peers	1650–99	20.0	1700–50	19.4
				1750–99	18.3
Nobility[9]	Provincial nobility	1600–49	23.8	1710–39	21.6
		1650–79	24.5	1740–69	22.8
Rouen city[10]	Merchants & officials	1640–1792	25.0		
	Legal profession		25.7		
	Lesser merchants		25.8		
	Shopkeepers		26.9		
	Artisans		26.1		
	Workers/Laborers		26.2		

Switzerland

Geneva[11]	High-mid bourgeoisie	1625–44	19.7	1650–74	25.2
	Petite bourgeoisie		23.2		24.9
	Employees and workers		26.8		27.1

Italy

Florence[12]	All brides	1437–79	19.9
		1480–1519	20.4
	Richer brides	1437–79	18.4
		1480–1519	19.8

Data are drawn from family reconstitution studies, except for the nobility which are based on family genealogies. All dates refer to marriage cohorts, except for those marked (B) which refer to birth cohorts.

1. Peller, "Births and Deaths Among Europe's Ruling Families," 88.
2. Hollingsworth, "Demography of the British Peerage," 25.
3. Roger Finlay, "Population and Fertility in London, 1580–1650," *Journal of Family History* 4 (1979): 31–32.

TABLE A5   *Continued*

4. Pamela Sharpe, "The Total Reconstitution Method: A Tool for Class-Specific Study?" *Local Population Studies* 44 (1990): 48; data based on family reconstitution, but should be treated with caution since social status could be determined for only roughly half of the women marrying (53 known for the first period, 128 for the second, and 114 for the third).

5. Van Dijk and Roorda, "Het patriciaat in Zierikzee," 37.

6. Knodel, *Demographic Behavior in the Past*, 133.

7. Jürgen Schlumbohm, "Micro-History and the Macro-Models of the European Demographic System in Pre-Industrial Times: Life Course Patterns in the Parish of Belm (Northwest Germany), Seventeenth to Nineteenth Centuries," *History of the Family* 1 (1996): 89; status is that of the husband.

8. Louis Henry and C. Levy, "Duc et pairs sous l'Ancien Régime. Caractéristiques démographiques d'une caste," *Population* (1960): 813.

9. Houdaille, "La noblesse française 1600–1900," 507; data drawn from family genealogies.

10. Bardet, *Rouen*, 255; data based on family reconstitution of 3,244 marriages and the status refers to the bride's family.

11. Perrenoud and Zumkeller, "Caractères originaux de la démographie genevoise du XVIe siècle," 131; data based on family reconstitution.

12. Anthony Molho, *Marriage Alliance in Late Medieval Florence* (Cambridge, Mass.: Harvard University Press, 1994), 307; the age at marriage is the reported age of the wife when the husband collected the dowry. "Richer brides" were those whose dowry amounts were in the top fiftieth percentile.

Contributors

JUDITH M. BENNETT is professor of history at the University of North Carolina at Chapel Hill. She is the author of *Women in the Medieval English Countryside: Gender and Household in Brigstock Before the Plague* (1987), *Ale, Beer, and Brewsters in England: Women's Work in a Changing World, 1300–1600* (1996), and a forthcoming book, *A Medieval Life: Cecilia Penifader of Brigstock, c. 1297–1344.*

MONICA CHOJNACKA received her Ph.D. in European history from Stanford University in 1994, and she is currently completing a book on women, family, and community in early modern Venice. She teaches at the University of Georgia.

SHARON FARMER is associate professor of history at the University of California, Santa Barbara. She is the author of *Communities of Saint Martin: Legend and Ritual in Medieval Tours* (1991), and she is currently completing a monograph entitled *Gender and Poverty in High Medieval Paris.*

AMY M. FROIDE received her Ph.D. from Duke University in 1996. She is an assistant professor of history at University of Tennessee at Chattanooga. She is currently working on a book about singlewomen and the meanings of singleness in early modern England, and she has a forthcoming essay on elderly singlewomen in *Old Women in England, 1500 to the Present*, ed. Lynn Botelho and Pat Thane (1999). In 1998–99 she will hold a Rockefeller Foundation Fellowship for research on women in premodern Europe.

MARGARET R. HUNT is associate professor of history and women's and gender studies at Amherst College. She is the author of *The Middling Sort: Commerce, Gender, and the Family in England, 1680–1780* (1996), and of numerous essays on women's history, lesbian and gay history, and the history of sexuality.

RUTH MAZO KARRAS is the author of *Common Women: Prostitution and Sexuality in Medieval England* (1996), and of numerous articles on gender and sexuality in medieval history. She is professor of history at Temple University, and currently working on a project on the construction of masculine identities in the later Middle Ages.

MARYANNE KOWALESKI is professor of history at Fordham University and author of *Local Markets and Regional Trade in Medieval Exeter* (1995). Coeditor of *Women and Power in the Middle Ages* (1988), she has also published articles on women and work, urban families, port towns, and maritime trade in medieval England.

ROBERTA L. KRUEGER, professor of French at Hamilton College, is author of *Women Readers and the Ideology of Gender in Old French Verse Romance* (1993) and the editor of the forthcoming *Cambridge Companion to Medieval Romance*. Her current research is on women's education and the literature of conduct in late medieval France.

SUSAN S. LANSER is professor of comparative literature and English and affiliate professor of women's studies at the University of Maryland at College Park. Her published works include *The Narrative Act* (1981); *Fictions of Authority: Women Writers and Narrative Voice* (1992); *Women Critics 1660–1820*, an anthology of primary writings coedited with the Folger Collective; and numerous essays in journals and books ranging from *Feminist Studies* to *Eighteenth Century Life*. Her current project, a book-length study entitled "Sapphists, Spinsters, Friends: Female Economies in the Long Eighteenth Century," was also the topic of her Folger Institute seminar in 1995.

SUSAN MOSHER STUARD is a medieval historian concerned with social and economic questions. She received her Ph.D. from Yale University and is professor of history at Haverford College. She is the editor of *Women in Medieval Society* (1976) and *Women in Medieval History and Historiography* (1987), and coeditor of the third edition of *Becoming Visible: Women in European History* (1998). She is also the author of *State of Deference: Ragusa/Dubrovnik in the Medieval Centuries* (University of Pennsylvania Press, 1992), and she won the Berkshire Prize for 1996 for her article, "Ancillary Evidence on the Decline of Medieval Slavery," *Past and Present* 149 (1995).

MERRY E. WIESNER is professor of history and former director of the Center for Women's Studies at the University of Wisconsin-Milwaukee. She is one of the editors of *Sixteenth Century Journal*, and the author of *Working Women in Renaissance Germany* (1986), *Women and Gender in Early Modern Europe* (1993), *Gender, Church, and State in Early Modern Germany: Essays by Merry E. Wiesner* (1998), and over thirty articles on various aspects of women's lives and gender structures in early modern Europe, especially in Germany.

Index